MW01040270

Phallacies

Phallacies

HISTORICAL INTERSECTIONS OF DISABILITY
AND MASCULINITY

Edited by Kathleen M. Brian
and
James W. Trent Jr.

OXFORD
UNIVERSITY PRESS

OXFORD
UNIVERSITY PRESS

Oxford University Press is a department of the University of Oxford. It furthers
the University's objective of excellence in research, scholarship, and education
by publishing worldwide. Oxford is a registered trade mark of Oxford University
Press in the UK and certain other countries.

Published in the United States of America by Oxford University Press
198 Madison Avenue, New York, NY 10016, United States of America.

Library of Congress Cataloging-in-Publication Data
Names: Brian, Kathleen M., editor. | Trent, James W., Jr., 1948– editor.
Title: Phallacies : historical intersections of disability and masculinity /
edited by Kathleen M. Brian and James W. Trent, Jr.
Description: New York : Oxford University Press, [2017] |
Includes bibliographical references and index.
Identifiers: LCCN 2017002544 (print) | LCCN 2017032788 (ebook) |
ISBN 9780190459000 (updf) | ISBN 9780190458997 (alk. paper)
Subjects: LCSH: Men with disabilities. | Masculinity.
Classification: LCC HV1568 (ebook) | LCC HV1568 .P53 2017 (print) |
DDC 305.9/080811—dc23
LC record available at https://lccn.loc.gov/2017002544

9 8 7 6 5 4 3 2 1
Printed by Sheridan Books, Inc., United States of America

CONTENTS

LIST OF ILLUSTRATIONS

Chapter 5

Chapter 6

Chapter 7

Chapter 9

ACKNOWLEDGMENTS

This volume began as a panel titled "Rehabilitating the Fin de Siècle: Masculinity and Disability in Comparative Perspective," presented at the 2014 annual meeting of the American Historical Society. Organized by Kathleen Brian, the panel brought together papers that investigated how manliness and ability were debated in the long nineteenth century and how these debates structured and constrained economic and political possibilities. The papers combined analyses of popular print media with studies of archival sources, such as medical case files and institutional records, to explore this twining in several distinct geographical locations.

From this panel, the editors developed the current volume as a collection of papers that explore historical intersections of masculinity and disability beyond the nineteenth century. Indeed, the volume draws together historical material from diverse time periods and different western European and North American societies.

The interdisciplinary fields of masculinity studies and disability studies have burgeoned over the past forty years. Emerging in the 1970s, both fields began with scholars casting doubts on long-held claims about the exact nature of sex and the body. From these doubts, masculinity studies, emerging out of the wider field of gender studies, questioned the assumption that femininity and masculinity could be reduced to uncontaminated binary categories of male and female. Likewise, disability studies challenged the assumption that disabilities were merely medical, physiological impairments. As such, both fields began by challenging claims made for the essential *nature* of sex and the body.

From this beginning, the language of masculinity studies, like the more prominent feminist studies (or sometimes merely gender studies), made a distinction between female and femininity, and male and masculinity. Similarly, disability studies designed a distinction between impairment and disability. Male and female, like impairment, became the essential, objective categories of physiological differences, while masculinity and femininity, like disabilities, became the categories of socially constructed differences. In both cases, the emerging fields claimed that masculinity and disability contained no essential reality apart from the socially constructed, relative, and changing shapes that both concepts assumed at the present, had assumed in the past, and might assume in the future.

Despite their common assumptions, the historical studies in the fields of masculinity studies and disability studies have drawn on different material, artifacts, and sources. Most obviously, masculinity studies depend on material from gender studies, while disability studies have tended to rely on studies of particular disabilities and of individuals (sometimes prominent individuals) who have lived with one of these disabilities. Likewise, masculinity studies have emphasized constructions of gender among "typical" men, albeit sometimes in specific settings, associated with a particular class, status, and sexual orientation and often during a specified time. Disability studies, unlike masculinity studies, have focused most often on the "atypical," on groups of people who find themselves outside of corporal or cognitive norms. In short, masculinity studies have emphasized "ordinary" men by deconstructing their ordinariness whereas disability studies have emphasized "atypical" people by deconstructing their difference.

Our book has as its central aim the merging of these two, otherwise separate, fields of study. As such, much of the book focuses on disabled men, who negotiate their masculinity as well as their disability. To accomplish this goal, we first acknowledge the contributors to the volume. Their efforts have produced a group of diverse and fascinating collection of essays. We also acknowledge our OUP editor, Dana Bliss, for his counsel and patience.

Kathleen M. Brian and James W. Trent Jr.

Phallacies

Introduction

David Serlin

In the summer 2014, while visiting London, I took a brief detour down Old Compton Street—for decades the symbolic and historic heart of gay male culture in Soho—and found an unfamiliar face staring back at me. In one shop window, placed amidst familiar sexualized commodities on display—rainbow flags, fetish toys, calendars of shirtless rugby players—I observed an advertisement for Jack Adams underwear featuring former US Marine Alex Minsky. In the years since serving in the Iraq War, Minsky has become a well-known model and spokesman for veterans' empowerment following his recuperation from brain trauma and below-the-knee leg amputation. He has also become one of the premiere male objects of the erotic gaze: images of Minsky, both in his underwear and in sporty athletic gear, depict the veteran as a palimpsest of coded messages about the contemporary male body in which his muscled, tattooed, and tanned body shares the visual field with his prominently displayed advanced prosthetic leg or else his stump's amputation sleeve (see Figure 0.1).

The proliferation of images of disabled veterans, often chosen for their normative beauty as much as for their capacity to perform disability for the camera, is certainly not new, as many of the superb chapters in *Phallacies: Historical Intersections of Disability and Masculinity* will attest. Indeed, Minsky is but one of many veterans who has become part of a constellation of eroticized images of disabled male veterans used across advertising and social media. US photographer Michael Stokes, for instance, who has also taken images of Minsky, initiated a calendar campaign titled "Always Loyal" featuring recent US veterans posed nearly naked—here a pair of Ray-Ban sunglasses, there a Scottish kilt—alongside their visible stumps and prosthetic devices. As with images of Minsky, Stokes's photographs juxtapose manicured disabled bodies alongside both athletic and military gear, this time with the added patriotic resonance of dog tags, Jeeps, missile warheads, and industrial chains. In one prominent example, a bosomy Liberty figure, draped in a Greek toga and bandolier, brandishes a semi-automatic machine gun

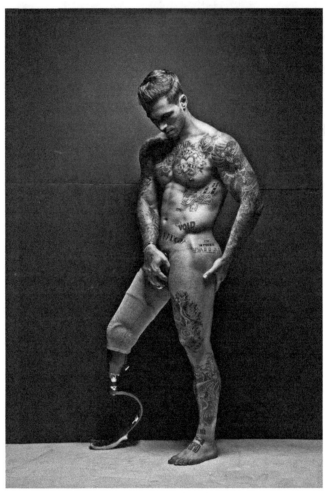

FIGURE 0.1 Veteran and model Alex Minsky, photographed by Michael Stokes, c. 2013. Initially appearing on Facebook, the photograph was taken down, then reinstated with an apology after public outcry, before finally being removed. Reprinted with permission of Michael Stokes.

while cradling a hunky double above-the-knee amputee, Pietà-style, in her lap (see Figure 0.3).

The production of these images of disabled veterans, in which patriotism and homoeroticism are extensively and overtly intertwined, would seem to suggest a new cultural frontier. We are in a different universe from the one, as documented by the late Paul Longmore, that gave us mid-twentieth-century campaigns like the March of Dimes, featuring conservatively dressed young boys and girls hobbling on braces and smiling for the camera, or those a generation later who were subjected to the exploitative televisual gaze of Jerry Lewis's decades-long participation in the Muscular Dystrophy Association's annual Labor Day telethon.[1]

By contrast, Minsky and his fellow veterans could be described as exemplars of new ways of embodying and representing disabled masculinity that have resulted in more complex, and perhaps more ambivalent, images of disabled men in the popular sphere. While this also could be said to be true of other celebrated examples of disabled masculinity, such as Paralympic runners Oscar Pistorius (South Africa) and Jonnie Peacock (England), Stokes's images seem more intentionally crafted to upend the binary claims that attach to traditional, and often essentialist, understandings of disabled men as the opposite of ablebodied men: that is, weak, vulnerable, dependent, and even feminine. As such, they force the viewer to question the presumed hegemony of ablebodied masculinity's claim to certain kinds of privileged bodily codes.

Yet it is also true that, in contrast to the kinds of patriotically charged, though often quite erotic, images of disabled men that have typically proliferated after periods of war—veterans of World War I operating industrial machinery, for instance, or veterans of World War II performing desk work to demonstrate their productive roles in the service economy—the disabled men in Stokes's photographs seem to reflect the kinds of images associated more often with queer nondisabled (and, importantly, nonmilitary) men. These are images less concerned with promoting autonomy or, for that matter, titillating the opposite sex than with serving iconically as equal-opportunity objects of visual pleasure. These are men whose performance of disability, independent of their actual sexual orientation, shares a corner of the same representational universe as those men whose willing exhibition of their desirability takes place not *despite* the indeterminate gender of their viewers but *because* of it: from contemporary actors and performers like James Franco, Nick Jonas, and Jaden Smith, to athletes like David Beckham, or the Warwick Rowers, whose nude calendars have not only ignited the fantasies of millions of fans but have inspired similar projects by numerous cash-strapped organizations. To this end, the Stokes photographs could be said to share the same imaginative space occupied by ostensibly straight actors who proliferate in gay male pornography and inspire the same curiosity—*is he or isn't he?* —that is accorded to those who are identified with the surreptitious sexual activity known as "living on down low."[2]

It would be naïve to think, however, that all challenges to the seemingly unassailable power of heterosexual, gender-normative, ablebodied masculinity are subversive—or, for that matter, successful. The association between disability and masculinity fixated on the relationship between gender norms and bodily norms is itself a historical production that fails to take account of the wider worlds within which disabled masculinities are circulated and maintained. Cognitive functional disabilities, such as the result of brain trauma or posttraumatic stress disorder, or affective disabilities such as autism—so-called "invisible" disabilities—may have their own conventions within clinical or commercial photography or other forms of image making. But since they tend to concentrate on facial and gestural affect more than the rest of the body, they do not fit analogously within older conventions

of disability representation, thereby allowing physical impairments such as amputation to take center stage as an "authentic" container of disability in the public
imagination. Even technological examples that challenge the status of the "natural" body or the "natural" characteristics of gender are, at their core, inflected with
conventions and presumptions shaped by ideas drawn from attitudes toward disability. How, for instance, do we reconcile the contemporary association between
male athleticism and steroid use, which not only causes chronic health problems
but has been used by gender theorists to expose the inherent bankruptcy of using
the "natural" male body as a physical gauge of "authentic" masculinity? Similarly,
how do we understand a controversy within the female-to-male trans* community
in which medical professionals encourage some F2Ms to self-identify with a diagnosis of gender dysphoria, a psychopathological classification rejected by many
trans* and genderqueer activists, to secure their daily regimen of testosterone?
The notion that merely invoking disability in the context of gender roles results in
the outright destabilization of the essential categories associated with normative
models of masculinity and/or ablebodiedness is thus at best a pliable argument
rather than a fact etched in stone.

In many ways, commercial images of disabled male veterans and athletes are
easy prey for anyone conducting contemporary analyses of disability and masculinity. These are images that the late Austrian journalist Stella Young might have
identified as "inspiration porn": that is, they are images framed visually and affec-
tively by sentimental and feel-good motivational rhetoric that make the nondisabled feel better about themselves while they simultaneously hold the disabled
body to an impossibly high standard.[3] And images of war veterans, whether commercial or ideological, continue to be exploited for all kinds of purposes through
no fault of their own. Yet one can see in such "inspiration porn" masculinity's ability to reconstitute its power by subverting cultural codes that disguise the authority that such codes ultimately hold. Indeed, it may be worth comparing eroticized
images of disabled male veterans like Minsky not with figures like David Beckham
but with their most immediate counterparts: the self-generated videos made by
ablebodied military men mimicking the dance moves of pop divas like Beyoncé
and Taylor Swift that have been uploaded to YouTube and other social media sites
to the delight and/or consternation of millions of viewers. As Mickey Weems has
described them, these are videos that depict "military men . . . dancing with each
other like female strippers, bent over with butts waving around (sometimes grind-
ing in the crotch of a buddy)."[4] But rather than merely reveling in such scenes
as extensions of boyish behavior, as the videos' commentators and defenders are
often wont to do, Weems goes on to enumerate the ways in which such

> homoerotic scenes involving a man in an outdoor shower lip-syncing a disco
> song, a man in the latrine, and men dancing together (often with sensuous
> dance moves) are mingled with scenes of a tattered Iraqi flag fluttering in
> the wind, Iraqi captives, children running behind patrol vehicles, armed

personnel in helicopters, a camel, distant explosions, and general grab-ass behavior (including two friendly dance scenes with civilian and military Iraqi men) strung together in a painfully poetic narrative, all of it unspoken.[5]

What might we say is the "unspoken" narrative put forward by queer images of disabled male veterans like Minsky? As standard-bearers for male sacrifice and commitment to nation, veterans have for generations occupied a central role in reproducing certain normative codes of masculinity, just as certain normative conventions of male activity—whether through gym workouts or endurance rituals like fraternity hazing—are indexical for particular bodily ideals associated with masculinity. Such indexes may well be understood for what they are: performative and self-referential spectacles that must be reproduced and reanimated by every conversation, gesture, activity, and image in order to consolidate their normative power. Yet what is exposed by provocative representations of disabled masculinity, such as those curated by Stokes or the dancers in the videos analyzed by Weems— and what is concealed? How do such images traffic in the privileges of ablebodied masculinity, let alone their corollary effects—those of whiteness, or empire, or the aesthetic tyranny of normative male beauty?[6]

Western culture expects and even insists that men with disabilities look like and behave like "real men," often against impossible odds, suggesting that confronting gender normativity is perhaps the ultimate stage of development for disability activism. In the post–"Don't Ask, Don't Tell" era, even images of openly gay and openly disabled veterans—such as Eric Alva, the Marine famous for being the first seriously injured veteran at the beginning of the war in Iraq in 2003—assiduously avoid any associations in which the recognizable contours of an identifiably normative masculinity might be suspect. The recuperative fantasies of contemporary gender politics exert enormous pressure upon disabled men to perform masculine normativity to disavow the appearance of weakness, vulnerability, or dependence. Thus, the capacity of disabled men to perform masculine normativity to be virtually indistinguishable from their ablebodied counterparts is directly proportional to their capacity to flaunt the features of that normativity, or so such recuperative fantasies seem to compel us to believe. In doing so, disabled men become more like ablebodied men who do not have to account for, nor even make efforts to change, cultural presumptions to heteronormative masculinity lest they lose the stature that has been accorded to them as their biological birthright: the presumptive authority of male power (see Figure 0.2).

In this sense, the queering of disabled masculinity may serve more than titillating the libido. As scholars such as Rod Ferguson and Robert McRuer have argued, queering masculinity is not in and of itself an automatically subversive act or even progressive tactic; such actions must be understood in relation to the historical periods and cultural environments in which they were initially generated.[7] During the late 1960s and early 1970s, for instance, radical feminists and gay liberationists of various political stripes and theoretical orientations routinely

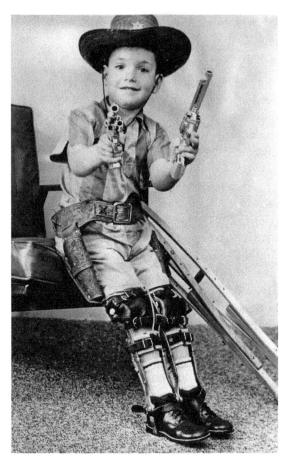

FIGURE 0.2 Disabled boys, like their adult male counterparts, are routinely expected to perform the signifiers of able-bodied masculinity. In this 1962 fundraising campaign photo for the March of Dimes, Jimmy Boggs of Coy, Arkansas, poses in cowboy hat and holster, with drawn pistols, alongside visible leg braces and crutches. Boggs's pose playfully mimics contemporary Cold War images such as Elvis Presley's iconic pose for the film *Flaming Star* (1960), which became better known through Andy Warhol's silk screen *Double Elvis* (1963), itself a playful deconstruction of able-bodied masculinity. Photograph dated October 29, 1962. Courtesy of the author.

argued that patriarchy comes in a wide variety of flavors and is not automatically compromised by differences of race or ethnicity or class or sexual orientation. Categorical opposites stereotypically assigned to certain forms of male behavior— vulnerability and hardness, emotionalism and rationality, sexual bravado and erotic sensitivity—could be interpreted as different sides of the same coin of the realm.[8] During the civil rights era, white female activists in "the Movement" could point to the inherent chauvinism found among their male counterparts. A decade later, second-wave feminists building a case for the Equal Rights Amendment could point to the hypermasculine gay male clone that emerged following the depathologizing of homosexuality by the American Psychological Association in 1973. New configurations of gender and sexual politics promised by the momentum of the 1970s were followed by a carefully orchestrated reactionary backlash during the Reagan-Thatcher years, much of it in reaction to the strides made by women's and men's liberation movements but also to the sobering arrival of AIDS. The parodic elements of *Real Men Don't Eat Quiche* (1982), Bruce Feirstein's bestselling takedown of conventional masculinity, dissolved as newer touchstones for free-range heterosexual male anxiety appeared, including the rediscovery of Joseph Campbell's *The Hero with a Thousand Faces* (1949) in the mid-1980s. Along with cultural phenomena like the *Star Wars* films and Robert Bly's massively influential *Iron John* (1990), public conversations about masculinity began to shift from Freudian exegesis to Jungian archetype, giving shape and cultural legitimacy to mythologies of essential gender roles and the tendentious position that men and women came from altogether different planets other than Earth. Thus followed a new era of highly performative spectacles of communal masculinity—from the rise of evangelical Christian men's groups like the Promise Keepers, to African American participants who galvanized the Million Man March on Washington, DC, to gay political conservatives who founded the Log Cabin Republicans, all syncopated to the emotive weeping of former Speaker of the House John Boehner.[9]

One could argue that the emergence of such groups over the past three decades has only served to reinforce the capacity for hegemonic masculinities to contain varieties of gendered behavior and ablebodied status. The evidence of this, especially in recent years, has been staggering. One need only to consider the 2016 election of President Donald J. Trump, a person who has singlehandedly sutured together the bodily and social privileges of white heterosexual ablebodied masculinity in his public humiliation of disabled journalist Serge Kovaleski and his private sexual degradation of women. The astonishingly misogynist and ableist dimensions of Trump's behavior in each of these instances should be regarded neither as isolated nor as merely coincidental. As journalist Drake Bauer has written, "Trump is *such* an ableist that when he mocked [Kovaleski], his defenders said it was a general, rather than specific insult. . . . In Ann Coulter's estimation, Trump wasn't mocking Kovaleski, 'he was doing a standard retard, waving his arms and sounding stupid.' "[10] "As a defense for Trump's bad behavior, "standard retard" sounds very much like an ablebodied equivalent to "locker room talk," Trump's own phrase of choice in defending the language he used when it was revealed to the nation that he believed his celebrity entitled him to "grab [women] by the pussy."

Trump's electoral victory capitalized, both literally and figuratively, on forms of populist rage and racial insecurity that reach back to a pre–civil rights past; indeed, the Trump–Pence campaign's promise to "Make America Great Again" is devoted to reclaiming and restabilizing the normative privileges of white heterosexual Christian masculinity. But however much we may want to attribute such rage to Trump's rise to power, none of this began with the lead up to the 2016 election or even with the nearly decade-long opposition to Barak Obama. Since the early 1990s, following upon the "zero tolerance" policies enacted by urban mayors like Rudolph Giuliani and then spreading after the events of September 11, 2001, institutional and often bureaucratic forms of power exerted through technologies of surveillance, torture, and imprisonment have been cast globally as the vital antidote to the ostensible excesses of dangerous masculinities, whether cast as ghetto or immigrant, local or transnational, terrorist or jihadist. For two decades, such attitudes have been organized around the perceptions that corruptions or inversions of normative white Christian masculinity are vectors of domestic and international menace. From the prisons of Guantanamo and Abu Ghraib to the streets of Ferguson, Missouri, challenges to the seemingly preternatural codes of ablebodied masculinity have been and continue to be met by a vociferous and often punishing reactionary backlash involving forms of racial violence, sexual predation, and political terrorism against those who do not or will fit within recognizable scripts of gender and physical normativity. Under the administration of Donald Trump and Mike Pence, these attitudes—toward the profiling and prosecution of minorities, religious adherents, and trans* individuals—will continue to not only flourish but deepen.

Yet one must hold steadfast to hope and remember the legacies of our collective past for inspiration—the kind of public outpouring of outrage that has taken shape across the nation and the globe since Trump's inauguration in January 2017. This is because moments of social crisis and political transformation give shape to a host of individuals and communities whose works have deliberately taken on and unpacked the spectacles of normativity with which they are routinely confronted. Within academic culture, tectonic disciplinary and intellectual shifts of the 1960s and 1970s gave rise to the fields of ethnic studies and critical race theory, women's and gender studies and men's studies, LGBT studies and queer studies, and disability studies, and crip theory. Scholars in these fields have not always been in alignment, of course, but they do increasingly recognize each other as workers and activists in adjacent and overlapping fields of critical inquiry, cultural production, and social justice.[11] For almost two generations, scholars and activists in gender studies and disability studies have produced an assortment of both academic and popular works—from books and journal articles to websites and documentaries—within which masculinity and disability are regarded not as symmetrical forms of embodied identity but as intersectional positions to be problematized and questioned on all fronts. And while a significant component of their collective strength is the trepidation with which they assert forms of power, be it personal or institutional, for many scholars the breakdown of the carefully cultivated stature accorded to ablebodied normalcy or heterosexual masculinity is not automatically diminished by challenging or deconstructing the natural order of things. Like Dorothy Gale remembering to click the heels of her ruby slippers, there is a recurring awareness that hegemonic masculinity under duress simply reconstitutes itself to enjoy the power it has always enjoyed from long before the civil rights revolutions of the mid-twentieth century. One thus begins to understand why the enduring legacies of hegemonic masculinity continue to hover uneasily on the margins of any academic or cultural interrogation of disability, masculinity, and the male body.

The authors in *Phallacies* demonstrate how any analysis of the relationship between disability and masculinity always must be understood as a recuperative historical process. Although the chapters deal with a wide-ranging set of themes—some specialized to historical subfields, others common to the broader field of disability history—one shared point of departure is the utility of the medical model of disability. Broadly speaking, the medical model of disability treats the disabled body as damaged, pathological, or lacking wholeness, a position that is anathema to disability rights activists and critical disability scholars. For historians grappling with ontologies of disability, the rise of the medical model is roughly historically concurrent with numerous medical, legal, and moral campaigns to protect and rehabilitate the (often literally) wounded male body and psyche. The nineteenth century bequeathed the basic vocabulary terms of the medical model of disability: the rhetorical and technological tools of rehabilitation and repair that address the specific concerns of the imperiled male body. These included men with frail constitutions—those who suffered from alcoholism or gambling, for example, or those who succumbed to the vice of masturbation—as well as those who were physically wounded through war, accidents, or the new conditions of industrial modernity, such as living in dangerous proximity to railroads and streetcars.

In her chapter on photographs of male hysterics institutionalized in nineteenth-century France, for instance, Daniela Barberis gives us an overview of the work of Jean Martin Charcot, who revolutionized the study of male frailty (in the form of the category of male hysteria) by taking and reading photographs as material evidence of their pathological condition. For Barberis, the gender performance of disabled masculinity was inextricable from the physical evidence of neurotic behavior exhibited, and ultimately captured, by the scientific photograph. Here we have science's claim to neutrality operating on two distinct but overlapping levels: the ability to capture the body in a seemingly neutral way and the ability to freeze a moment of pathological behavior for the ages, not only verifiable to anyone with "common sense" but useful for building an archive of similar artifacts. Barberis thus builds upon the pioneering scholarship of Allen Sekula, whose classic 1986 essay "The Body and the Archive" introduced to critical theorists and historians of visual culture the importance of thinking about photography—both its science and its artifacts—as a tool both of state surveillance and the exertion of state power.[12]

Barberis takes the substance of Sekula's groundbreaking insights and updates them through the important differentials of gender and disability, expanding them not only for the field of disability studies but also for those engaged with the relationship between visual technologies and power dynamics. That many of these grow out of the ubiquitous influence of clinical photography during the nineteenth century is not surprising; but it is equally important to bear in mind the role that medicalization of the disabled male body both predates military medicine and was galvanized by it, producing a rich palimpsest for scholars of disability and masculinity to excavate.

Barberis's chapter on the production of pathology through visual media finds a more benign, but no less insidious, parallel in Anna Creadick's chapter on the creation of the category of "the normal" by the US military in the first half of the twentieth century.[13] As Creadick demonstrates, the normal male recruit was constructed in opposition to the abnormal or pathological male recruit who would be unable to fulfill his role in military service due to his failure as a man. The introduction in the early twentieth century of rigorous psychological and physical tests, combined with the deployment of psychological categories such as homosexuality or neurosis to describe defective mental functioning, gave the military the same imprimatur of objective authority as that used by Charcot and his colleagues a half century earlier. Like Barberis, Creadick is fully aware that the category of the normal is neither neutral nor even self-evident but a truth claim that must be perpetually defended and naturalized for its power to seem like the most obvious thing in the world. Importantly, Creadick cites specific institutions, such as Harvard, and various military hospitals, such as Walter Reed, as cocreators (and thus coconspirators) in the production of military masculinity as both ablebodied and gender normative, with an astonishingly long run that continues to shape both professional and everyday understandings of what it means to be a recruit, a soldier, a veteran, and a hero.

Of course, the language of pathology is not only the province of military recruitment manuals or the clinical practices of medical science; pathology, and its relation to the production of categories of difference, is everywhere one looks in the modern period. In the compelling chapter by Ivy George and James Trent Jr., the authors move the site of pathology from laboratory to the courtroom by conducting a close reading of the 1944 trial of John F. Noxon Jr., arrested for killing his son in a brutal act of murder that shocked the nation. As George and Trent point out, it was not so much the murder of a disabled baby that was shocking—euthanizing babies and sterilizing women with physical or cognitive disabilities had been practiced for generations, with the latter constitutionally protected after the 1927 Supreme Court decision in *Buck v. Bell*—but because the defendant was a wealthy attorney, father of the child, and, most notably, himself a "polio survivor." George and Trent take us through all the various and contradictory elements involved in the prosecution of Noxon for his heinous crime: not just surrounding the violent act of infanticide but the asymmetries involved in attributing infanticide to a disabled man during a historical period in which disabled parenting was not thought to be in and of itself antithetical to raising healthy citizens. In this sense, George and Trent demonstrate how the Noxon case marked a fundamental shift in the ways in which disabled men who were not veterans were equally scrutinized for their capacities to be temperate, responsible members of the social sphere. The pathologization of the disabled male body, as documented in Charcot's photographs or in the statistical data gleaned and mobilized by scientists, was no longer the exclusive domain for understanding the textures (or the limitations) of disabled masculinity.

Clearly, the disabled male body is, and remains, both a physical object as well as a psychic space onto which are repeatedly projected definitions of bodily norms that have emerged from the "objective" fields of medicine and law as well as traditional expectations and social conventions of masculinity. Yet disability, as an ontology with its own religious, moral, and legal vectors of meaning making, should be identified apart from its military standing. That is, for all the scholarship on disability and masculinity in relation to the military body, it is important to recognize that while war has profoundly shaped our understanding of disabled masculinity, it cannot always serve as disabled masculinity's singular point of origin. As with Barberis's analysis of Charcot's photographs, it is urgent that we try to defamiliarize disabled subjects rather than domesticate them—if we want to try to understand them as the enigmatic outliers that they were rather than as standard bearers for masculinity under duress.

The prevalence and authority accorded to the medical model of disability is the central analytical pivot for understanding why disability has been, and remains, directly proportional to the ways in which the male body and psyche were, and continue to be, treated by authorities, experts, and professionals. In the chapter by Kathleen Brian—a historical as well as critical rumination on the strange phenomenon of "suicide clubs" in late-nineteenth-century America—the author challenges the investment that historians make in invoking the male historical subject as rational, deliberate, and in full control of his own agency, whatever the subject's gender presentation or bodily status may be. Brian uses the example of male participants in these suicide clubs to admit, in quite certain terms, that neither the historical record nor the tools of the scholar can make much sense of such fundamentally unknowable historical actors. For Brian, the male body as well as the institutions and professional relationships in which such bodies are embedded must be understood within a historical framework in which conventional associations, such as ruggedness with ablebodiedness and dependence with disability, make sense only until such associations no longer serve the cultural narratives for which they were originally intended. Masculinity, in her example, is not cited merely as a social construction or example of false consciousness but as a precarious invention that inextricably binds "masculinity" or "ablebodiedness" to structures of knowledge making, thus obviating the basis on which they qualify as knowledge in the first place. In this way, Brian sees suicide clubs as a space of historical precariousness and even epistemological precariousness—forms not only for regarding the integrity of men but also for regarding the integrity of history

itself. This sense of underlying precariousness is ultimately what makes the aesthetic and ideological conceits embedded in images of disabled veterans or athletes such powerful cultural objects.

Since all the chapters in this collection follow a historical trajectory from
within canonical understandings of masculinity and disability particular to
Western culture, it is important to recognize the power and influence that such
ideals and values have accrued over time. Many of the contemporary codes of ablebodied masculinity, for instance, are drawn from early Christianity beginning in
the early first century AD, built upon religious understandings of the body as well
as civic and legal codes of civic behavior derived from the Greeks and Romans.
As a result, Christian institutions, such as charities, orphanages, hospitals, and
schools became, and remain, pivotal institutions of care across both the Western
world, as well as those parts of the world colonized by missionaries and nation-
states beginning in the sixteenth century. In the medieval period these were primarily the charge of religious orders, such as that of the Priory of St. Mary Spital,
founded in the late twelfth century outside of the walled City of London (today the
core of the Spitalfields neighborhood in the East End) to tend to those with infec-
tious and chronic illnesses. Since the eighteenth century, the so-called care industries, administered traditionally by women from religious orders, charities, and
civic-minded reform groups as well as from their college-educated counterparts
in the often gender-segregated worlds of nursing and social work, have become
instrumental in administering and sustaining various iterations on the medical
model of disability. Indeed, it would be difficult to overstate the important inter-
penetration of the medical model of disability and the religious model of charity
in the historical development of the care industries—in particular, the investments
made by professional caregivers in their subjects' gendered normativity and social
and spiritual well-being.

The conflicts and contradictions produced at that conjuncture of religious
and spiritual ideals are precisely those which are examined by Meghan Henning
in her chapter on bodily suffering in early Christian thought. Early Christian
authors, adapting the surviving works of Greek and Roman physicians like
Hippocrates and Galen, tried to infuse these older scientific texts with newer,
church-derived values associated with Christian piety, such as sacrifice, auster-
ity, and devotion to the body. As a result, they helped to construct ideas about
virtuous practices associated with masculinity that focused on healthy activities such as taking care of one's body, exercise, nutrition, and abstaining from
vice. This bequeathed to future generations a restrained version of manliness
that would be understood and celebrated as distinct from the excesses of the
ancients and their tolerance of gender and sexual deviance, among other bodily
perversions. Henning's reading of disability and masculinity in early Christian
theological texts also helps to demystify the naturalized category of male bodily
suffering, differentiating between the ways it can be both a spiritual value and
an expression of effeminacy. There are, in other words, types of suffering that

make one act more like a man, and types of suffering that make one act less like a man; and Henning, like her counterparts in this volume, shines an antiseptic light on these bodily constructions to show how religion continues to exert itself on forms of public behavior more typically associated with the secular ideals of post-Enlightenment culture.

Henning's chapter has interesting symmetries with Rebecca Ellis's chapter on the education and care of boys and young men at a school for the blind in early-twentieth-century Argentina. Ellis demonstrates how the charity model associated with Roman Catholicism, which included not only improving the lot of the poor but often controlling their behavior and reforming their identities, was applied by the Román Rosell Institute and Asylum for the Blind, an organization made possible through the generosity of Rosell, a Spanish businessman and philanthropist who immigrated to Buenos Aires in 1933. Ellis argues that Rosell's widow, joined by the reform-oriented wives of wealthy Argentinean businessmen, saw an opportunity to use the Institute to not only educate blind children to become productive citizens but also to underscore the idea that Christian values and social reform were synonymous, thus affirming the role of charity beyond business or political models and into the world of disabled children and adults. Ellis, however, takes this analysis one step further by showing how the investments in care along gendered lines played a significant role in shaping understanding both the objects of education (blind orphan boys) as well as their advocates and protectors (able-bodied wealthy women). Clearly, rehabilitating and normalizing forms of gendered behavior ostensibly linked to the failures of disabled experience is one of the primary foci of the helping professions.

As Ellis's story unfolds, the case of the Román Rosell Institute becomes not a unique outlier in histories of masculinity or disability but, rather, an extraordinarily instructive model that sheds light on the work of nineteenth- and twentieth-century charitable organizations as galvanized by the medical model of disability and its constitutive elements of moral and physical reform. While disability itself is always coproduced in conjunction with norms and conventions of gender, class, race, sexuality, and citizenship, disabled masculinity, especially for those associated with institutions of care, often receives the lion's share of social, political, and economic attention. One could make the argument that this is because we value men and boys over women and girls; therefore, the education and reform and care of those categorized as male will always be elevated above those who occupy the opposite gender. But such a platitude ignores the ways in which neither disability nor masculinity are static categories, neither essential nor commonplace. Care, whether by individuals or institutions, is historically specific in that people in different times and places (and bodies) think about disabled masculinity in different and often contradictory ways. And just as no generation thinks of disability and masculinity in quite the same way, no generation thinks of the experience of disabled masculinity as wholly separated from aspirations to able-bodied masculinity or to physical and gender normativity.

Disabled masculinity, under the rubric of the state and its facilities of care and rehabilitation, constitutes one of the most powerful conjunctions for understanding the production of gender and disability—precisely because they are so naturalized and reinforcing and because they are examples against which all definitions and recalibrations of gender and disability are measured. Veterans, for instance, have enjoyed specialized and often elevated forms of care for centuries, owing perhaps to the state's recognition of disabled veterans as occupying a separate stratum of state munificence. In 1670, for instance, Louis XIV mandated the building of the Hôtel des Invalides in central Paris, a hospital complex created to house and maintain French war veterans. The Hôtel, along with the small pensions awarded to veterans and their counterparts in later wars, produced an enduring association between the care of the male body and the need to ameliorate the assaults on masculinity that may have been compromised on the battlefield. It also inadvertently created, whether by design or default, an understanding that the forces of modernity value and protect some disabled bodies more than others.

What happens, however, when the activities of a social or demographic group are no longer seen to represent the interests of a charitable organization, an entrepreneurial elite, or a nation-state? Robert Bogdan takes up this question in his chapter on the experiences of survival among disabled men in early-twentieth-century American cities. Following roughly the same historical period as that charted by Ellis, and inspired by the work of Susan Schweik's groundbreaking book *The Ugly Laws*, Bogdan describes the economic and social activities of disabled men for whom institutional care was no longer available and, further, was materially inaccessible due to their defiance of the passive models of pity and charity that helped to domesticate disabled identity in the popular imagination.[14] Bogdan adds to our collective knowledge of disabled masculinity by drawing upon not only written sources but also photographs and other visual materials that depict these men as embedded in the street life of urban America. Liberated from the protective (albeit paternalistic) gaze of reformers and clergy, disabled men were portrayed as a danger not only to themselves but to the social worlds they inhabited due to their necessary alliances with the urban *demimonde*. As Bogdan shows, disabled beggars joined the diverse mosaic of itinerant workers, immigrants, grifters, prostitutes, homosexuals, con men, and the so-called dangerous classes who helped redefine urban landscapes as Petri dishes of pathological behavior for sociological study for the next half-century.

In his chapter "Black and Crazy," Lawrence Holcomb expands many of the concerns about pathology raised by Bogdan and also returns us to many of the concerns raised by Daniella Barbers by examining scientific coproduction of masculinity and mental illness in the nineteenth century. But whereas Barberis's subjects, all French inmates, could have their ethnic or national identities subsumed under the political banner of French *fraternité*, Holcomb uses the example of African-American masculinity to chart exploitations of race and disability in the construction of a national Other. Drawing inspiration from disability studies scholar such as the late Christopher Bell as well as historians such as Jonathan Metzl, Holcomb demonstrates that both disability and masculinity use, as their silent foil, understandings of normalcy that are predicated on the white, nondisabled body.[15] When Princeton professor John Dilulio Jr. coined the word "superpredator" in 1995 to characterize the pathological statures of urban black men and boys, he was exploiting fears and fantasies of the black male body pathology that have persisted in the United States for centuries, and which in particular moments (such as the Black Power movement during the late 1960s or the #BlackLivesMatter movement during the mid-2010s), certain forms of black visibility have become naturalized as the domain of urban sociopathy. Holcomb also gestures to the important insights made by historian W. E. B. Du Bois, whose book *The Souls of Black Folk* (1903) introduced to readers the concept that African Americans live with the burden of "double consciousness," a condition of internalized racism and cognitive dissonance. Holcomb's goal, however, is not to promulgate associations between race and pathology (physical or cognitive); rather, it is to provide a critical framework in which tacit assumptions about masculinity and normalcy are understood as part of the elusive kingdom of white privilege.

Race also marks, albeit implicitly, the analysis of John M. Kinder, whose chapter on the marketing of disabled manhood since the Civil War engages with the idea that the white veteran holds the ontological key to disabled citizenship. Read in tandem with Holcomb's claims about the way that black masculinities have been historically pathologized, Kinder's chapter renders whiteness and disability as mutually reinforcing markers of social status. Kinder deploys an archive of advertising images drawn from the 1860s forward to underscore the value of the disabled veteran to commercial and cultural enterprise, and his examples routinely show the way that certain commodities, such as automobiles, were used to draw out connections between the innovative or comfortable benefits of their product with the kinds of innovations and comforts a disabled veteran might experience with a prosthetic device. Capitalism's genius routinely exploits these connections between forms of national sacrifice and forms of conspicuous consumption, and Kinder shows that even the most contemporary examples of this—whether promoting the Paralympics or the latest wheelchair design—is a story that has been told before by industrial capitalism many, many times.

While Kinder and Holcomb focus on the confluence of disability and masculinity as deeply racialized as well as commercially profitable, Jessica Meyer examines disabled masculinity in the context of Britain after the First World War—in particular, the kinds of stories told by medical caregivers in the British Royal Army Medical Corps. Whereas Holcomb examines elements of popular culture and Kinder examines aspects of commercial culture, Meyer takes an approach to ontologies of care that is more archeological. In her unearthing and analyzing letters, diaries, and memoirs, Meyer evaluates not only the status of disabled veterans but also the lives of medical caregivers who attended to these men. In dialogue with the work of British historians of disability such as Deborah Cohen, Sanatu

Das, and Jeffrey Reznick, Meyer conveys the ways in which gendered assumptions about care have been seen, historically, as female (and, therefore, feminine) until the emergence of a stratum of professional care giving that redefined the parameters of empathy through a rational, and thus, masculine sensibility.[16] British medical caregivers shared with their disabled charges the burden of defining themselves as gender normative despite assumptions that the masculine power of a veteran or a caregiver was somehow compromised, either socially or professionally, from their ablebodied male counterparts. Meyer's chapter thus helps us rethink a strain of scholarship within disability studies, popularized by the feminist philosopher Eva Feder Kittay, whose critical association between caregiving and female labor has influenced scholarship on disability and gender for over two decades.[17] What Meyer contributes does not challenge Kittay's insights but, rather, expands and deepens them to include men whose experiences and ambitions cannot be defined solely by the privileges of normative masculinity.

One of the recurring tropes within contemporary historical assessments of disabled masculinity—either empirical or imagined—is the presumption that the condition of disability results inevitably in male sexual frustration. During the first half of the twentieth century, concerns about impotence and performance, combined with concerns about physical and emotional fragility and dependence on caregivers, became a phenomenally powerful point of professional and social consternation. One only has to invoke the memory of Harold Russell, the real-life veteran and double amputee who won the Academy Award for Best Supporting Actor for his performance in William Wyler's *The Best Years of Our Lives* (1946), to remember how, in the years before the disability rights movement of the early 1970s, popular culture regularly seized upon images of the disabled veteran as metonymic of the recuperation of disabled masculinity.[18] Less well known, however, is the fact that Wyler first saw Russell in a film produced by the US Army to train veterans with disabilities how to take care of themselves and become physically and socially independent. Wyler, among many other cultural producers and interpreters of the period, worked vigilantly to disassociate disabled veterans like Russell with any images of dependency or vulnerability, tapping into a Cold War unconscious that sought out dominant male archetypes in order to survive a future of social and sexual uncertainty.

Beth Linker's and Whitney E. Laemmli's chapter, which focuses on the same postwar period charted by Wyler's film, examines the construction of a "science of paraplegic impotence," in which medical and psychiatric experts perceived male vulnerability as a crisis tantamount to the crisis of national defense. Impotence, Linker and Laemmli argue, was not merely an individual or familial problem; it was, in fact, a national problem with repercussions for national security and civic health. For many scholars of gender and sexuality during the postwar period, concerns over impotence and reproduction were the base-superstructure dialectic that animated scientific and social endeavor; as historians like Margot Canaday have demonstrated, heterosexual reproduction

FIGURE O.3 Unnamed Iraq veteran and ex-Marine, injured by an improvised explosive device, with model of "Liberty." Photographed by Michael Stokes ca. 2014 and published in his book *Always Loyal* (2015). Reprinted with permission of Michael Stokes.

and the benefits of citizenship, as codified in the G.I. Bill of 1944, were proof that American society elevated masculinity's status to the forefront of domestic concern.[19] Disabled veterans might not be able to reproduce, or might have to endure years of physical and psychological therapies, but the weight of ablebodied masculinity and all of its powers of persuasion would shape daily experiences and life ambitions. Like Kinder and Meyer, Linker and Laemmli examine materials drawn from archival collections as well as those from popular culture to show how impotence was fought on the home front and the clinical front as a danger parallel to and indexical of incursions that threatened the domestic sphere and, by extension, the global political sphere.

Disability has never been, nor ever will be, segregated from the social because of the way that the social has always needed disability in order to define the parameters of what is ablebodied. This is the lesson that the late Eve Kosofsky Sedgwick taught us more than three decades ago: that which is designated as "homosexual" or "queer" has no inherent properties of its own except its relationship to that which is understood to be familiar and normative.[20] Sedgwick's work, both her literary scholarship as well as her political activism, stemmed from her belief in the power of narrative to both convey as well as expose these properties. Narrative structures, whether produced by a single author or by a national mythology, have been instrumental in producing and representing the properties of disability and masculinity as both mutually exclusive as well as mutually coconstitutive. This is beautifully expressed by Susan Schweik in her chapter on the classic American musical *Porgy and Bess*. Schweik examines the figure of Porgy, represented on stage as a black disabled man, to explore how author Dubois Hayward exploited black disabled masculinity in a period when, as Holcomb makes so evident in his work, blackness was more closely aligned with the pathologies of disability than it was with properties of manhood. By performing a close reading of Heyward's novel, a text much less well known now than the Gershwin musical based upon it, and by contextualizing both the novel and the musical with other narratives of black disabled masculinity, Schweik shows us that to ignore historical constructions of disabled masculinity within a racial framework is to ignore the importance of narratives of oppression even *within* histories of disability. Schweik concludes her chapter with a generative rereading of "Summertime," the musical's iconic song, the lyrics for which Hayward provided to the Gershwins. Schweik argues that most interpreters of the song align its importance to histories of race over those of histories of disability, much to the diminution of the song's cumulative power as a text with intersectional impact.

Like Schweik, Carolyn Slaughter takes an approach to a well-known subject—Ernest Hemingway—to uncover the relationship between an author's use of narrative to characterize disabled masculinity and the cultural contexts in which that use of narrative emerges. Slaughter, like Schweik, is invested in biography and uses Hemingway's relationship to his family (which, Slaughter tells us, routinely effeminized and humiliated young Ernest) as a corollary to Hemingway's perpetual association between effeminacy and social abjection. Using a psychoanalytic framework shaped and expanded by the insights of critical disability studies, Slaughter uses Hemingway's *A Farewell to Arms* as well as his posthumously published *The Garden of Eden* to draw associations between Hemingway's wounded psyche and his persistent desire to assert his heterosexual masculinity.

As Schweik's and Slaughter's chapters demonstrate, content analysis of texts can provide rich opportunities for interpreting the multiple and contradictory aspects of representations of disabled masculinity. But scholars focused on content analysis have also delivered certain critical tools to the study of media that are not necessarily language-based, which provide scholars and artists with numerous opportunities to lift the veil off or cultural narratives embedded in other forms of artistic production. We can find this in Mary S. Trent's wonderfully rich chapter about Henry Darger, the Chicago janitor and Ür-outsider artist whose creative works, produced in secret during the mid-twentieth century, were discovered in the early 1970s and which have come to critical and popular attention over the past two decades. Although Darger's artistic *oeuvre*, centered around his unpublished fifteen-thousand-page dystopian magnum opus *The Realms of the Unreal*, has been the source of much art historical scholarship, Trent takes the necessary steps of situating Darger and his work in relation to his longstanding relationship to disability as a source of artistic production. For instance, Trent argues that Darger's infamously provocative multimedia paintings—which combine watercolor paints, photographs, commercial advertisements, and industrial detritus to depict young children, especially girls, in violent and often apocalyptic sexual settings—must be understood in relation to his experience as a young man who was institutionalized in the Illinois Asylum for Feeble-Minded Children and his adult desire to serve as a protector to vulnerable children. Rather than merely gawk at or else exploit the artist's eccentric worldview, as many critics and commentators have tended to do in the absence of a more sophisticated vocabulary for thinking through disability, Trent helps avoid the impulse to marginalize Darger by explicating some of the elemental contradictions at the core of his erotic fantasy world, especially as shaped by his own complex relationship to institutional exertions of patriarchal masculinity.

Like Trent, film scholar Murray Simpson shows the power of disability studies' approach to patriarchal masculinity's power in his provocative chapter about filmmaker Russ Meyer and the director's most (in)famous film, 1965's *Faster Pussycat! Kill! Kill!* While typically viewed as a notorious example of the "sexploitation" genre of cult films from the 1960s, Simpson argues that such an approach puts more emphasis on the objectification of female characters and the prurient heterosexual gaze of the director. Simpson offers, by contrast, a more nuanced reading that puts disability front and center, allowing both female and male characters to occupy positions along a horizontal continuum in which assumptions about femininity and masculinity in relation to disability and pathology converge and diverge. In applying a disability critique of male characters and their differences (both embodied and affected), Simpson suggests that what makes the film a "cult classic" is less about its heaving bosoms and camp sensibility and more about its embedded presumptions about compromised and damaged masculinity—presumptions that are inextricably linked to the exploited elements of women's sexuality for which the film is well-known.

Taken together, the chapters in *Phallacies* persuade us that any historical narratives that discuss the male body but that fail to engage with the presumptively "natural" categories of ablebodied normativity along with gender normativity are not only incomplete but deeply impoverished. Like the advertisements adorning shop windows featuring Alex Minsky in his underwear, such narratives demonstrate how the conjuncture of disability and masculinity, far from fixed, is the wet clay out of which contemporary forms of embodied knowledge continue to be molded. The authors in *Phallacies* thus ask us to contemplate what it means to be a man and what it means to have a disability not as identities or subjectivities that are fixed in time and space but, rather, as ways of traveling in the world—side by side, consciously and even warily, all the while resisting the temptation to be subsumed and defined by each other.

Notes

1. Paul Longmore, *Telethons: Spectacle, Disability, and the Business of Charity* (New York: Oxford University Press, 2016).

2. See, for example, J. L. King, *On the Down Low: A Journey into the Lives of Straight Black Men Who Sleep with Men* (New York: Broadway Books, 2004).

3. Stella Young, "We're Not Here for Your Inspiration," *The Drum* (July 3, 2012), http://www.abc.net.au/news/2012-07-03/young-inspiration-porn/4107006.

4. Mickey Weems, "Taser to the 'Nads: Brutal Embrace of Queerness in Military Practice." In Eric A. Eliason and Tad Tujela, eds., *Warrior Ways: Explorations in Modern Military Folklore* (Logan: Utah State University Press, 2012), 155.

5. Weems, "Taser to the 'Nads," 155.

6. See Aaron Belkin, *Bring Me Men: Military Masculinity and the Benign Façade of American Empire, 1898–2001* (New York: Oxford University Press, 2012).

7. Rod Ferguson, *The Reorder of Things: The University and Its Pedagogies of Minority Difference* (Minneapolis: University of Minnesota Press, 2012), and Robert McRuer, "We Were Never Identified: Feminism, Queer Theory, and a Disabled World," *Radical History Review* 100 (Winter 2006), 148–154.

8. For a provocative recent exploration of this, see Jane Ward, *Not Gay: Sex Between Straight White Men* (New York: New York University Press, 2015). See also Michael Kimmel, *Guyland: The Perilous World Where Boys Become Men* (New York: HarperPerennial, 2009).

9. Robert Bly, *Iron John: A Book About Men* (New York: Addison Wesley, 1990).

10. Drake Baer, "Let's Talk About Trump's Ableism," *New York Magazine* (published online October 18, 2016), http://nymag.com/scienceofus/2016/10/lets-talk-about-trumps-ableism.html; italics in original.

11. For important examples of men's studies scholarship, see R. W. Connell, *Masculinities*, 2nd ed. (Berkeley: University of California Press, 2005), Michael Kimmel, *Manhood in America: A Cultural History*, 3rd ed. (New York: Oxford University Press, 2011), and Todd W. Reeser, ed., *Masculinities in Theory: An Introduction* (New York: Wiley-Blackwell, 2010).

12. Allan Sekula, "The Body and the Archive," *October* 39 (Winter 1986), 3–64.

13. Julian Carter, *The Heart of Whiteness: Normal Sexuality and Race in America, 1880–1940* (Durham, NC: Duke University Press, 2007), Anna G. Creadick, *Perfectly Average: The Pursuit of Normality in Postwar America* (Amherst: University of Massachusetts Press, 2010), and Sara Igo, *The Averaged American: Surveys, Citizens, and the Making of a Mass Public* (Cambridge, MA: Harvard University Press, 2008).

14. Susan Schweik, *The Ugly Laws: Disability in Public* (New York: New York University Press, 2009).

15. Christopher Bell, "Introducing White Disability Studies: A Modest Proposal." In Lennard J. Davis, ed. *The Disability Studies Reader*, 2nd edition (New York: Routledge, 2006), 275–282; Jonathan Metzl, *The Protest Psychosis: How Schizophrenia Became a Black Disease* (Boston: Beacon Press, 2011).

16. Deborah Cohen, *The War Come Home: Disabled Veterans in Britain and Germany, 1914–1939* (Berkeley: University of California Press, 2001), Sanatu Das, *Touch and Intimacy in First World War Literature* (New York: Cambridge University Press, 2008), and Jeffrey S. Reznick, *Healing the Nation: Soldiers and the Culture of Caregiving in Britain During the Great War* (Manchester, UK: Manchester University Press, 2011).

17. See, for example, Eva Feder Kittay, *The Subject of Care: Feminist Perspectives on Dependency* (New York: Rowman & Littlefield, 2003).

18. David Gerber, ed., *Disabled Veterans in History* (Ann Arbor: University of Michigan Press, 2000).

19. Margot Canaday, *The Straight State: Sexuality and Citizenship in Twentieth-Century America* (Princeton, NJ: Princeton University Press, 2011).

20. See, for instance, Eve Kosofsky Sedgwick, *Epistemology of the Closet* (Berkeley: University of California Press, 2008 [1990]).

PART I

Is He Normal?

1

Disability's Other

THE PRODUCTION OF "NORMAL MEN"
IN MIDCENTURY AMERICA

Anna Creadick

"Leaders of the people should rise from among those who are well and fit."

—CLARK W. HEATH, *HARVARD GRANT STUDY OF NORMAL MEN, 1945*

This past autumn I returned home to North Carolina to visit my father who was suffering from late-stage, terminal cancer. Each day I sat at his hospital bedside, observing his strength come and go, watching doctors talk to him and nurses care for him and machines track each of his failing systems. Each night, I returned to the tiny textile-mill town of Mebane to spend the night with a dear aunt and uncle. One bright morning, I decided to take a walk to clear my head. Crossing the railroad tracks to enter Mebane's small commercial district, I stopped short before the plate-glass window of a stylish antique shop. I couldn't believe what I was seeing: two plaster statues, sculpted at half-size, anthropometric models of the "normal" midcentury American male and female body.

Dubbed "Normman and Norma," these statues had inspired my first book.[1] I had first seen them on temporary display in a German Hygiene museum, next to plans for the Nazi death camps. Although the original statues were kept in the Cleveland Health Museum, I knew plaster reproductions had been sold to doctor's offices across America. This was the only possible explanation for how these copies had landed in Mebane, to stare out at me now like a pair of hipster tchotchkes. The juxtaposition of Norm's "divine average" physique and my own father's frail, failing form shook me again, this time to the core. Like small sentinels at the boundary between beauty and frailty, health and disease, function and dysfunction, these inanimate objects made concretely visible so much of what the "normal" has historically been designed to include and exclude (Figure 1.1). Once again, and even more personally, now, those boundaries seemed a matter of life and death.

FIGURE 1.1 "Normman" model (courtesy of the Dickinson-Belskie collection, Cleveland Health Museum).

Like "disability," "normality"[2] is an epistemological category with a specific and traceable history. This chapter tracks one watershed moment in that history, a moment in which normality was powerfully positioned as disability's Other. In the United States in 1945, a felt need for a "return" to normal after decades of depression and war worked in tandem with more insidious forces of science, medicine, industry, and the military to produce powerful definitions of normality. In 1945, the Normman and Norma models, mathematically defined and sculpted in three dimensions, were acquired for permanent display in the Cleveland Health Museum. That same year, an interdisciplinary team of scientists published the findings of their Harvard Grant Study of Normal Men, detailing everything from blood pressure to personality to home life to hair color in a popular volume titled

Young Man, You Are Normal.[3] Precisely as hundreds of thousands of veterans began to return from World War II variously altered, injured, impaired, or disabled by battle, the nation's medical and scientific communities greeted them and their families with a powerful new discourse about "normal men." It was knowledge designed to include and exclude, and it was a knowledge these same veterans had inadvertently helped to generate.

In Cleveland, the science used anthropometric methods to sculpt the normal American body, and nearly 4,000 local citizens sized themselves up against its dimensions. At Harvard, the science determined not just the fitness of the normal man's body but the normality of his mind and spirit. In both cases, disability existed either explicitly or as a shadow presence, and masculinity became the hallmark of postwar citizenship. By both gendering normality and defining it with such supposed precision, this postwar science of "normal men" quietly invoked then loudly excluded disabled bodies from the social body.

The New Normal

During the war, the "normalizing" power of the Selective Service had already rejected nearly 30 percent of enlistees and draftees as either "mentally or physically unacceptable."[4] But as the war ended, the physical and psychological effects of combat made certain kinds of impairments undeniably visible, nationwide. Some 671,000 Americans returned wounded, 300,000 of them seriously enough to require long-term care and rehabilitation. "Neuropsychiatric casualties" mounted steadily during the final years of the war, with up to 500,000 men hospitalized for neuropsychiatric reasons in 1945 alone.[5] With more than three times the number of troops deployed in World War II as in the First World War, the challenges of reintegration reached every corner of American life. Even Hollywood worked to address the crisis with the film *The Best Years of Our Lives.* With plotlines that addressed unemployment, alcoholism, divorce, and the poignant experience of a football hero-turned double amputee, the movie grossed $10 million in the year after its 1946 release to become the second largest moneymaker in movie history, surpassed only by *Gone with the Wind.* The film's near-record seven Academy awards included a Best Supporting Actor as well as a "special" Oscar for the amateur actor and Army vet Harold Russell, for "bringing hope and courage to his fellow veterans" through his portrayal of double-amputee Homer Parrish. The prominence of his performance helped invoke not only the 15,000 men who lost hands or arms in combat[6] but the struggles of all veterans to reintegrate, whether their scars were visible or hidden.

If war had in this way produced "disability," war was also a determining force in the production of a new "normal." The mass mobilization of thousands of soldiers during World War II and, to a lesser degree, World War I, enabled the gathering of voluminous "facts" and statistics. Hundreds of thousands of minds and bodies could be, and were, measured up one side and down the other, and the data was applied not only for wartime but, increasingly, for postwar purposes. One "hasty study" completed in 1944, for example, measured 1,000 Women's Army Corps volunteers and nurses to standardize better-fitting uniforms. Those findings were supplemented with postwar measurements of WACs and nurses passing through Army separation centers, where 8,859 women were measured in 65 different ways "from length of body to breadth of nasal root." These postwar figures, with their veneer of science, were then taken up by "Harvard-trained" anthropologist Francis E. Randall who "settled down in the R & D branch of the Quartermaster General's office and began to sift [the] reams of new figures . . . to determine how American women differ in size and appearance." Eventually, this scientist hoped to determine "whether married women are heavier than single, and whether the WAC officers as a whole were taller than the enlisted women."[7]

Similar studies accumulated in the immediate postwar context: the heads of more than 3,000 GIs were measured by the Chemical Warfare Service to find "the most comfortable gas mask," but the results were to be applied in civilian life for "fitting eyeglasses, the production of hats, dental and medical service; telephone headsets . . . goggles and eye-shields, as industry and the spacings in planes and land vehicles to accommodate the body of *the average man*."[8] In such scenarios, bodies already preselected by the armed forces for their fitness were measured *en masse* to produce "standard" spaces and equipment to fit the bodies of what was termed the "average man." This normal/standard/average postwar American body was thus always-already conceived as able-bodied, and usually, as male.

As the wartime availability of docile bodies and aggregate measurements made new investigations possible, a curious obsession took hold. Doctors, psychiatrists, scientists, and physical anthropologists began to isolate the "normal" as a subject and began to gather data to measure the normal with increased precision. These researchers offered passionate defenses of their work, pointing urgently to the "fatal lack of norms" that had preceded their own historical moment. William H. Sheldon, for example, made just such a case in introducing his infamous 1954 somatotyping handbook *Atlas of Men*:

> Everywhere the rudimentary efforts toward formulating a science of man have been blocked by an almost fatal lack of norms. . . . Much of the waste [in research] is traceable to failure to record who the subjects in various experiments were . . . in terms of a taxonomy that would give them identification tags capable of systematizing and relating the whole flow of research on human beings. The somatotype is intended as a kind of identification tag aimed at precisely this goal. The somatotype identifies a person as belonging to a biological group or family . . . providing a universal frame of reference . . . a general human taxonomy."[9]

Taxonomic thinking, designed to produce division and difference, was characteristic of this "new normal" of the 1940s and 1950s. As the lead researcher of the

Harvard Grant Study of Normal Men argued, "Study of the normal person, who is not seriously afflicted with some disease or defect and whose behavior does not get him into difficulties in society, has been comparatively neglected."[10] Conceiving *normal* as the absence of illness, "defect," or criminal behavior, this science was rife with bias regarding race, class, sexuality, gender, ethnicity, and ability. An atmosphere of midcentury scientism allowed ableist and patriarchal notions to be embedded into the idea of the normal with particular potency.

Normality's emergence in 1945 is best described as a re-emergence, since the epistemology of normality stretches back at least to the Enlightenment's rise of statistics, the emergence of the "normal curve," and Adolphe Quetelet's concept of *l'homme moyen*, or the "average man."[11] Lennard Davis notes that the use of the word *normal* to mean "standard, regular, usual" emerged surprisingly recently, in 1840. The term *norm* emerged "in the modern sense" around 1855, and *normality* and *normalcy* only appear in 1849 and 1857, respectively.[12] By the 1920 presidential campaign, Warren G. Harding famously won the election by promising a "return to normalcy." That post–World War I invocation of the normal stitched the concept to the nation itself, a usage that would make sense anew following World War II. In 1945, the word *normality* began to appear in the *Reader's Guide to Periodical Literature*, and a proliferation of essays on the concept would be indexed in the *Reader's Guide* consistently across the next two decades.[13] In this midcentury discourse, we see the coalescing of all of the term's previous associations: the normal as middle or average, as typical, as fit, as stable, as ideal, and as national condition.

It is important to acknowledge that the "new normal" of the mid-twentieth century emerged alongside its own critique. Even the two scientific projects I discuss next operated from functional definitions of *normal* that were not indisputable but in fact hotly debated. "In medical practice, 'normal' is almost clinical shorthand for 'nothing abnormal found upon examination,'" complained Clark Heath, lead researcher for the Harvard Grant Study.[14] His group instead worked from a definition of *normal* that leaned more toward *optimal*: "'Normal' is defined as the *balanced*, harmonious blending of functions that produce good integration."[15] Peer experts like Yale neuro-anatomist C. Daly King protested the sloppiness with which research like the Grant Study employed the term, arguing that "[w]hat is, in fact, normal can never be ascertained simply by the use of any mathematical tool, because its essential dependence is upon qualitative considerations, and mathematics deals with quantitative data."[16] King was particularly critical of the way the field of psychology increasingly employed "statistical methods" with a tendency toward "the fallacious and deceptive misuse of norm and normal in the psychologically mistaken sense of typical or average." The normal, King maintained, is "objectively, and properly, to be defined as that which functions in accordance with its design."[17] Debates over the concept simmered across disciplines and contexts until the early 1960s, when the critique of the normal actually became the dominant mass culture discourse.[18]

In 1945, however, the "new normal" was pursued with great confidence. This science, of which Normman and the Harvard Grant Study were emblematic, was striking for its attention to *men* in particular. The anthropometric experiment that produced Normman and the interdisciplinary study that measured "normal men" in body, mind, and spirit were both products of a general (re)turn to normality at this time. The focus on manhood and masculinity was amplified by the specific context of the end of World War II.

Normal Bodies

Judith Butler has argued that we must ask "how bodies which fail to materialize provide the necessary 'outside,' if not the necessary support, for the bodies which, in materializing the norm, qualify as bodies that matter."[19] In 1945, bodies "outside" such as the disabled or wounded body of war were epistemologically necessary for the scientific materialization of the normal body. Yet the normal body also seems to have helped constitute a collective disabled body as its Other. Lennard Davis notes that the mid-nineteenth-century emergence of the normal set the stage for a new discourse on disability to emerge by the late nineteenth and early twentieth centuries.[20] Can "normality" be said to have produced "disability" again in the mid-twentieth century, in a genealogy similar to what Foucault described as the clinical "invention" of homosexuality producing heterosexuality as its effect?[21] After World War II, "normal" was so thoroughly quantified, measured, materialized, and defined that it became one "necessary support" for the materialization of disability in the later twentieth century.

The midcentury science of the normal body was epitomized by the fields of anthropometry and somatotyping. Anthropometry, or the science of comparative measurement of the human body, had existed since the late eighteenth century but had become a method favored by the booming midcentury field of physical anthropology. Somatotyping, a method introduced by W. H. Sheldon in 1940, was essentially anthropometry using photographs of nude bodies rather than live subjects. Both fields understood the body through the precision of measurements and the numerical logic of bell curves. Both fields produced taxonomies of the body that separated fit, fitter, and fittest.

The methods of anthropometry were combined with sexology, physical anthropology, and art to produce Normman and Norma, the two model bodies of the "average" American form that made their debut in 1945. Produced along with a number of other medical models from data gathered by the physician and renowned sexologist Robert L. Dickinson, the statues were sculpted in alabaster by his colleague Abram Belskie as part of a series of gestational and childbirth models designed for education and display. A selection of the birth models was shown by Dickinson at the 1939 World's Fair, where he met Bruno Gebhard, curator for the Cleveland Health Museum. A German émigré, Gebhard had formerly been the curator of the Hygiene Museum in Dresden from 1927 to 1935.[22] Out of admiration and a shared interest in public health education, Dickinson donated his collection to Gebhard's Cleveland Health Museum for permanent display, and in July of 1945, their acquisition was announced to the press, which focused on the Norm and Norma, the final and most newsworthy of the models.

Produced from the largest number of anthropometric measurements ever assembled for such a purpose (over 15,000, taken from a variety of sources, including the military and the garment industry), Normman and Norma were sculpted at half-size, with the label "native white American" on their pedestals. "Nation's Ideal Boy and Girl Come to City in Sculpture," read the headlines in the *Cleveland Plain Dealer*, and soon the *Dealer* and the museum together sponsored a "Norma Look-Alike Contest," around which dozens of local newspaper features were written and for which some 4,000 Ohio-area women sent in their measurements in hopes of winning war bonds. When a local theater cashier won the contest, the news revealed that her measurements did not exactly match Norma's; they only came closest.[23]

The main spokesperson for Normman and Norma in the national media was physical anthropologist Harry L. Shapiro. In his 1945 essay "A Portrait of the American People" written for *Natural History*, Shapiro began by discussing "Norma—the average American girl" but soon turned to "'Normman,' her male counterpart" to discuss how bodies have changed over time.[24] Shapiro contrasted Normman somewhat unfavorably against classical sculpture *Doryphorus, the Spear Thrower*, "a Greek ideal of about 400 B.C.," whose "massive torso and well-proportioned limbs, combined to give an appearance of power rather than agility or speed," and then more favorably to Dudley Sargent's late-nineteenth-century sculptures of shorter, slimmer "average young man and woman of the Gay Nineties."[25] Shapiro celebrated the fact that the postwar Normman, while not the classical ideal, was, at least, larger than his grandparents: "our average now surpasses those of the various European countries from which our population is derived." With "melting pot" metaphors and a sense of national pride, Shapiro considered, "How far the American people are evolving a characteristic American type fundamentally distinct from those of our European contemporaries." His answer was mathematical but also unmistakably eugenicist: "The American of today remains a close derivative of the stocks that have settled here . . . [h]is deviations . . . are either the results of mixture . . . or the consequence of an increased size with the attendant changes in bodily proportion that follow on such a quantitative expansion."[26] On the eve of the end of World War II, Shapiro understood and described bodily strength and power in nationalistic terms, intertwining the fit male body with a sense of national fitness.

Gender tensions appeared in the press over whether Norm or Norma would be the public embodiment of postwar normality. While in some contexts Normman was foregrounded, in others Norma was emphasized either through the focus of the newspaper story or the prominence of her photograph. Significantly, the

Norma figure was understood as female but not necessarily described as *feminine*. In fact, much of Shapiro's discourse dwelt on the distinctions between Norma's form and that of the "ideal" woman of the day, the fashion model or pin-up, or the "wasp-waisted" women of past eras. Articles in the *Cleveland Plain Dealer* focused on Norma's physical strength and prowess, specifically in contrast to her Victorian-era "grandmother."[27] Such distinctions suggest that what Norma may have embodied was what Jack (formerly Judith) Halberstam has called *female masculinity*.[28] Such a conception makes sense, particularly in the context of figures like Rosie the Riveter and the general national turn toward female masculinity in the late 1930s and early 1940s. If women's strength was seen as a powerful way to buttress the nation while so many men were battling economic depression and then fighting the enemy abroad, Norma's soldier stance and muscular physique can be seen as a remnant of that moment before the more baroque gender divisions that would characterize the 1950s. The strength and health of the woman worker body was both resonant and malleable, however. As part of a series of birth models, Norma was also likely foregrounded for her reproductive function. As a "fit" and able-bodied figure, she could and did become an "ideal for which to strive" in terms of hard-bodied national fitness: one Cleveland physical education teacher even considered Norma's measurement a new goal for high school students.[29] Norma's youth and whiteness allowed her to fit eugenicist fantasies of postwar citizenship.[30]

If Norma was a vehicle for the alignment of (female) masculinity with the normal in 1945, what, then, was Normman's specific function? Feminist theorists have charted how the female body has been subject of and subject to science since the seventeenth century. Susan Bordo points specifically to the links between the quantification of women's bodies and patriarchal control. She notes that frequently, "on the other side" of such science stands " 'an innocent and dignified 'he' . . . to represent the part of the person that wants to stand clear of the flesh, to maintain perspective on it,' "[31] In this sense, since Norma was frequently emphasized as the "figure . . . figured out by science," Normman could simply stand for the unmarked and unremarkable "normal" body. His masculine ability, his phallic power (usually concealed by a fig-leaf in the popular press), his quiet stature and broad-shouldered strength could seem less situational and more transcendent, more permanent. Normman could embody the normal *human*.

With an explicit focus on "normal men," masculinity and ability were encoded in the Harvard Study of Normal Men from its conception. Between 1940 and 1944, the study looked at between 60 and 70 men per year for a total of 268 subjects.[32] The results were published in 1945 in two versions, an academic text *What People Are: A Study of Normal Young Men*, and a popular volume, *"Young Man, You Are Normal": Findings from a Study of Students*. The popular volume was authored by the well-known provocateur, eugenicist, and Harvard physical anthropologist Earnest Hooton, who described the design of the study:

First each individual went through a medical examination and physiological tests, then an anthropological examination. Next the psychologist investigated his higher mental processes and the social worker interviewed him about his home environment, his college activities, etc. Finally he had a series of hour meetings with one of the psychiatrists, who studied his personality traits. In nearly every case, the social worker interviewed the parents of the boys at their homes. After the first intensive studies, the subjects were seen again from time to time during the rest of their college residence, and an annual postgraduate follow-up was instituted. ... Data on the continuing careers of the Grantees are available for 259 individuals out of the 268 who participated in the study.[33]

To chart the contours of the normal man's body, the study relied on somatotyping, but rather than describe their subjects' body build in Sheldon's language of "endomorph, mesomorph, ectomorph," the Grant Study developed its own terminology. Dr. Carl Seltzer, anthropologist to the Grant Study, produced the new classification, ranking the bodies from "strong masculine component" to "moderate masculine component" to "weak masculine component." The new somatotype classification according to "masculine component" was necessary, Hooton argued, to "avoid the direct imputation of femininity to persons who, after all, are primarily male."[34] While Hooton acknowledged that masculinity and femininity occur "in varying degrees" in both men and women, the terminology of the study aligned gender and sex, masculinity and manhood, and assigned normality to that constellation.

A picture is worth a thousand words in understanding the power of these classifications, and photographs were included in both the academic and popular books on the Grant Study (Figure 1.2). Faces and genitals were omitted in Hooton's text, but genitals were displayed in Heath's academic tome for Harvard University Press.

Fully 90 percent of the Grant Study subjects fell into the "strong masculine component" categorization with the "remaining 10 percent distributed over the weaker categories."[35] As the pictures make clear, "weakness" of masculine component simply translated to a softness and femininity of form (Figure 1.3). Yet while the "normal boys" were "usually well endowed in the masculine characteristics of their physique," according to Hooton," they were "mediocre to poor in physical condition" and in fact "with an average physical fitness index of 63.8 [were] evidently below war standards in physical conditioning."[36] Irony of ironies, during wartime, these most "normal" of men would have been unfit for service.

After using somatotyping to classify the students' physical forms, the Grant Study scientists subjected the young men to more evaluations. The "normal men" had their pulse and metabolic rates measured, and they took Scholastic Aptitude tests. The researchers counted the hours of "sleep [the men] obtained nightly," their "multiplicity of colds per year," and their "endocrine secretions."[37] Dr. Seltzer

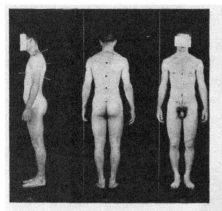

FIG. I. STRONG MASCULINE COMPONENT

Note: 1. General angularity and ruggedness of the body outline.   6. Narrower hip breadth relative to shoulder breadth.
2. Sharply outlined musculature.   7. Absence of feminine abdominal protuberance.
3. Interspace between thighs with heels close together.   8. Constricted distribution of pubic hair running upwards
4. Freely dependent arms.   towards navel.
5. Greater inner than outer curvature of calf muscles.   9. Flatness in mammary area.
                                                   10. Good muscle firmness.

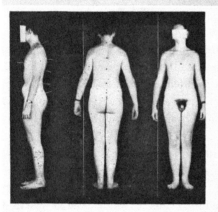
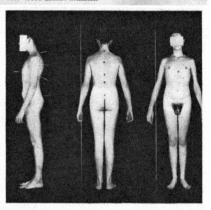

FIG. III. WEAK MASCULINE COMPONENT

Note: 1. Pronounced roundness and softness of the body outline.   6. Feminine abdominal protuberance with suggestion of
2. Absence of sharply defined musculature.   abdominal folds.
3. More extensive approximation of thighs with heels close   7. Lateral distribution of pubic hair along inguinal folds.
    together.   8. Fullness in mammary area.
4. Greater outer curvature of calf muscles.   9. Softness in musculature.
5. Markedly greater hip breadth relative to shoulder
    breadth.

FIGURES 1.2 AND 1.3 "Strong" and "Weak" masculine component somatotype photographs, Harvard Grant Study of Normal Men. Reproduced from *What People Are: A Study of Normal Young Men* by Clark W. Heath et al. Copyright © renewed 1973 by Clark Wright Heath. Courtesy of Harvard University Press.

classified hair color into nine different shades; 14.5 men were found to be without appendixes. The general fitness of the sample was clearly a reflection of the selection process, as "some boys who had serious health difficulties were excluded from the Study for this reason," and the deck was stacked and stacked again as the authors of the study found that "'normal' boys include more individuals of what is ordinarily called 'athletic' build."[38] The Grant Study was explicit in naming disability as normality's Other by excluding most subjects with any illness or marked difference from their sample.

While the Grant Study attached normality to the male body, it did, at least, name gender as a limit. The "normal man" in this case was an impossible ideal, already youthful and able-bodied in form, and drawn from the highly racialized and class-specific sample of Harvard sophomores. In preselecting "normal" bodies to determine knowledge about human beings, the Grant study and, to a lesser degree, the Norm and Norma models, take strikingly different approaches than did later research on the body. This later research took tissues from bodies of individuals who were the least likely to represent "normality" in 1945. For examples, there was the impoverished African American woman Henrietta Lacks who, in 1951, unwittingly provided the first immortal cell line for biomedical research, and the executed Texas murderer Joseph Paul Jernigan, whose cadaver, donated to science, was sliced and scanned to become one of biomedicine's "prime models of normal human anatomy."[39]

While somatotyping might seem a pseudoscience employed by the Grant Study, it was the "reigning school" of the time. As Ron Rosenbaum's research on the "Ivy League Photo Scandal" revealed, "whole generations of the cultural elite"—including George Bush, George Pataki, Meryl Streep, Wendy Wasserstein, Hillary Rodham, and Diane Sawyer—were made to pose for somatotype photos at their Ivy League colleges.[40] As leaders of the field, Earnest Hooton of Harvard and W. H. Sheldon together "directed an institute for physique studies at Columbia University" and

> held that a person's body, measured and analyzed, could tell much about intelligence, temperament, moral worth and probably future achievement. The inspiration came from the founder of social Darwinism Francis Galton, who proposed such a photo archive for the British population . . . The Nazis compiled similar archives analyzing the photos for racial as well as characterological content.[41]

In both cases, then, the investigation of normal bodies was correlated with claims about normal minds.

Normal Minds, Normal Spirits

With its opening paragraph, Earnest Hooton's book *"Young Man, You Are Normal": Findings from a Study of Students* brought its 1945 readers up close and personal:

> So you are passed as fit for induction into the armed services of the United States. Doctors have tested your eyes, examined your nose, ears, and throat, listened to your heart before and after hopping, counted your teeth, analyzed

your urine, tried your reflexes, checked up on possible hernia, found out that you are not syphilitic, nor mentally deficient, nor psychopathic, nor illiterate. You are absolutely O.K. and can train to shoot and be shot at.[42]

Speaking in terms that evoked a wartime culture of measurement and selection, Hooton pointed out that while the GI may have been "passed" in the past, those findings were "purely negative." Worse, while a "really able physician" might be able through the "clinical hunch" to better determine whether someone is a "well man," that hunch would be more "magic than . . . science." Further trips to a psychiatrist, psychoanalyst, "professor of sociology," or even a "spiritual adviser," Hooton argued, would function in domains too discrete to be able to fully evaluate wellness.[43] Hooton then sets up the Grant Study as unprecedented for its integrative approach, "carried on by persons trained in various scientific techniques: medicine, physiology, anthropology, psychiatry, mental measurement, and sociology."[44] The postwar nation would need to understand normality not only in terms of physical fitness but through what was now termed "mental health."

In part because of the high numbers of psychological casualties following the First World War, enlistees during World War II were subjected to psychological testing on a scale not been seen before. While such testing was largely designed to weed out recruits deemed unfit for service, the data collected both reflected and constituted a midcentury shift in psychiatric discourse and approach, toward greater investigation of "mental health," or of "normal" psychology. Prior to the midcentury, as one scholar recalled decades later "there were relatively few psychiatrists actively engaged in studies of normal behavior."[45] But around the same time as the news of the Harvard Grant Study was announced, another major study at Berkeley was funded by the Rockefeller Foundation, this one to study normal personality.[46]

The Grant Study researchers investigated the "normal mind" with the same energy as the normal body. Personality classifications were made in terms of general "soundness," but with barely concealed homophobia, the "affect" of personality was categorized as "vital, bland, or sensitive."[47] Social backgrounds were considered, but even after admitting the Harvard sample skewed toward the upper class, Hooton reported that the data indicated that "little or no relationship [exists] between trait complexes and socio-economic factors of the individual's background, but a strong association [exists] between his physical characteristics and such personality traits."[48]

While ablebodiedness, physical health, and masculinity spoke to a need for a renewed social body after the war, there was also a perceived need for the psychological strength to guard against fascism or the creep of communism as the Cold War heated up after 1948. As cultural historian Jackson Lears has argued, when "the public world outside the self becomes diffuse, distant, governed by institutions we cannot control or even influence, the body remains important as an arena we actually can control."[49] The context of the looming and unknown postwar world gave an urgency to the Grant Study's work, and the researchers were explicit about their sense that "normal men" were the best candidates to make that world. The lead researcher, Clark Heath, stated openly in the introduction to his Harvard University Press book on the Grant Study that "Leaders of the people should rise from among those who are well and fit."[50] That the study was published at a time when the leader of the United States used a wheelchair lends special irony to this claim. Further irony comes from knowing that one of the Harvard sophomores being studied was John F. Kennedy, who would be injured during his own service in World War II and would, like FDR, hide his physical impairments for most of his presidency.[51]

The significance of eugenics as a context for the emergence of the "normal man" in 1945 cannot be overstated. I first saw the original Normman and Norma statues on loan to the German Hygiene Museum's *Der Neue Mensch* exhibition in Dresden, where they were positioned in a clear genealogy between phrenology charts, images of exercising Aryan youth, and blueprints for the concentration camps. R. L. Dickinson's and sexology's ties to the birth control movement and Cleveland Health Museum curator Bruno Gebhard's nationwide American lectures on race hygiene and sterilization programs[52] make clear the links between the production and display of these models and widely held eugenicist beliefs about breeding a more perfect population. As has been well documented, the Nazis studied American sources for expertise on eugenicist practices. By 1944, thirty US states with sterilization laws "reported a total of more than 40,000 eugenic sterilizations—with those sterilized reported as insane or feebleminded," and state-sponsored sterilizations "continued long after the war, totaling approximately 22,000 in 27 states between 1943–63."[53] The science of "normal men" was one manifestation of American eugenic thought in the 1930s and 1940s.

The author of the popular volume on the Harvard Grant Study Earnest Hooton was a longstanding member of the American Eugenics Society and was openly supportive of eugenics; his previous books included the tellingly titled *Apes, Men, and Morons*. As a leading physical anthropologist in the country, Hooton advocated for eugenic sterilization and, more controversially in 1943, even suggested breeding the "war strain" out of the German population.[54] Hooton's views were notably "transitional" in terms of race, moving away from nineteenth-century ideas about racial determinism and craniometry toward a mid-twentieth century view of human variation occurring within racial categories. But his eugenic views on disability were clear: "Racial purity is desirable in one sense only. Every racial strain in our country should be purified through the sterilization of its insane, diseased, and criminalistic elements."[55] Hooton concluded his text on the Harvard Grant Study of Normal Men with a pronouncement of the scientific "progress" such studies of normality could serve: "If the way were cleared for better breeding by measures taken to prevent obvious genetic inferiors from having offspring, progress could then be made toward a positive science of eugenics."[56]

The Harvard study, in correlating bodies and minds, layered the seemingly objective veneer of science and statistics over attitudes already present in the culture: "the creative and intuitive are strongly in excess among the individuals with weakness of the masculine component . . . the he-men are most likely to be 'pragmatic.'" Countless throw-away lines are very telling of such biases in the study: "It is thus suggested that relatively flat chests go with the less expansive and rounded personality traits." As Hooton quipped, "Your carcass is the clue to your character . . . from the material and the easily measureable, the spiritual and the intangible may be predicted."[57]

In this way, discourse in these studies of normal men moved blithely from the realms of body and mind toward diagnosing a kind of normality of spirit. The scientific inquiry became inextricable from anxieties about masculine citizenship and the fitness of the postwar American nation. These studies spoke to concerns about the vulnerability of American bodies after war and American minds after the near-victory of fascism. For this reason, the obsession with defining the "normal" continued to be carried out by postwar science and social science, in collaboration with the data produced by a new military-industrial complex. The scientific pursuit of this knowledge after World War II was not simply defining "normal men"; it was proclaiming a postwar nation.

The Trouble with Normal

The 1945 discourse on "normal men" was not just generated; it was disseminated. Shapiro wrote about Norm and Norma for *Natural History* but also for *American Weekly* and CBS television. The Norma Look-Alike Contest was featured in dozens of articles in the *Cleveland Plain Dealer*, and local physical education teachers used the statues' measurements as a new physical fitness goal for their students. The Grant Study of Normal Men was touted in both a popular press and a university press format, shaping understandings of normality both within and beyond the academy. Its results did not fade away after 1945 but were simply renamed and folded into a longitudinal study, the results of which are still being published today.[58]

If normality was the dream of a postwar nation, it was also tied to the production of "disability" in the twentieth century. The "new normal" produced deviance, difference, and disability, not simply through the Othering process of making disability into its "necessary outside" but by highlighting the "*abnormality*" embedded even in those populations expected to embody normality the most. In the Norma Look-Alike Contest, for example, "abnormal" bodies were produced when an entry-form grid ruled out thousands of bodies from the start. Next, the contest produced thousands more "losers," whose bodies were not quite "normal" enough to win. Finally, with measurements close to but not precisely the same as the "perfectly average" sculpture Norma, even the contest *winner* did not measure up.

The 1945 "normal men" research seems a necessary precondition for the way mental hospitals and eugenic sterilization policies, the 1952 *Diagnostic and Statistical Manual of Mental Disorders*, and other forces would function to isolate and pathologize "disability" across the second half of the twentieth century. Yet it is also worth considering whether the consolidation of the normal may have helped to produce not just disability as Other but disability as a collectivized and, therefore, politicized identity and disability rights as an emergent agenda of the twentieth century. After only a few watershed events before 1940, the following decade saw a steady stream of important legislative and activist steps toward increasing disability rights nearly every year.[59]

In his introduction to the academic book on the Grant Study, lead researcher Clark Heath stated the main "thesis" of his book was "that normal people can be studied profitably *for themselves* in a clinical manner."[60] Despite the "evidence" of his research and the materiality of the Norm and Norma models, "normal people" were not studied by this research; they were invented by it. The anthropometric instrument *makes* measurements; the mathematical process *determines* an average figure (of the average *figure*), then the scientist and sculptor *make* that mathematical figure into a three-dimensional object. In Cambridge, there was no "normal man" to begin with, nor were "normal men" present after the fact.

Nevertheless, "normality" influenced real people's lives, and striving to be "normal" became a powerful postwar pursuit. One 1952 physical fitness textbook includes a telling example. Training her readers to internalize the normalizing gaze as part of the health curriculum, the author gives an assignment:

> Stand before a full-length mirror. Study your appearance as critically as if you were a stranger looking at you. Is your posture attractive? Would you like to alter it? Consciously study the appearance of the people you see the next two days. In your mind hold a secret contest for the best posture, the best walk, and the best general pattern of movement. Briefly describe the winner. . . . Glancing in a plate glass window, which everyone does either consciously or unconsciously, gives an image of the balanced or unbalanced posture and should create an urge to correct any deficiencies.[61]

This haunting lesson in the plate-glass window takes us back to my Mebane, North Carolina, meeting with the Normman model and to my father who, like many if not most purportedly "normal" men of his generation, spent much of his adult life feeling miserable in his skin, out of shape, overweight, never up to par. Born in 1942, he was the product of a culture that had produced "normal men" as an impossible ideal. And he died feeling pleased that cancer had at last brought him back to his "ideal weight."

Notes

1. Anna Creadick, *Perfectly Average: The Pursuit of Normality in Postwar America* (Amherst and Boston: University of Massachusetts Press, 2010).

2. Being highly charged and constructed concepts, both "normality" and "disability" should rightly have quotation marks around them at all times. But to avoid the irritation of constant scare quotes, I will acknowledge the constructed-ness of these terms at the outset and ask that readers imagine them whenever the terms are used henceforth.

3. The Grant Study results were published in two formats, an academic press volume by lead researcher Clark W. Heath et. al, *What People Are: A Study of Normal Young Men* (Cambridge, MA: Harvard University Press, 1945) and also a popular press volume written by Earnest Hooton called "*Young Man, You Are Normal*": *Findings from A Study of Students* (New York: Putnam, 1945).

4. Michael C.C. Adams, *The Best War Ever* (Baltimore: Johns Hopkins University Press, 1994), 78. See also Allan Bérubé, *Coming Out Under Fire* (New York: Penguin/Plume, 1990), especially chapter 1, "Getting In," on the new Selective Service psychiatry aimed largely at screening out suspected homosexuals from military service.

5. David A. Gerber, "Heroes and Misfits: The Troubled Social Reintegration of Disabled Veterans in *The Best Years of Our Lives*" *American Quarterly* 46.4 (December 1994), 549.

6. Gerber, "Heroes and Misfits," 556; 570–571, fn16.

7. "What Size Americans?" *Newsweek*, November 4, 1946, 61.

8. "Army Makes a Study of Head Shapes," *The New York Times*, June 3, 1945, 9. Emphasis added.

9. William H. Sheldon, "Wanted: A Biological Identification Tag," *Atlas of Men* (New Yorker: Harper, 1954), 3–5. A Columbia University psychologist, Sheldon, developed three categories—endomorph, ectomorph, and mesomorph—to catalog human physique. Similar to Harvard physical anthropologist Hooton, discussed later, Sheldon developed a theory of constitutional psychology and aligned these physical differences with differences in temperament, intelligence, and other traits. Sheldon's ideas were widely accepted in the eugenics community of the1940s but were beginning to be discredited by the mid-1950s.

10. Heath, *What People Are*, 4–5.

11. Lennard Davis, *Enforcing Normalcy: Disability, Deafness and the* Body (London: Verso, 1995). Davis's first chapter (6–27) contains the first and best etymology of the term I have found. See also Charles J. Marsh, "The Anniversary of the Normal Curve" *Science* 77.2007 (June 16, 1933), 583–584.

12. Davis, *Enforcing Normalcy*, 24.

13. While the term did appear once in 1932 to index a debate over the scientific use of the term, the proliferation of entries falls clearly between 1945 and 1963. See Creadick, *Perfectly Average*, 1–15.

14. Heath, *What People Are*, 3.

15. Hooton, *Young Man*, 12.

16. C. Daly King, "A Note on the Meaning of Normal," *Science* 1104 (July 26, 1945), 88. See also his earlier "The Meaning of Normal," *Yale Journal of Biology and Medicine* 17 (1944–1945), 493–500.

17. King, "The Meaning of Normal," 497–498.

18. Creadick, *Perfectly Average*, 1–14.

19. Judith Butler, "From: *Bodies that Matter: On the Discursive Limits of 'Sex'.*" In Lizbeth Goodman, ed. *Routledge Reader in Gender and Performance* (London and New York: Routledge, 1998), 286.

20. Davis, *Enforcing Normalcy*, 23–50.

21. Michel Foucault, *History of Sexuality, Vol. 1: An Introduction* (New York: Vintage, 1980), 43.

22. Though Gebhard refused to join the Nazi party, he lectured in the United States on "positive eugenics," thus promoting race hygiene and sterilization programs. Bruno Gebhard helped organize the production of another "normal" body—the Transparent Man exhibition in Dresden, whose counterpart "Juno" the Transparent Woman, was installed in the Cleveland museum in 1950. See Creadick, *Perfectly Average*, 25–27.

23. For more on the "Norma Look-Alike Contest" see Creadick, *Perfectly Average*, 28–38.

24. Harry L. Shapiro, "A Portrait of the American People," *Natural History* (June 1945), 248–255. Shapiro also wrote a Science Guide featuring the models for the American Museum of Natural History and presented Normman and Norma on the television program *Adventure* in 1953. See "The American Look," *Adventure* [television program] CBS/AMNH [American Museum of Natural History] Production, November 15, 1953, American Museum of Natural History Film Archives, New York.

25. Shapiro, "A Portrait," 252–253.

26. Shapiro, "A Portrait," 254–255. See also Harry L. Shapiro, "The American Figure Figured Out by Science," *American Weekly* (February 3, 1946), 26–27. Although this essay communicated the same basic content as the *Natural History* piece, Shapiro focused here more on women's bodies in keeping with the likely audience for Hearst's *American Weekly*.

27. Shapiro, "The American Figure," 26–27. Norma editor Josephine Robertson wrote a number of articles about Norma for the *Cleveland Plain Dealer* over a two-week period to promote the Look-Alike Contest. See, for example, "Nation's Ideal Boy and Girl Come to City—in Sculpture," *Cleveland Plain Dealer*, July 6, 1945, 1; "Norma Wants Her Posture to Be Perfect," *Cleveland Plain Dealer*, September 13, 1945, 1, 3; "Norma in '45 Styles," *Cleveland Plain Dealer*, September 18, 1945, 20; "3,700 Send Measurements in Ohio Search for Norma," *Cleveland Plain Dealer*, September 20, 1945, 1; and the final "Theater Cashier, 23, Wins Title of 'Norma', Besting 3,863 Entries," *Cleveland Plain Dealer*, September 23, 1, 4.

28. Jack Halberstam, *Female Masculinity* (Durham, NC: Duke University Press, 1998), 1–44.

29. Josephine Robertson, "High Schools Show Norma New Way to Physical Fitness," *Cleveland Plain Dealer*, September 23, 1945, 1.

30. By the late 1950s, female or feminine embodiments of the "normal" became the target of an increasingly virulent critique. It was a feminized suburban populace that, in striving to be "normal," was seen as a threat to modernity and to progress. See Creadick, *Perfectly Average*, 7–9; 138–141.

31. Dorothy Dinnerstein, quoted in Susan Bordo, *Unbearable Weight: Feminism, Western Culture, and the Body* (Berkeley and London: University of California Press, 1992), 4–5.

32. Hooton, *Young Man*, 180.

33. Hooton, *Young Man*, 14, 169.

34. Hooton, *Young Man*, 81.

35. Hooton, *Young Man*, 82–83.

36. Hooton, *Young Man*, 86, 84.

37. Hooton, *Young Man*, 125, 127–128, 112.

38. Hooton, *Young Man*, 18–21.

39. Lisa Cartwright, "The Visible Man: The Male Criminal Subject as Biomedical Norm" in Jennifer Terry and Melodie Calvert, eds. *Processed Lives: Gender and Technology in Everyday Life* (New York and London: Routledge, 1997), 123–137, 125. See also Rebecca Skloot, *The Immortal Life of Henrietta Lacks* (New York: Broadway Books, 2011), and subsequent scholarship on the bioethics of that case.

40. Ron Rosenbaum, "The Great Ivy League Nude Posture Photo Scandal: How Scientists Coaxed America's Best and Brightest Out of Their Clothes," *The New York Times*, January 15, 1995, 26.

41. George Hersey, quoted in Rosenbaum, "The Great Ivy League," 30.

42. Hooton, *Young Man*, 1.

43. Hooton, *Young Man*, 1–2.

44. Hooton, *Young Man*, 8.

45. Daniel Offer and Melvin Sabshin, *Normality: Theoretical and Clinical Concepts of Mental Health* (New York: Basic Books, 1973), xiii.

46. The 1949 Rockefeller Foundation study was led by Donald W. MacKinnon. The funding report stated "We should study effective and happy people to try to find out what makes them so" (58). See Chester I. Barnard, "President's Review," *Rockefeller Foundation Annual Report for 1949*, 1–73. Media coverage of the study included "Getting Back to Normal," *Collier's*, August 20, 1949, 74.

47. Hooton, *Young Man*, 43.

48. The fact that the subjects were "Harvard men" should be uncontroversial, Hooton declared, defensively: "It would be foolish to include Negro babies and inmates of a home for old men, with Radcliffe seniors in a study designed to explore the structure of personality. . . . The investigators have merely taken their guinea pigs out of the nearest cages." See Hooton, *Young Man*, 8–9, 67.

49. T. J. Jackson Lears, "American Advertising and the Reconstruction of the Body, 1880–1930" in Kathryn Grover, ed. *Fitness in American Culture: Images of Health, Sport, and the Body, 1830–1940* (Amherst: University of Massachusetts Press, 1989), 62.

50. Heath, *What People Are*, 5.

51. See Creadick, *Perfectly Average*, 160 n.17. See also Davis, *Enforcing Normalcy*, 91–99, for a fuller discussion of the erasures of these presidents' disabilities.

52. Creadick, *Perfectly Average*, 26.

53. Jacqueline Weaver, "Study Finds Similarities in U.S. and Nazi Eugenics Efforts," *Yale Bulletin & Calendar*, February 18, 2000, 1–2, http://www.yale.edu/opa/v28n.21/story.10.html.

54. Earnest Hooton, *Apes, Men, and Morons* (New York: Putnam's, 1937); see also Hooton, "Breed the War Strain out of Germans," *PM Daily* 3.172 (January 4, 1943), 2–3.

55. "Hooton Finds No One Type of 'American': Anthropology Professor Shows Nine Racial Types Intermingled in New Haven Address Last Night," *Harvard Crimson*, May 1, 1936, http://www.thecrimson.com/article/1936/5/1/hooton-finds-no-one-type-of/.

56. Hooton, *Young Man*, 208.

57. Hooton, *Young Man*, 95, 97, 102.

58. See Creadick, *Perfectly Average*, 60. See also George Vaillant, *Aging Well* (Boston: Little, Brown, 2002).

59. The force of war, alongside the fierceness of activism, seems to have historically been linked to upsurges in disability rights. For example, there were the veterans' pensions and widows' benefits programs established for Civil War veterans in the late nineteenth century; the Congressional charter of the first college for the deaf and blind at the end of the Civil War (1864); the Smith-Sears Veteran Rehabilitation Act of 1918, which focused on the vocational rehabilitation and employment of military veterans of World War I; and the Disabled American Veterans organization established in 1920. Although timelines can distort, one timeline I consulted showed major federal actions and activist organizations emerging in 1940, 1943 (the 1943 Lafollette-Barden Vocational Rehabilitation Act), 1945, 1946 (three events that year including Truman's establishment of the National Institute of Mental Health and the Hill-Burton Act), 1947, and 1948. Amendments to the Social Security Act in the mid-1950s would help protect disabled workers and their dependents.

60. Heath, *What People Are*, 15.

61. Eleanor Metheny, *Body Dynamics* (New York: McGraw-Hill, 1952), 8–9, 189.

2

Henry Darger and the Unruly Paper Dollhouse Scrapbook

Mary S. Trent

Grown men do not play with paper dolls, or, at least, they are not supposed to. These two-dimensional toys belong to children, most often girls, who dress them up in different paper outfits and accessories and drop them into a variety of printed scenes to construct imaginary fantasies. For a grown man to play with these toys would associate him with a girlish immaturity and thus divest him of the authority society often automatically grants men. Nevertheless, self-taught Chicago artist Henry Darger (1892–1973) worked over many decades to create an elaborate fictional world illustrated by his own unique version of paper dolls. In a series of collage paintings that probably date to the late 1940s through the early 1960s, Darger depicted paper-doll-like girls playing in long shallow domestic interiors akin to paper doll vignettes. In this chapter, I examine these paintings to consider the significance of paper dolls to his art. I argue that domestic space and its girlish childhood crafts offered Darger opportunities for creative expression that were otherwise inaccessible to him in the public sphere due to his designation by society as a sexually degenerate man. In the privacy of his own apartment away from society's judgments, however, Darger was free to appropriate the girlish craft of paper dolls to create a fictional world. As this chapter will show, his art offers an alternative to the restrictive sexual norms of his time by celebrating ambiguously gendered children.

Darger was born in Chicago to a German immigrant father, Henry Darger Sr., and a mother of American birth, Rosa Fullman. His father worked as a tailor, and the family lived in a part of the city inhabited primarily by immigrants. In 1896, his mother died of complications during childbirth and his newborn sister was immediately put up for adoption. His father, now single, had limited means to care for the baby while also providing for himself and his son. Added to his problems, Darger's father was physically disabled. By 1900, the sixty-year-old man found himself in such poor health that he could no longer care for his son and himself. Darger's father entered Chicago's St. Augustine Poor House and his son was admitted to The Mission of Our Lady of Mercy orphanage, known locally as the "News Boys' Home" because its children sold newspapers to help pay for their care. There, Darger joined around five hundred other previously homeless children. During his stay, he attended a local Chicago public school.[1]

In an autobiography written toward the end of his life, Darger wrote that he earned the nickname "Crazy" while living at the Mission because he had disciplinary problems, including making odd, repetitive motions with his hands and disruptive noises with his mouth, nose, and throat. Though he was quite intelligent and excelled at his studies, his irregular behavior led the Mission in 1904 to have Darger examined by a doctor who arranged for him to be sent away to the Asylum for Feeble Minded Children in the rural town of Lincoln, Illinois. The state-run institution housed around 1,200 "feeble minded" children and adults, many of whom would be described today as having intellectual and developmental disabilities, including mental retardation, epilepsy, cerebral palsy, and autism. On his intake form, the reason listed for Darger's institutionalization was "self-abuse," a euphemism for masturbation.[2] This is the only known official diagnosis of mental disability Darger ever received. Many doctors at the time, especially those influenced by eugenics, believed masturbation to be an unhealthy use of bodily force and a waste of powerful masculine energy.[3] Turn-of-the-century anxieties about the waning of rugged American masculinity with the close of the western frontier aligned masturbation with fears of feeble masculinity and the supposed weak self-discipline of the lower classes. Thus, a child (especially one of already suspicious socioeconomic stock) who had no recorded disability other than masturbating could be cast out of society and indefinitely institutionalized as feeble-minded in order to keep his supposedly degenerate genes out of society.

Though the thought of being confined against one's will in a Victorian asylum may conjure up grim visions—and the Illinois Asylum certainly had its share of controversies around the time of his stay—Darger's writing asserts that he enjoyed living there much more than at the Mission and that he considered it home.[4] His writing does state that, even as a child, he recognized his intelligence and at first resented being classified as "feeble-minded." Yet, his writing also suggests that he developed many positive experiences and feelings toward the institution after his arrival. In his autobiography, he reported having a fairly active social life at the asylum, and he paid tribute to several fellow patients by using them as characters in his work. At Lincoln, his peers and authority figures did not shun Darger as the odd "Crazy" kid, and, in fact, he was one of the higher functioning patients. Living there exposed him to a diverse population of individuals with differing levels of social, physical, cognitive, and emotional abilities, and this exposure may have helped him to contextualize his own social difference within a wider field of diversity than the normative codes offered in the Chicago public schools and the Mission. Spending his formative years there, he may have grown to appreciate the comforts of living in an environment where neurodiversity flourished.

In the summers, high functioning members of the Asylum were sent to the institution's farm to work. Darger did not like working on the farm, and he decided to run away in the summer of 1909. He succeeded and walked over 150 miles to Chicago. After his escape, with the help of his godmother he found work in the city. From 1909 until his retirement in 1963, Darger performed menial jobs in a handful of city hospitals as a janitor and bandage roller. He lived a modest but self-sufficient life by himself in a small apartment in Lincoln Park, on the north side of the city. During his last ten years, he survived off a meager social security check and the kindness of others, including his landlord, Nathan Lerner, a noted Chicago photographer. He never faced institutionalization again, but he lived a much more isolated life outside of the institution where his place remained on the bottom rung of the socioeconomic ladder. Looking back in his later years, he wondered if he had been a fool to leave the Asylum since his life there had been "like in a sort of heaven."

Darger's writings and the personal articles left in his apartment at his death confirm that he developed a few social relationships in his adulthood—he had a "pal" named William Schloeder and remained close with his kindly former landlords named the Anschutzs. Yet, there is no evidence in his papers of any sexual or romantic relationships, suggesting that he lived a largely solitary life especially compared to the group-living situation in the Asylum.[5] Outside of the Asylum he was again treated as different and less than others. The quirky social behaviors that isolated him as a child in the Mission and the public schools likely encouraged him to isolate himself from others. Additionally, some of his employers knew of his stay at Lincoln and taunted him as "Crazy," even threatening to send him back to the institution if he did not do his job properly. Toward the end of his life, when his few friends had died or moved away, he was quite alone, destitute, and physically pained by a bad leg. Seen talking to himself and rummaging through neighborhood trash bins (probably, in part, for supplies for his art) he was again considered mentally disabled by many around him. These later-life impressions strongly influenced the reception of his art, which was only discovered in 1973 at his death by Lerner.[6]

It is a challenge to know what, if any, diagnosis Darger would receive today. Masturbation, of course, is not considered a sign of mental disability in children but a normal, healthy activity. Taking into account elements from his biography—his social awkwardness, repetitive hand gestures and noises, and intellectual precocity—Darger scholar and trained psychoanalyst John MacGregor suggests that the artist might have had Asperger's syndrome.[7] From a medicalized perspective, this suggestion is certainly plausible. Yet, if we recognize that disability is a social construction based on historically-specific definitions of physical and mental norms—of which the terms "self-abuse" and "feeble minded" are excellent examples—there is little value in diagnosing Darger with a contemporary psychological disorder.

For the purposes of this chapter, it is more useful to acknowledge that, during Darger's lifetime, those who wielded social and medical power considered him mentally disabled and a threat to the overall healthy functioning of society. Throughout his life, teachers, caretakers, and peers called him "Crazy." And doctors were responsible for his confinement and treatment in the asylum. At this time, many American doctors were influenced by eugenicist fears for the negative impact of delinquent and immigrant youth on the nation's genetic health. In fact, eugenicists often confined poorly behaved homeless adolescents—many of whom were immigrants or children of immigrants, like Darger—in institutions like the Illinois Asylum to keep them off the streets and inhibit their contribution to the American gene pool.[8] It is certainly possible that Darger was one such case.

MacGregor left his discussion of Asperger's to a note in the back of his book. Much of the bulk of his lengthy text is in fact a rather imaginative psychoanalytic reading of the symbolism and characters in Darger's art. MacGregor loosely applies psychoanalytic terms and theories to interpret the art as representing the fantasies of a dangerously disturbed man who, never getting over the loss of his sister to adoption, developed a perverse fixation on girls that may have even led him to murder one or more children. MacGregor identifies Darger with the villains in his art—evil adult men whose hatred of children leads them to enslave, overwork, and even murder them—rather than with the children. Much like the doctor who originally confined Darger to an institution for "self-abuse," MacGregor uses medical knowledge and authority to assert over the voiceless Darger (deceased in 2002 when MacGregor's book was published) a diagnosis that reads his nonnormative masculinity as dangerously perverse.

For Darger, his art offered freedom from the restrictive social and gender conventions that had originally cast him out of society as weak and degenerate. His paintings hybridize female and male genders to create an empowered alternative to the forced norming of boys and men as the keepers of rugged masculinity. Darger's art embraces the creative powers of the feminine domestic realm and the experience of a girlish childhood. As an adult male, he had no trouble engaging with the crafts of girlish paper dolls to construct his elaborate fictional world; these crafts helped him transcend societal expectations for normative masculinity.

For many decades, during his leisure hours in his apartment, Darger devoted himself to creating an alternate world. Working privately over the course of sixty years, he wrote thousands of pages, including multivolume novel of over 15,000 pages. The story is set on an imaginary planet characterized by extreme weather patterns and tells an epic tale of heroic children fighting evil adults: *The Story of the Vivian Girls, in What is Known as the Realms of the Unreal, of the Glandeco-Angelinian War Storm, Caused by the Child Slave Rebellion.* He crafted numerous visual works inspired by his writings, including large canvases filled with rich color, pattern, and compositional complexity. The imaginary planet's lightning storms, large cloud formations, and abundant plant life translate into stunning visual backgrounds in the paintings.

In Darger's story, evil adults from the nation of Glandelinia and its allied countries are engaged in a war with Angelinia and its allies over their horrific practice of child slavery. The Glandelinians hate children: they enslave them, make them work, and punish them severely, including torturing and killing them, if they rebel. The Vivian Girls are the main heroines of Darger's novel and art. These seven beautiful sisters are princesses of one of the allied nations fighting the child-enslavers. The girls are no damsels in distress; they are powerful heroes who negotiate treaties, go undercover to spy on the enemy, endure humiliation and torture, and fight vigorously on the battlefield for the cause of freeing child slaves. Darger's concern for broad-scale, institutionalized abuse of children by adults no doubt resonated with his own childhood experiences in turn-of-the-century Illinois schools, an orphanage, and the Asylum. The Vivian Girls represent his heroic ideal of children fighting against oppression.

Like Darger in his youth, the Vivian Girls do not fit society's norms. Darger's "girl" characters (the Vivian Girls as well as many of the other children in his art) have the unique quality of having penises. The artist does not reference this transgender identity in his text but reveals it in art scenes where Glandelinians punish children by making them go naked outdoors, exposed to the elements. In these works, we see that, for example, pigtailed "girls" have penises under their dresses. Granting them a penis associates them with the biologically male Darger, and with his specific story of victimhood, as one who was institutionalized for "self-abuse." In both the Vivian Girls' and Darger's stories, their penises are the cause of adults shaming and punishing them. Darger likely identified with the transgender girls in his art rather than with their adult male oppressors, contrary to MacGregor's claims.

Transgender people would have been considered mentally disabled and "Crazy" in most American social contexts of Darger's time. Pioneering German physician and sexologist Magnus Hirschfeld had coined the term transvestite in 1910 and oversaw the first sex reassignment surgeries in his *Institute of Sexual Research* in Berlin during the nineteen-thirties. Yet, most of American society remained unaware of transexuality during this time. The issue was brought to light in America during Darger's lifetime with the highly publicized 1952 case of Christine Jorgensen, an American Army private who transitioned to female by receiving help from a doctor in Denmark. Yet, trans issues were still very foreign to most Americans and transgender people remained unprotected without any medical, legal, or human rights. And, today, it only takes a quick glance at a comment book in an American exhibition of Darger's art to see that his young transgender heroines still confuse categories and cross comfort zones, leaving many viewers perplexed, disturbed, and even infuriated by his art. Yet, in the alternate world he created, the transgender girls are the norm and the adults who violently persecute them are the evil enemies. Darger's fictional world transforms children perceived by society as disabled and sexually degenerate into powerful heroes fighting their oppressors, and it makes society's dominant male adult authorities the evil, perverse enemy. Darger, though he was himself an adult male while making this art, related much more to the girlish heroines.

Darger's art has been lauded around the world since his death and now sits in many important museum collections. It has achieved such acclaim partly because today a lively market exists in so-called outsider art, art made by individuals whom gallerists often discover. These artists usually work without connection to the fine art market and are often of low socioeconomic status, with no or minimal art education and possibly with social or mental quirks or disabilities. Many galleries specialize in this art, and there are annual art outsider art fairs in several cities at which Darger's art often features. Art that radically challenges gender and sexual norms is also now a regular topic in contemporary fine art, which has helped Darger's work find a home in several contemporary art collections. Additionally, with small steps, society has grown more accepting of gender and sexuality diversity.

For most of Darger's life, however, his art would not have received the positive reception that it has earned since his death. It is true that interest in the art made by patients of mental institutions grew among European surrealists. Max Ernst and André Breton led the charge in the 1910s followed in 1922 with the German publication of Hans Prinzhorn's *Artistry of the Mentally Ill,* and continued in the 1940s with Jean Dubuffet's development of the Art Brut movement. Yet, there was no real parallel in the more conservative art establishment of United States until the final decades of the twentieth century. During Darger's lifetime, American interest in art created outside of the fine art world, to the degree that it existed at all, was limited to the appreciation of American folk art. In 1938, for example, the Museum of Modern Art's founding director Alfred Barr declared the abstracted and simplified forms of folk and self-taught art to be a vital tradition within modernism and championed the paintings of artists like Grandma Moses. Yet, few early- to mid-twentieth-century American art professionals shared Barr's beliefs, and none dedicated themselves to the art of the insane or "outsider art" until the late 1960s and 1970s. Fine art professionals like Barr may have celebrated folk art for its simple forms and values, but they did not look to it for the radical approaches to social and sexual norms that the European surrealists and Dubuffet found so liberating in the art of the insane. Thus, in the professional American art world during most of Darger's life, there was no real place for his transgender characters.

Showing his art to a more conservative public might have even earned Darger the kind of attention that could have landed him in another institution. In fact, his lifetime was punctuated by regular, heighted panics about threats to American masculinity and the dangers of nonheteronormative "sex deviants." Especially at mid-century when fears of sex crimes reached a crescendo, it is hard to image the nation's art world embracing imagery that could easily be cast as promoting dangerous and "deviant" sexual identity. Even in today's more socially accepting climate, much of the response to his work has continued to focus on inferences about its suppressed sexual content and fears about the artist's perversion and possible danger to others.

Darger's vernacular materials also set his work apart from that of his fine art contemporaries. Darger lived off a meager salary and consumed simple, cheap materials at hand: watercolor, graphite, and collage on paper. He also had limited drawing skills and no real access to advanced art education, so he developed a collage and tracing process to transform mainstream American media images into his art. To make his paintings he would take an image from a mass print source (such as newspaper ads, coloring books, *LIFE, Saturday Evening Post,* or other magazines), insert a piece of transfer paper in between it and his paper canvas, and then trace over the lines of the original source so that a carbon outline of the form would be left on the canvas. Sometimes, if he needed to alter a figure from its original form, such as by changing its clothing or the position of its limbs, the artist would first trace a copy of the original figure onto a new piece of wax or tracing paper. Then, he could alter that copy and (once finished) use transfer paper to trace this altered, wax paper copy onto his canvas. He could change a figure's outfits and add accessories by cutting out other mass print images of clothes or accessories and then adding them to the original source. Once he finished, he would paint the traced imagery with watercolors and acrylic. Darger's canvases could be quite large, even over 10 feet in length. Sometimes he would have the original media source enlarged at a drug store to reach the larger scale he needed before tracing it in his canvas. By tracing mass print representations of people, clothing, and accessories into his images, he could imagine all kinds of scenarios for his fictional world. Though fine artists like Robert Rauschenberg and Andy Warhol also began using mass print media in art in the 1950s and 1960s, Darger did so not to engage in a dialog with the formalist conventions of 1940s fine art but as part of his process of using simple everyday materials and domestic craft techniques. Rather than breaking formalist conventions, he was interested in expanding the imaginative, world-making potential of girlish craft traditions he likely learned as a child.

Darger's process of tracing clipped figures into his paintings over and over and making alterations to their clothing or accessories echoes the craft of paper doll making. This craft was popular in the late nineteenth and early twentieth century, and Darger likely practiced it as a child.[9] Sheets of paper dolls, clothes, and accessories were sold as toys in the late nineteenth century and sometimes were given away for free on trade cards or other advertisements. Children also made homemade paper dolls by drawing figures and clothing from scratch on paper, or clipping out people and clothes from mass print sources. In fact, one 1899 article, "Dolls Which Cost Nothing," argued that this was a great example of a toy for families of limited income, like Darger's.[10] It is also possible that paper doll making could have been a low-cost craft promoted in the institutions that cared for Darger as a child. As an adult, Darger kept both paper dolls and scrapbooks in his apartment and collected paper dolls as source materials for his art.[11] His archives include newsprint paper dolls of a mother, daughter, and son in bathing suits and a book of paper dolls—"Quiz Kids Paper Dolls"—that he retitled a "Book of Vivian Girls," indicating his association of paper dolls with the characters in his novel and illustrations. Darger would trace many stock figures repeatedly in his images, changing their clothes or accessories from one imaginary scene to another as if they were paper dolls. Like paper dolls, most of the figures in his paintings face forward. The girls in some of his paintings even retain the look of paper dolls. The feet of the two girls in the foreground of *At Torrington. Imperiled by terrific explosions* appear to have stands attached to them as if they were paper dolls with supports for standing up.[12]

In addition to learning crafts at school and the News Boy's Home, Darger also likely encountered arts training at the Lincoln Asylum. His autobiography states that a typical day at the asylum consisted of schooling: "We all retired to bed at eight o'clock in the evening, got up at six AM in the morning and went to school across from the asylum."[13] The school employed up-to-date methodologies for educating its children and taught not only "the simpler elements of instruction usually taught in common schools" but also skills that could lead to self-sufficiency: "habits of decency, propriety, self-reliance, and the development and enlargement of a capacity for useful occupation."[14] Training in arts, crafts and music, including "clay modeling, basketry, needle-work, cardboard constructions, red, raffia, sloyd and Venetian iron work" was emphasized over "book-learning." The asylum also scheduled leisure activities including sports and musical activities. The institution, in fact, gave regular public concerts featuring its "excellent" student orchestra, band, and chorus, which were sometimes accompanied by poetry recitations and readings.[15] Considering its prominence as a low-cost craft for children at the time, it is probable that Darger made paper dolls at some point during his stay at the Asylum. It is also possible that he may have learned the specific craft of paper dollhouse scrapbooking, a craft that shares important similarities with several of his painted tableaus.

Paper dollhouse scrapbooking was popular in America from the 1880s through the 1920s. Children made these scrapbooks by cutting images of furniture, appliances, art, plants, pets, and other objects from mail order catalogs, magazines, and newspapers. Then they would paste these clippings across the pages of a blank book. The child treated each set of open pages as a two-dimensional "room" in the overall scrapbook "house." The first set of pages, for example, would be the entry foyer; the next set, the parlor then perhaps a ladies' sitting room, billiard room, art gallery, dining room, kitchen, and so on. The scrapbook might also include rooms on the upper floors and might end in a garden outside the back door.[16] After completing the scrapbook, children could play in it with their paper dolls. Often, they would store their dolls between the pages when not in use, and sometimes children would even paste paper doll figures in each room to create permanent tableaux. An example from the Winterthur Library shows a young women pasted into a sumptuous Victorian sitting room strewn with commodities clipped from the pages of catalogs.

For parents in late-nineteenth-century America, paper dollhouse scrapbooks allied with the values of the "household arts" movement. This middle-class cultural campaign promoted the virtues of decorating a home with beautiful objects that constructed a positive moral and spiritual milieu for the family outside of the demands of modern industrial life.[17] Though children at this time had no or very minimal roles as consumers in selecting the actual objects that adults purchased for the home, they increasingly had access to the visual advertisements of trade cards and illustrated catalogs, and advertisers began to construct ad images that would appeal to them.[18] Parents and educators thus became concerned with guiding children toward a productive and restrained interaction with this growing field of mass visual marketing and consumption.

Middle-class child raising guidebooks from the late nineteenth and early twentieth centuries, and magazine and newspaper articles concerned with the household arts argued that scrapbooks could help girls exercise skills important

FIGURE 2.1 Anonymous, Paper Dollhouse Scrapbook. c. 1880–1900, mixed media, 35 cm.
Courtesy Winterthur Library: Joseph Downs Collection of Manuscripts and Printed Ephemera.

for their future roles as wives and mothers in charge of nurturing a positive domestic environment:

> The child who has any conception of the "house beautiful" will unconsciously lean toward good models and strive to make a harmonious picture—and for her the making of a paper-doll home becomes a pure joy, for she acquires at an early age the discriminating taste of an embryo collector.[19]

The reference here to collecting reveals another hope of the household arts movement that scrapbooks helped girls develop good consumer taste:

> There is an opportunity for training the child's eye in regard to good taste, choice, and color of pictures while arranging a page. A catalogue of a large furniture store has page after page of pictures from which to choose the furniture for different rooms. Any furniture store of a large city will send a catalogue upon request.[20]

According to the guidebooks, by carefully selecting and arranging visual scraps into books, children will learn to restrain themselves and make proper, reasonable shopping and decorating selections.

Though scrapbooking played an important role in helping middle-class children manage mass print media, it was not a craft restricted to the middle and upper classes. Charitable and Progressive organizations employed the craft in campaigns for lower-class children. A 1914 study of social service activities in Sunday school classes, for example, lists the outreach activities of youths from Christ Church, Chicago as having seventh-graders construct scrapbooks and sew simple articles for St. Mary's Home for Children. Eighth-grade volunteers from the church made "homemade games [and] home-made candy" for the Chicago Home for the Friendless and sixth- and seventh-graders for the Chicago Home for Boys. Likewise, children from the Sunday school class at the Hyde Park Baptist church craft "tiny scrapbooks" for their sick classmates.[21] On the one hand, the household arts movement promoted the craft as a tool for training middle-class taste in a time of expanding visual mass print media. On the other, it was a low-cost activity that poor children could make or receive as charity. Many American children made these crafts, and it would not at all have been surprising for Darger to have done so as well.

The items preserved in Darger's studio include many scrapbooks filled with comics, images, and articles clipped from newspapers and magazines. These articles testify to the artist's lifelong appreciation for scrapbooking. There are no examples of paper dollhouse scrapbooks in the Darger archives, but it is quite possible that he made some as a child. Girls were the most common practitioners of the craft, yet considering the popularity of scrapbooks and paper dollhouse scrapbooks, it would not be surprising if instructors at the Asylum included them in the curriculum at some point during Darger's five-year stay. In fact, a teacher on staff by 1908, Miss Hatch, who taught "clay modeling, painting and art work," was a graduate of the Chicago Art Institute.[22] This is significant because several

FIGURE 2.2 Henry Darger, *Untitled (Aqua tinted interior with multiple figures of girls and Blengins)*. c. 1940s–1960s, mixed media, 56 × 286 cm. © 2016 Kiyoko Lerner/Artists Rights Society, New York. Photo courtesy of the Estate of Henry Darger/Art Resource, NY.

surviving paper dollhouse scrapbooks in the archives today were made by students of the Chicago Art Institute, which has led a historian of the craft to speculate that it might have been taught as part of the institution's art educator training.[23] The strongest evidence that he learned the craft as a child, however, comes from Darger's art itself.

Darger created a series of paintings of his transgender girls in domestic space that share the horizontal compositions and middle-class decoration of the paper dollhouse scrapbook rooms. This series of paintings presents the strongest link with the specific craft of paper dollhouse scrapbooks. One untitled work, for example, constructs a long horizontal foreground divided from a back wall. A solid blue carpet establishes the foreground space and a continuous stretch of wood paneling indicates the back wall. Often, the artist placed decorative objects in the rooms to mark the space as a well-appointed, middle-class home. In this example, Darger decorates the back wall with paneling, multipaned windows with lush curtains, and large paintings. It is likely that Darger created such shallow stages to be like paper dollhouse scrapbooks.[24] Since children would have used paper dollhouse scrapbook rooms to play make-believe with paper dolls, these pages needed a shallow stage to allow the dolls to move on top of the page/room. Even if one eventually planned to paste down one's paper dolls, the shallow composition provided a means to keep the dolls and room close to one's eye and hand. Darger's painting similarly pushes the action up to the front of the picture plane, where multiple girls crowd the page, running, playing, and resting with friends.

FIGURE 2.3 Henry Darger, *171 At Jennie Richee. Mabel introduces her Blengin sisters to the little Vivians One PM*. c. 1940s–1960s, mixed media. © 2016 Kiyoko Lerner/Artists Rights Society, New York.

Though Darger primarily traced girl characters into his scenes, he also occasionally collaged mass print clippings directly into his works. This collage process recalls children's pasting of homemade paper dolls into their scrapbooks. *171 At Jennie Richee. Mabel introduces her Blengin sisters to the little Vivians. One PM.* includes such an example. This room holds fine interior decorations—a wall clock sits between two small, framed images above a shelf holding a blue and white vase. One of the frames presents a large home, a symbol of the American dream. The work also includes large framed portraits of girls that appear to be traced from coloring books. Additionally, Darger collaged on the page five clippings of girls taken from contemporary magazines. Aside from their obvious difference in medium, the collaged girls fit with the scene. They are engaged in indoor activities appropriate for this middle-class home: they read books and make handicrafts.

Like paper dollhouse scrapbooks, Darger's domestic paintings show a concern for appointing rooms with aesthetically pleasing art, wallpaper, and other decorative objects. The wall clock, paintings, vases, and shelves of *171 At Jennie Richee* are good examples. Progressive reformers may have instructed Darger in principles of the household arts in his youth, which carried influence in this later work. He also likely picked up additional elements of middle-class taste from the many magazines he consumed.

Yet, the girls in Darger's interiors also disrupt the orderliness of the ideal middle-class home. The untitled work with the aqua rug, for example, mixes middle-class taste and unruly play. The children in the foreground engage in both appropriate and inappropriate indoor activities. The girl at the table toward the center of the image carefully stirs something in a mixing bowl, practicing skills important to a future homemaker. Yet, several others behave more wildly—running through the house and even swinging from swings hanging from the ceiling. It is as if they have taken over the space from adults and transformed it into a funhouse. The raucous ballet of disorderly girlish play in the foreground overpowers the tranquility and tidiness of the curtained windows decorating the back wall. Darger's paintings thus suggest a mix of adult ideals and actual children's desires for paper dollhouse scrapbooks. His scenes display elements of a proper middle-class household decorated in a manner informed by the household arts movement. Yet, they also present children inhabiting the space in a way that makes room for fantasies of wild play.

After all, just because parents and Progressive reformers hoped that paper dollhouse scrapbooks would cultivate proper middle-class taste does not mean that children actually experienced the craft this way. Scholars of the history of childhood and youth have explored many ways children's actual experiences often differ markedly from adult writings about childhood ideals. The scrapbooks children actually produced reinforce this point. Some albums are fairly well organized so that rooms appear clean, orderly, and in keeping with middle-class domestic taste. Yet, others crowded scraps into cluttered, messy rooms. Many paper dollhouse

scrapbook makers also ordered their scraps in a manner that creates illogical dis-
continuities in the size of objects and spatial perspective between them. That there
is a broad range of orderliness and spatial congruity to the rooms of the existent
paper dollhouse scrapbooks makes a strong case for the suggestion of material
culture historian Beverly Gordon that older female relatives had a hand in making
the most orderly, well-crafted albums. The messier albums, in contrast, probably
resulted from less adult assistance.[25] Thus, the messier the scrapbook and the less it
reflected the values of the household arts movement, the more likely it was created
by a child without adult assistance.

Middle-class educators encouraged children to arrange scraps logically not
only in paper dollhouse scrapbooks but also in scrapbooks in general. Writers
from the period instructed children to "not crowd [pasted scraps] together or have
different ideas mixed on the same page."[26] The ideal scrapbook page, according
to this advice, would be completely devoted to one subject and presented with
harmonious organization. For example, a page might just include trade cards
from one company, such as Pear's Soap, positioned in a grid with no alterations to
the cards, or one image related to a single theme such as the World's Columbian
Exhibition. Such tidiness would indicate that the reformers' goals for developing
children's restrained consumption of media had been fulfilled.

Yet, children often broke from these guidelines. One example of a delight-
fully unruly scrapbook from the Winterthur includes pages cluttered with
clipped images. The anonymous maker of the book pasted large clippings of
mass-produced prints in each of the page's corners: a portrait of an upper-class
young woman, a girl and boy playing, a barefoot boy street urchin, and five well-
dressed women. Under three of these prints, the scrapbook maker pasted captions suggesting that she or he imagined these mass-reproduced characters as
familiar figures, perhaps alternatives for real family members: "Jessie," "Little
Beth and Cousin Ben at the Wedding," and "Ned, the Little Match-Merchant."
In between the pictures, in no logical order, the scrapbook maker stuck a variety
of delights: red and blue alphabet letters, pointing human hands, a cow, horses,
chickens, a male in Turkish dress, a camel, and lambs surrounded by an elaborate gold and blue frame. The page playfully mixes the familiar and the fantastic,
offering up imaginative associations between the rural and urban and people of
different classes and nationalities.

Perhaps scrapbooks, when approached with such rowdy creativity, offered
children and young adults fantasies of escaping their own family and the constraints of proper middle-class domesticity. In contrast to their parents' wishes,
these books may have provided girls with a means for creating exciting alternatives
to the propriety and pragmatism of the middle-class domestic arts. Visual culture
and mass media, in fact, often allow children and young adults paths for widening
their world beyond what they are exposed to by their parents, and this is precisely
why parents often feel the need to control and order their children's access to them,
by attempting to channel media into appropriately instructive activities.[27]

FIGURE 2.4 Anonymous, Scrapbook. c. 1870s, mixed media, 38 cm. Courtesy Winterthur Library: Joseph Downs Collection of Manuscripts and Printed Ephemera.

Reading against the instructional guidelines of the period to focus more on the playfulness of the actual paper dollhouse scrapbooks, Gordon describes these books as an "aesthetic outlet": "A complex, ultimately satisfying activity [that] was a way of making a world—fashioning a complete, unified living entity out of literal scraps and organizing it according to one's own fantasies and ideas."[28] Paper dollhouse scrapbooks thus created fantastic worlds, even though adults frequently discussed the craft in terms of the domestic arts.

FIGURE 2.5 Henry Darger, Untitled (Part 2 of 205). c. 1940s–1960s, mixed media, 61 × 267 cm. © 2016 Kiyoko Lerner/Artists Rights Society, New York. Photo courtesy of the Estate of Henry Darger/Art Resource, NY.

The relation of Darger's work to these paper dollhouse scrapbooks suggests a similar disruptive use of mass-print sources. Like the young girls' unruly play with abundant color imagery, Darger's paintings present fantasies of things familiar and foreign. They present homes decorated with middle-class objects, but the active play of the girls who inhabit these spaces exceeds middle-class propriety and creates an alternative world. And, of course, they disrupt the middle-class propriety even further by depicting the girls as not biologically female. In spite of the fact that many of the girls' forms were borrowed from conventional mass print sources where they were presented as unquestionably female—coloring books, sewing patterns, advertisements, *Parents Magazine*—Darger's art reimagines their gender identity as fluid and not irrevocably attached to biological identity.

An additional similarity between Darger's paintings and paper dollhouse scrapbooks can be found in the rooms' windows, doors, and framed pictures. These openings enliven domestic space and allow for additional imaginative opportunities. Windows punctuate the back walls of several of Darger's interior scenes. As the artist was fascinated by weather patterns, especially storms, it should come as no surprise that these windows often showcase dark skies and lightening, such as in *171 At Jennie Richee*. Windows also show pouring rain, as in the example *Part 2 of 205*. Sometimes, Darger positions figures or structures outside the windows, such as the little girl holding an umbrella in the far-right window in *Part 2 of 205*. These windows suggest that, despite his focus on the domestic, Darger was also interested in openings to the outside.

FIGURE 2.6 Henry Darger, "While inside they await developments," c. 1940s–1960s, mixed media © 2016 Kiyoko Lerner/Artists Rights Society, New York. Photo courtesy of the Estate of Henry Darger/Art Resource, NY.

The fascinatingly complex back wall of *While inside they await developments* includes an elaborate tripartite portal repeated three times. The top two-thirds of the portal includes an arched window with paneling below it. The portal's bottom section consists of an opening supported by two thin columns mostly covered by a red curtain decorated with white flowers. The curtain parts in the middle of the section to reveal a passageway that progresses back into space, also visible through the portal's upper window, at the end of which is a closed door. Most of the girls in the foreground face frontally and pay no attention to these portals. The one exception is a girl in a yellow dress and red jacket who stands in front of the left portal. Her body faces the parted curtain and her right-hand gestures to the opening, while her head has turned to the viewer as if to invite him or her to imaginatively pass beyond the curtain to reach the far door. These mysterious, veiled doorways suggest the possibility of traveling beyond the shallow room to other spaces.

Doors and windows played an important role in paper dollhouse scrapbooks. Children sometimes manipulated these flat books to allow for three-dimensional play. Makers would cut pages so that doors in rooms could be opened. Paper dolls could then pass through the door to go from one room into the next as the page was turned. Children also cut out windows so that they could see through one room to the next one in the album. A page from an album in the Winterthur Library collection, for example, shows a fine Victorian dining room in which a table with food and sideboard sit on top of a floor constructed from patterned wallpaper. The back wall of the room consists of a print clipping of a wall of decorative wood paneling punctuated by a fireplace and a wooden door. The scrapbook maker cut the clipping and album page along three sides of the door so that it could be opened and closed. When the door opens, one sees a glimpse of the kitchen page that follows. While playing with loose paper dolls in the dining room page, a child could thus have a doll exit through the dining room door and enter the kitchen.

Though Darger did not cut open the doors and windows in his paintings, the works nevertheless achieved something similar to the openings of paper dollhouse scrapbooks in their original form. Darger bound his paintings in a very large volume. The paintings are double-sided, like the pages of a paper dollhouse scrapbook, and would have originally been viewed by turning the pages of the bound volume. After his death, his paintings were cut out of the bindings so they could be framed, exhibited, and sold as traditional two-dimensional artworks., Unfortunately, scholars have not yet been able to reconstruct the original order of the pages.[29] Nevertheless, keeping in mind that his paintings were originally pages in an album, we may presume that the openings and exits in some of his domestic scenes could have constructed associations between pages. Darger's domestic scenes create another kind of opening on their back walls. Frequently a twinning exists between the characters in the foreground and those in frames on the back

FIGURE 2.7 Anonymous, paper dollhouse scrapbook with cut door. c. 1880–1900, mixed media, 35 cm. Courtesy Winterthur Library: Joseph Downs Collection of Manuscripts and Printed Ephemera.

wall. His interior images repeat figures across the foreground and background of their shallow stage sets. The untitled work with an aqua rug for example, extends from the thirty-five girls in the shallow foreground to the four paintings on the back wall. One of these paintings contains a figure derived from the same source material as a character in the foreground: the blond girl with outstretched arms in the second painting from the right. Darger has traced her from the same source material as the girl with a red bow in her hair in the right of the foreground. He has altered the two girls' clothing and colored them differently to distinguish them, yet they clearly mirror each other and stem from the same source.

Sometimes it is unclear whether figures on the back wall are simply a piece of hung art or are real characters standing in a passageway that extends the space of the room. A striking example occurs with the figure of the girl standing on a ladder hanging a window curtain in *While inside they await developments*. At first it might appear as if this girl is merely a figure in one of the many decorations on the back wall. However, unlike other hung pieces of art on the back wall, this picture has no nail and wire above it. Additionally, the figures in the picture other than the girl hanging the curtain seem to be peering out from within the pictorial space and communicating with "real" girl characters in the foreground. Considering these facts, it appears that the "framed picture" is actually a large framed window through which we see girl characters in another room. But the piece is ambiguous. The wallpaper in the room extends unbroken into the space behind this window, and the bottom of the wooden frame juts out from the back wall. The ceiling is particularly confusing, as the space behind the wooden frame shows a ceiling even though the back wall of the larger room extends above the top of the wooden frame, offering no room for a real ceiling to exist. In this example and others, Darger has constructed confusing spaces on the back wall.

Complicating the viewer's attempts to decipher the location of the girl with a curtain in *While inside they await developments* is the fact that the scene appears again in another work: *171 At Jennie Richee*. This time the girl stands in the foreground of the scene. Is she also a character in *While inside they await developments* and Darger has just dealt with the perspective in a manner that makes little logical sense? Or is the frame in *While inside they await developments* a portal to *171 At Jennie Richee*? If scholars are one day able to reconstruct the original order of the pages in Darger's bound album of works from the remaining binding, it would not be surprising to discover that the framed image of the girl hanging a curtain *in While inside they await developments* was on a page close to *171 At Jennie Richee* where she also appears. Darger might have playfully constructed the framed image to indicate a passageway to a nearby page in his large album. If so, this process recalls the paper dollhouse scrapbook's use of doorways and windows to connect rooms.

Because the pictures on the back walls often include figures also found in the foreground, these works construct a *mise-en-abyme*, a picture within a picture. *Part 2 of 205*, for example, presents three elaborately framed scenes of children at play behind a foreground of children at play. Darger places a long beam at its center that suggests dramatic progression into space, though everything else in the shallow foreground denies such depth. By inserting the beam, Darger encourages the viewer to imagine the visual shift from the shallow foreground to the representational space of the paintings as a physical movement into depth. Pictures, his work suggests, are intimately connected to the real world, so much so that one can even imagine them extending and expanding the real space of one's domestic environment.

Darger's treatment of doors and windows in his paper dollhouse scrapbook paintings suggests a radical reinterpretation of domestic space. In contrast to the original, Progressive intentions for the craft, Darger's art allows imaginative journeys to other worlds where raucous, childlike play transcends middle-class propriety and constraint. His use of the craft champions a rowdy freedom within domestic space not intended by the craft's original designers.

Darger and his apartment were hardly middle class; he worked long hours at low paying jobs and lived alone in a small, enclosed space. Yet, his creative reworking of mass print media caused his home to overflow with openings to imaginative spaces to which he could travel at will. The walls of his small apartment did not confine him; they provided him with the protection and privacy to develop imaginative self-expression. Similar to what he had found in the sequestered Asylum, which was "like a sort of heaven," he established an escape from the restrictive social norms that labeled him a sexual degenerate and a threat to society. In the privacy of his meager home, he could rework mass media to create an alternative world populated by transgender antiheroes who fight their evil oppressors.

Working class, minimally educated, and considered "Crazy," Darger had little chance of achieving much public appreciation for his art during most of his life. Yet, he pursued it with great passion anyway, creating a massive, private body of work over the span of more than five decades. Domesticity and its attendant girlish crafts provided this grown man with opportunities for self-expression and rebellion against social and gender identity norms. Not having empowering opportunities available to him in the broader public sphere, Darger played with paper dolls to find outlets for creativity and rebellion within the bounds of home life. By bending the format of the paper dollhouse scrapbook into much larger-scaled and less orderly paintings with unexpected openings between spaces, his girlish art celebrates the abilities for creativity and the imagination to flourish within the home. Though the flexible gender identities of his characters have led viewers to interpret his art as reflecting a dangerously degenerate masculinity, we can now appreciate its suggestion of the potential we all have to use media within domestic space in unruly ways to open up alternatives to social norms.

Notes

1. John MacGregor, *Henry Darger: In the Realms of the Unreal* (New York: Delano Greenidge Editions, 2002); Michael Bonesteel, *Henry Darger: Art and Selected Writings* (New York: Rizzoli International, 2000).

2. MacGregor, *Henry Darger*, 45.

3. Victoria Bates, *Sexual Forensics in Victorian and Edwardian England: Age, Crime and Consent in the Courts* (Basingstoke, UK: Palgrave Macmillan, 2015), 84–85.

4. See James W. Trent Jr. *Inventing the Feeble Mind: A History of Intellectual Disability in the United States* (New York: Oxford University Press, 2016), 116–120.

5. James Elledge has suggested (on the basis of conjecture more than evidence) that Darger's relationship with Schloeder may have been a long-term romantic partnership. James Elledge, *Henry Darger, Throwaway Boy: The Tragic Life of an Outsider Artist* (New York: Overlook Press, 2013).

6. Lerner first brought the work to public attention. When he died in 1997, his widow Kiyoko oversaw the estate.

7. MacGregor, "Appendix A: On the Problem of Diagnosis," in *Henry Darger*, 656–665. The 2015 *Diagnostic and Statistical Manual of Mental Disorders* removed Asperger's syndrome, shifting the diagnosis of autistic individuals with no intellectual or language disabilities to being grouped within autism spectrum disorders.

8. On the influence of eugenics on the institutionalization of feeble-minded children see Trent, *Inventing the Feeble-Mind,* 63–83, 96, 129–177.

9. As a poor boy cared for by Progressive institutions, Darger might have been taught low-cost crafts as a way of keeping him busy or of training middle-class taste. Arts and crafts training helped fulfill Progressive goals of experience-based learning and became especially important for settlement houses in Chicago, most notably Jane Addams' Hull House, that taught skills to poor immigrants and their children. Teaching hands on skills in these institutions instilled proper middle-class American values and taste. Mary Ann Stankiewicz, "Art at Hull House, 1889–1901: Jane Addams and Ellen Gates Starr," *Woman's Art Journal* 10.1 (Spring–Summer, 1989), 35–39.

10. Eugenie Edgar, "Dolls Which Cost Nothing," *The Ladies' Home Journal* xvii.1 (December 1899), 43.

11. Examples are preserved in the Henry Darger Room at Intuit: The Center for Intuitive and Outsider Art and the Henry Darger Study Center at the American Folk Art Museum.

12. This work is reproduced in MacGregor, *Henry Darger,* 444.

13. Henry Darger, *The History of My Life,* 16.

14. C. T. Wilbur, "Illinois Institution for the Education of Feeble Minded Children" *Medical Examiner* 13.13 (July 1, 1872), 204.

15. Trent, *Inventing the Feeble Mind,* 99–101.

16. On the tendency for the rooms of scrapbook houses to unfold successively see Beverly Gordon, "Scrapbook Houses for Paper Dolls: Creative Expression, Aesthetic Elaboration, and Bonding in the Female World," in *The Scrapbook in American Life* (Philadelphia, PA: Temple University Press, 2006), 117. Examples of period instructions for how to make a scrapbook houses are "A Scrap-Book House" *New York Evangelist,* November 18, 1897, 29; Marion Dudley Richards, "Fun with Paper Dolls," *Ladies' Home Journal,* September 1902, 41; Emily Hoffman, "Homes for Paper Dolls," *Harper's Bazaar,* January 1904, 84–87; Carolyn Sherwin Bailey, "A Doll's House," *Harper's Bazaar,* July 1910, 474.

17. Gordon "Scrapbook Houses for Paper Dolls" 126–127. A period source cited by Gordon is Charles Eastlake, *Hints on Household Taste* (London: Longmans, Green and Co., 1868).

18. Lisa Jacobson, *Raising Consumers: Children and the American Mass Market in the Early Twentieth Century* (New York: Columbia University Press, 2004).

19. Hoffman, "Homes for Paper Dolls," 85. Rodris Roth also discusses this in "Scrapbook Houses: A Late Nineteenth-Century Children's View of the American Home," in *The American Home: Material Culture, Domestic Space, and Family Life,* ed. Eleanor McD Thompson (Hanover, NH: University Press of New England, 1998), 308–309.

20. Lucy Wheelock, *The Kindergarten Children's Hour, Children's Occupations* (New York: Houghton Mifflin, 1920), 122.

21. William Norman Hutchins, "Graded Social Service for the Sunday School," *The Biblical World* 44.2 (August 1914), 65–148.

22. "Report of the Special Investigating Committee of the Illinois State Legislature," quoted in MacGregor *Henry Darger,* n. 136, 676.

23. Roth, "Scrapbook Houses," 316; Gordon, "Scrapbook Houses for Paper Dolls," 122 and 127.

24. Though lack of artistic skill might seem like a possible explanation for Darger's shallow compositions, many of his other works show successful progressions into depth.

25. Gordon, "Scrapbook Houses for Paper Dolls," 122.

26. Wheelock, *The Kindergarten Children's Hour,* 122.

27. Ellen Wartella and Byron Reeves, "Historical Trends in Research on Children and the Media: 1900-1960" *Journal of Communication* 35.2 (1985), 118–133; Peter Stearns, "Historical Perspectives on Twentieth-Century American Childhood," in *Beyond the Century of the Child: Cultural History and Developmental Psychology*, ed. Willem Koops and Michael Zuckerman (Philadelphia: University of Pennsylvania Press, 2003), 97. For a specific study of this trend in Darger's period, see Bart Beaty, *Frederic Wertham and the Critique of Mass Culture: A Re-Examination of the Critic Whose Congressional Testimony Sparked the Comics Code* (Jackson: University of Mississippi Press, 2005).

28. Gordon, "Scrapbook Houses for Paper Dolls," 124–125.

29. Fortunately, the binding of the original album is preserved in the Henry Darger Study Center at the American Folk Art Museum. Once a scholar is able to take on the task of carefully matching the remaining quarter-inch of each image on the binding to the now-separated paintings, he or she will be able to reconstruct the original ordering of the paintings.

3

Black and Crazy
THE ANTINOMIAN BLACK MALE IN
NORTH AMERICAN CONSCIOUSNESS
Lawrence E. Holcomb

The Antinomian Black Male

In his important book, *All God's Children: The Bosket Family and the American Tradition of Violence*, Fox Butterfield claims that after Reconstruction a new breed of folk hero emerged for black Americans. As daily life became more problematic for post-Reconstruction Afro-Americans, this newly minted cultural icon would dominate the consciousness of both blacks and whites. However, the racial castes would receive him very differently. Unlike American folk heroes Johnny Appleseed, Daniel Boone, and Davy Crockett, who graduated to mythic status because of their elevated social position in American life and perhaps perceived culturally productive deeds, late-nineteenth- and early-twentieth-century Afro-American folk heroes were based on a different type of societal luminary. The black American icons were actually antiheroes, constructed in the image of real life criminals that were often "hard, pitiless toughs who dispatched their opponents without remorse."[1] The appeal was their lawless nature.

Despite this character-type, many law-abiding, God-fearing black Americans revered these antinomian figures. Others had a hard time categorically rejecting them. This reality, of course, requires explanation. The historical era when the antinomian black male came to the forefront of the nation's collective conscience was during the waning years of the nineteenth and the beginning of the twentieth centuries, a very challenging time for black Americans. During this era, the United States finally closed the chapter on its Reconstruction efforts in the South. Much of the Reconstruction effort was aimed at incorporating the freemen into American society.

Whereas most Americans believe that there was a radical cessation of Afro-American rights at the end of Reconstruction and beginning of Redemption period in the South (c. 1877), this was not the case. According to historian C. Vann Woodward, the Black Codes did not take full effect all over the South until some two decades later.[2] And it was during this time that the antinomian black male made his contradictory presence felt in American popular culture. The Black Codes demonstrated that American society did not respect the constitutional rights of its black citizens. For all practical purposes, regional laws informed Afro-Americans that they inhabited an alternate universe, outside of the purview of national law. Despite the post–Civil War Fourteenth Amendment to the US Constitution guaranteeing all Americans equal protection under the law and the promises of the distribution acreage from the estates of the slave-owning rebellious white aristocracy to former black slaves who had fought in the Union army, the Black Codes made it clear to African Americans that they would not be able to appeal to their nation's social contract. In other words, they were on their own.

By the late 1870s, every individual black American lived in an extremely vulnerable position because of the Black Codes. During the antebellum period, when blacks were treated as chattel-slaves, slaveholding whites had an incentive to protect the lives and well-being of their investment against strangers, who were intent on doing the bondsmen harm. After the Emancipation Proclamation, that incentive was lost. During Reconstruction, occupying Union officials stepped in to fill the custodial void. It was during this era that callow black American citizens, despite the existence of the Black Codes, made great strides toward full inclusion into American society. However, when the Union forces began their retreat from the South in 1877, the position of black Americans became much more precarious. By the dawn of the twentieth century, when the North completely turned its back on the interests of black Southerners, the promise of Reconstruction was foreclosed and blacks were left to fend for themselves among a hostile people that had formerly condoned or profited from their enslavement.

This meant that vulnerable Southern American blacks were left to figure out a way to defend themselves against a hypersensitive, hypermasculine, militarily humiliated, politically defeated but culturally privileged racial caste bent on redemption through vengeance. Any unbiased observer would come to the conclusion that the prospects for Southern blacks were not good. The advent of lynching blacks as a regional pastime during this era confirms the observation.

This reality had dire implications for black people. The undemocratic imposition of the Black Codes meant that Afro-Americans were incapable of appealing to a societal institution if their legal rights were violated. It meant that blacks had no rights that whites need respect. For our purposes, it meant that at the beginning of the twentieth century, a black male's attempt to protect his person, his family, or his property against any violation a white aggressor could imagine could result in that black male's death.

Social circumstances are ripe for the production of antiheroes. In a subculture composed of individuals who cannot appeal to the law or law enforcement for the protection of their natural rights, it is the strong who survive while the lawless seem to thrive. In a world where the established laws are rigged against a particular subaltern group, those subalterns will eventually begin to revere the lawless. Butterfield informs us this is what happened in the black community at the turn of twentieth century, the time when the antinomian black male became heroic to many Afro-Americans.

One such antinomian male was Morris Slater. According to Butterfield, this nineteenth-century outlaw was the inspiration behind the mythic folk-hero Railroad Bill. Apparently, Slater was an extremely troublesome individual; "a black turpentine worker . . . who in 1893 killed a policeman during an argument [and] . . . escaped on a freight train" then spent the rest of his short life "robbing trains, threatening poor African-Americans who lived along the tracks," and killing law-enforcement officers who pursued him.[3] Before Slater's murderous, impoverished, and itinerant activity ended in ambush that resulted in his own death, the only thing that seemed to qualify the outlaw for saintly treatment was his unwillingness to be cowed by cultural norms and social authorities. Apparently, for many black Americans at the beginning of the twentieth century, Slater's reckless courage, especially after his death, was more than enough for him to win their admiration.

Afro-Americans folk heroes at dawn of United States history were, like Slater, antinomian black males. They were not nice guys. Ordinary people would not want to invite a "crazy" antinomian Afro-American man over for dinner. In fact, if people truly revered an antinomian black man, and they saw him coming toward them on the street, respect would dictate that they lead their loved ones in running as fast as their legs would carry them in the opposite direction. Antinomian black men did not privilege some social groups over others, rob from the rich and give to the poor, or think it worthwhile to protect women and children. They were governed by no worldview, had no wish for a brighter tomorrow, and harbored no secret desire to lead an enlightened vanguard into an egalitarian future. Their very lawlessness made them "crazy."

Antinomian black men were quintessential bad bad-guys. They were anarchists, nihilists, and equal opportunity destroyers. According to Lawrence Levine, antinomian black men were "pure force, pure vengeance, explosions of fury and futility. They were not given any socially redeeming characteristics simply because in them there was no hope of social redemption."[4]

The antinomian black male's action in the world suggested to black Americans that he saw the world for what it was. And for the overwhelming majority of Afro-Americans at the turn of the twentieth century, life in the presence of the actual, and especially the ideational, milieu of European Americans was a constant exercise in physical insecurity, intellectual condescension, relational domination, and spiritual insignificance. Black Americans' social and cultural life, when engaged with the dominant caste, was an alternative universe where none of the social norms, cultural values, ethical requirements, and spiritual principles governing the dominant caste members' interactions with one another applied. In fact, paradoxically, the more the black American worked to achieve those things that the dominant culture valued, the more he was mocked as being engaged in a futile exercise.

The antinomian black male responded to this untenable social position by fully embracing it. If the dominant culture perceived him as an animal with no natural rights no matter how he behaved, he reasoned it was fruitless to live otherwise. In fact, the antinomian black male could easily point out that peers who respected the rules of the dominant culture were not revered by its members. On the contrary, these subalterns were simply mocked for acting "above their station," ridiculed for "attempting to be white," and served up a heaping dose of insult to add to their already considerable injury.

Afro-American folk heroes like Stagolee, also known as Stagger Lee, Railroad Bill, also known as Morris Slater, and Jack Johnson were not having it.[5] They responded to these cruel facts by accepting the dominant culture's stereotypical image and running with it. The lawless, "crazy" black male as Levine points out, acted purely out of "force and fury" and has no socially redeeming characteristics.[6] In Freudian analysis—rhetoric developed by Freud during the same time period, the antinomian black male's character type was all id and devoid of super-ego. And if the black man has yet to develop a super-ego, one may as well consider him a primitive, hedonistic, unrestrained, and even "crazy" beast.

Given our understanding of the premium placed on hypermasculinity and honor that a majority of the Afro-Americans imbibed as they were socialized into American culture by the Scottish-Irish whites, it makes sense that both Afro-American men and women, and grudgingly even some white Americans, would come to respect and revere the antinomian black male. However, this was a pyrrhic victory for the black American male who was lionized by his subculture.

To be sure, any black American male that took the lead would become a hero for the black community at large. And certainly, the nihilistic black male achieved a sort of fame and notoriety that eluded most blacks. He defied a cruel and unjust authority. This has been the path of hero-worship throughout human history. However, the nature of the authority that the antinomian black male was compelled to defy was so powerful, and total, that in order to abrogate it he had to extricate himself from all forms of ordinary social life. Like Slater, the antinomian black male was forced to cut ties with all of his most vital personal relationships, could not help himself or his subculture through legitimate forms of employment or community service, was compelled to adopt a criminal identity and lifestyle in order to survive, and was reduced to a dishonest, antisocial, isolated, noncommunal form of existence because of the constant pursuit of legal authorities.

Since Émile Durkheim's discussion of egoism and anomie in his first major work, *Suicide,* social scientists have examined the perils of living outside of the bounds, or apart from the regulation, of normative social interaction. However, few have improved upon the insights of the nineteenth-century French theorist. There is something about living ungoverned by social norms that is not good for the mental health of the individual. Erich Fromm, Kingsley Davis, Phillip Zimbardo, and Nikita Duncan have each explored the implications of social isolation and the feeling of increasing alienation from that which is normative (or "normal") in social life.[7] It has become an axiom of the social sciences that an extended experience of isolation or feelings of alienation from normative social life has deleterious psychological and emotional consequences for the individual. Aberrant, antisocial thoughts and behaviors are known to express themselves when one is subjected to extended periods of social isolation.

These facts suggest that the black antinomian male suffered greatly not only socially for his behavioral choices but psychologically and emotionally as well. Whereas the antinomian black male may survive for a time acting outside the rules of civilized society, the laws governing social life are still operating on him. Ultimately, this means that the antinomian Afro-American male, while jettisoning man's law, is paying the ultimate price in terms of his psychological well-being.

Identifying such figures as "heroes" also has a significant cost. In privileging the attitudes and behaviors of those who live outside the norms of society, those who identify with antinomian figures experience difficulty developing the psychological wherewithal necessary for day-to-day survival, if not success, in the dominant culture. Such identifications are bound to have serious emotional consequences for those who choose them. This reality begs the question: How does Afro-American culture, specifically, and American culture at large receive and respond to the deleterious behavior of Afro-American males who champion the antinomian male character type and demonstrate disturbing psychological attitudes, dispositions, and behaviors?

The Afro-American Injunction: "Don't Bring Me No Bad News"

Throughout their history in the United States, black Americans have faced an extraordinarily daunting set of institutional, structural, and psychological barriers while attempting to integrate themselves into the larger, predominantly white society. No other American ethnic group that sought civil integration has experienced the obstruction reserved for Afro-Americans. Given the unique history of the United States and its revolutionary, modern claim that all human beings are entitled to equal treatment and respect by those who govern them, it is arguable that Afro-Americans have had a more challenging psychological and spiritual experience contending with their own society than any other American group. This challenge has been especially true for the black man.

If one takes a cursory look at American history, one will soon discover that black Americans' fellow countrymen did not perceive events in this way. Most Euro-Americans never acknowledged the significant strides blacks made after the abolition of slavery. Nor did they own up to the extraordinary institutional and structural barriers erected to turn back this progress. Instead, most Euro-Americans—Northerners and Southerners, conservative and progressive, friends and foes—turned their collective backs on the Afro-Americans and blamed them for the poverty, disease, and crime that plagued their communities at the turn of the century. It was an egregious example of blaming the victim.

The sentiments of the early twentieth century Virginia academic Paul B. Barringer, who regarded black Americans as abject failures in everything except "as a source for cheap labor for a warm climate," were not produced in a vacuum.[8] They bubbled to the surface in a cultural space that had intellectuals, academics, and writers like Thomas Dixon publishing multiple editions of best-selling, scurrilous tomes with race-baiting titles such as *The Leopard's Spots: A Romance of the White Man's Burden–1865–1900*, *The Clansman: An Historical Romance of the Ku Klux Klan*, and *The Traitor: A Story of the Fall of the Invisible Empire*.[9]

C. Vann Woodward points out the emerging social sciences of the period, particularly "its sociology, anthropology, and history," suggested that Afro-Americans themselves, not whites who set up the institutional and structural barriers to assimilation, were the cause of the problems blacks faced. The titles of texts such as Charles Carroll's *"The Negro a Beast" or In the Image of God*; William B. Smith's *The Color Line: A Brief in Behalf of the Unborn*; and Robert W. Shufeldt's *The Negro, A Menace to American Civilization* provide an indication regarding the tone of the scholarship.[10] All of these works were academically sanctioned manuscripts; all ignored the significant strides that Afro-Americans made in the South during Reconstruction; and all blamed the poverty, overcrowded slums, and ignorance that plagued black Americans at the turn of the century on some ontological deficiency within blacks, not the imposition of social policies meant to exploit, oppress, and disenfranchise them.

Jumping from the beginning of the twentieth century to its end, we find a similar phenomenon taking place. In the wake of advances related to the civil rights acts of the 1960s, a political backlash by former Dixiecrats took place. These Southern reactionaries were joined by a group of Northern conservative academics, writers, and pundits who produced a spate of texts suggesting that the issues facing Afro-Americans in the post–civil rights era were brought on by either their own intellectual or cultural deficiencies. They suggested that the progressive multicultural movements and liberal social policies, which, as they saw it, were encouraging black Americans to see themselves as victims and become dependent on "big" government, were the central explanations for the plight of Afro-Americans.

Although none of the more recent writers of the latter half of the twentieth century appealed to the overtly racist element in the American public as their reactionary predecessors had done at the beginning of the century, all of them followed their forebearers' lead by using racialized tropes familiar to the American public to appeal to and manipulate the "racial" passions of white Americans. Additionally, the well-worn political sentiment that "big" governmental efforts (this time, via the legislative branch) on behalf of blacks were imperiling not only Afro-Americans but all of American culture was dusted off and powerfully employed by Charles Murray, Alan Bloom, Shelby Steele, and Dinesh D'Souza in their respective works. Moreover, the merit of educating black Americans to standards above the vocational and industrial levels were, once again, examined and mocked by Bloom, Richard Herrnstein and Charles Murray, and D'Souza. Like landless and primarily rural Afro-Americans who were blamed for the cultural and political demise of the Confederacy at the beginning of the century, post–civil rights urban blacks were blamed for threats to the entire Western world's hegemony at its end, leaving the antiquated, problematic cultural practices and the political activity of American white elites to go unexamined.[11]

Finally, like Booker T. Washington at the beginning of the century, academics of color like Steele, D'Souza, and John McWhorter attempted to rationalize white supremacy and mock those black Americans who believed that liberty, justice, and equality were meant for all and not just reserved for the privileged upper-class few. By doing so, the heirs of Booker T. Washington facilitated their white counterparts' belief that all reasonable people, black and white alike, felt that only irrational political operatives and ignorant Afro-Americans could not see that most of the problems blacks faced during American history had to do with a Western, North American culture that refused to face up to its history of duplicity regarding the human rights of black Americans; its severe economic, political, and cultural oppression of that particular ethnic group; and its violent resistance to their hard-fought political gains when earned. Instead, these new-day scholars of color continued to allow the dominant culture to believe that black Americans brought the majority of the problems they experienced upon themselves.

Race, Mental Health, and Denial

Because of their first-hand familiarity with the treatment of Afro-Americans by intellectuals, academics, and scholars throughout United States history, black Americans in general, and black men in particular, have not been disposed to avail themselves of the offers of Euro-American leaders and professionals for interventional help. This is especially true of mental health intervention. Additionally, Afro-American men, collectively and individually, are not likely to welcome the explanation that the pain and distress they are experiencing may be a result of their own psychological maladjustment—that may reside, at least in part, within themselves. Moreover, black American men often have a difficult time believing that the lion's share of the anxiety they feel, the frustration and anger they undergo, and the sense of helplessness and depression they experience will ever go away because they know that the dominant culture appears only able to explain black men's "craziness" by blaming the victim. Black men know, because they have experienced it, that whites (including white academics and professionals) will still fault black Americans and their "culture" for the psychological upheavals that black men (and black women) experience.

It is hardly surprising, then, that American blacks are more likely to believe that the social and psychological pain they experience results from their interaction with America's professional classes and could not possibly be ameliorated by their further interaction with these groups. When one considers the reluctance of Afro-Americans to be open to insights of "the scholarly community" in general, and to that part of the academic and medical professions that deal with psychological disorders in particular, it is hard to ignore the fact that black Americans, throughout their sojourn in North America, have been consistently pilloried with "scientific" information "proving" their ontological inferiority. For over a century, commentators have chronicled the systematic, sustained, and pervasive onslaught conducted by major institutions entrusted with the physical, emotional, intellectual, and spiritual development of the American citizen to demean the character of black Americans. Black men have especially experienced the effects of this belittling.

The spheres of US-style apartheid are far reaching and are found in various sources of the media, in the practice of medicine, and in public transportation, restaurants, law enforcement, and the prisons. All of these American institutions oppressed black men at all levels.[12] As a result, many black men, including Afro-American male scholars, became defensive and circumspect regarding the identification of social or cultural problems facing themselves in the black American community in particular as well as in the general national culture.

Numerous contemporary progressive Afro-American and white scholars, such as Nancy Denton, Robert Massey, John Hoberman, and Orlando Patterson, have pointed out that since the Moynihan Report of 1965, when Daniel Patrick Moynihan maintained that Afro-Americans suffered from a "matriarchal" form of social organization, most black academics, scholars, and intellectuals have been reluctant to discuss issues that might reflect negatively on individual blacks or the black community at large. However, the mistrust goes back much further than 1965. As we have noted earlier, white Western professionals, and a few blacks, who have examined "the Negro question" and communicated their findings in scholarly articles and essays, have not endeared themselves to the Afro-American community. As a result, many contemporary black academics respond with reflexive rage when white or black scholars propose theories that touch upon the issue of Afro-American "personal problems" and link that issue to black social, psychological, intellectual, and cultural ill-health.

This lack of trust in American authorities by Afro-Americans and the attitude of protection regarding black America extends itself to those Afro-American males whom purveyors of popular culture have identified as antinomian. The disposition toward women, attitudes regarding criminal activity and violence, and aspirations regarding advanced education attest to this distrust. The fact that several of the same black men celebrate gunplay, claim that they have "pimped" women, advocate illegal drug use, and have served multiple sentences behind bars only reinforces the idea that these men should exist in a special place, apart from the rest of society. Instead, some of Afro-America's most esteemed political, cultural, and scholarly figures come to the defense of antinomian black males.[13]

Henry Louis Gates, for example, was called as a witness for the defense in the 1990 case of the members of the puerile, prurient, and perverse 2 Live Crew in their 1990 obscenity trial. On the stand, Gates argued that 2 Live Crew were creative music artists expressing African American culture in a distinctive manner. Moreover, he claimed that the lyrics in their song were serving a political means by talking about "popular racist stereotypes about Black sexuality." In her reporting of the trial, Kimberle Crenshaw states, "Gates found a form of 'sexual carnivalesque' freighted with the promise to free us from the pathologies of racism."[14] Likewise, several black women and men came to the defense of real life antinomian male ear-biting, wife-punching, school-girl raping, boxer Mike Tyson when the former heavyweight champion was accused of raping Desiree Washington. After Tyson was convicted and served a three-year sentence for raping Washington, former Democratic presidential candidate Jesse Jackson Sr. led a well-attended parade in Harlem for the convicted rapist upon his release. Cultural critic, political pundit, and Baptist minister Michael Eric Dyson has been known to mimic the cadence and rhyme flow of weed-smoking, prostitute-slapping, gangster-shooting Snoop Dogg at his speaking engagements. Crowds of Afro-American college students cheered for black comics like Cedric the Entertainer, and Chris Rock empathized with O. J. Simpson when a jury found the wife-abusing former Heisman Trophy winner not guilty of the 1994 murders of his ex-wife Nicole Simpson and her alleged lover, Ronald Goldman. Feminist writer and pundit Melissa Harris-Perry featured crack-selling, "ho-slappin," women-bashing Sean Carter in her writings without uttering a word about the misogyny that is featured in his most popular music.[15]

Antinomian black males are given license in Afro-American culture and in the society at large that white males do not have. It seems that we expect more of white stars than we do their black peers. Mel Gibson's career came to a screeching halt after he yelled a few unpleasant obscenities at the mother of his child. Eminem was boycotted by gay-rights groups at the 2001 Grammy Awards. Bill Maher is regularly referred to as a misogynist. Tom Cruise takes a beating the press and loses "q" points because he is a control freak, who has divorced two wives. All of these Euro-American men have said, done, and been convicted of much less than the aforementioned Afro-American men whom black Americans and much of white American culture lionize.

Putative black feminists like Oprah Winfrey and her bestie, Gayle King, swoon at the mention of an upcoming Sean Carter concert. Calvin Broadus, an admitted member of the L.A. Crips, who was arrested but found "not guilty" of the murder of a rival gang-member shot in his presence, actually gets booked by children's shows like *Sesame Street* and is allowed to coach children in his son's football league. At the time of this writing, convicted rapist and serial screwup Mike Tyson is performing a one-man show on Broadway and being feted by female journalists on womencentric television shows such as *The View* and *Entertainment Tonight*. When presented with this evidence, it is difficult to gainsay the fact that American culture has a curious relationship with the antinomian black male.

Given the fact that these behaviors are considered outrageous when exhibited by white males and acceptable when carried out by Afro-American men and boys, how does this affect the way that antisocial, psychologically disturbing behavior is perceived by parents, friends, teachers, and intimate others of the Afro-American community? How about the Afro-American male himself? Does this cultural acceptance of the antinomian black male influence the psychologically disturbing behaviors that go unquestioned or tolerated among black American males in general? Might it cause parents, teachers, and friends to tolerate behaviors that would be identified as problematic in another cultural context? Might black boys and men who own up to the problematic behavior they exhibit be considered soft, effeminate, or oversensitive if they are disturbed by their hyperaggressive disposition or their feelings of guilt for antisocial attitudes and behaviors that are perceived as normative for members of their group? Finally, might any of the scenarios associated with the antinomian black man contribute to black males not seeking out the help that they need, or to civil authorities and medical professionals not recommending psychiatric treatment for disturbing behaviors exhibited by Afro-American males?

Acknowledgment

This chapter represents a compilation of the journals that Lawrence E. Holcomb wrote shortly before his death in 2014. Ivy George, Liam Adams, and James Trent provided editorial assistance in its preparation.

Notes

1. Fox Butterfield, *All God's Children: The Bosket Family and the American Tradition of Violence* (New York: Knopf Doubleday, 2008), 63–64.

2. C. Van Woodward, *The Strange Career of Jim Crow* (New York: Oxford University Press), 35–44. In the United States, the Black Codes were laws first enacted by the southern

states in period after 1866 but were especially prominent in legislation after 1877. These laws had the intent and the effect of restricting Afro-Americans' freedom and of compelling former slaves to work in a labor economy based on low wages or debt. The most notorious of the Black Codes were the vagrancy laws, which allowed local authorities to arrest blacks who could not identify a white sponsor and subject them to involuntary labor.

3. Butterfield, *All God's Children*, 64.

4. Butterfield, *All God's Children*, 64.

5. John Edgar Tidwell and Steven C. Tracy, *After Winter: The Art and Life of Sterling Brown* (New York: Oxford University Press, 2009).

6. Butterfield, Butterfield, *All God's Children*, 6464.

7. Eric Fromm, *Escape from Freedom* (New York: Henry Holt, 1941); Kingsley Davis, "Extreme Social Isolation of a Child," *American Journal of Sociology* 45 (1940), 554–565. http://www.jstor.org/stable/2770265; and Philip Zimbardo and Nikita Duncan, *The Demise of Guys: Why Boys Are Struggling and What We Can Do About It* (Amazon Digital, 2012).

8. Paul B. Barringer, "Negro Education in the South," in *Report of the Commissioners of Education for the Year 1900–1901*, Vol 1. (Washington, DC: Government Printing Office 1902), 522. See also Kevin Gaines, *Uplifting the Race: Black Leadership, Politics, and Culture in the Twentieth Century* (Chapel Hill: University of North Carolina Press, 2012).

9. Thomas Dixon Jr., *The Leopard's Spots: A Romance of the White Man's Burden—1865–1900* (New York: Doubleday Page, 1902), *The Clansman: An Historical Romance of the Ku Klux Klan* (Lexington: University Press of Kentucky, 1970), and *The Traitor: A Story of the Fall of the Invisible Empire* (New York: Doubleday Page, 1907).

10. Charles Carroll, *"The Negro a Beast," or In the Image of God* (St. Louis, MO: American Book and Bible House, 1900); William B. Smith, *The Color Line: A Brief in Behalf of the Unborn* (New York: McClure, Phillips & Co, 1905); Robert W. Shufeldt, *The Negro, A Menace to American Civilization* (Boston: Badger, 1907).

11. Among these books were Charles Murray's *Losing Ground: American Social Policy 1950–1980* (New York: Basic Books, 1984), Charles Murray and Richard Herrnstein's *The Bell Curve: Intelligence and Class Structure in American Life* (New York: Free Press, 1994), Alan Bloom's *The Closing of the American Mind* (New York: Simon & Schuster, 1987), Shelby Steele's *The Content of our Character: A New Vision of Race in American* (New York: Harper Perennial, 1991), Dinesh D'Souza's *The End of Racism* (New York: Free Press, 1995) and his *Illiberal Education: The Politics of Race and Sex on Campus* (New York: Free Press, 1998), Stephen and Abigail Thersnstrom's *America in Black and White: One Nation Indivisible* (New York: Simon & Schuster, 1997), and John McWhorter's *Losing the Race: Self Sabotage in Black America* (New York: Harper Perennial, 2001).

12. Including W. E. B. DuBois, Carter G. Woodson, Gunnar Myrdal, John Hope Franklin, C. Vann Woodward, Stephen Jay Gould, James Cone, Howard Zinn, Michael Banton, and Jonathan Kozol.

13. Calvin Broadus (Snoop Dogg), Curtis Jackson (50 cent), Kanye West, Sean Carter (Jay-Z), Dwayne Michael Carter Jr. (lil Wayen), and Clifford Joseph Harris Jr. (T.I) in the music that made them famous should have most American fathers, black and white, urban and suburban, locking their doors and grabbing a shotgun. I am aware that Marshall Mathers (Eminem), Fred Durst, and Paul Michael (Paul Wall) as well as other white, male performers I am not familiar with would evoke a similar response. However, in this chapter, they are not my concern.

14. Kimberle Williams Crenshaw, "Beyond Racism and Misogyny: Black Feminism and 2 Live Crew," in *Feminist Social Thought: A Reader*, edited by Diana Tietjens Meyers (New York: Routledge, 1997), 246–263.

15. See note 13 and E. R. Shipp, "Tyson Gets 6-Year Prison Term for Rape Conviction in Indiana," *The New York Times*, March 27, 1992, B12; T. Denean Sharpley-Whiting, "When a Black Woman Cries Rape: Discourses of Unrapeability, Intraracial Sexual Violence, and the *State of Indiana v. Michael Gerard Tyson*," in *Spoils of War: Women of Color, Cultures, and Revolutions*, edited by Renee T. White and T. Denean Sharpley-Whiting (Lanham, MD: Rowman & Littlefield, 1997), 47–58; Michael Eric Dyson, *Open Mike* (New York: Basic Books, 2003); "'Melissa Harris-Perry Show' for Sunday, April 14th, 2013" [Transcript], http://www.today.com/id/51543956/ns/msnbc/.

4

Masculinity or Bust

GENDER AND IMPAIRMENT IN RUSS MEYER'S *FASTER PUSSYCAT! KILL! KILL!*

Murray K. Simpson

Whether in lived experiences, social norms, or literary representations, connections between disability and sexuality are particularly complex, all the more so when intersection with other dimensions, such as gender and race, are factored in.[1] Shuttleworth, Wedgwood, and Wilson problematize the field still further by emphasizing the fact that neither masculinity nor disability are generic categories and that most studies revolve around heterosexual men with adult-acquired physical impairments, leaving little scope for congenital and prepubescent impairments or nonphysical conditions and other sexual and gender identities. That said, the authors still regard the specific intersection of disability and masculinity as inherently problematic, "what we term the *dilemma* of disabled masculinity."[2] Whether, in fact, the masculine "ideal," of sexual potency and economic and personal independence is quite so ubiquitous as is supposed is moot. However, it does seem to be well established that disability sits in a complex, arguably "compromised," certainly oppressive, relationship with masculinity.[3]

Equally as complex, cinema does not conveniently or straightforwardly reflect these societal norms or capture embodied experiences. Neither can it be regarded uncomplicatedly as a reflection of dominant social attitudes toward disability and masculinity. Meeuf's study of John Wayne's performance in *The Wings of Eagles* (John Ford, 1957), for instance, highlights the way in which his character, Frank Wead, a disabled naval pilot, extends his underlying pre-established masculinity and overcomes his disability in the fashion of the "super-crip." Indeed, his disability allows him to forge, what Mead calls, a specific "hard" masculinity, free of domestic and family attachments—"soft" masculinity—in the exclusively male environment of the navy.[4] Similarly, the presence of corporeal variance, including monstrosity, and prostheses function in a multiplicity of ways in superhero and horror film genres, often in ways that cannot be called "disability" in any singular or straightforward sense.[5]

Snyder and Mitchell observe that film derives a good deal of its cultural status from the "its willingness to recirculate bodies typically concealed from view."[6] Nowhere is cinema's potential to utilize extraordinary bodies in ways that disrupt prevailing norms and construct new narratives more apparent than in relation to paracinema, where breaching normativity is its defining feature. Indeed, Mathijs and Sexton go so far as to argue that

> one of the key components of cult viewing's oppositional attitude is its empathy with the "little people," with which not only is meant those in disadvantaged socio-economic and cultural positions, but also literally little people (the non-normative physical body) and by extension every example of the anomaly, the persecuted, the outcast, and the victim.[7]

However, their own focus on the taboo-breaking tendencies of cult cinema through the presentation of deviant bodies tends to suggest that the nonnormative body functions as a narrative device—a "prosthesis"—that is deployed precisely in order to breach normative boundaries.[8] Whether this is compatible with the asserted "empathy" is debatable. Nonetheless, portrayals of disability, gender, sexuality, and race in paracinema invariably do rupture conventional expectations, and for that reason they are often pregnant with significance often lacking in mainstream films. It is to just such a cult movie that this chapter turns in order to explore such irruptions into deviant cultural spaces.

Russ Meyer and the Desert of Disability

Released in 1965, *Faster Pussycat! Kill! Kill!* was directed by the infamous movie maker Russ Meyer, coscripted with Jack Moran and coproduced by his second wife Eve. This low-budget film—there are only ten characters with lines—is widely held to be a definitive classic of the "exploitation" genre and by many to be Meyer's best film.[9] At first glance, this cult film is little more than a stage for sexploitation and gratuitous violence. When read as a gendered Western and held up to the light of disability studies, however, the film reveals a complex struggle leading ultimately to Meyer's dismal but telling surrender to hetero- and corponormative[10] uniform domesticity. Deviant narratives of sexuality and disability explode into brilliant shards throughout the movie, before finally being smothered by the blanket of normalcy.

From the outset, Meyer's directorial career, after a stint as a photojournalist in World War II, centered on sex and, to a lesser extent, violence. However, whilst it may seem convenient to dismiss Meyer as a mere pornographer, it would be inaccurate; he does not bear suitable comparison with other film-makers in that category. Meyer was technically more skilled than many of his contemporaries even in mainstream cinema, particularly as an editor.[11] Meyer was also a cinematic pioneer, first, of the "nudie-cutie" genre with *The Immoral Mr. Teas* in 1959 and, later, the sexually violent "roughie," with *Lorna* (1964).[12] Also, at least for his post-1964 output, Meyer's films do not rush through direction or disrupt narrative structure simply in order to titillate the audience.

Meyer's creations are neither aimless nor dull. The sex and violence, whether by innuendo or display, are thoroughly woven into his stories, again with the exception of the early nudie cuties. His methods are often so crude as to seem intentional, but whether or not this is true, his cinematic aim is always sure and his target consistent. For Meyer, it is the American ideal of middle-class domesticity—sexless and passionless—that he holds in his sights. Reflecting the optimistic experimentation of rebellion against social convention in the 1960s, he breathes life into a counterculture bubbling underneath the facade of the postwar suburban family unit. In this world, free-love, ambisexuality, and open display of desire are rampant (see, e.g., *Up!*, 1976; *Beneath the Valley of the Super-Vixens*, 1979). Meyer's views of women and sex are undoubtedly highly problematic, reflecting a complex sociocultural shift, but his films and characterizations are by no means straightforward.

Filmed largely in the Mojave Desert, with frugal scenic back-drops of mountains and wilderness, Meyer's story, not a new one, unfolds as the process by which the civilized world tackles and domesticates a lawless and untamed land.[13] The film centers on the exploits of the three outlaw drifters—a trio of go-go dancers, true harpies who gleefully ignore social constraints, taking delight in delinquent destruction. Typically, for Meyer, this troupe, varyingly flexible in their sexual preferences, are all extraordinarily voluptuous. Their enormous breasts, barely restrained by flimsy clothing, are balanced by their menacingly swaggering, powerful hips. They are glamorous, exotic, and sassy, pushing both their predatory lust and lustful violence to the extreme. With neither nudity nor realistic violence—we see very clearly that no karate chop actually makes contact—*Faster Pussycat!* is tame by both Meyer's later and earlier standards. It is tame also by modern standards; most of the sexually suggestive script would pass as fairly conventional innuendo. Today, in the age of surgical body modification, we are not even shocked by the exaggerated hourglass shape or the impossibly toned musculature of the women.[14]

The film was a commercial failure, even by the more modest expectations of grindhouse movies. Costing around $45,000 to make, it is estimated to have grossed just over $36,000 at the box office (*Mr. Teas* had grossed over $1 million and cost less to make than *Faster Pussycat!* took in). The reasons for this probably have little to do with the hammy acting, camp script, or unsatisfactory resolution, but more likely because it was neither extreme enough for the grindhouse crowd nor mainstream enough for a general audience. Whilst the lesbian themes were apparently too extreme for many promoters, audiences grumbled that Satana had remained fully clothed throughout—the fact that the movie was in black and white is also unlikely to have helped commercially.[15]

Nonetheless, the female characters are undoubtedly highly sexualized and objectified. However, they are also a confusing trio: their breasts nearly spill out of their skimpy clothes as they swagger around, but their voices, their actions, and their insouciance suggests empowered, and certainly powerful, females, or, perhaps they read as empowered, powerful men. Are we supposed to gawk at their antigravitational breasts, be disgusted by their unladylike penchant for thrills and murder, or both? We do not identify with or admire any of them—no one should be *that* brutal—but we are fascinated by them in the same way as we are fascinated seeing magnetic male villains in Westerns—no-one is really particularly "good" in *The Good, the Bad and the Ugly* (Sergio Leone, 1966), for instance. This double reflex is at the heart of the film, both as a box office failure in the 1960s and as an artifact of cultural analysis fifty years later.

The Bland, the Bad and the Ugly

Led by the ruthless Varla, neither landscape nor law hinders or binds the go-go desperados, though even the wildest 1965 cultural imagination could not stretch to allow these unbridled women or their relationships with each other to survive. Despite repeatedly insisting that she was her own woman and refusing to bow entirely to Varla's command—"nobody owns me . . . yet"—Billie, the free spirit splashing in the water hole, finds she is not as free to walk away from the others as she supposes. In the end, she dies trying, literally stabbed in the back by Varla. Rosie, ever subservient to Varla, finds herself riven with jealousy by her lust for Varla, who will sacrifice everything for money and kicks. The consequences for these violently adventuresome, recklessly disobedient women are didactic: striding out of heteronormative patriarchal bounds—or at least mimicking the characteristics of the heteronormative patriarchy by strapping them on—might seem rebelliously fun but will only lead to destruction. Whether or not Meyer intended this to be the outcome, he was trapped by his characters' inevitable defeat the moment he set the scene.

Whilst, if Meyer's leading men are female, his males are (sometimes pretty) always weak stage props, illustrated particularly well by the short-lived, lackluster Tommy. Clean-cut, college boy Tommy likes to go out into the desert from time to time to race his car. Unlike the women whose space he invades, however, his interest is as arid as the desert dust he raises in his time trials. Content to beat the clock, he is no match for Varla and her posse on the track or in hand-to-hand combat. Even his girlfriend Linda, who pops cheerfully out of Tommy's car clad only in a bikini, is temporarily frenzied as she dances with the maenads, forgetting her single assignment to time him.

The audience is not expected to muster sympathy for Tommy, even as Varla karate chops him to the ground and cracks his neck for good measure, as an impulsive afterthought. He should not have ventured into the desert, certainly not wearing preppy Bermuda shorts. This is not his world, and the women do not welcome visitors. This efficient murder is a graphic but cartoonish plot device and is rarely mentioned, save an occasional perfunctory screamed remark by the perpetually horrified Linda—kidnapped by the gang—when she is not tranquilized or gagged.

When the women are forced to interrupt their drag racing and games of murder to stop for fuel, light-hearted music signals that this will be a comic interlude. The gas station attendant, functioning as herald, chats garrulously, oblivious to Varla's disdainful sneer and Linda's drugged state. He, too, is a prop, a bit of comic relief in his simplicity, and a vehicle for narrating the story. Fumbling ineffectively with Varla's sophisticated equipment, he cannot manage to insert his hose even after he has found the opening. Varla humiliates him with insults that he is too dense to understand, leaving the audience to choose between sharing the private joke or rejecting her callousness, but our allegiances are not guided, and this forced decision is uncomfortable.

Billie, both prey and predator among the women, leers at a muscled hunk, as he carries his father, the Old Man to their truck. This prompts the attendant to spill the whole story. The beefcake is the intellectually disabled son of the Old Man, a reclusive miser who has hidden his vast wealth, acquired, the attendant offhandedly adds, in a settlement by the railroad after the Old Man was injured assisting a young girl trying to board a moving train. Varla snaps to attention, raises an eyebrow, and the plot, such as it is, thickens.

The narrative then moves out to the Old Man's ranch—where it will remain. The *mise-en-scène* accentuates the themes of disability, violence, and sexuality. Nothing appears to grow on the Old Man's ranch; no cattle are raised; not even a chicken pecks the dust. Only dead cars and the scabs of rusting machinery pock its surface. Even the use of black and white—though a commercially driven decision—makes the setting seem all the more arid. Nothing good inhabits this country. The wealth of the ranch is hidden from the visitor and viewer; it is the cash compensation settlement, manifested only in the visual reminder of the wicker wheelchair in which the Old Man sits, legs akimbo.

The grizzled Old Man is key in this frontier struggle, the sadistic owner of the junkyard ranch, who is pitted against most humanity, all women, and in particular against Varla. The Old Man's greed and misanthropy are crystalized by the all too familiar trope of physical impairment, which serves a double function. His acquired impairment, paraplegia, resulting from a mixed act of charity, assisting a young woman onto a moving train—is one of two main wellsprings of his misogynistic rage and miserliness. As we are told by the gas station attendant the act, "Kind of queered his mind too, especially about women."

Second, his disability showcases his moral sadistic wreckage, brought on by the rage he has for the younger of his two sons, the intellectually disabled "Vegetable," a boy whose enormous size is blamed for the "killing" in childbirth of the Old Man's wife.

Yeah, he's my seedling, I can't deny that, but he ain't no son to me. He's a piece of mutton, a blob of flesh. He's no use to no-one. . . . Hell he's an instrument, he's a means, he's for using in things that humans can't do.

Disability thus posits itself in multiple ways and draws the film together, not as a box office success but as a cultural artifact. Whilst it is tempting to dismiss the significance of the impairments of the Vegetable—"the hunk who can't fuck"—and the Old Man—"wizened cripple-with-a-secret who can't fuck"—as Morris does, this glosses over the characters' multilayered complexity.[16] In addition to the cliché theme of loss, disabilities intersect curiously in *Faster Pussycat!* As noted, the Old Man's physical impairment plays several standard narrative functions. The function of his second son's disability is a bit more interesting. The Vegetable, fantastically strong, displays a cognitive impairment of some vague unspecified nature. He is unfazed by his father's bitter accusations that he killed his mother at birth and appears to have some kind of condition expressed in a hulking muteness—except when it is absolutely necessary to the plot that he blurt out a few halting words. He is unable to think rationally for himself, but he takes orders as an instrument for his father's household needs and serves as the object of his hatred and scorn. He does not even reap the questionable benefits of Billie's lust, for the passing train interrupts her sexual maneuvers.

Ultimately, regret helps him discern right from wrong, or at least to mimic a kind of rage/guilt-inspired morality—"I can't do it. I don't mean to . . . I'm sorry. I don't know. Nothing right." He says haltingly to Linda, unable to follow through his father's command to attack her. Shortly afterward he stabs Rosie with her own blade for the murder, by Varla, as it happens, of Billie. However, we are not invited to regard the Vegetable as meriting love, nor does he find it. His caring brother is largely ineffectual, and when he does step in, he is impotent to stop their father's abuse. Although he does try to remove himself from Varla's path of murder (literally, by pushing back the car she is driving into him at full force), only the fraternal promise of institutionalization at the end saves him from the more familiar self-sacrifice normally reserved for such characters.

At the film's denouement, we discover the secret, sought by Varla and her gang, as to the whereabouts of the Old Man's money. It is not buried in the desert, as the gas station attendant had speculated, but rather, built into a hidden compartment in his wheelchair, as we learn when Varla runs him down and the wad of cash explodes. The accident in which he lost the use of his legs became the source of both his gnawing resentment and hatred of the world and also the source of his wealth from a compensation payout. The Old Man's fury, his disability, and his money all intersect physically and figuratively in the wheelchair. In several scenes, the spectator is presented with views of the Old Man in his chair, framed by close-up rear shots of Varla and Varla and Rosie together. Their voluptuous bodies are further highlighted in repeated camera angles that partially capture their bodies: their curvaceous hips and behinds, Varla's cleavage, a rear shot of Varla showering. All of these further emphasize the Old Man's neutering, as symbolized by his wheelchair, as well as the accompanying Vegetable's asexuality, which the audience is invited to regard as the result of his intellectual disability. The women become a frame of literal and cultural reference for both of the film's disabled characters, creating a double layer of spectacle: the dangerously sexualized women and the sexually damaged and limited men.

The Old Man's disability is also interwoven with that of his son in their interdependence. The audience must assume, first, that physical disability is the equivalent of confinement and loss and, second, that intellectual disability means the lack of adulthood and determination. In 1965, these were safe assumptions. Fifty years later, the assumptions about disability are interwoven with assumptions about gender and sexuality. Any one thread pulled from this tapestry unravels the whole story, revealing the sociocultural foundations against which Meyer fought, and lost.

The Queer, Queer West

Whilst undoubtedly an exploitation movie, not a call for social justice, *Faster Pussycat!* is certainly a crossover of genre. Meyer's main vehicle is the classic American Western—a "Westernsploitation,"[17] as Bennett would say. Though the setting is less obviously a Western than his earlier nudie cutie *Wild Gals of the Naked West* (1962) or Francis Ford Coppola's, *Tonight for Sure* (1962), *Faster Pussycat!* and several of its Meyer contemporaries are much more in the Western or postwestern mold.[18]

In *Faster Pussycat!* the open expanse of uncharted territory is dotted with only a few marks of civilization, even if a gas station stands in for the general store. There is the Old Man, a grizzled misanthropic old drunk, the ruthless gang of outlaws, the damsel in distress—whose very presence is a negation—and the hero who, somewhat insipidly, comes to the rescue. Like the classical Western, *Faster Pussycat!* takes the expanding space of the American West as a fulcrum for the construction of American mythology, a feature that typifies the Western genre. In this sense, *Faster Pussycat!* and several of its Meyer contemporaries (*Lorna, Mudhoney,* 1965, and the later *Cherry, Harry and Raquel,* 1970) are far more in the Western mold despite all being set in the twentieth century. Indeed, it is only with *Lorna* (1964) that Meyer takes a decisive step forward with the exploitation genre by setting up his own camp in desert topography and claims the Western genre. Once asked why he loved the desert, Meyer is reputed to have replied "Because you can die there"—an ambition shared by the Old Man.[19] All of this results in a twisted Western that verges on a queered Western.

Adopting one especially familiar Western trope, the landscape is cut by the railway, which brought both disaster and prosperity to the ranch. The railway haunts the film's prehistory, lurks occasionally throughout the film, and is the setting for the closing scene, as a weakened Varla tries to kill Kirk and Linda. The tracks are the literal borderline of the ranch, signifying frontier lands in need of moral authority—on one side the ranch, on the other the town. The tracks also mark the long, painful, and largely unsuccessful journey to the land's civilization. Stretching out into the wilderness with promise and hope, the shot of a railway in a Western indicates upheaval and disruption to the land, followed by order and domestication. Here, the wail of the train's daily passage is the Old Man's daily tormentor, mocking the injuries it has bestowed upon him. The Old Man fulminates against the sound of the passing train: "Sound your warning . . . send your message . . . huff and puff and belch your smoke . . . and kill and maim and run off *unpunished*." The railway proves as indifferent as the desert to the march of civilization and everything crushed in its path.

In the Wild West only the strong survive, and only the morally upright prosper. Propping up the beleaguered moral majority in the story is the Old Man's ineffectual older son, Kirk. *Faster Pussycat!* is in a class of its own in that, whatever reservations and "deserved" fate we may accept for Meyer's outlaw bandits, there are simply no admirable characters whatsoever, particularly among the men. Whilst we may muster some obligatory sympathy for the murdered Tommy, the kidnapped Linda, or the unloved younger son, they elicit pity at worst and annoyance at best but never admiration. Kirk, perhaps even more boring than Tommy had been, and thoroughly interchangeable with him, eventually becomes Linda's savior, and as such, her beau. When being seduced by Varla he can only mumble pitifully, "You're a beautiful animal and I'm weak." In formulaic conformation, the spoils of battle will ultimately belong to this vacuously generic heteronormative couple. Without the saccharine *deus ex machina, Faster Pussycat!* would not be a Western, or maybe an "American" movie of any sort. These conventional restrictions are the horns of Meyer's ultimate dilemma; though it seems clear that he desperately wishes to subvert the familiar narrative, he is ultimately constrained to reproduce it. No matter how vapid, the morally—and physically—unblemished will always win out.

Also notable by its absence from *Faster Pussycat!*'s landscape is any form of authority. At no point is there any possibility that Tommy, and then Linda, will be rescued, and there seems scarcely any chance that their tormentors might be punished by the law—"They'll have to yell damn loud [for the police], there ain't a phone for five miles." The Old Man taunts Varla. In Meyer's West, no fearless sheriff imposes lawful order by standing up to outlaws, drunks, or bullies. Instead, Meyer's victors impose a thoroughly domestic moral order by default. It is an outcome, however, with which Meyer seems clearly dissatisfied. The civilization that Kirk and Linda represent is not one that Meyer could ever inhabit even if he cared to—a couple "so unctuously proud it makes you want to throw up."[20] Like the creeping desert, he is left to find refuge only in oases that stage rebellion against numbing domesticity.

It is noteworthy that the film was made at the time when the Western itself was shifting, particularly due to the influence of John Ford's body of work, toward a "postclassical" age, in which the commitment in films to their protagonists and the idea of the West became more complex—*Faster Pussycat!* was released in the same year as Sergio Leone's *For a Few Dollars More* and just three years following Sam Pekinpah's seminal *Ride the High Country*.[21] In this respect, Meyer can be interpreted as part of this shift, utterly destroying any hint of nostalgia for a passing West. It also predates one of the most definitive postwesterns, *Easy Rider* (Dennis Hopper, 1969) by several years.[22]

These observations notwithstanding, Meyer's Western reads more like a perverse inversion, with gender roles reversed and deviant and disabled bodies to the fore. "The Western," write Bandy and Stoehr, "is typically preoccupied with notions of masculinity, marked by chivalrous deeds and noble daring, and the classic westerner is traditionally male."[23] As they suggest, some notable exceptions do break this general rule. Even strong female characters, such as Vienna in *Johnny Guitar* (Nicholas Ray, 1954), however, have to demonstrate their interest in respectability and, in the eyes of the audience at least, achieve it. Hence, as Westbrook notes, "women are not, as many feminist critics have argued, 'erased' from the classic Western; there is literally no room for them in the first place."[24] The only two heteronormative women in *Faster Pussycat!* are the Old Man's late wife, who is an entirely absent presence—in the kitchen and as a block on his vicious misogynist propensities—and the bland, characterless figure of the kidnapped Linda.

The outlaws, by contrast, are cast in the film's most "masculine" roles. As the Old Man wryly notes, Varla is, "More a stallion than mare ... Then again, you never can tell, she might just gentle down real nice with the right halter." Westbrook observes that Western protagonists require a certain relationship and potential in relation to the frontier space—the capacity for freedom of movement and the perpetual imminence of violence, particularly in its perpetration. Such expectations have, therefore, excluded women from the frontier narrative.[25] Women in Westerns are typically supplementary enablers: prim fiancées or newlywed wives in danger who may or may not join the violence as a last resort; the much more interesting tarts with hearts; and an occasional put-upon shopkeeper. The primary qualities of the typical cowboy, however, are precisely what define Varla and company; their cars are their horses, and they have no roots, whilst confrontation is sought out both for its own amusement, as well as for whatever other rewards it might bring.

Taking *Faster Pussycat!*, then, as a gendered, queered postwestern allows us to see more clearly than what might be true in a more mainstream film the ways in which the insertion of radically deviant bodies into cultural spaces in which they do not belong might produce tears in the fabric sufficient to tell a transgressive tale. However, normalcy is restored by the end, and all tears have been sewn up once more.

Treacherous Masculinity: Fe-Males and (Fe)Males

For the final showdown, the film inevitably returns to the ranch steading, since what is centrally at stake is the future of the American home and family. Will it continue to grow, nourished only by death and crippling hatred? Will the outlaws defeat the Old Man and either turn the American home into a den of vice or simply take the money and run? Or will the homely couple win the day with their simple love and morality of the hearth? The formula is straightforward enough: whilst the outlaws trump the Old Man's misanthropic rage, they have no defense against the power of domestic banality.

In a classic Western move, the film climaxes with its own version of the Mexican standoff. But a standoff only holds until someone pulls the trigger. At the opening of *The Wild Bunch* (Peckinpah, 1969), a group of children torture scorpions by dropping them into an ants' nest. Peckinpah portrays an elaborate variant of rock-paper-scissors, with the scorpion as the stinger of humans, humans the crusher of ants, and the ants which swarm the scorpion. Varla the scorpion, having dispensed with the Old Man, has fired the first shot. But having removed the power that held in check the relentless advance of domesticity, Kirk and Linda overwhelm Varla with the formic bite of apple-pie.

Though Varla, Rosie and Billie are not presented as "disabled" in any way, their bodies do not conform to any conservative notions of femininity. Their bodies and the manner of their presentation—through their clothing, behavior, camera shots—are thoroughly hypersexualized and brutal. In this respect the deviance of their bodies is as significant—albeit in different ways—as the Old Man and the Vegetable are with their disabilities. Whilst the Vegetable's intellectual capacity seems to render him largely asexual, the Old Man's disability, and the manner of its acquisition, leave him not so much emasculated, at least not in any straightforward way, as retaining a sadistic kind of sexuality involving tag team carnal violence with his younger son. Interpreting these five characters as five varied and specific instances of similar processes—connecting deviant bodies and perverse sexualities and gender roles—accords with Mollow's suggestions that disability can be found linked to both hyper- and hyposexuality, as well as her psychoanalytically rooted contention that sex *is* disability. Certainly, Meyer's brigands do bear witness to the claim that there is a ruinous impulse "inherent in sexuality."[26]

Meyer not only documents the mirage of a clear-cut appeal for equality and liberation, however unintentionally, but, consciously or not, he also exposes the war against oppression as just that: a war, complete with violent confusion where it is hard to separate the heroes from the villains or the winners from the losers. Whilst Muller and Faris may be correct to observe that Meyer's view was of "a sexual battlefield [in which] . . . women didn't lie back and take it; they dished it out—but good," they fail to deal with the fact that his Amazonian rebels rarely come out well in the end.[27]

Following Linda Williams, Snyder and Mitchell note that "body genres," of which sexploitation is clearly one, function primarily through the stimulation of emotional reactions in the audience, the more extreme the better—horror, revulsion, arousal. As with horror cinema, *Faster Pussycat!* operates through the production of "excessive" bodies, something that would be true of all five of the film's main protagonists, albeit for different reasons.[28] Where the narrative structure fails to deliver in its normative expectations, it succeeds, eminently, in the production of excess. The bodily excess of the watusi-gang requires little further explication. Just as what made us respect Peckinpah's wild bunch, the thing that draws us to Meyer's trio is not that they were good or admirable but that they are authentic.[29] The exposure of their already extravagantly erogenous frames is calculated to provide an illicit titillation, safe in the knowledge that they will pay the price for the lust of the (typically straight male) audience. The Old Man's excesses lie, first, in his own unrestrained misogyny and, second, in the repugnance generated in the spectacle of his vengeful hatred, as he crawls through the dust—in the only scene in which he is not in his wheelchair—shouting his imprecations and invective at Linda and the Vegetable. Where Frank Wead had become exaggeratedly masculine in *The Wings of Eagles*, within the specific and approved disciplined normativity of the US Navy, the traits incubated within the Old Man, though masculine in many ways—he is aggressive and domineering and regards women as utterly subservient and as sexual objects—lie beyond the pale of what patriarchy would *admit* to being acceptable or normal. The Vegetable, by contrast, shows a bodily excess in his muscular physique that only serves to further emphasize his intellectual disability. His is the only male body displayed in the film—when he lifts weights shirtless, scarcely comprehending the none too subtle seductive innuendo of Billie. Despite being the physically active element in his father's schemes of sexual violence, the only emotional reaction the Vegetable invites from the audience is pity, and that only to a degree. Of all the corporeal variation on show, it is intellectual disability that remains the least compelling, precisely because it is least excessive.

Ultimately, the conflict between Varla, Rosie, and Billie on the one hand and the Old Man, aided by his younger son, on the other, is not a war of the sexes. Rather, it is presented as a struggle for the rights to male power. The femininity of the three women becomes bracketed by Meyer and made subservient to the masculine authority that they seize and claim—(fe)males. Their bodies are used instrumentally, deadly weapons in the conflict they are only too happy to enter. Both the Old Man and the Vegetable, by contrast, are men for whom the entitlement to masculinity is made precarious, at best, as a result of their disability. Both are compelled to acquiesce to a feminine dependency on a man, albeit one another, and they are accorded only limited sexual potency. Their problematic manhood, linked, of course, to their disabilities, constitutes them more like fe(minized)-males.

When the dust of battle begins to settle, of the five deviant forms, four lie dead, with only the Vegetable remaining—only barely—standing. Varla, Rosie,

Billie, and the Old Man declined the yoke of civilized normalcy and paid the price. The Vegetable's survival was predicated not on his own agency but, because of his feminization, on the authority assumed by his brother, *in loco parentis*, or, perhaps, *in loco maritus* would be more suitably feminizing.[30]

All that might implicitly have enchanted the go-go bandits to their audience, or made the Old Man a figure of ghastly fascination, explicitly damned them—for not even Meyer, the cinematic *enfant terrible*, can escape the demand for domestic, gender, moral, and sexual certainty and certainty has no room for anything but binaries. Whilst Meyer has taken his glorious gang into queered and cripped cultural spaces, he has no time for queers and crips other than for their disruptive potential, and he cannot even make that last. Meyer has his romp, but ultimately capitulates. In the end, artists must eat and baddies must die.

And so we find ourselves at the edge of Meyer's West. Meyer, himself the cinematic and cultural outlaw, invites us to band eternally with his sexually liberated creations and follow them into the desert and endless fulfilment: "Reject pissy compromise and live forever in the untamed frontier lands." Instead, however, Meyer is doomed to destroy his intoxicating creatures by the very domestication he so clearly loathes. As for the victors, Meyer chokes on his own script as he submits to insipid heteronormativity and hands them, without fanfare or enthusiasm, the future. Manifest Destiny mandated that the Wild West be free of cripples, savages, and any variation whatsoever. Through the double lens of disability studies and genderqueer reading, we see that beyond a schlocky cult film, *Faster Pussycat!* is a marker in US cultural history, where the taming of the lusty and the loathsome marks the taming of the land.

Notes

1. Tom Shakespeare, "The Sexual Politics of Disabled Masculinity," *Sexuality and Disability* 17.1 (1999), 56; R. Noam Ostrander, "When Identities Collide: Masculinity, Disability and Race," *Disability & Society* 23.6 (2008), 594–595.

2. Russell Shuttleworth, Nikki Wedgwood and Nathan J. Wilson, "The Dilemma of Disabled Masculinity," *Men and Masculinities* 15.2 (2012), 175, emphasis added.

3. That is, by heteronormative standards. Robert McRuer, *Crip Theory: Cultural Signs of Queerness and Disability* (New York: New York University Press, 2006).

4. Russell Meeuf, "John Wayne as 'Supercrip': Disabled Bodies and the Construction of "Hard" Masculinity in *The Wings of Eagles*," *Cinema Journal* 48.2 (2009), 89.

5. Michael Bérubé, "Disability and Narrative," *PMLA* 120.2 (2005), 569; Petra Kuppers, "The Wheelchair's Rhetoric: The Performance of Disability," *The Drama Review* 51.4 (2007), 84–88; Angela Smith, *Hideous Progeny: Disability, Eugenics, and Classic Horror Cinema* (New York: Columbia University Press, 2011), 3–7.

6. Sharon L. Snyder, and David T. Mitchell, *Cultural Locations of Disability* (Chicago: Chicago University Press, 2006), 158.

7. Ernest Mathijs and Jamie Sexton, *Cult Cinema: An Introduction* (Oxford: Wiley-Blackwell, 2011), 97.

8. David Mitchell and Sharon Snyder, *Narrative Prosthesis: Disability and the Dependencies of Discourse* (Ann Arbor: University of Michigan Press, 2000); see also Rosemarie Garland-Thomson, *Extraordinary Bodies: Figuring Physical Disability in American Culture and Literature* (New York: Columbia University Press, 1997).

9. David K. Frasier, *Russ Meyer: The Life and Films: A Biography and a Comprehensive, Illustrated, and Annotated Filmography and Bibliography* (Jefferson, NC: McFarland, 1998), 89–91, for a selection of reviews, not all positive; Jimmy McDonough, *Big Bosoms and Square Jaws: The Biography of Russ Meyer* (London: Jonathan Cape, 2005), 175–176; John Waters, "Russ Meyer: Master," in *The Very Breast of Russ Meyer*, ed. Paul A. Woods (London: Plexus, 2004), 42, Waters goes so far as to call it the greatest film ever made.

10. Namitha Kumar, "Corponormativity and Marking Apart," *Italian Journal of Disability Studies –Marzo* 2.1 (2014), 63.

11. Gary Morris, "*Faster, Pussycat! Kill! Kill!,*" *Bright Lights Film Journal* 16 (April) (1996) http://brightlightsfilm.com/16/pcat.php#.UytnX16UnC8.

12. McDonough, *Big Bosoms.*

13. Neil Campbell, *Post-Westerns: Cinema, Region, West* (Lincoln: University of Nebraska Press, 2013), 11.

14. Victoria Pitts, *In the Flesh: The Cultural Politics of Body Modification* (New York: Palgrave Macmillan, 2003), 168–169.

15. McDonough, *Big Bosoms.*

16. Morris, "*Faster, Pussycat! Kill! Kill!*"

17. On this term, see Timothy Bennett, "The Legacy of Corman," *Check Out My Checkout* (2007), http://checkoutmycheckout.blogspot.com/2007/01/legacy-of-corman.html.

18. A term coined by Philip French, *Westerns* (London: Carcanet, 2005), 84.

19. McDonough, *Big Bosoms,* 153.

20. Russ Meyer, quoted in McDonough, *Big Bosoms,* 169.

21. Mary Lea Bandy, and Kevin Stoehr, *Ride, Boldly Ride: The Evolution of the American Western* (Berkeley: University of California Press, 2012), 216–237.

22. Neil Campbell, *Post-Westerns: Cinema, Region, West,* 134–135.

23. Bandy and Stoehr, *Ride Boldly Ride,* 40.

24. Brett Westbrook, "Feminism and the Limits of Genre in *A Fistful of Dollars* and *The Outlaw Josey Wales,*" in *Clint Eastwood, Actor and Director: New Perspectives,* ed. Leonard Engel (Salt Lake City: University of Utah Press, 2007), 26–27.

25. Westbrook, "Feminism and the Limits," 27.

26. Anna Mollow, "Is Sex Disability? Queer Theory and the Disability Drive," in *Sex and Disability,* ed. Robert McRuer and Anna Mallow (Durham, NC: Duke University Press, 2014), 286.

27. Eddie Muller and Daniel Faris, *That's Sexploitation!! The Forbidden World of "Adults Only" Cinema* (London: Titan Books, 1997), 100.

28. Snyder and Mitchell, *Cultural Locations,* 159.

29. This was the time when the existential Western was coming into vogue, Bandy and Stoehr, *Ride Boldly Ride,* 216–217.

30. In place of her husband.

PART II

War, Manhood, and Disability

5

Marketing Disabled Manhood

VETERANS AND ADVERTISING SINCE THE CIVIL WAR

John M. Kinder

On November 11, 2015, the action camera manufacturer GoPro released a nearly eight-minute promotional film as a tribute to Veterans Day. Hosted on the company's Facebook page and YouTube channel, it features the story of Ian Parkinson, a skateboard fanatic-turned-soldier who was severely injured while serving in Afghanistan (Figure 5.1).

Light-haired and boyishly handsome, Parkinson was leading a small headquarters element when suddenly the "ground erupted from underneath" him. An explosion shattered his arm and tore off parts of both legs. In the moment, he felt completely "useless" and anticipated a quick death. However, he was swiftly evacuated to a Kandahar hospital and spent the next two years stateside recovering from his wounds.[1]

Much of the film documents Parkinson—now a bilateral above-the-knee amputee—attempting to relearn how to skate on his new artificial legs. Instead of natural feet, he controls his board using flat rubberized pads attached to the bottom of metal prosthetics. It is tough going, as the film makes all too clear. Over the course of several minutes, Parkinson falls, picks himself up, and falls again. (At one point, he breaks one of his rubber "feet" and patches it with duct tape and Gorilla Glue.) Despite his many setbacks, Parkinson eventually manages to stay upright, cheered on all the while by his supportive wife and an assortment of childhood pals. The ad ends with a shot of Ian carving on his skateboard down an empty two-lane highway in the Arizona desert. The sun is setting just above the horizon; an acoustic guitar plaintively accompanies his voiceover. "No matter what you put your mind to, you can accomplish it," Parkinson assures the viewer. "And just to know you can be yourself, and it's absolutely okay—I think it's the best feeling in the world." He has barely finished speaking when the screen cuts to black, followed by an image of a camera and the GoPro slogan: "Be a HERO."

FIGURE 5.1 Ian Parkinson, a veteran of the war in Afghanistan, returns to skateboarding in a promotional film released by the video camera manufacturer GoPro on Veterans Day 2015. Like most commercial representations of disability, the film downplays the structural dimensions of disability. Instead, it frames Parkinson's life as a story of personal triumph—over both injury and the feelings of uselessness stereotypically associated with disabled manhood. *GoPro: For All the Good Times—An Army Veteran's Return to Skateboarding.* November 11, 2015. Courtesy of GoPro Camera.

Recent decades have seen a growing body of scholarship on the relationship between disability and commercial advertising. Although very little of this work focuses on disabled veterans per se, a number of scholars have drawn attention to the way advertising reinforces (and, in rare cases, challenges) long-held beliefs about the marginalized status of disabled people in American society.[2] They are right to do so. More than a mere vehicle for pumping up sales, advertising is a "cultural force with an influence that has permeated all aspects of American life."[3] In their efforts to chart new directions in disability advertising, however, scholars have paid only limited attention to gender. This is especially the case when it comes to advertisers' representations of *disabled manhood,* a concept traditionally viewed as something of an inherent contradiction.[4] In a path-breaking essay from 1988, Adrienne Asche and Michelle Fine observe that, in many people's eyes, "Having a disability [is] seen as synonymous with being dependent, childlike and helpless—an image fundamentally challenging all that is embodied in the ideal male: virility, autonomy and independence."[5] Throughout much of US history, disability has been viewed as anathema to true manhood, a shameful stigma that few advertisers would want to associate with their products or messages. Yet, as Ian Parkinson's GoPro ad suggests, commercial advertisers have not always equated disability with masculine inadequacy. In fact, advertising history reveals a long tradition of companies trying to exploit perceptions of disabled veteran manhood to gain commercial advantage or establish their patriotic bona fides.

This chapter sketches a brief overview of disabled veterans in American advertising. Specifically, it charts the efforts of businesses to market disabled veteran manhood from the Civil War to the United States' current wars in the Middle East. Although the history of disabled veteran advertising covers more than 150 years of images, commercial testimonials, and TV ads, most advertisements featuring disabled veterans can be lumped into a handful of categories. In wartime, businesses have frequently sought to link their products and campaigns to the hypermasculinity often associated with injured servicemen. During the world wars, in particular, wartime advertisements lauded the heroic sacrifice and noble suffering of America's wounded warriors, often to develop a sense of shame and obligation among those at home. In war's wake, however, advertisers have historically pursued a different path, either seeking to capitalize on disabled veterans' fears of diminished manhood or—as was the case in the GoPro ad—narrating disabled men's successful triumphs over their physical and mental impairments.

On the whole, disabled veteran advertising has served a largely conservative purpose. Although many ads challenge the myth that disabled men are somehow emasculated by their bodily impairments, they tend to reinforce hegemonic ideals of masculinity that lionize such virtues as toughness, physical sacrifice, and autonomy. Many disabled veteran ads rely upon the stereotype of the "supercrip," the disabled person whose "Herculean achievements . . . obscure the day-to-day needs of the disabled majority—a barrier-free environment, an end to job discrimination, and at the most fundamental level, simply being thought of as human beings."[6] Just as significant, commercial advertising—like American visual culture in general—offers up a misleading view of the nation's disabled veteran population, overrepresenting the most visually striking disabled veterans (e.g., amputees, wheelchair users) while all but ignoring the vast majority with "invisible" wounds. Finally, and perhaps most disturbing of all, disabled veteran advertising contributes to a widening rift between veterans and other disabled populations, singling them out for special recognition and status above all others.[7] In this way, even the most benign advertisements contribute to the very sort of martial cheerleading that will endanger the bodies and lives of future generations of American troops.

Disabled Veterans as Pitchmen

Historically, advertisers have shied away from using disabled veterans as pitchmen. Indeed, until recent decades, American commercial advertising has largely ignored disabled people as whole.[8] This paucity can be traced, in part, to the historical context in which the advertising industry took root. Although the earliest advertisements date back hundreds of years, advertising as we think of it today did not emerge until the nineteenth century.[9] It was spawned, as pioneering disability scholar Harlan Hahn has argued, by the requirements of the new capitalist order itself, which demanded not only higher profits and expanded markets but also a fundamental reorientation of previous attitudes toward (conspicuous) consumption. In Hahn's words, "advertising slowly became the leading apologist and proponent of the mass consumption that seemed to be a natural corollary of mass production in a capitalist economic system."[10] During the nineteenth century, the burgeoning advertising industry sought to market various goods and services, but it also sought to teach Americans to view themselves as potential consumers—people whose lives would be dramatically improved with the latest product.

As a number of scholars have shown, early advertisers focused much of their efforts on transforming American attitudes toward the human body.[11] Starting in the Victorian era, historian Jackson Lears notes, ad men played a crucial role in "redefining the body as a universe of discourse—recasting the ways Americans conceived of sensual pleasure, physical attractiveness, and bodily health."[12] Fueled by a growing cultural investment in what disability scholar Lennard J. Davis has deemed the "normal body," nineteenth- and early-twentieth-century advertisers promoted a new iconography of physical appearance—a model of bodily citizenship that excluded all but a small swath of the population.[13] Racial minorities, the aged, the poor, and others were rendered virtually invisible, a status that mirrored their marginalized status in American society. As sociologist Robert Bogdan recently summarized, "Advertisers developed the image of the average American to promote their products, and people with disabilities did not fit that prototype."[14]

Although disabled veterans would occasionally buck this trend, they too have been largely excluded from general advertising campaigns, especially during peacetime. Before the 1980s, disabled veterans were typically found in only two types of advertisements: fund-raising and war bond campaigns and advertisements aimed specifically at disabled consumers. Even these, moreover, tended to focus on a narrow segment of the disabled veteran population—namely, amputees or men with easily identifiable signifiers of injury. That advertisers would single out these particular vets should come as no surprise. As a rule, advertisements deal in stereotypes, not subtlety; in order for an ad to work, viewers must be able to comprehend its message in the few seconds it takes to glance up at a billboard or scan a page in a magazine. Amputees and other visibly wounded vets have a significant advantage in this regard. They are easy to represent visually (unlike, for example, veterans disabled by psychological stress or disease). This is one of the reasons why visually striking casualties, particularly amputees, have been over-represented in American culture as a whole since the Civil War, if not earlier.[15] At times, advertisers have tried to represent "invisibly" disabled veterans, often by using accompanying text to illuminate disabilities or impairments that the viewer cannot see. However, ads featuring vets with nonvisible wounds are few and far between. Favored, instead, is a small set of disabled veteran *types*: amputees (with or without prosthetics), men wrapped in bandages or dressed in hospital gowns, veterans seated in wheelchairs, and men leaning on canes.

As much as anything else, the dearth of disabled veterans in commercial advertising is a product of Americans' complex and often contradictory attitudes toward disabled veterans themselves. On the one hand, there is a long tradition in the United States of celebrating disabled veterans as paragons of civic virtue and manly sacrifice. Louisa May Alcott's *Hospital Sketches* (1863), a thinly fictionalized account of the author's stint as a nurse at a Georgetown hospital, exemplifies this perspective. In one oft-quoted passage, the author encounters a disfigured Yankee soldier—shot through the cheek and missing an eye—fretting about his fiancée's reaction to his new appearance. Without missing a beat, Alcott reassures him that his wife-to-be would "admire [his] honorable scar, as a lasting proof that he had faced the enemy, for all women thought a wound the best decoration a brave soldier could wear."[16] To this day, the US military routinely deploys uplifting images of disabled veterans to laud the virtues of military service and cast wounded warriors as national heroes.

Throughout much of American history, however, this practice of celebrating disabled veterans' sacrifices has been overshadowed by a radically different vision of war disability, one that associates disabled veterans with unmanly dependency, aesthetic deviance, and—in some cases—national failure. Exiled to an old soldier's home or dependent upon government pensions to make ends meet, severely disabled veterans have often struggled to exhibit the economic autonomy, social aggressiveness, and corporeal "wholeness" that have traditionally been associated with hegemonic manhood.[17] Moreover, disabled veterans have long functioned as symbols of loss—living reminders of conflicts (World War I, the Korean War, the Vietnam War, the War on Terror) many Americans would rather forget. Attempting to capitalize on such anxieties, opponents of American militarism have regularly turned to graphic (and often pitiful) images of disabled veterans to debunk romantic myths of war's glory and highlight the lingering traumas—bodily or otherwise—of military conflict.[18] In the hands of peace groups, disgruntled veterans, and other war critics, disabled veterans are not icons of martial citizenship; they are *anti-advertisements*, striking arguments about why war should be avoided. (Think Ron Kovic, not Ron Popeil.)

Remaking Disabled Veteran Manhood after the Civil War

Given the many factors working against them, it is little wonder that disabled veterans scarcely made an appearance in advertising in the first eight decades of American history. Dispersed across the country, with few organizations or social occasions to tie them together, disabled veterans of the Revolutionary War, the War of 1812, and the Mexican-American War demanded public support, but they lacked the numbers and political clout to win widespread visibility. That began to change in 1860 with the onset the Civil War, a conflict that left more than a million ex-soldiers—Union and Confederate—disabled as a consequence of injury and sickness. For five bloody years, disabled veterans occupied a conspicuous place in American visual culture (Figure 5.2). Photographs of disabled veterans circulated throughout the United States, and magazines like *Harper's* routinely featured illustrations of recently injured American troops. Newspapers published the results of left-handed writing contests for recent amputees, and US cities teemed with disabled veterans peddling pencils and war almanacs. Desperate to solicit public donations, a small number of men even distributed "begging cards," small slips of paper containing photographs and brief narratives detailing their impairments.[19]

In the war's aftermath, hundreds of thousands of disabled veterans struggled to pick up the pieces of their shattered lives. In the North, disabled veterans were given employment preferences in federal jobs, along with monetary pensions based upon their perceived inability to perform manual labor. Yet such measures hardly amounted to a quick fix. As Kim E. Nielsen points out, the Civil War

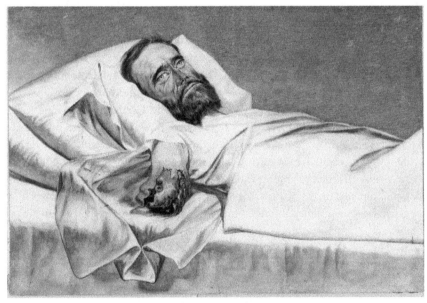

FIGURE 5.2 In the aftermath of the Civil War, commercial advertising tended to shy away from images of disabled veterans. Nevertheless, disabled veterans occupied a conspicuous place in post–Civil War visual culture—in cartoons, photographs, and medical illustrations. This particular illustration, originally published in *The Medical and Surgical History of the War of the Rebellion* (1870–1888), shows Milton E. Wallen, a Union private who developed "hospital gangrene" after his arm was amputated by Confederate surgeons. Unlike most public imagery of disabled veterans, medical illustrations made no attempt to disguise or euphemize the bodily damage suffered during the Civil War. Courtesy of Otis Historical Archives, National Museum of Health and Medicine, Silver Spring, MD.

pension system relied heavily upon biased (and frequently racist) criteria when it came to awarding benefits. African American veterans, for example, were often denied their pension claims, as were disabled veterans lacking immediately visible evidence of injury. Even if granted monetary recognition, many vets viewed their disabilities as evidence of a kind of "masculine deficiency," one that excluded them from the employed (and employable) brotherhood of Victorian manhood.[20] At a time when economic independence and male identity were frequently conflated, vets' reliance upon pension relief threatened to undercut their prestige as masculine role models. Matters were especially difficult for disabled veterans of the former Confederacy. Having failed spectacularly in their traitorous campaign to secede from the United States, they could not turn to the federal government for support. What few provisions they could muster came from charity groups or the individual states, all nearly bankrupt after years of fighting.

While disabled veterans were rarely seen in advertising imagery during this era, there was one exception: advertisements for prosthetics. The Civil War was a boon for the American prosthetics industry. Though figures remain imprecise, Civil War surgeons performed roughly 60,000 amputations over the course of the war, often using little more than a bone saw and muscle power. The 45,000 patients who survived the ordeal constituted the largest number of war amputees in American history.[21] Union amputees were granted cash allowances for the purchase of artificial limbs ($50 for a foot or arm, $75 for an entire leg). Eventually, the federal government authorized provisions for amputees to purchase new prosthetics every five years.[22] Eager to tap this new market of recently mutilated amputees, American prosthetic manufacturers waged fierce campaigns to design—and publicize—the latest and most "natural" artificial limbs. Between 1861 and 1873, the federal government issued patents for more than a hundred artificial limbs, including designs for prosthetic arms, forearms, hands, and legs.[23] Ads for prosthetic limbs appeared in newspapers and popular journals, and a number of limb manufacturers published lengthy pamphlets detailing their newest products.[24]

Prosthetic makers were perhaps the earliest industry to exploit disabled veterans for commercial gain, but their advertisements set the tone for much that would follow. Consider, for example, the advertising materials produced by A. A. Marks, the nation's premier prosthetic manufacturer throughout the second half of the nineteenth century. Founded in New York City in 1853, A. A. Marks produced scores of advertising cards, illustrations, and publicity pamphlets aimed at demonstrating both the value of their limbs and—no less significant—the importance of maintaining a proper (i.e., nondisabled) appearance. On this latter point, the company was emphatic:

> That a person will make a better appearance with an artificial arm properly dressed than with an empty sleeve, is obvious. To conceal any physical defect is a natural aim. There is nothing so distressing, especially to a sensitive person, as the exhibition of any imperfection in his anatomy.

An artificial arm was more than a tool, A. A. Marks assured would-be customers. If properly fitted and maintained, it will "conceal the loss, restore a natural appearance to the person, avoid observation and comment, and after it has been worn a short time will become companionable and necessary to the wearer's mental comfort."[25]

To drive this message home, A. A. Marks produced a wide range of advertising images, including of series of black-and-white illustrations (collectively titled "From Stump to Limb") documenting the various stages of the manufacturing process (Figure 5.3). The series depicts scenes from Marks's workshops and drawings of amputees being fitted with braces or artificial limbs. In all of illustrations, the disabled men are sketched as generic figures—neatly dressed, white, with no distressing evidence of physical anomaly—presumably meant to illustrate the "typical" customer.[26] On occasion, however, A. A. Marks incorporated photographs of amputees in its advertising material. One especially striking advertising card from the late 1800s features a "before-and-after" image, a visual trope commonly used in charity campaigns (Figure 5.4).[27] The left side of the card shows a bilateral leg amputee seated on a wooden chair, his two artificial legs propped up against

FIGURE 5.3 In its "From Stump to Limb" advertising campaign (c. late 1800s), manufacturer A. A. Marks took potential customers on a visual tour of the prosthetics business. This particular illustration depicts the A. A. Marks's showroom, where a well-dressed salesman displays the company's latest designs. Such scenes were designed to transform public attitudes toward prosthetics: from rough-hewn "peg legs" to individually fitted bodily accessories suitable for Victorian businessmen. Courtesy of Warshaw Collection, Archives Center, National Museum of American History, Smithsonian Institution.

FIGURE 5.4 Using a before-and-after trope common to commercial ads and charity campaigns, this A. A. Marks advertising card from the late 1800s illustrates one of the central claims of prosthetics' manufacturers: to help disabled customers "conceal the loss" of amputated limbs. Courtesy of the National Library of Medicine.

him and the naked stumps of his amputated legs exposed (almost obscenely) from beneath his suit jacket. The left side shows the same man standing upright on his artificial legs; the prosthetics themselves are hidden beneath the man's trousers and he holds his right arm across his torso in a pose of masculine propriety.

Although veterans were not the only targets of limb manufacturers (industrial and railroad workers were disabled at alarming rates throughout the late 1800s), companies like A. A. Marks routinely included testimonials from ex-soldiers in their advertising materials. A. A. Marks's 1906 publicity manual featured product endorsements from both sides of the Mason-Dixon Line, evidence of the spirit of reunion and reconciliation that swept much of white America at the turn of the century.[28] V. B. Clark of Jones County, Georgia testified:

> I lost my foot in the battle of Spotsylvania, May 10th 1864, and have been wearing A. A. Marks' artificial limbs for some twenty years, tried other kinds, none suited me half so well as yours, for comfort and durability; I do not believe there is any made on earth to equal Marks' limbs.

A. H. Gibbs, a native of Washington, DC, was a more recent convert:

> My leg was amputated in 1888 as the result of a gunshot wound received at Antietam in 1862. I attempted to wear a leg of another make but was unable to do so and after about one and a half years abandoned it and returned to crutches, which I used until I got the leg you made. I would not change back to crutches under any consideration.[29]

In the aftermath of the Civil War, prosthetics manufacturers established many of the tenets of twentieth century disabled veteran advertising, drawing upon popular notions of veteran pain and sacrifice to add symbolic weight to their products. Just as significant, prosthetics ads reinforced—and offered a resolution to—what Russell Shuttleworth, Nikki Wedgewood, and Nathan J. Wilson call the "dilemma of disabled masculinity."[30] At a time when disability was increasingly associated with a loss of manly independence, prosthetics promised not only to restore disabled veterans' manhood but also to render their physical differences virtually invisible to the naked eye. As such, prosthetics advertising helped construct a new mechanistic understanding of the male body, one that still governs the discourse of rehabilitation that dominates federal disabled veteran policy. "Fixed up nearly as good as new by the same system that crippled him," writes cultural studies scholar Erin O'Conner, "the prosthetic man became a symbol of all that was possible in the modern world of manufacture, a walking advertisement for the personal and social benefits to be had from a full-scale embrace of machine culture."[31]

Marketing Disabled Manhood in the World Wars

The world wars represented the highpoint of disabled veteran advertising in the United States. Throughout both conflicts, advertisers turned to images of wounded and disabled combatants with greater frequency than at any other time in US history. In *Fables of Abundance*, Jackson Lears singles out the world wars as an important turning point for the ad industry. In 1917–1918, "spokesmen for national advertising began to formulate what has since become a reflexive analysis of government policy: they began to trace political success or failure to the success or failure of particular marketing strategies." Messages mattered, ad spokesmen argued, and it was incumbent upon advertising professionals to shape the government's publicity efforts. Throughout the war, commercial advertising firms fused corporate interests and patriotic sentiment into a business-friendly ideology of national "morale"; in the process, industry attained unprecedented status, especially in the minds of advertisers themselves.[32] A statement published by *Printers' Ink*, the nation's first advertising trade magazine, three days after the Armistice testified to the industry's new sense of confidence: "The war has been won by advertising, as well as by soldiers and munitions."[33]

After the United States entered World War I in April 1917, war casualties quickly popped up in advertisements for a range of commercial products, from Swan pens to Santanogen, a topical disinfectant. Most of the images were distinctly upbeat in tone, mirroring the stories of cheerfully wounded soldiers that filled wartime newspapers. A Wrigley's gum ad from 1918 typifies the genre with its scenes of happily convalescing casualties waited on by demure Red Cross nurses (Figure 5.5).[34] In the illustration, two recovering soldiers chat (and chew gum) on a bench, while several more hobble about on crutches. Like many ads of its kind, it downplays the long-term effects of war injury; instead, it situates doughboys' injuries within a visual narrative of healing and hope. There is little sense that any of the men will be permanently disabled as a result of wartime trauma. Indeed, were it not for the strategically placed crutches and bandages (both common signifiers for wartime injury), a viewer would never know that the men had been wounded. Wrigley's and other companies hoped to use advertisements like this one to tap into nationalist sentiment and align their brands with the values often associated with wartime service: courage, sacrifice, heroism.

The few advertisements that actually acknowledged the permanent nature of veterans' disabilities were no less manipulative, combining calls of patriotic consumption with images of manly sacrifice. Most were produced in conjunction with war-related fundraising drives, a pattern that continued in World War II. Since the United States' entry in the Great War in 1917, the nation's propaganda ministry, the Committee on Public Information (CPI), had made a habit of using gender to bludgeon the American people. CPI posters crowed "The Army Builds Men!" According to government propagandists, male youth who shirked their wartime duties were not only unpatriotic but also unmanly, deserving of public ridicule and scorn. As icons of wartime masculinity, disabled veterans were considered especially powerful tools for shaming their less-than-heroic fellow citizens. A newspaper photograph associated with the 1919 Victory Liberty Loan campaign, for example, typifies the CPI's practice of using disabled veterans to guilt Americans into monetary donations.[35] The image features a grainy photograph of three bilateral leg amputees sitting in wheelchairs. Each man points an accusatory finger at the viewer. The photograph makes no effort to disguise the soldiers' injuries, nor does it attempt to explain how the additional victory loans will help such men. All the viewer is meant to understand is that the three amputees—men whose bodies are permanently altered by military service—are "A Powerful Argument to Buy Victory Loan Bonds" (Figure 5.6).

During World War II, advertisers rediscovered the usefulness of America's war-wounded as marketing figures, fundraisers, and spokesmen for martial values.

FIGURE 5.5 During World War I, Wrigley's and other companies attempted to cash in on wounded soldiers' heroic image by featuring convalescing troops in their advertising campaigns. *The Red Cross Magazine* (c. 1918).

FIGURE 5.6 As World War I drew to a close, government fundraisers used photographs of disabled male veterans to shame the public into purchasing victory bonds. "A Powerful Argument to Buy Victory Loan Bonds" (c. 1918). Scrapbook of Cora G. Stahl, Box 2, OHA 371, National Museum of Health and Medicine, Washington, DC.

Casualty-themed advertisements from World War II can be grouped into two broad categories. The bulk focused on wounded or convalescing soldiers—men, one is led to believe, with little likelihood of lifelong disability. Such ads invariably downplay the physical and psychological toll of war injury. In a 1945 ad from the *Saturday Evening Post*, for example, the Pullman Car Company assures readers that American casualties are the "best cared for wounded in the world"; backing up the claim is a photograph of smiling convalescents relaxing in a Pullman sleeping car (Figure 5.7a). Other companies sent similar messages, touting the relative health and happiness of the United States' injured troops. In 1945, the Chicago-based American Meat Institute sponsored a color ad depicting a pajamaed convalescent fighter tucking into a massive steak dinner (Figure 5.7b). Best known for using celebrities (Ronald Reagan, Gregory Peck, Joan Crawford) to hawk its trademark Chesterfield cigarette, the Liggett and Myers Tobacco Company also jumped on the wounded soldier bandwagon. An especially memorable ad from 1947 spotlighted a stop on the Sporting News Sports Caravan, a tour of New York veterans' hospitals cosponsored by Liggett and Myers and *The Sporting News*.[36] In

(a)

The best cared for wounded in the world

The men in this Pullman car were wounded in Europe.

Now, in an almost unbelievably short time after they received their first medical attention at aid stations right on the battlefield, they are in America—on their way to General Hospitals near their homes.

No other wounded in the world are cared for with the skill and devotion which the men and women of the Army Medical Corps give American wounded. No other wounded in the world are brought home so speedily.

Motor vehicles, ships, planes and trains all play a part in getting them here *fast*.

And Pullman—working with the railroads through its "pool" of sleeping cars—is privileged to contribute to their comfort.

Pullman's part of the job is providing sleeping cars to supplement the Army's special hospital trains. These cars—like the one in the picture—may have to be taken out of regular passenger service in order to meet Army needs as promptly and fully as possible.

So please—if you should be unable to get

the Pullman space you want exactly when you want it—remember this:

About half the Pullman fleet is assigned to carrying out mass troop movements and transporting other military personnel.

The other half is carrying more passengers than the whole fleet carried in peacetime.

And from this half must be drawn the *increasing number* of sleeping cars in which the wounded ride.

PULLMAN

For more than 80 years, the greatest name in passenger transportation

FIGURES 5.7a AND 7b During (and immediately after) World War II, a number of companies used images of wounded or convalescing servicemen to sell products and demonstrate their patriotic bona fides. Pullman Company, "The Best Cared for Wounded in the World," T2484—Courtesy of Ad*Access Digital Collection, John W. Hartman Center for Sales, Advertising and Marketing History, David M. Rubenstein Rare Book and Manuscript Library. Meat Institute, Duke University; American Meat Institute, "Meat for the Convalescent Fighter," *Life*, November 5, 1945, and "Meat for the Convalescent Fighter," *Life*, November 5, 1945.

(b)

Meat
for the convalescent fighter

Our men in convalescent hospitals are being rebuilt to health with a speed never known before. An excellent example is the far-sighted program of the Personnel Distribution Command of the Army Air Forces.

One way the recovery of these men is hastened is by feeding them generous quantities of meat containing the protein substances (amino acids) to make up for the protein they have lost.

When the body loses protein excessively (as in wounds, severe burns and infections) or when the diet does not provide enough protein (as with starved prisoners) the body literally "eats itself."

Meat proteins contain all ten of the essential amino acids needed to maintain and rebuild the body.

This emphasizes anew the rightness of our age-old liking for meat.

AMERICAN MEAT INSTITUTE
Headquarters, Chicago • Members throughout the U.S.

MEAT FOR A MAN FOR A WEEK

Here is a typical week's supply of meat served to patients of the Convalescent Hospital of the Army Air Forces at San Antonio—one of 12 such hospitals in the United States. Meat is served three times a day. The week's assortment shown above includes fresh pork, beef, lamb, ham, bacon, liver, sausage and cold cuts.

This Seal means that all nutritional statements made in this advertisement are acceptable to the Council on Foods and Nutrition of the American Medical Association

FIGURES 5.7a AND 7b Continued

the ad, Pete Petropoulos, a minor league baseball player and decorated Army sergeant, hands a copy of the sports daily and a carton of Chesterfields to a smiling (and smoking) young patient.

All three ads feature idealized versions of GI masculinity. Clean-shaven and boyish in appearance, with little visual evidence of physical disability or psychological trauma, the wounded men look more like college frat boys than the war-weary "dogfaces" of cartoonist Bill Mauldin or reporter Ernie Pyle. The equation of American GIs with youthful innocence was—and continues to be—a central feature of the "Good War," the mythologized version of World War II constructed by military propaganda, Hollywood, nostalgic historians, and others.[37] Just as important to the Good War myth was the perception that American private industry valued patriotism over profits, especially when it came to helping the nation's fighting men.

All three ads touch on this message as well. The Pullman ad not only highlights the company's contributions to the war effort but also attempts to curtail public complaints about the lack of available space in its sleeping cars. The small print beneath the photograph chides disgruntled passengers to remember that

> **About half the Pullman fleet** is designed to carrying out mass troop movements. . . ..
>
> **The other half** is carrying more passengers than the whole fleet carried in peacetime.
>
> **And from this half** must be drawn the increasing number of cars in which the wounded ride.[38]

In an obvious effort to deflect public criticism about food rationing, the Meat Institute insists that convalescing soldiers need "generous quantities of meat" to recover from their injuries. (Without it, the viewer is told, the wounded soldier's body "literally 'eats itself.'") The Chesterfield ad sends two messages, both meant to help the bottom line. Like countless advertisements of its kind, it suggests that cigarette smoking is conducive to good health. Just as important, it aligns the company with the nation's wounded soldiers, many still recovering from a traumatic yet ultimately triumphant war. On this latter point, Don Legg, the fresh-faced recipient of the free smokes, leaves little room for doubt: "Chesterfield never forgets the Veterans."

As opposed to wounded soldiers, disabled veterans rarely appeared in commercial advertisements during World War II. Like their World War I-era predecessors, they were largely consigned to war bonds campaigns, where they were used to inspire both admiration and shame on the part of civilians. Sponsored by the Gruen Watch Company, an ad from 1943, for example, uses an image of a disabled veteran to warn Americans against cashing their war bonds (Figure 5.8a). It instructs viewers to emulate Steve, an uncomplaining amputee who gave both of his legs fighting on the nation's behalf. "When you cash any War Bond now," the viewer is told, "you just pull your money out of the fight. You make deserters out of your dollars—a coward out of your cash." Most damning of all, the ad explains, "You refuse to let *your* money help give millions of Steves the things they need to stay safe—win fast—come home soon." Like many similar images, the ad celebrates disabled veterans as paragons of national sacrifice and manly duty. Moreover, despite its scolding tone, it seems to downplay any future difficulties for men like Steve. Smiling and striding across the picture, Steve seems to epitomize vigor and strong health; only his cane and the accompanying text suggest that his body has been permanently altered by military service.

(a)

FIGURES 5.8a AND 5.8b Permanently disabled veterans were far more likely to be found in ads for war bonds, where they were used to leverage viewers' feelings of guilt into monetary contributions. Gruen Watch Company, "Tell Steve You Cashed Your War Bond" (1944), W0353; and Revere Copper and Brass, "Their Supplies Seemed Endless" (1944), W0355—Courtesy of Ad*Access Digital Collection, John W. Hartman Center for Sales, Advertising and Marketing History, David M. Rubenstein Rare Book and Manuscript Library, Duke University.

FIGURES 5.8a AND 5.8b Continued

Not all fundraising advertisements were quite so cheery. In this regard, one particular set of war bond ads deserves special notice. They were sponsored by Revere Copper and Brass Incorporated of Rome, New York, and featured photographs of disabled veterans accompanied by brief testimonials. Their commitment to using disabled vets to shame American audiences is notable, even by World War II standards. A 1944 ad shows a disabled vet clutching a cane and asks, "If he can smile, why should you cry?" In another ad from the same year, an amputee seated in a wheelchair attempts to curb complacency on the home front. Citing the deaths of seventy-six of his fellow shipmen (along with the loss of much of his right leg) in a recent attack, Chief Signalman Willard A. Murphy declares, "The Japs aren't as cross-eyed as you think." Perhaps the most memorable of Revere's World War II ads centers on a photograph of Lt. John G. Kuhn, a Marine pilot in the Pacific (Figure 5.8b). He wears a thick canvas brace on his chin, and he glares reproachfully at the viewer. Describing a series of deadly air battles against a seemingly endless supply of Japanese fighter planes, he admits that he "can't understand how folks at home can keep even one spare dollar in their pockets. They must know that, every day, good American boys are being killed, who might have lived if the weight of supplies had been on their side."[39] All three ads rely upon gendered ideas of martial citizenship to elevate disabled veterans' status as both *experts on* and *evidence of* patriotic sacrifice. And their collective message is clear: disabled veterans contribute their bodies to the war effort; the very least the rest of us can do is pay the bills.

The Disabled Veteran Market in Midcentury America

Women by the millions were yearning for evidence that they were still basically feminine; and men by the millions were yearning for evidence they were still indisputably and virulently masculine. Merchandisers were quick to see the possibilities of offering both products that would serve as reassurance symbols.[40]

— VANCE PACKARD, *THE HIDDEN PERSUADERS* (1957)

Disabled veterans did not disappear entirely from American visual culture at the end of World War II. The Veterans Administration cranked out numerous illustrated pamphlets, flyers, and films detailing the benefits of government-sponsored programs. Award-winning Hollywood films such as William Wyler's *The Best Years of Our Lives* (1946), Delmer Dave's *Pride of the Marines* (1945), and Fred Zinnemann's *The Men* (1950) cast a sympathetic eye on the physical and emotional hardships of disabled veterans. Magazine articles with titles like "They May Be Disabled—But Man! Can They Work!" (1951) and "They Call *Him* Disabled" (1953) profiled disabled veterans' successful integration into the postwar economy. And, in a few cases, businesses mounted advertising campaigns to tap the suddenly swollen market of convalescing or disabled vets.

How many disabled veterans were there? The answer is not entirely clear. Between 1941 and 1945, 678,000 US servicemen sustained nonfatal injuries, including 300,000 whose injuries required extensive hospitalization and convalescent care. A million more men suffered debilitating psychiatric symptoms, while countless others were haunted by traumatic memories for the rest of their lives.[41] For World War II's disabled survivors, reintegration was not easy. Decades before the passage of the Americans with Disabilities Act (1990), antidisability prejudice ran deep. Congressional investigations found disabled vets languishing in run-down treatment centers, and some communities (especially those located near

Veterans Administration hospitals) complained openly about the sight of disabled patients walking the street.[42]

Nevertheless, marketers were eager to reach disabled veteran customers—and not just because of their numbers. The passage of the Serviceman's Readjustment Act of 1944—better known as the GI Bill—provided health care, low-interest home loans, and university education to millions of vets, swelling the middle class for the next half-century. Thanks to the boom in the postwar economy, World War II veterans, even disabled ones, were likely to be better off than their Civil War and Great War counterparts. Plus, martial sentiment continued to infuse mid-century American culture, especially once the Cold War threatened to turn hot. Animated by postwar "victory culture," many companies were eager to associate their products—and their corporate images—with the men who had endangered their bodies to defeat Hitler and avenge Pearl Harbor.[43]

Although ex-combatants were featured in a wide variety of advertisements, disabled World War II veterans were usually relegated to "community specific" advertisements—ads aimed to address the fears and desires thought to be unique to the disabled (veteran) community.[44] Not surprisingly, male disabled vets featured heavily in ads for canes, artificial limbs, and other prosthetic technologies, as they had following the Civil War. Ads of this sort typically pitched their products as tools for disabled veterans' successful reintegration into mainstream society. In doing so, they presented narratives of manhood lost and regained—stories of vets resolving the "dilemma of disabled masculinity" with the help of modern consumer products. A Sonotone hearing aid advertisement from 1946, for example, tells the story of Bill, a young GI whose hearing was "blasted" in the invasion of Normandy in June 1944 (Figure 5.9a). During his stay in the hospital, the Army "taught him to hear again" using the latest technology. Now, armed with his Sonotone brand hearing aid, Bill has been "Honorably Discharged—From Deafness" and is ready to reenter the workplace. More than an illustration of one man's success, the Sonotone ad is framed as an open letter to employers on behalf of thousands of hearing-impaired vets: "Throughout the war, great numbers of men with similar hearing 'disabilities' have licked nearly every kind of job from production line to executive office...*unhandicapped, thanks to Sonotone!*"

At least one major industry went out of its way to market to disabled veterans: auto manufacturers. Thwarted by nearly two decades of depression and war, the US automotive industry boomed in the late 1940s and 1950s. For postwar Americans, cars were *the* national product—familiar yet exotic, luxurious yet suddenly within the reach of millions of potential motorists.[45] Writing in his bestselling book, *The Hidden Persuaders* (1957), Vance Packard remarked,

> The automobile has become far more than a mere means of conveyance. In the words of Pierre Martineau, "The automobile tells who were are and what we think we want to be. . . . It is a portable symbol of our personality and our

(a)

HONORABLY DISCHARGED—FROM DEAFNESS!

BILL'S HEARING WAS BLASTED IN NORMANDY—and the Army moved right in to help him. Soon he found himself in an elaborate rehabilitation hospital, where prompt and intelligent treatment promised well for his future—

THE ARMY TAUGHT HIM TO HEAR AGAIN—realising how much more there is to hearing again than just having a hearing aid. The background of his case was painstakingly studied. Audiometric tests gave an accurate picture of his tone loss—

THESE TWO BUTTONS say. *"Ready for immediate employment!"* One is the official emblem of honorable service in the armed forces. The second is the Sonotone button that puts good men back into good jobs.

The thousands of veterans whose hearing injuries are compensated with efficient modern hearing instruments have the right to expect *real futures.* Throughout the war, great numbers of men with similar hearing "disability" have licked nearly every kind of job from production line to executive office . . . *unhandicapped, thanks to Sonotone!*

The veteran can do the same. Recent technical advances in hearing instruments, including far greater power and closer fitting to the individual's needs, now bring effective hearing even to many degrees of hearing loss that have been considered "hopeless". The new Sonotone "600" is a truly amazing instrument . . . *but even more important to uninterrupted good hearing on the job is Sonotone's unique nation-wide system of personal service.* 207 Sonotone offices across the country are always available to the veteran in your firm who wears a Sonotone—so he may come in anywhere, anytime, for instrument refittings and repairs, or for personal help and counsel in maintaining the best possible hearing.

And so, Mr. Employer, when you meet this young man with two badges, you may repay a great service and do another for yourself. One large firm reports typically on 1800 rehabilitated World War II veterans . . . *"Our most conscientious men . . . less liable to accident and absence than the average."*

SONOTONE "600"
with BI-FOCAL CONTROL

Look in your telephone directory, or write Sonotone, Elmsford, N. Y. 207 Sonotone offices and 1511 regularly held Sonotone Hearing Centers in the U. S. In Canada—Sonotone, 929 Yonge Street, Toronto.

© 1946 Sonotone Corp.

BILL CHOSE A SONOTONE, LEARNED NEW Navy and Army veterans get their choice of finest modern instruments. Bill chose because, besides good hearing, it offered service and help across America *for life—*

HE HEARS WELL AND WANTS A GOOD Armed with the Service's wonderful start, advanced Sonotone "600" and continuing from Sonotone Consultants, there are jobs Bill can't perform as well as anybody

2

FIGURE 5.9a Following World War II, manufacturers of assistive devices regularly featured disabled veterans in their advertisements. In this ad, a D-Day veteran is "discharged from deafness" thanks to the use of a Sonotone 600 hearing aid. Sonotone, "Honorably Discharged—From Deafness," *Life*, February 4, 1946.

position. [In buying a car] you are saying in a sense, 'I am looking for the car that expresses who I am.'"[46]

The automotive industry marketed its vehicles in highly conventional terms, often relying upon gendered stereotypes to reach customers. Ads aimed at women typically stressed such "feminine" characteristics as comfort, safety, and ease of use; ads for men took a different route, highlighting the speed, girth, and horsepower of their vehicles. Above all, cars were advertised as vehicles for fantasy and self-expression. One Buick ad promised, "It makes you feel like the man you are."[47]

Shortly after World War II, several car brands—Ford, Buick, Oldsmobile, and others—launched campaigns to target disabled World War II veterans, especially amputees. Each highlighted available modifications to car's control system (steering, braking, acceleration) to help put disabled veterans behind the wheel. Buick offered modification packages for four types of disabilities: right-hand amputations (or right- and left-hand amputations), left-hand amputations only, right- or left-leg amputations, or right- and left-leg amputations.[48] Oldsmobile went further, advertising five possible modification packages as part of its newly designed "Valiant" driving control system (Figure 5.9b). According to a fifty-page publicity brochure Oldsmobile released in 1950, the driving system was named after seriously disabled World War II veterans: "These men, popularly known as 'Valiants,' faced the stark realization that they might never again be able to drive." Before the war, such men would have been left helpless and hopeless, unable to live out their dreams of auto-mobility. However, thanks to Oldsmobile, disabled veterans had a chance to "lead, as nearly as possible, normal lives."[49] The company even advertised a priority purchase plan for World War II disabled veterans. Men whose injuries were incurred in wartime service—and who were unable to operate a car with "conventional driving controls"—were given "priority rights" on an Oldsmobile with Valiant steering and a Hydra-Matic Drive transmission.[50]

All of the modifications were free of charge. Indeed, car companies framed their offers as part of an unspoken social contract with disabled veterans and the American people. Disabled veterans had sacrificed their bodies and future prospects in the nation's time of need. Now, it was incumbent upon all Americans to ensure that disabled veterans regained something of what they had lost. In *So That Disabled Veterans Can "Take the Wheel Again,"* a publicity pamphlet published shortly after the end of World War II, auto baron Henry Ford summed up this attitude in a quote printed prominently on the back of the cover:

> The least we can do for these men is to be sure that they get an even break with those who come back without major disabilities, and we do not want any profit incentive to enter into this picture. No man who lost a limb in the armed services of our country during the war is going to have to pay anything extra to drive a Ford automobile.[51]

"Valiant" DRIVING CONTROLS

Bright New Horizons

Oldsmobile, co-operating with the Surgeon General's Office of the Army and Navy, designed and built an experimental car equipped with these Special Driving Controls. This car was placed at the disposal of one of the largest Army hospitals, in a sincere attempt to aid in the rehabilitation and recovery of Valiants. The results were extremely gratifying. Even men who had lost both legs or both arms found that they, too, could handle the car very satisfactorily by means of the driving controls provided.

Immediate response from Army and Navy hospital authorities and the sincere gratitude of the veterans themselves, prompted Oldsmobile to assemble a fleet of "Valiant Cars". These were then placed at the disposal of the rehabilitation officers of major Army and Navy hospitals throughout the country.

So urgent have been the appeals from "Valiants" and civilians alike, for these Driving Controls, that Oldsmobile has made them available as accessories for 1941, 1942 and 1946 Oldsmobile Hydra-Matic equipped cars.

Thus, through these Driving Controls, thousands of "Valiants" will be able to overcome what appears to be insurmountable handicaps and will soon be looking forward to Bright New Horizons.

3

FIGURE 5.9b Immediately after World War II, American auto manufacturers attempted to tap the new market of recently disabled military veterans. In this advertising brochure, Oldsmobile suggests that driving is an integral part of disabled GIs' masculine reintegration into postwar society. Oldsmobile, "Oldsmobile's 'Valiant' Driving Controls: For Disabled Veterans and Other Handicapped Persons" (1946), 20111104_Oldsmobile_Controls_for_Disabled_Vets_001.JPG, http://cdm15017.contentdm.oclc.org/cdm/ref/collection/p15017coll26/id/5191, Z. Taylor Vinson collection of transportation ephemera (Accession 20100108.ZTV), Audiovisual Collections and Digital Initiatives Department, Hagley Museum and Library, Wilmington, DE 19807. Courtesy of General Motors Corporation.

Disability Advertising in the Shadow of Vietnam

> If you watched television or opened a magazine in the late 1980s, you
> probably remember Bill Demby.
>
> —CHAD STEWART, *ON PATROL MAGAZINE* (2014)[52]

In the 1970s, disabled veterans were too polarizing to make good pitchmen.
As Americans grappled with the United States' military defeat in Vietnam, commentators across the ideological spectrum pointed to disabled vets as evidence
of what went wrong—and how best to recover. Conservatives claimed them as
icons of old-fashioned patriotic sacrifice, a sentiment that would eventually be
enshrined in country music artist Merle Haggard's 1990 ballad "Me and Crippled
Soldiers":

> Has the holocaust been so long? Is Hitler really gone
> As we burn our only cause for Vietnam?
> There's the mom who lost her son
> Is this the freedom that we won?
> For only me and crippled soldiers give a damn[53]

Antiwar protestors, on the other hand, mobilized disabled veterans as symbols
of war's trauma. At the 1972 Republican Convention, recent veteran Ron Kovic,
a paraplegic wheelchair user and member of the Vietnam Veterans Against the
War, captured the national spotlight. "What's happening in Vietnam is a crime
against humanity," he told CBS reporter Roger Mudd. "If you can't believe the veteran who fought the war and was wounded in the war, who can you believe?"[54] In
the ensuing years, revelations about post-traumatic stress disorder and war crimes
further stigmatized disabled Vietnam War veterans (and Vietnam vets in general).
Throughout the late 1970s and early 1980s, films such as *Taxi Driver* (1976), *The
Deer Hunter* (1978), and *First Blood* (1982) sent the message that Vietnam vets were
not only dangerous but, more often than not, mentally deranged, seething against
a lost war and an uncaring public.

The situation was no better for the greater disabled community—at least as
far as advertising was concerned. Although disabled activists staged high-profile
protests throughout the 1970s, Madison Avenue took little notice.[55] Sandra
Gordon, who would later become a senior vice president for the National Easter
Seal Society, recalled, "It was the mid-1970s when I first started trying to get companies interested in using someone disabled. I went and talked with them and you
would have thought I had suggested they put a dog in there."[56] That attitude dominated advertisers' thinking for the next decade until a landmark ad campaign in
1987 set the stage for a new era of disability advertising. The advertisement's sponsor was DuPont, a chemical company best known for the slogan "Better things for
better living." Its star was about as unlikely a media icon as one might expect: a
balding, 6'1" African American, double amputee named Bill Demby (Figure 5.10).

For Bill Demby, the difference means getting another shot.

When Bill Demby was in Vietnam, he used to dream of coming home and playing a little basketball with the guys.

A dream that all but died when he lost both his legs to a Viet Cong rocket.

But then, a group of researchers discovered that a remarkable DuPont plastic could help make artificial limbs that were more resilient, more flexible, more like life itself.

Thanks to these efforts, Bill Demby is back. And some say, he hasn't lost a step.

At DuPont, we make the things that make a difference.

Better things for better living.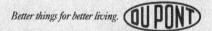

FIGURE 5.10 In the late 1980s, DuPont launched an award-winning set of ads featuring Bill Demby, a middle-aged African American veteran whose lower legs were amputated during the Vietnam War. The campaign predated the growing trend of disability-related advertisements. In doing so, however, DuPont's print and television ads sent a familiar message: that disabled men could restore their masculinity with hard work and technological intervention. DuPont, "For Bill Demby, the Difference Means Getting Another Shot" (c. 1987).

Demby's road to media fame began in the early 1950s.[57] He grew up in a poor community on the eastern shore of Maryland. In high school, he averaged 16 points per game on the Queen Anne's County basketball team, but when it came time to graduate, his school guidance counselor told him he was not college material. Demby took a job in a factory and received his draft notice a few months later. On March 26, 1971, he was riding in a gun truck in Quang Tri Province (Vietnam), when a rocket slammed into the vehicle. "It was like a quarter hit the side of my door—there was a 'ping' sound," he told *People* magazine in 1988. "All I remember is smoke filling the truck, and I saw my leg on the floor." On the flight to the hospital, Demby wondered how his family would react when they saw him. "I knew I wasn't going to change inside, but society judges you physically," he reflected wistfully.[58] Surgeons amputated much of his remaining leg and, upon returning home, he sunk into depression. He spent the next decade trying to numb the pain with drugs and booze. Eventually, he turned his life around through what his media profilers often describe as sheer masculine will. Rejecting group therapy, he embraced sports and the world of rough-and-tumble competition. He taught himself to ski, took up drag racing, and became a world-class Paralympic athlete in track and field.

Demby was competing in the National Amputee Games in Nashville when he was discovered by a New York ad firm, Faces & Places, which specialized in locating "real people" for television commercials.[59] In the resulting 30-second commercial, Demby plays in a pickup basketball game on New York's Upper West Side. He wears a pair of artificial legs cushioned by a tough yet pliable form of plastic developed by DuPont researchers. In the middle of the ad, Demby is knocked to the concrete, exposing his prosthetics, but he quickly rejoins the game. In case viewers failed to grasp the full implications of Demby's achievements, the narration intones:

> When Bill Demby was in Vietnam, he dreamed of coming home and playing a little basketball. A dream that all but died when he lost both legs to a Viet Cong rocket. Now Bill's back and some say he hasn't lost a step.

The commercial and accompany print ad were instant hits. DuPont received thousands of enthusiastic letters in its first week, and the TV spot ran on commercial networks for three years. It won a Clio, the advertising industry's top honor, and the National Easter Seal Society's first ever EDI (Equality, Dignity, Independence), an award meant to recognize "communications judged to enhance the independence of people with disabilities."[60] The Disabled American Veterans named Demby 1990's Outstanding Disabled Veteran of the Year. He hired an agent and became a popular motivational speaker, making over 150 public appearances a year. Journalists and industry insiders praised the campaign's "inspiring story" and ability to heal the ideological wounds of Vietnam.[61] "Regardless of how people felt about the war," reflected one marketing reporter in 1991, "the humanity of the commercial won the hearts of many viewers."[62]

Nevertheless, it is clear that much of the campaign's appeal came from the message it sent about disability, masculinity, and recovery. In highlighting Demby's triumph over a "Viet Cong rocket" attack, the commercial makes no reference to the legal and environmental barriers that limit disabled people's access to power and social opportunity. [63] Rather, it frames Demby's story as a triumphalist narrative of overcoming life's obstacles. Once emasculated by war injury, Demby had pulled himself up by his leg straps to rejoin the bruising world of male athletics. Much like A. A. Marks's ads a century earlier, Demby's commercial frames the "dilemma of disabled masculinity" as a personal project, to be resolved not by group activism but by individual action and consumption. Indeed, Demby exemplifies many of the characteristics of the "hard body" masculinity that, according to film scholar Susan Jeffords, characterized Reagan-era conservative culture. During the conservative upsurge of the 1980s, Jeffords writes, "The depiction of the indefatigable, muscular, and invincible masculine body became the linchpin of the Reagan imaginary; this hardened male form became the emblem not only for the Reagan presidency but for its ideologies and economies as well."[64] His disabilities (missing legs, drug addiction, postwar depression) now seemingly eliminated, Demby embodies the values of manly competition, hard work, and free enterprise that Reagan and others touted as the core values of conservative social and economic policies. Thanks to technology (and the help of companies like DuPont), both Demby and America are "now back"—wholly recovered from the traumas of a failed war.

Selling Disabled Veteran Masculinity Today

Disabled veterans remain outsiders in the world of advertising. Even so, many industry followers are increasingly optimistic about the future. Writing in *We*, a publication aimed at disabled audiences, in 1999, John M. Williams noted advertisers' growing willingness to challenge the long tradition of casting only "perfect" people in television ads. Indeed, at that time, companies were already spending more than $150 million with ad agencies on disability-related products and advertising campaigns.[65]

What accounted for this sudden eagerness to reach disabled customers? Federal policy played a part. The passage of the Rehabilitation Act of 1973 and the Americans with Disabilities Act of 1990, along with relentless pressure from disability organizations, has led to a greater awareness of disabled people in American society. However, the rise of disability advertising has also been driven by far less noble factors, including a new awareness of disabled people as a large and virtually untapped market (a situation some wags have deemed "handicapitalism").[66] According to Williams, advertisers are increasingly aware that "the 54 million Americans with disabilities have never been targeted in campaigns as rigorous and sophisticated as those used to reach smaller minority groups."[67]

The resulting ads are by no means perfect. Many adhere to the same kinds of disqualifying stereotypes that have plagued disability representation throughout US history.[68] Still, media scholars Beth Haller and Sue Ralph see reason for hope. "Although many businesses are learning to use disabled models in advertising due to capitalistic motivation for profits," they observed in 2001, "this crass commercialism is actually producing some good disability images in advertising."[69]

Recently, the shopping giant Nordstrom—which has been using imagery of disabled people since the early 1990s—published a photograph of Alex Minsky, an Afghanistan War veteran and amputee, in its summer 2014 catalog (Figure 5.11). In the image, the dark-haired model is squatting on one leg, his metal prosthetic limb balanced out in front of him. He is wearing the uniform of a hipster gym-rat: low-top Nike sneakers, workout clothes, stubble, and, of course, elaborate tattoos running up both arm sleeves and his remaining leg. His photo is not featured in a "community specific" ad campaign but on a page promoting the latest sneaker designs. In fact, were it not for his prominently displayed prosthetic, Minsky looks exactly like one of the impossibly handsome hunks one would expect to find in upscale fashion campaigns. (From the waist up, he could easily pass for a European soccer star.)[70]

And that, ultimately, is part of the problem. For as much as such advertisements are a welcome sight in an advertising landscape dominated by white, able-bodied blandness, they do little to challenge hegemonic notions of masculine appearance, which treat chiseled abs and flexing muscles as the ultimate signifiers of male physical attractiveness. If anything, ads like Minsky's reinforce the belief that disabled veterans (indeed, all disabled men) can—and thus should—attempt to reshape their bodies to fit a very narrow ideal of embodied masculinity. Moreover, such ads—in their eagerness to push the boundaries of advertising acceptability—tend to obscure an important truth: that the vast majority of disabled veterans do not have lost limbs or visible scars. In February 2013, *Wired* writer Spencer Ackerman reported that, in eleven years of fighting, the latest generation of American troops had undergone over 1,700 limb amputations. But far more disturbing is the number of recent combatants who struggle with the burden of invisible wounds such as post-traumatic stress disorder and traumatic brain injury. In 2013, their population topped—by the government's own estimates—more than 370,000, and it has been growing ever since.[71]

In twenty-first-century American warfare, the most representative image of war disability is not a heroic amputee standing proudly on his shiny metal prosthetic. It is a CT scan, and we are not likely to see one of those in a commercial any time soon.

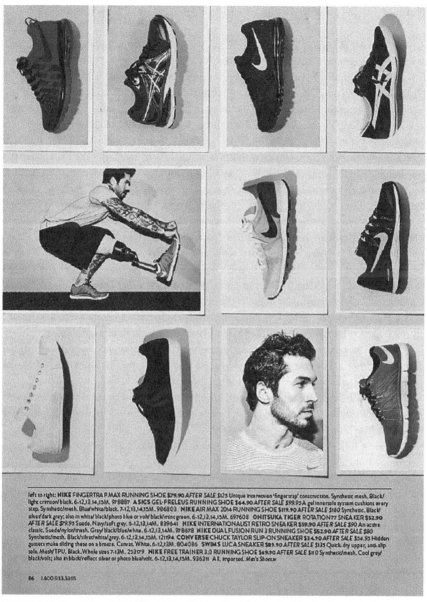

FIGURE 5.11 Since the early 2000s, a growing number of commercial advertisements have included images of disabled veterans. Such ads invariable challenge many of the gendered stigmas associated with disability, including the equation of bodily impairment and diminished masculinity. With few exceptions, however, disability-themed advertisements continue to reflect the same narrow set of beauty standards that has dominated the ad industry for decades. Nordstrom Summer 2014 Catalog. Courtesy of Nordstrom Inc.

Notes

1. "For All the Good Timxes—An Army Veteran's Return to Skateboarding," https://www.youtube.com/watch?v=Wr6DhLKYol4.

2. In 2001, *Disability Studies Quarterly*, the premier journal in the field of disability studies, dedicated an entire issue to the topic of advertising. Beyond the essays contained in that issue, other important discussions of disability in advertising and other forms of commercial media include Rosemarie Garland-Thomson, "Seeing the Disabled: Visual Rhetorics of Disability in Popular Photography," in *The New Disability History: American Perspectives*, eds. Paul K. Longmore and Lauri Umansky (New York: NYU Press, 2001), 335–374; Beth Haller and Sue Ralph, "Are Disability Images in Advertising Becoming Bold and Daring? An Analysis of Prominent Themes in US and UK Campaigns," *Disability Studies Quarterly* 26.3 (2006); Beth Haller, *Representing Disability in an Ableist World: Essays on Mass Media* (Louisville, KY: Avocado Press, 2010); Sarah Heiss, "Locating the Bodies of Women and Disability in Definitions of Beauty: An Analysis of Dove's Campaign for Real Beauty," *Disability Studies Quarterly* 31.1 (2011); Olan F. Farnall and Kelli Lyons, "Are We There Yet? A Content Analysis of Ability Integrated Advertising on Prime-Time TV," *Disability Studies Quarterly* 32.1 (2012); Robert Bogdan, with Martin Elks and James A. Knoll, *Picturing Disability: Beggar, Freak, Citizen, and Other Photographic Rhetoric* (Syracuse: University of Syracuse Press, 2012).

3. Harlan Hahn, "Advertising the Acceptably Employable Image: Disability and Capitalism," in *The Disability Studies Reader*, ed. Lennard J. Davis (New York: Routledge, 1997), 181.

4. For an overview of current directions in the study of disability and masculinity, see Russell Shuttleworth, Nikki Wedgewood, and Nathan J. Wilson, "The Dilemma of Disabled Masculinity," *Men and Masculinities* 15 (2012), 174–194.

5. Adrienne Asch and Michelle Fine, "Introduction: Beyond Pedestals," in *Women with Disabilities: Essays in Psychology, Culture, and Politics*, ed. Michelle Fine and Adrienne Asch (Philadelphia: Temple University Press, 1988), 3.

6. Joe Clark, quoted in Haller and Ralph, "Are Disability Images in Advertising Becoming Bold and Daring?"

7. On efforts to carve out an exceptional status for disabled veterans in American culture and policy, see John M. Kinder, *Paying with Their Bodies: American War and the Problem of the Disabled Veteran* (Chicago: University of Chicago Press, 2015).

8. The only exceptions were advertisements aimed at disabled consumers. See Bogdan, *Picturing Disability*, 104.

9. Volney B. Palmer established the United States' first advertising agency in Philadelphia in 1842. Winston Fletcher, *Advertising: A Very Short Introduction* (New York: Oxford University Press, 2010), 21. For more on the development of advertising in America, see Roland Marchand, *Advertising the American Dream: Making Way for Modernity for Modernity, 1920–1940* (Berkeley: University of California Press, 1985); T. J. Jackson Lears, *Fables of Abundance: A Cultural History of Advertising in America* (New York: Basic, 1994).

10. Hahn, "Advertising the Acceptably Employable Image," 179.

11. See Hahn, "Advertising the Acceptably Employable Image," 172–186; Stewart Ewen, *Captains of Consciousness: Advertising and the Social Roots of the Consumer Culture*, 25th anniversary edition (New York: Basic Books, 2001), 46; T. J. Jackson Lears,

"American Advertising and the Reconstruction of the Body, 1880–1930," in *Fitness in American Culture: Images of Health, Sport, and the Body, 1830–1940* (Amherst: University of Massachusetts Press, 1989), 47–66.

12. Lears, "American Advertising and the Reconstruction of the Body," 49.

13. On the emergence of the normal body, see Lennard J. Davis, *Enforcing Normalcy: Disability, Deafness, and the Body* (London: Verso, 1995).

14. Bogdan, *Picturing Disability*, 104.

15. Kinder, *Paying with Their Bodies*, 23.

16. Louisa May Alcott, *Hospital Sketches* (Boston: James Redpath, 1863), 36.

17. On the feminization of dependency in modern America, see Nancy Fraser and Linda Gordon, "A Genealogy of *Dependency*: Tracing a Keyword of the U.S. Welfare State," *Signs: Journal of Women in Culture and Society* 19.2 (Winter 1994), 309–336; Mary Klages, *Woeful Afflictions: Disability and Sentimentality in Victorian America* (Philadelphia: University of Pennsylvania Press, 1999), 1–9.

18. Kinder, *Paying with Their Bodies*, 216–252.

19. Bogdan, *Picturing Disability*, 31–32.

20. Kim E. Nielsen, *A Disability History of the United States* (Boston: Beacon Press, 2012), 83, 86.

21. Lareann Figg and Jane Farrell-Beck, "Amputation in the Civil War: Physical and Social Dimensions," *Journal of the History of Medicine and Allied Sciences* 48.4 (1993), 454.

22. Dixon Wecter, *When Johnny Comes Marching Home* (Cambridge, MA: Riverside Press, 1944), 213.

23. Figg and Farrell-Beck, "Amputation in the Civil War," 454.

24. Guy R. Hasegawa, *Mending Broken Soldiers: The Union and Confederate Programs to Supply Artificial Limbs* (Carbondale: Southern Illinois University Press, 2012), 16.

25. A. A. Marks, *Manual of Artificial Limbs: An Exhaustive Exposition of Prosthesis* (New York: A. A. Marks, 1906), 183, 184.

26. Images from the "From Stump to Limb" campaign are held in the Warsaw Collection, Archives Center, National Museum of American History, Smithsonian Institution, Washington, DC. They have been reproduced in *Honorable Scars*, a digital history exhibition produced by the US National Library of Medicine. See https://www.nlm.nih.gov/exhibition/lifeandlimb/honorablescars.html.

27. Bogdan, *Picturing Disability*, 106.

28. See David W. Blight, *Race and Reunion: The Civil War in American Memory* (Cambridge, MA: Belknap Press of Harvard University Press, 2001).

29. A. A. Marks, *Manual of Artificial Limbs*, 280, 308.

30. Shuttleworth, Wedgewood, and Wilson, "Dilemma of Disabled Masculinity," 174–194.

31. Erin O'Connor, "'Fractions of Men': Engendering Amputation in Victorian Culture," *Comparative Studies in Society and History* 39.4 (October 1997), 767.

32. Lears, *Fables of Abundance*, 219, 221.

33. Quoted in Lears, *Fables of Abundance*, 220.

34. A copy of the advertisement can be found in the December 1917 issue of *Red Cross Magazine*.

35. A copy can be found in the scrapbook of Cora G. Stahl, Box 2, OHA 371, National Museum of Health and Medicine, Washington, DC.

36. This ad is discussed in an online exhibit produced by Stanford Research into the Impact of Tobacco Advertising. Locate the advertisement by searching in the theme "Doctors Smoking," subtheme "Hospitalized Patients." See http://tobacco.stanford.edu/ tobacco_main/index.php.

37. On the myth of the "Good War," see Michael C. C. Adams, *The Best War Ever: America and World War II*, 2nd ed. (Baltimore: Johns Hopkins University Press, 2015).

38. Bold in original.

39. All three Revere Copper and Brass Incorporated ads are available in the Ad*Access Online Project, John W. Harman Center for Sales, Advertising and Marketing History, Duke University David M. Rubenstein Rare Book and Manuscript Library.

40. Vance Packard, *The Hidden Persuaders* (New York: Pocket Books, 1957), 74.

41. David A. Gerber, "Heroes and Misfits: The Troubled Social Reintegration of Disabled Veterans in *The Best Years of Our Lives*," in *Disabled Veterans in History*, ed. David A. Gerber (Ann Arbor: University of Michigan Press, 2000), 73.

42. Kinder, *Paying with Their Bodies*, 272.

43. On post–World War II "victory culture," see Tom Engelhardt, *The End of Victory Culture: Cold War America and the Disillusioning of a Generation* (New York: Basic Books, 1995).

44. On the difference between "community specific" and "general" ad campaigns, see Beth Haller and Sue Ralph, "Profitability, Diversity, and Disability Images in Advertising in the United States and Great Britain," *Disability Studies Quarterly* 21.2 (Spring 2001).

45. On the Americans' obsessions with automobiles after World War II, see Karal Ann Marling, *As Seen on TV: The Visual Culture of Everyday Life in the 1950s* (Cambridge, MA: Harvard University Press, 1994), 129–162.

46. Packard, *The Hidden Persuaders* 43.

47. Quoted in Packard, *The Hidden Persuaders*, 43.

48. *Buick's Special Driving Controls for Disabled Veterans of World War II* (Flint, Michigan: c. 1946), vinson_2011_0511_00045, Series I. Automobile Makes, Box 1-140, Z. Taylor Vinson collection of transportation ephemera (Accession 20100108.ZTV), Published Collections Department, Hagley Museum and Library, Wilmington, DE 19807 (hereafter Hagley); available in the Hagley Digital Archives.

49. *Oldsmobile's "Valiant" Driving Controls . . . For Disabled Veterans and Other Handicapped Persons* (Lansing, MI, 1946), 20111104_Oldsmobile_Controls_for_Disabled_Vets, Series I. Automobile Makes, Box 1-634, Hagley; available in the Hagley Digital Archives.

50. "Announcing Priority Rights for Disabled Veterans," *The New York Times*, September 8, 1946, E8.

51. Quoted in *So That Disabled Veterans Can "Take the Wheel Again"* (c. 1946), 20111104_Ford_Disabled_Vets, Series I. Automobile Makes, Box 1-319, Hagley; available in the Hagley Digital Archives.

52. Chad Stewart, "Advances in Prosthetics, Wheelchairs Help Wounded Vets Push Past Obstacles," *On Patrol*, Summer 2014. http://usoonpatrol.org/archives/2014/07/14/ advances-in-prosthetics-wheelc

53. Merle Haggard, "Me and Crippled Soldiers," *Blue Jungle*, Curb Records, 1990.

54. Ron Kovic, *Born on the Fourth of July* (New York: Pocket Books, 1976), 180.

55. On the disability activism in this period, see Nielsen, *Disability History*, 157–183.

56. Alan L. Adler, "TV Ads Make a Pitch to the Disabled," *L.A. Times*, February 2, 1992.

57. The subsequent biographical sketch is gleaned from details derived from the following sources: George Vecsey, "Still Living on the Line," *The New York Times*, August 19, 1988, D19; Ted Johnson, "Anaheim: Disabled Athlete Lauded for Fortitude," *L.A. Times*, July 30, 1990; Thomas Petzinger Jr., "The Front Lines: Bill Demby Attaches his Name, and Pride, to Product He Needs," *The Wall Street Journal*, Eastern edition, December 29, 1995, B1; Mike Trask, Reading [Pa] *Eagle*, February 23, 2006.

58. Andrew Abrahams, "An Amazing 'Foot' Puts Legless Vet Bill Demby Back in the Ballgame," *People* 29.13 (April 4, 1988).

59. Bruce Horovitz, "Finding 'Real' People for Ads Takes Real Effort," *L.A. Times*, June 20, 1989.

60. David Baroza, "National Easter Seal Announces Awards," *The New York Times*, November 13, 1996.

61. Adler, "TV Ads Make a Pitch to the Disabled."

62. Bruce Horovitz, "With Peace, Look for Ads to Lighten Up," *L.A. Times*, February 27, 1991.

63. Demby was so adamant about downplaying the social limitations of "disability" that he often spelled the term with a "lowercase 'dis' and a capital 'A.'" Maria C. Johnson, "By the Time He Heard It, It Was Too Late," *Greensboro* [NC] *News*, March 9, 1992.

64. Susan Jeffords, *Hard Bodies: Hollywood Masculinity in the Reagan Era* (New Brunswick, NJ: Rutgers University Press, 1994), 25.

65. John M. Williams, "And Here's the Pitch," *We*, July/August 1999, 28.

66. Quoted in Haller and Ralph, "Profitability, Diversity, and Disability Images."

67. Williams, "And Here's the Pitch," 29.

68. Media scholars Kim Wolfson and Martin F. Norden have described ten disability stereotypes in twentieth-century Hollywood film: the "civilian superstar," the "comic misadventurer," the "elderly dupe," the "high-tech guru," the "noble warrior," the "obsessive avenger," the "saintly sage," the "sweet innocent," the "techno marvel," and the "tragic victim." Although such stereotypes, in Wolfson and Norden's words, "typically bear little resemblance to the actual experiences and lifestyles of people with disabilities," they nevertheless have proliferated across a wide range of media, from television and film to advertising and popular art (295). See Kim Wolfson and Martin F. Norden, "Film Images of People with Disabilities," in *Handbook of Communication and People with Disabilities: Research and Application*, eds. Dawn O. Braithwaite and Theresa L. Thompson (Mahwah, NJ: Lawrence Erlbaum Associates, 2000), 289–305.

69. Haller and Ralph, "Profitability, Diversity, and Disability Images."

70. On his personal website, Minsky attempts to downplay his physical appearance (it seems real men are not supposed to care about such things) but to little effect. His biography, clearly authored by a publicist, declares, "He was a good-looking guy with a perfect body covered in badass tattoos. But it was his blasé attitude towards his prosthesis that captured people's imagination. Minsky became a role model for those living with disabilities, redefining long-held standards of beauty and perfection." See http://www.alexminsky.com/about-me/.

71. Spencer Ackerman, "The Cost of War Includes At Least 254,330 Brain Injuries and 1,700 Amputations," *Wired*, February 13, 2013, http://www.wired.com/2013/02/cost-of-war/.

6

Half a Man

THE SYMBOLISM AND SCIENCE OF PARAPLEGIC IMPOTENCE IN WORLD WAR II AMERICA

Beth Linker and Whitney E. Laemmli

At the conclusion of the Second World War, more than 600,000 men returned to the United States with long-term disabilities, profoundly destabilizing the definitions, representations, and experiences of male sexuality in America. By examining an oft-neglected 1950 film, *The Men*, along with medical, personal, and popular accounts of impotence in paralyzed World War II veterans, this chapter excavates the contours of that change and its attendant anxieties. While previous scholarship on film and sexuality in the postwar period has focused on women's experiences, we broaden the analytical lens to provide a fuller picture of the various meanings of male sexuality, especially disabled sexuality. In postwar America, the paralyzed veteran created a temporary fissure in conventional discussions of the gendered body, a moment when the "normality" and performative features of the male body could not be assumed but rather had to be actively defined. To many veterans, and to the medical men who treated them, sexual reproduction—not function— became the ultimate signifier of remasculinization.

"One reason people aren't going to the movies anymore," famed actress Gloria Swanson complained in 1951, is that "Hollywood deals too much with the problems of paraplegics and the blind people."[1] The decade after World War II witnessed a flurry of reintegration dramas, films that featured permanently wounded soldiers overcoming their disabilities to fit back into a well-ordered society. The genre was by no means new: films depicting blinded and deaf World War I soldiers were also popular in the 1920s and 1930s. As film scholar Martin Norden points out, however, post–World War II films differed from their predecessors in one important way: a tendency to eschew the "repaternalizing miracle cure" trope.[2] Post–World War II audiences no longer naively bought into the rosy picture of frictionless reintegration, and Hollywood responded with increased realism. World War II reintegration dramas, therefore, embodied lofty hopes that veterans might be seamlessly reincorporated into civil society, while also conceding that these men's feelings of anger, alienation, and frustration could easily undermine ideals of postwar harmony.[3]

In many of these World War II–era dramas, women appeared to shoulder the burden—practical, emotional, sexual—of reintegration. In the enormously popular *The Best Years of Our Lives,* double amputee Homer Parrish is rescued from self-pity and depression by the unconditional love of Wilma, his fiancée.[4] In a climactic scene, Homer allows Wilma into his bedroom and accepts her help in removing his prosthetic hooks. Wilma shows no horror at the sight of his stumps but rather kisses him passionately and gently tucks him into bed. Many scholars see this scene as the crucial element in Homer's reintegration, the instant when viewers become certain that Homer will indeed triumph over adversity. "If women played their prescribed role in the demobilization drama," historian David Gerber writes, it was assumed that "all would work out well for the nation, their loved ones, and themselves."[5] The assumption that women could and should play a central role in bringing about postwar order extended into advice literature of the day as well. Women's magazines and marriage manuals encouraged would-be wives to engage in "serious study of the veteran and his psychology"[6] in order to establish stable heterosexual unions with men coming home from the war.

Gender historians have found such postwar demands on—and portrayals of— women to be highly problematic.[7] Susan Hartmann criticizes post–World War II advice literature for its tendency to push newly independent women back into stereotypically gendered structures:

> While women were assigned the crucial responsibility for solving this major postwar problem, they were to do so in terms of traditional female roles. Through self-abnegation, by putting the needs of the veteran first, women might successfully renew their war-broken relationships, but they would do so at the price of their own autonomy.[8]

Historian Sonya Michel finds the denial of women's sexual agency most troubling. "Though the soldiers' sexual longing was a persistent theme in wartime popular culture," Michel claims, "women were instructed to temper expressions of their own sexual needs and behave submissively." Michel notes that, in *The Best Years of Our Lives,* Wilma's sexual desire was expressed only "through her demure, quasi-maternal affection toward Homer."[9] Like other young wives and sweethearts of the era, Wilma's role as a restorer of lost masculinity required that she tailor her own gratification to Homer's physical and psychological needs and limitations.

Such critiques of postwar film and advice literature are valid, but these analyses almost uniformly sidestep the question of how we are to understand male sexuality, and in particular disabled-male sexuality. At the conclusion of the Second World War, more than 600,000 men returned to the United States with long-term disabilities, contributing to a profound destabilization of the definitions, representations, and experiences of male sexuality in America. For many, the unprecedented number of paraplegic veterans was particularly disorienting. Prior to World War II, few soldiers with spinal cord injuries survived longer than a handful of days or weeks, frequently felled by infections of the urinary tract, respiratory system, and pressure sores; mortality rates during World War I hovered around 80 percent. By the end of World War II, however, blood transfusions, the mass production of penicillin and sulfa drugs, new techniques of catheterization, and innovations in hospital procedure had decreased mortality rates to around 10 percent.[10] But while, to some, such improvements in care made paraplegic veterans "living memorials to the skill of medical officers during World War II," the survival of this new patient group also raised potentially troubling questions.[11] What did it really mean to be paralyzed below the waist? Would these men be able to experience sexual pleasure, satisfy their partners, reproduce?

These questions seemed particularly pressing because, while sex experts of the early twentieth century measured "successful" heteronormative intercourse by the achievement of female orgasm, during the Second World War, attention shifted toward male performance, with men increasingly regarded as the "more fragile and sexually vulnerable" sex. As a man's sexuality became increasingly "entangled with his sense of self-worth," any inability to perform— reproductively or romantically—became a serious threat to his masculinity.[12] For disabled veterans, such anxieties were often particularly severe, threatening not only their manhood but also their marriages and thus the larger project of national rehabilitation.[13]

The specific link between erectile function and masculinity was not, of course, entirely unique to the postwar period. In a recent issue of *Osiris*, Leah DeVun shows us that as early as the Middle Ages, physicians used "impotency tests" (in which a prostitute was used to test a man's capacity for arousal) to assess masculinity. When a patient failed this test, DeVun writes, he was deemed "less than a 'real man'" and dismissed as "lacking in hardness, substance, and maleness." Nathan Ha demonstrates that twentieth-century scientists made similar associations, using the rings and pressure cuffs of phallometry to gauge both masculinity and sexual orientation.[14]

For veterans with spinal cord injuries, however, fears about "impotence" extended far beyond simple measures of penile function. To more deeply explore the contested nature of masculinity, heteronormative sexuality, and disability during the World War II years, this chapter focuses on an oft-neglected reintegration film of the postwar era: Fred Zinnemann's *The Men* (1950).[15] Starring Marlon Brando as Ken "Bud" Wilcheck, a World War II soldier who returns home with a sniper bullet wound to the thoracic spine, the film is one of the first to feature a paraplegic veteran bound to a wheelchair. By featuring paraplegic men on the silver screen, Zinnemann tapped into postwar fears of impotence as no other reintegration film had before.[16] In theater posters and advertisements, the film was billed as "a completely new experience between men and women!" (Figure 6.1).

Significantly, the film crew conducted weeks of research at the Birmingham Veterans Administration (VA) Hospital in Los Angeles, California, where they observed (and in some cases lived with) dozens of paraplegic veterans and their treating physician, Dr. Ernst Bors.[17] At Birmingham, the film crew also encountered the Paraplegic Veterans of America (PVA), a group of spinal cord injured veterans who formed their own association to advocate for better medical care,

FIGURE 6.1 Original theatrical poster advertising *The Men* (1950).

pensions, and adaptive equipment that would meet their needs and rights as disabled citizens. Zinnemann became especially close to paraplegic Ted Anderson, the president of the PVA, on whom "Bud" Wilcheck was based.[18]

Toggling between filmic representation and published literature produced by the PVA and by medical researchers, this chapter shows that impotence was not only a symbolic concern but an immediate physical and emotional issue for patients and for the medical scientists who treated them. Because the film closely tracked a historical situation that we have been able to reconstruct from published records, *The Men* offers a unique opportunity to look at both the symbolism and the science of impotence during the immediate post–World War II years in America.

By looking at paraplegic impotence, we hope to deepen existing discussions of gender representation and male sexuality in midcentury America. Our focus on disabled-male sexuality is a particularly productive way of excavating this history, in part because the disabled body—for better or for worse—has frequently served as a site of gender fluidity and complication.[19] In postwar America, the paralyzed veteran created a temporary fissure in conventional discussions of the gendered body, a moment when the standard measures of sexual performance and the male body could not be assumed but rather had to be actively defined.[20] While this chapter demonstrates that there was a chorus of opinions and conflicting views on what constituted paraplegic masculinity and sexuality, many paraplegic veterans—and especially their treating physicians—wished to downplay the centuries-long emphasis on sexual performance and instead define masculinity in terms of the ability to sire children.

Symbolism of Impotence in *The Men*

In many ways, *The Men* was a standard American post–World War II rehabilitation film. Bud goes off to war and, in the course of an act of military heroism, is felled by a German sniper's bullet. Paralyzed below the waist, Bud is consigned to a VA hospital, where he struggles to regain his former self through a slow and painful course of physical and psychological rehabilitation. As Beth Linker has argued elsewhere, inherent to the ethic of rehabilitation is the demand for remasculinization, a process whereby a man is viewed as a hero for having struggled to recover from a debilitating wound to become "whole" again.[21] This process was by no means unique to the United States. Frances Bernstein, for example, shows the extremes to which the Soviet Union went in order to erase the potentially emasculating "problem" of World War II disabled veterans.[22] Similar to earlier US rehabilitation efforts, the USSR focused its efforts on remaking—or, as Bernstein puts it, "unmaking"—amputee veterans, a group that became a model for how a war-torn nation could overcome the physical and economic realities wrought by years of battle. Just as amputees could "fix" themselves through the simple flip of a prosthetic strap, so too could a nation paper over the past with a new political image of normalization and vitality.[23]

The director and producers of *The Men* took a risk by filming paraplegic veterans who, by virtue of their wheelchair dependency, could not be made to appear as "normal" again. But Zinnemann knew that the severity of the disability would add to the film's dramatic effect and, if anything, allow him to embellish the struggles inherent in reintegration stories. The concern of *The Men*—as with most films of the genre from this time period—was how to reconcile Bud's wartime valor with his postinjury paralysis and symbolic emasculation. Tellingly, like so many films and novels before it, *The Men*, too, speaks of rehabilitation using gender-infused battle metaphors. The film opens with a deep-voiced narrator intoning a heroic dedication over the sound of martial drumming:

> In all wars, since the beginning of history, there have been men who fought twice. The first time they battled with club, sword, or machine gun. The second time they had none of these weapons. Yet, this by far, was the greatest battle. It was fought with abiding faith and raw courage and in the end, victory was achieved. This is the story of such a group of men.

It was this "second" and "greatest" battle that structures the majority of the plot. Though the viewer gets a brief glimpse of Bud sustaining his battle wound, the bulk of the film follows a group of paraplegic men recuperating under the watchful and disciplinary eye of Dr. "Bowels and Bladder" Brock (Everett Sloan), a man who barks medical orders like an impatient first sergeant. He is assisted, quite predictably, by an equally disciplined and trustworthy nurse, Nurse Robbins (Virginia Farmer), who ministers care with great concern but without overindulgence, a reflection of midcentury mothering ideals.[24]

But for all of Nurse Robbins's motherly coaxing and Dr. Brock's staunch patriarchal demands, Bud remains depressed, withdrawn, and uncooperative. Only when his fiancée, Ellen (Theresa Wright), enters the picture does Bud begin his campaign of self-improvement and remasculinization. Taking his lead from fellow paraplegic Angel Lopez (an actual paraplegic played by a nonactor, Arthur Jurado), Bud engages in upper body training, first with a hospital trapeze bar, then with modified pushups. Once he gains enough strength, Bud graduates to a wheelchair and participates in sports such as water polo, bowling, and wheelchair racing. Eventually, Bud learns how to drive a car, further fostering the masculinization process. As historian Christina Jarvis writes,

> The frequent portrayals of [Bud] driving help to rephallicize his body. Just as wartime advertisements and recruitment posters fused soldiers' bodies with weapons in an attempt to portray their strength and "steel-like qualities," the speed and technology of the specially designed car help counter some of the weakness associated with [Bud's] disability, rendering him both whole and mobile.[25]

It is important to note that, like other films of the era, *The Men* relied upon its female characters as crucial elements in the rehabilitative process. Though it is Bud who sweats through workouts and checkups, without Ellen—and the symbolic prospect of heteronormative family life she represented—he would have had little motivation to engage in the arduous process of recovery. As already suggested, this tendency has made *The Men* a target for scholars who see it as a participant in the postwar subjugation of women. Norden, for example, tells us that the "Hollywood mentality of the time . . . encouraged women on the domestic front to give up their interests and accommodate the returning veterans"[26] and further notes that "female figures . . . do not represent women, but the needs of the patriarchal psyche."[27]

But while *The Men* replicated many of these postwar tropes, it also differed from other films of the genre in significant ways. For though Bud does recover much of his physical prowess and some of his confidence by the end of the story, a truly full and glorious recuperation never arrives. The catharsis of a happy ending is withheld. To be sure, much of the film revolves around Bud's relationship with Ellen, particularly her efforts to convince him to resume their engagement despite his paraplegia. There is, however, a sense of unease—and indeed failure—at all the crucial moments when Bud and Ellen attempt to formalize their relationship, first through marriage, and then as a wedded couple. Their wedding ceremony, which takes place not in a church but in the hospital chapel, is laced with feelings of doom and dread. Ellen marries Bud against her parents' wishes and, thus, in their absence. Just before the wedding vows, Bud, seated in his wheelchair, struggles to stand upright (with the assistance of leg braces and canes) but quickly falters and has to be held up by Brock. Unlike *The Best Years of Our Lives*, there is no bedroom scene where wedding night vows would be physically consummated. Instead, Bud and Ellen's honeymoon night ends in a fight. Rather than Bud carrying Ellen over the threshold, as a nondisabled man would do, Ellen swings open the door and enters the living room with a diminutive Bud trailing behind, his wheelchair's disruptive squeaking announcing his disability. A bottle of celebratory champagne explodes prematurely, Bud's leg begins to tremble, and he erupts with rage. As Ellen bends over to clean up the spill, Bud is shot from below, looking almost inhuman. The whole scene can be easily read as a metaphor for Bud's frustration over his symbolic—and perhaps anticipated—failure to perform sexually and Ellen's fear that she has made a mistake. This catastrophic attempt to enact domestic heteronormativity behind him, Bud returns "home" to the VA hospital, seeking safety and comfort in the fraternity of his fellow paraplegic veterans.

Not until Dr. Brock reveals his own personal commitment to paraplegic reintegration (Brock's wife was paralyzed in a car accident and "medical science couldn't save her") does Bud give his own marriage another try. In the closing scene of the film, Bud appears at his in-laws' house unannounced. Busy with gardening outside, Ellen sees Bud and says, "You've come a long way," clearly referencing both a physical and emotional distance. As Bud wheels himself to the front porch, a set of concrete steps impedes additional movement. "Do you want me to help you up the steps?" Ellen asks. "Please," Bud replies, uttering the final words of the film. Bud and Ellen do reunite, but the peace that both of them make is an ambiguous and uneasy one, owing much to popular understandings and taboos concerning paraplegia and sexuality in this period.

In fact, the portrayal of paraplegic veterans' sexuality throughout the movie does much to underscore its rather atypical ending. Although the production codes of the era meant that the frank depiction or discussion of sexual subjects was forbidden, sexuality—and in particular male sexuality—appears to be *The Men*'s central anxiety.[28] Take, for example, the first scene that brings the concern of resexualization— and in turn Bud's remasculinization—to the fore. When Ellen first lays eyes on Bud in the hospital, he is prostrate in a bed, with disheveled hair and crumpled sheets. Upon seeing Ellen, Bud reacts with anger and fear, proclaiming, "I'm not a man. I can't make a woman happy." Taken out of context, Bud's assertion of unmanliness could mean many things. Adjusting to his new reality as a paraplegic, Bud might feel incapable of fulfilling his manly duties in an economic sense; though the film takes care to establish that the men were enormously well-provided for by the government, he might doubt that he could hold down a traditional job. He might also doubt his masculinity because of an identification with his dependent, infantile state. He is immobile and, like most paraplegics immediately after injury, has no control over his bladder and bowels. Bud might be defining his manhood in contradistinction to childhood.

But the setting in which Bud utters these lines is key to understanding the symbolic meaning of manliness in *The Men*. As the conversation continues, Bud—still lying in bed—dramatically unveils the lower half of his body, whipping back the hospital bed covers and shouting: "All right, I'll give you what you want. Want to see what it's like? All right, look. I said look at me. Now get a good look. . . . Is that what you want?" The reference is not explicitly sexual, but context makes it clear that Bud's concern is not solely his atrophied legs but also his potentially incapacitated genitalia. Significantly, the camera never reveals exactly what Ellen sees, allowing viewers' phobic imaginations to fill in the gaps.

Ellen's response, though similarly veiled, also suggests an undercurrent of sexual tension. After Bud reminds her that he will never walk again, Ellen—who has until this point been standing upright next to Bud's bed—lowers herself next to Bud and, leaning forward until they are nearly nose to nose, pleads: "But you could do lots of things. Oh please, please, try. Don't you see? I need you. There will never be anyone else. Oh darling, don't you want us to be happy?" She collapses into his arms, sobbing, while Bud's eyes fill with tears. "Sure I want us to be happy, honey, but I don't know. I don't know." The conversation itself is ambiguous, but Ellen's body language implies that this discussion was a particularly intimate one. In this scene, Ellen establishes herself as a figure both maternal and sexual. This dual role, we are told by film scholars and historians, was seen at the time as necessary for

Bud's recuperation. Perhaps even more interesting than the film's negotiation of Ellen's sexuality, however, is the way in which *The Men* deals with Bud's sexuality—and, in turn, the sexuality of disabled men more generally.

To date, the sexuality of disabled veterans has been understudied, as most scholars have assumed that it is identical to that of nondisabled males (itself often erroneously understood as historically stable in its meaning and manifestation).[29] Moreover, male sexuality is frequently assumed to be dichotomous: a man is either potent or impotent, with few intermediary gradations. This rather crude understanding seems to have been fueled by a scholarly fascination with "symbolic castration," a theoretical framework that is applied ubiquitously to novels and films, especially when a disabled male figure is involved. However, much nuance and insight can be gained if we move beyond symbolism and train our eyes on those men who have the power to castrate or cure other men, even if "symbolically," as well as on the men who are being rendered impotent.

The Science and Subjective Experience of Paraplegic Impotence

It is difficult in retrospect to fully appreciate the depths of uncertainty that accompanied a diagnosis of spinal cord injury in the immediate post–World War II years. Most contemporary understandings of paralysis came from polio patients, the most prominent of whom was the recently deceased Franklin D. Roosevelt, but spinal cord injury was distinctly different in that it affected both sensory and motor functioning. The working (albeit vague) definition of paraplegia was complete motor and sensory paralysis of the entire lower half of the body.[30] World War II paraplegic Kenneth Wheeler described the subjective feeling of paralysis as one in which he was "chained to a body that was only half, or less than half a man."[31] Other paraplegic memoirists spoke in terms of being "half dead."[32] Immediately after Bud sustains his injury from a German sniper in the opening scene of *The Men*, he tells his fellow comrades that he is only "half alive."

While paraplegic veterans mourned the possibility of never walking again, the expressions of being only "half alive"—with everything below the waist dead to feeling and purpose—speak also to lost sexual capacity. In this sense, World War II paraplegics joined the ranks of military men who dreaded genital injury above all else. About traumatic wounds to the groin, Wheeler wrote: "Nothing much worse can happen to a man this side of death."[33] The men who fought during the Second World War heard tales of soldiers privileging the safety of the penis over the rest of the body, protecting their genitalia by crossing their legs under shell fire and using helmets to shield sexual organs instead of eyes and heads.[34] This concern for genital integrity can still be seen today. Recounting her work as a nurse in an Army intensive care unit that treats US soldiers injured in Afghanistan, Kathryn Gillespie explains that when a wounded soldier initially regains consciousness, he first asks: " 'Is my junk all together?' " "They want to check their 'package', first," she says, "then they check their arms and legs. This all happens probably within 15 minutes of being off sedation."[35]

While not precisely the same kind of injury as genital amputation, paraplegics—and their families and doctors—had similar concerns about sexual potency, in terms of both physical functioning and fertility. The concern for potency is addressed most directly in *The Men* during a scene in which Dr. Brock conducts a question-and-answer session in the hospital chapel with the wives, mothers, and fiancées of paraplegic men in his care. For the film's purposes, this scene was meant to educate the audience on the basic medical facts of spinal cord injury. After several rounds of questions regarding mobility— "the word *walk* must be forgotten," barks Brock—one woman from a back pew slowly stands and says, "But doctor, my husband and I want a large family." With knowing concern in his eye, Brock answers in a low voice, "In some cases it is possible, but we can't discuss it here."

In real life, Dr. Ernst Bors (the actual physician-urologist upon whom *The Men*'s Dr. Brock was based) researched paraplegic sexuality quite extensively, as did other physicians who specialized in the treatment of spinal cord injuries. Bors joined the Army Medical Corps in 1943 and was originally stationed at Hammond Army Hospital in Modesto, California, as assistant chief of urology on the transverse-myelitis ward. Bors earned his medical degree at the University of Prague in 1924 (he was Czechoslovakian by birth) and spent his early career as a surgical assistant at the University of Zurich. He had little experience with paralysis before taking up his post at the Birmingham VA in Van Nuys, just outside of Los Angeles. "In the 20 years that I had practiced prior to coming to [California]," Bors wrote, "I had seen possibly a total of eight paraplegics—no more."[36]

At the time Zinnemann began filming *The Men*, Bors had just completed a study on fertility in thirty-four paraplegic men at Birmingham.[37] He was not the first physician in charge of a spinal cord unit to do so. Donald Munro, a neurosurgeon at Cushing VA Hospital in Boston, had conducted multiple studies on sexuality and paraplegia in the immediate postwar years. Munro made plain that for spinal cord injured patients, the loss of sexual ability was "one of the most difficult psychological [problems]" they had to encounter.[38] Similar to Bors, Munro sought to conduct research on paraplegic sexuality because he had no answers for the questions that his patients posed. "Doctors," Munro lamented, "either admit their ignorance or make up explanations and prognoses out of whole cloth."[39]

The prevailing popular assumption concerning paraplegic and sexual capacity at the time was that a severed spinal cord would render a man entirely impotent, flaccid, and unable to sire children.[40] Scientists steeped in animal experimentation and physiology, on the other hand, believed that paraplegics would experience priapism, a reflexive, "persistent abnormal erection of the penis, usually without sexual desire."[41] Indeed, earlier generations of doctors sometimes used symptoms of priapism to diagnose high cord lesions.

Neither of these stereotypes reflected clinical or, for that matter, personal experience on the part of World War II paraplegic veterans. Recounting his recuperation experience in a Memphis VA hospital, paraplegic Terry McAdam wrote in 1955, "The sexual abilities of each patient were eagerly discussed, for strangely enough, some of these boys could still function sexually. . . . In some cases there was an absolute end to any form of sex," McAdam continued, "in some there was a continuing ability to perform the mechanical act itself, but without any physical pleasure on the part of the man. . . . In still others," he described, "the feeling was mysteriously present in advantageous localities even though the level of the injury was far above."[42]

The clinical picture, then, was far from clear. However, systemic ignorance of the actual situation was not helped by the pervasive stigma attached to disability and sex.[43]

Alfred Kinsey, often lauded for his progressive views on sexuality, all but ignored the disabled, even though he gathered data for *Sexual Behavior in the Human Male* during the war years. The one mention he makes on the subject of disability in his 800-page book demonstrates that while Kinsey was eager to normalize other forms of ablebodied "deviant sex" (i.e., masturbation, homosexuality, and bestiality), he found the sexual needs of the physically disabled aberrant, beyond the possibility of normalization. He wrote:

> Persons who are deformed physically, deaf, blind, severely crippled, spastic, or otherwise handicapped, often have considerable difficulty in finding heterosexual coitus. The matter may weigh heavily upon their minds and cause considerable psychic disturbance. There are instances where prostitutes have contributed to establishing these individuals in their own self esteem by providing their first sexual contacts. finally, at lower social levels there are persons who are . . . so repulsive and offensive physically that no girl except a prostitute would have intercourse with them. Without such outlets, these individuals would become even more serious social problems than they already are.[44]

In his quest to find the normal or average American sex life, Kinsey continued to categorize disabled sex as abnormal, stripping away sexual agency from a large swath of the population, while labeling the very existence of disabled persons a "social problem."[45]

Because so few sex researchers devoted their studies to disability in midcentury America, paraplegic sexuality continued to raise more questions than could be answered. To begin, it rekindled an old debate about where male sexuality was located in the body and what anatomical and/or physiological processes were essential to potency. Was male potency located in the endocrine system, where androgens were produced? Was it to be found in the testes, where spermatozoa were stored? Or was potency situated in the psyche, where desire, lust, as well as "perversions" resided? The new population of men with spinal cord injuries inspired yet another direction of inquiry: What role did the neuromuscular system play in potency?[46]

Early findings concerning paraplegics and their potency were actually quite encouraging. As early as 1948, Munro reported that 74 percent of the paraplegic veterans at Cushing VA Hospital retained the ability to have erections after injury. In 1950, Bors estimated that 88 percent of his patients at Birmingham had a return of erections within a few months after injury. In the same study, paraplegic veterans reported having sexual dreams, some of them "wet dreams with both orgasm and actual seminal emission."[47] Boston urologist Herbert S. Talbot came to conclusions similar to those of his colleagues. Out of the 408 paraplegics under his care, 66 percent had "erections in response to local stimulation." "About one-third of those having erections," Talbot concluded, "were able to have intercourse."[48]

The experience of injured veterans writing for the magazine *Paraplegia News* confirmed these medical findings. Indeed, for members of the PVA who had editorial control over *Paraplegia News*, maintenance of sexual capabilities after spinal cord injury was almost a given. Take, for example, a letter that the editor in chief, Robert Moss, wrote in 1951 to the newly paralyzed coming home from the Korean War: "Most of you will be physically capable of sexually satisfying your mate."[49] The editors of *Paraplegia News* also commissioned wives of paraplegics to offer testimony to a paraplegic's ability to maintain a healthy, postinjury sex life. The wife of one former Birmingham hospital paraplegic wrote: "My husband and I have a fairly normal sex life together, and I am satisfied with it."[50] In an attempt to further normalize paraplegic sex, veterans such as Moss insisted that all married couples, "paraplegic or not, have a 'sexual problem.'"[51] Paraplegia was just a different kind of "problem." This pluralistic view of a married sex life led another wife writing for *Paraplegia News* to conclude that the sexual "response of a man and a woman to each other takes many varied and beautiful forms."[52]

The ability to have a postinjury erection, however, seemed cause for little celebration among medical scientists. Even though Munro expressed irritation at the fact that most researchers conflated erectile function and fertility (and insisted that potency should not be defined exclusively by the latter at the expense of the former), he still considered reproduction to be the sine qua non of paraplegic sexuality. The privileging of reproduction over sexual capacity is most apparent in how Munro presented his research findings. Detailed medical case studies of paraplegics who fathered children far outnumber write-ups of men who had regained sexual function but remained sterile.[53] Here is one characteristic example of how Munro recorded the sexual recovery of his patients with paraplegia:

Patient is a 27 year old injured October 1944 by a bomb fragment which struck him in the region of the sixth to seventh thoracic vertebras. Three months after the injury his urethral catheter, which he had worn until then, was removed. ... About one month after injury he began to have spontaneous erections lasting from 1–20 minutes. They had no relation to cerebral activity. The patient then discovered that erections could be caused by local stimulation of the penis. About 10 months after his injury, he attempted masturbation for the first time. After this stimulation he obtained a brownish-red ejaculate. A week later he repeated the procedure with essentially the same result. Since then ejaculations have been described as being normal in appearance, substance, and quality. During ejaculation, the patient's spasms increase momentarily, but no other sensation occurs. He was married to a nurse, aged 25 years old in May 1946. Intercourse was timed to correspond with his wife's periods. His wife delivered a normal, full-term child on March 1, 1947.[54]

Although proof of phallic recovery is outlined on a step-by-step basis in this case study, it is clear that siring a child is the point of the clinical lesson.[55] Munro would not have published the details of this case study if the patient had recovered "merely" to the point of having an erection or being able to masturbate.

One reason for the focused attention on the reproductive paraplegic was that fathering a child after such an injury appeared to be a medical oddity. As late as 1952, Talbot concluded that only 7 percent of paraplegic men were capable of siring children.[56] Moreover, medical researchers found no reliable physiological predictors that would indicate whether or not a paraplegic would be fertile. In his attempt to study paraplegic fertility through sperm motility and testicular biopsies, Bors concluded, with disappointment, that there was no evidence of a relationship between biopsy findings and sex function.[57] Nor did ejaculations or seminal emissions seem to be reliable predictors of paraplegic fertility.

Another reason nondisabled male physicians heralded reproduction was that siring a child provided incontrovertible proof that medicine could cure paraplegic men of their emasculating injury. Sexual functioning was largely a private matter, with success being agreed upon between a particular husband and wife. Siring a child, on the other hand, offered physical proof for the public of a paraplegic's remasculinization and of medicine's role in assisting his sexual recovery.[58]

While physicians like Bors (and films like *The Men*) insisted that questions of paraplegic fertility were fueled by the "natural" desire of wives to have children, in actuality, the push toward reproduction came from both the medical men and the paraplegic men whom they treated.[59] Evidence from personal letters of women married to paraplegic men as well as studies of college-aged women's views on disability and marriage indicate that most women were more concerned about a man's sexual capabilities than his fertility. In an advice column written for paraplegic veterans considering marriage, one wife insisted that as long as the veteran felt like he could satisfy his wife sexually—even if he could not father children— "she would be content." "While some girls feel that their lives would not be complete without bearing a child," she wrote, "others are just as happy without ever being mothers." "For myself," she admitted, "I would love to have a baby, but . . . if the Lord does not see fit to let us have one, I will love my husband just as much."[60]

Penn State College psychologist Clifford Adams confirmed such testimonials. During the war, Adams developed a questionnaire that asked unmarried female college students whether or not they would marry a disabled veteran. The questionnaire included thirty-three different types of war disabilities to serve as possible scenarios.[61] Adams found that, on the whole, "older girls showed a greater willingness to marry injured men than the younger girls ... due to the fact," he surmised, "that the older girls are more concerned about their chances of marrying."[62]

Adams's research demonstrated, most tellingly, that college-aged women had clear opinions about which types of disabilities they believed they could adjust to in marriage and which they could not. Of the 500 college-aged women surveyed, a majority found the following disabilities (in rank order) serious enough to end their engagements: (a) impotence, (b) loss of both arms in such a way that they could not be replaced with artificial arms, (c) mental imbalance requiring institutional confinement for several months or longer, and (d) loss of both legs so that they are not replaceable. Knowing that impotence could be construed as both sterility and loss of sexual function, Adams drafted a follow-up questionnaire that was more sensitive to definitional variance. When asked to distinguish between fertility and sexual capacity, over 80 percent of the women questioned said that they "would marry, if they could have a normal sexual life, even though there was no possibility of conceiving children."[63] Only 16 percent of the respondents said that they would refuse to marry an ex-soldier who had become sterile. In other words, college-aged women found loss of sexual functioning more disabling than sterility.

In *The Men*, it is Ellen's father who insists on defining potency as reproduction, a mandate that Ellen rejects by the end of the film. Concern about Bud's reproductive capabilities comes to the fore in a scene in which Ellen visits her parents to tell them of her intent to marry Bud. The three dance gently around the topic for some time, until Ellen's father broaches the subject head on. "Love can be very fragile," he tells Ellen, "Even healthy people can't hold on to it. How long do you think that love is going to last after you've become his nurse? You're a young healthy girl." But the conversation truly breaks down when the subject of procreation emerges. Ellen's father entreats, "Is it so wrong for us to want a grandchild?" As soon as Ellen's father brings up the "problem" of reproduction, she storms out of the house and visits Dr. Brock to seek his counsel. Brock provides few answers to Ellen's queries and fails to disabuse her of the notion that procreation was the primary—if elusive—goal of paraplegic male sexuality. In the end, Ellen decides that procreation "really doesn't matter," and the wedding proceeds as planned. While scholars such as Michel have read this scene as Ellen relinquishing her sexual needs for the purpose of Bud's reintegration, it could just as easily be understood as Ellen choosing to define sexual function in contradistinction to her father and Dr. Brock, just as real-life wives of paraplegic veterans did at the time.

Men living with paraplegia remained divided on how potency should be defined and whether sexual capacity alone legitimated their manhood. Certain members of the PVA insisted that in order for a paraplegic man to readjust and make his way back into society, he had to absorb the fact that "paraplegics are different from the rest of the world in two respects: they are paralyzed and probably sterile."[64] Even if a paraplegic man could not produce children, the argument went, he could still assume a patriarchal role in society by being productive in other realms of life, such as finding a steady job, owning a home, and engaging in adaptive sports like water polo and wheelchair basketball.

Other paraplegics, however, were not as willing to give up sexual agency, seeing it as more essential to defining their masculinity than middle-class notions of productivity in the home and workplace. McAdam's memoir recounts a telling debate between two unmarried patients, Carl Fuller and Jerry Radcliff. When Jerry boasts that he has a date with a very special "gal" whom he plans to wed, Carl responds: "Damn it, I tell you a paraplegic's got no business getting married."[65] Jerry responds by making a plea for his desire and need for sexual intimacy: "Look, Carl, we know you can't feel nothing, but some of us guys can. Why the hell should we sleep alone from now on?"[66] Exasperated, Carl replies, "Look, for the last time. It hasn't got nothing to do with tail. A damn paraplegic can't support a wife. You guys [will] make some poor woman unhappy and frustrated for a normal life."[67]

Whereas lust, sexual desire, and being able to satisfy a wife were assumed to be essential components of ablebodied, heterosexual manhood in midcentury America, the same rules did not readily apply to disabled men.[68] Take, for instance, the story of Fred B. Woolsey, cartoonist for the *Paraplegia News* from 1946 to 1950. A paraplegic himself, Woolsey edified many readers with his depictions of "delicious looking Florence Nightingales" massaging veterans and pushing them in their wheelchairs (Figures 6.2 and 6.3).[69]

To be sure, such images contributed to the objectification of women—nurses, in particular—in a pinup style common in postwar America.[70] Yet Woolsey's cartoons also served the function of normalizing the paraplegic male in his sexual desire, insisting that they were no different than nondisabled men. His cartoons represented the potent, heterosexually functioning male, not the reproductive male.[71] In his "Head Nurse" cartoon, Woolsey depicted a flustered yet sultry (and scantily clad) ward nurse who had just encountered a paraplegic who had become erect while she was caring for him.

The ward nurse, bringing a complaint to the chief nurse, says in the caption, "And then he said 'I must have had a spasm.'" It was common for paraplegic men to experience reflexive muscle spasms in the legs and abdomen during intercourse and masturbation—this was a neurophysiologic response of which both paraplegics and their doctors were aware.[72] The joke, of course, was that a paraplegic could use his disability as an excuse for having an "inappropriate" sexual response to a professional nurse—something unthinkable for a nondisabled veteran according to social mores. In this sense, a paraplegic man could have a sexual advantage over nondisabled men. The "Head Nurse" cartoon also engaged in fantasies of

What do you mean . . . "you'd rather just watch" . . .?

(Fred Woolsey of Madison, Wisconsin, retains all reproduction rights of the above cartoon.

FIGURE 6.2 "Rather Just Watch," *Paraplegia News* 4 (May 1950), 6.

paraplegic sexual prowess, showing how, contrary to assumed paralysis and flaccidity, a paraplegic with priapism could outperform other men.[73]

But the sexual desire of disabled men created unease among the ablebodied public. Sexual desire, except when discussed in the most clinical of ways, was—and still is—anathema to disability. Even in a presumably safe place like *Paraplegia News*, Woolsey received mail condemning his "offensive" cartoons, and he eventually quit his post as the magazine's cartoonist because of such complaints. One reader wrote to the editorial board saying that although he and his wife "thoroughly enjoyed reading the *News* and ha[d] . . . endorsed the policies set forth therein," they found the "so- called humor of the cartoons offensive and in extremely bad taste."[74] Whereas such pinups would have been seen as "normal" among heterosexual ablebodied men, such lustful images in association with disabled men were taken to be deviant.

This double standard is particularly ironic given the advice of marriage and sex experts at the time. Historian Jessamyn Neuhaus explains that most sex experts of the interwar years geared their manuals toward the education of men, specifically teaching them how to become "good lovers," including the art of pleasuring their wives. Husbands were considered to be "bumbling, ignorant, insensitive clods,"

"Why won't you ever let one of the boys help you up the curb?"

(Fred Woolsey of Madison, Wisconsin, retains all reproduction rights of the above cartoon.)

FIGURE 6.3 "Help Up the Curb," *Paraplegia News* 4 (April 1950), 6.

writes Neuhaus, and thus needed instruction on how to properly stimulate women so that they, too, could reach climax.[75] Sex expert Oliver M. Butterfield believed that the biggest problem for a husband to overcome was his single-minded attention to his penis, and his rather simple animalistic urge for vaginal intercourse. In 1937, Butterfield wrote, the husband should have "more than his own desire to consider," warning against the tendency to be "carried away" by the penis's "automatic and reflex action."[76]

In some ways, the paraplegic man could ostensibly function better than his nondisabled counterparts. Take, for example, the case of "Dave," another ward mate featured in McAdam's memoir. "In Dave's case, he couldn't feel a thing," McAdam writes. "But for some strange reason he could go through the mechanics of the act itself so that it was pleasing to his wife." "At first," McAdam admits, "Dave was unhappy about it, but, because he really loved his wife, he gradually came to feel pleasure in the satisfaction he could give her."[77] At least one paraplegic

And then he said, "I must have had a spasm."
(*Fred Woolsey of Madison, Wisconsin, retains all reproduction rights of the above cartoon.*)

FIGURE 6.4 "I Must Have Had a Spasm," *Paraplegia News* 4 (February 1950), 7.

had, by virtue of his physical incapacity, become very much like the kind of man Butterfield wished for.

But the stigma of a paraplegic being "half-a-man" was prevalent among non-disabled medical professionals, sex experts, and even certain paraplegics themselves. To counsel an ablebodied, virile man who enjoyed full feeling and function to attend to a wife's needs was one thing; to give the same advice to a disabled man who had impaired feeling and function was quite another. In the latter case, the socially accepted binary of male and female blurred. The risk in such sexual relations was that the woman would become a dominant aggressor, while the man would be a passive supplicant whose main goal was to satisfy his partner. This fear of role reversal can be seen in the work of Columbia psychologist Stanley Berger, who in 1951 concluded that paraplegic men had "more difficulty in identifying with their own sex and often gave indications of stronger identification with the female."[78] About one paraplegic man in particular, Berger wrote: "Identifies more with the female figure, with marked confusion over his own social-sexual role in life. Has considerable tension in this area. . . . Confusion over sexual functions; strong oral tendencies. Regards psycho-sexual role in a very infantile way."[79]

In the eyes of medical experts, paraplegics veered toward the infantile and the feminine when it came to sexual capacity, and thus they remained incomplete men.[80] As a result, paraplegics were judged according to whether they could meet the conventional demands of reproduction in the realm of sexuality but not the newer, twentieth-century expectations of sexual satisfaction and mate gratification. Added to this was the Cold War belief that child rearing united American citizens. As Elaine Tyler May tells us, the nuclear family increasingly became the locus of both security and hope after World War II. In a country that felt besieged by outside forces beyond its control, parenthood—especially among permanently disabled veterans of that war—became the ultimate signifier of national identity, and the "problem" of infertility assumed a new status in medicine and in the public imagination.[81]

In many ways, the paraplegic man became the symbol of such Cold War fears of infertility. Even though medical research indicated that many paraplegics retained sexual function, and wives of these men reported sexual satisfaction, the stronger cultural perspective was to consider paraplegics completely impotent, refusing to see them as sexual agents in their own right. The power to define male paraplegic sexual agency rested, for the most part, with nondisabled men, from medical professionals who treated paraplegics to future fathers-in-law and Hollywood film crews. In all of these realms, male potency was synonymous with fertility, which left paralyzed men effectively exiled from ablebodied manhood, an exclusion that—while in some ways responsive to the real challenges certain paraplegic men faced— was determined more by cultural fears than physical realities.

Paralytic Impotence as Totalized Disability and Trope

Scholar Angus McLaren writes that, at base, the history of impotence is more about power relations among men than it is about a science of individual sexual performance.[82] This observation certainly holds true for *The Men* and the medical research and institutions upon which the film was based. The nondisabled men who directed the film (Zinnemann), wrote the screenplay (Carl Foreman), and produced it (Stanley Kramer) rendered Bud as a modern-day eunuch, when, in all likelihood, the real Bud (Ted Anderson) and other men like him were potent, at least partially so. Despite what may have been a sincere effort to honor the sacrifices of the war wounded,[83] the filmmakers in effect castrated the "lesser" men they portrayed. In doing so, *The Men* contributed to one of the most powerful—yet misinformed—tropes about paraplegic men: that they were completely sexually impotent, in terms of both function and fertility. This trope continued to appear for the remainder of the twentieth century in films such as Hal Ashby's *Coming Home* (1978) and Stone's *Born on the Fourth of July* (1989).[84]

Then and now, disabled individuals—whatever their particular physical, emotional, or intellectual characteristics—are regularly assumed to be somehow incapacitated in all areas of everyday life. Susan Wendell refers to this as a "totalizing" or "global" view of disability, whereby nondisabled onlookers assume that the disabled are more incapacitated than they really are.[85] Disability scholar Tobin Siebers points out that the totalizing view of disability often extends to ablebodied assumptions about both sexual desire and sexual function in the disabled. Disability, he states, "signifies sexual limitation, regardless of whether the physical and mental features of a given impairment affect the ability to have sex."[86] As such, the myth of "global" disability does a great deal of work in explaining the continued propensity of popular works to assume full incapacitation of sexual function, despite the fact that a significant number of paralyzed soldiers had partial or full use of their genitals. It also explains why outlets such as *Paraplegia News* were essential—both to paraplegic men and to the public—in reclaiming sexual agency among disabled veterans with a spinal cord injury.

Although the myth of global disability persists in the minds and phobic imaginations of nondisabled filmmakers and onlookers, the reality is much more complex, especially when the historian listens to the voices of those living with the actual impairment. Through outlets such as *Paraplegia News*, veterans expressed their sexual agency in myriad ways. Some boasted a sexual prowess that surpassed nondisabled men, others expressed a quiet satisfaction in their ability to pleasure their wives, and still others wished to sire a child in order to demonstrate their fertility to the rest of the world. With the ever-present threat of having their sexuality stripped away from them—as *The Men* did—paraplegic veterans continually reclaimed their sexual agency through advocacy and print. Rather than having a globally uniform view of masculinity and sexual performance, members of the PVA normalized disabled sex by insisting that all heterosexual relations varied, that the sexual response of a man and a woman "takes many varied and beautiful forms."[87]

In the past, the history of postwar sexuality has focused primarily on the experiences of women. As this piece demonstrates, however, an understanding of prevailing ideas about male sexuality—and, in particular, disabled-male sexuality—is equally crucial to comprehending sexuality, gender roles, familial relations, and popular culture during this period. Masculinity and femininity are never defined in isolation from one another but rather relationally, and both are complicated by questions of ability and disability. As Milam and Nye point out in the introduction to this volume, "social constructions of masculinity function simultaneously as foils for femininity and as methods of differentiating between kinds of men," a process clearly at work in the ubiquitous discussions surrounding paraplegic virility.[88] In an age anxious about shifting gender roles and fluid sexuality, Marlon Brando's Bud and his real-life compatriots were stuck at the intersection of seemingly irreconcilable social roles: the successfully reintegrated soldier, the virile husband, and the asexual paraplegic. These "half-men" may have helped win the war, but as *The Men's* title sequence suggested, the aftermath was, indeed, another battle entirely.

Acknowledgments

We wish to thank Erika Lorraine Milam, Robert A. Nye, the participants of the 2012 Masculinities in Science/Sciences of Masculinity workshop, Dominique Tobbell, and the anonymous *Osiris* reviewers for their helpful comments and suggestions on earlier drafts of this chapter. We would also like to thank Rebecca L. Davis and David Gerber for sharing their historical expertise in the areas of sexuality and disability, respectively.

Notes

1. "Gem of the Month," *Paraplegia News* 5 (August 1951), 7.

2. Martin Norden, "Bitterness, Rage, and Redemption," in *Disabled Veterans in History*, 2nd ed., ed. David Gerber (Ann Arbor: University of Michigan Press, 2003), 96–114, 105.

3. David Gerber, "Heroes and Misfits: The Troubled Social Reintegration of Disabled Veterans of World War II in *The Best Years of Our Lives*," in Gerber, *Disabled Veterans*, 70–95; Gerber, "Anger and Affability: The Rise and Representation of a Repertory of Self-Presentation Skills in a World War II Disabled Veteran," *Journal of Social History* 27 (1993), 5–27.

4. *The Best Years of Our Lives*, directed by William Wyler (1946; Los Angeles, 2000), DVD.

5. Gerber, "Heroes and Misfits," 552.

6. Willard Waller, "What You Can Do to Help the Returning Veteran," *Ladies' Home Journal*, February 1945, 94, as quoted in Rebecca Jo Plant, "The Veterans, His Wife and Their Mothers: Prescriptions for Psychological Rehabilitation after World War II," *American History* 85 (1999), 1468–78, 1475.

7. Jessamyn Neuhaus, "The Importance of Being Orgasmic: Sexuality, Gender, and Marital Sex Manuals in the United States, 1920–1963," *Journal of the History of Sexuality* 9 (2000), 447–473; Susan Hartmann, "Prescriptions for Penelope: Literature on Women's Obligations to Returning WWII Veterans," *Women's Stud.* 5 (1978), 223–239; Plant, "The Veterans."

8. Hartmann, "Prescriptions for Penelope," 236.

9. Sonya Michel, "Danger on the Home Front: Motherhood, Sexuality, and Disabled Veterans in American Postwar Dilms," *Journal of the History of Sexuality* 3 (1992), 109–28, 119.

10. Mary Tremblay, "The Canadian Revolution in the Management of Spinal Cord Injury," *Canadian Bulletin of Medical History* 12 (1995), 125–155; J. J. Mattelaer and I. Billiet,

"Catheters and Sounds: The History of Bladder Catheterization," *Paraplegia* 33 (1995), 429–433.

11. Robert Kennedy, "The New Viewpoint toward Spinal Cord Injuries," *Annals of Surgery* 124 (1946), 1057–1062, 1061.

12. Neuhaus, "Importance of Being Orgasmic," 450, 465. See also Rebecca L. Davis, *More Perfect Unions: The American Search for Marital Bliss* (Cambridge, MA: Harvard University Press, 2010).

13. As Angus McLaren notes, "Though every era has employed discourses to represent and control sexuality, certain ages clearly manifested a heightened anxiety about the issue of male sexual dysfunction," and the postwar period clearly falls within this category. McLaren, *Impotence: A Cultural History* (Chicago: University of Chicago Press, 2007), xiii.

14. See Leah DeVun, "Erecting Sex: Hermaphrodites and the Medieval Science of Surgery," *Osiris* 30 (2015), 17–37; Nathan Ha, "Detecting and Teaching Desire: Phallometry, Freund, and Behaviorist Sexology," *Osiris* 30 (2015), 205–227.

15. *The Men,* directed by Fred Zinnemann (1950; Los Angeles, 2009), DVD. While scholars like Gerber, Michel, and Norden have all made reference to *The Men* in their work on postwar cinema, a sustained analysis of the film—its production, its reception, and the historical realities it sought to reflect—is still lacking. Similarly, Andrew Huebner's discussion of *The Men* in the context of postwar representations of the American soldier provides suggestive, albeit brief, analysis. Huebner, *The Warrior Image: Soldiers in American Culture from the Second World War to the Vietnam Era* (Chapel Hill: University of North Carolina Press, 2008).

16. Oliver Stone's *Born on the Fourth of July* is often seen as the film that deploys the paraplegic veteran as the symbol for US national impotence in a war gone wrong (*Born on the Fourth of July*, directed by Oliver Stone [1989; Los Angeles, 2004], DVD). Zinnemann, however, delved into similar issues, albeit relatively indirectly, as early as 1950.

17. Brando reportedly lived three weeks with paraplegic veterans recovering at Birmingham before *The Men* was shot. for more on this and the filmography of *The Men,* see Fred Zinnemann, *A Life in the Movies: An Autobiography* (New York: Scribner's, 1992); *Fred Zinnemann: Interviews* (Jackson: University Press of Mississippi, 2005); Arthur Nolletti, ed., *The Films of Fred Zinnemann: Critical Perspectives* (Albany: State University of New York Press, 1999).

18. For more on Ted Anderson, see Anderson, "Paraplegic GI Relives War in Searing Scene," *Los Angeles Times,* February 26, 1950, D3; "13-Year Struggle Ended by Paralyzed Veteran," *Los Angeles Times,* October 5, 1958, A; "Paralyzed Vets Elect Officers," *Los Angeles Times,* June 12, 1948, A1; "Meet Ted Anderson," *Paraplegia News* 9 (June 1955), 4. Anderson also authored a column, "Paraplegia in Review," in *Paraplegia News* for several years. See, e.g., Ted Anderson, "Paraplegia in Review," *Paraplegia News* 9 (February 1955), 2.

19. See, e.g., Abby Wilkerson, "Disability, Sex Radicalism, and Political Agency," *National Women's Studies Association Journal* 14 (2002), 33–57; Tobin Siebers, *Disability Theory* (Ann Arbor: University of Michigan Press, 2008).

20. It is also interesting to note that this was a historical moment when the concept of gender as performance—and as potentially biologically modifiable—began to enter the American consciousness. See David Serlin, *Replaceable You: Engineering the Body in Postwar America* (Chicago: University of Chicago Press, 2004); Bernice Hausman,

Changing Sex: Transsexualism, Technology, and the Idea of Gender (Durham, NC: Duke University Press, 1995); Judith Butler, *Gender Trouble: Feminism and the Subversion of Identity* (New York: Routledge, 1990).

21. Beth Linker, *War's Waste: Rehabilitation in World War I America* (Chicago: University of Chicago Press, 2011).

22. Frances Bernstein, "Prosthetic Manhood in the Soviet Union at the End of World War II," *Osiris* 30 (2015), 113–133.

23. For more on how amputees became a model of the US rehabilitation effort precisely because they could be more easily normalized and "fixed" through prosthetic wear, see Linker, *War's Waste.*

24. Rebecca Jo Plant, *Mom: The Transformation of Motherhood in Modern America* (Chicago: University of Chicago Press, 2010). Robbins's maternal role is established early in the film as she wheels Bud, immobile on a gurney, into the ward where other paraplegics reside. As she enters the ward, with a diminutive Bud cradled in front of her as if he were in a pram, Robbins chimes to the other bedridden men, "I'm bringing you a playmate."

25. Christina S. Jarvis, *The Male Body at War: American Masculinity during World War II* (Dekalb: Northern Illinois University Press, 2004), 110.

26. Martin Norden, "Resexualization of the Disabled War Hero in *Thirty Seconds over Tokyo*," *Journal of Popular Film and Television* 23 (1995), 50–55, 51.

27. Norden, "Resexualization," 51.

28. Thomas Patrick Doherty, *Hollywood's Censor: Joseph I. Breen and the Production Code Administration* (New York: Columbia University Press, 2007).

29. For example, Thomas Laqueur writes that "it is probably not possible to write a history of man's body and its pleasures, because the historical record was created in a cultural tradition where no such history was necessary." See Laqueur, *Making Sex: Body and Gender from the Greeks to Freud* (Cambridge, MA: Harvard University Press, 1992), 22. Erika Lorraine Milam and Robert A. Nye express a similar sentiment, noting that historians have "left largely unexamined the discriminatory hierarchies within all-white male cultures, which advanced the careers of some men while excluding or marginalizing other men (and, by extension, women) on the basis of class, race, religion, or sexual orientation." See Milam and Nye, "An Introduction to *Scientific Masculinities*," *Osiris* (30), 3.

30. If a soldier sustained a high cord lesion and experienced paralysis of the arms and hands, he would sometimes be referred to as a quadriplegic, although many laypeople and spinal cord injured preferred the term *paraplegia.*

31. Keith Wheeler, *We Are the Wounded* (New York: E. P. Dutton, 1945), 13.

32. Jarvis, *The Male Body at War*, 90.

33. Wheeler, *We Are the Wounded*, 175.

34. Jarvis, *The Male Body at War*, 87.

35. David Brown, "Amputations and Genital Injuries Increase Sharply among Soldiers in Afghanistan," *Washington Post*, March 4, 2011, http://www.washingtonpost.com/wp-dyn/content/article/2011/03/04/AR2011030403258.html. Thanks to Nathan Ensmenger for bringing this source to our attention.

36. "Meet Dr. Bors," *Paraplegia News* 9 (October 1955), 4.

37. Ernest Bors, "Fertility in Paraplegic Males: Preliminary Report of Endocrine Studies," *Journal of Clinical Endocrinology* 10 (1950), 381–398.

38. Donald Munro, Herbert W. Horne, and David P. Paull, "The Effect of Injury to the Spinal Cord and Cauda Equina on the Sexual Potency of Men," *The New England Journal of Medicine* 239 (December 9. 1948), 903–911.

39. Munro, Horne, and Paull, "Effect of Injury," 903.

40. See Donald Munro, "The Rehabilitation of Patients Totally Paralyzed Below the Waist: with Special Reference to Making Them Ambulatory and Capable of Earning Their Living," *The New England Journal of Medicine* 250 (1954), 4–14. In his study of 408 paraplegic patients, urologist Herbert S. Talbot also insisted that the "popular belief that (spinal cord injured) patients are impotent is . . . unjustified." Talbot, "The Sexual Function in Paraplegics," *Journal of Nervous and Mental Disease* 115 (1952), 360–361. See also S. Leonard Simpson, "Impotence," *British Medical Journal* 1 (1950), 692–697.

41. Munro, Horne, and Paull, "Effect of Injury," 909.

42. Terry McAdam, *Very Much Alive: The Story of a Paraplegic* (Boston: Houghton Mifflin, 1955), 65.

43. Then and now, sex lives of the disabled have conventionally been ignored, stigmatized, and controlled through institutionalization as well as eugenic sterilization. For more on this, see David Serlin, "Touching Histories: Personality, Disability, and Sex in the 1930s," in *Sex and Disability*, ed. Robert McRuer and Anna Mollow (Durham, NC: Duke University Press, 2011), 145–162. See also Irving Zola, *Missing Pieces: A Chronicle of Living with a Disability* (Philadelphia: Temple University Press, 1982). Zola was one of the first sociologists to make this point about disability and sexuality. For eugenic sterilization and disability, see Molly Ladd-Taylor, "The 'Sociological Advantages' of Sterilization: Fiscal Politics and Feebleminded Women in Interwar Minnesota," in *Mental Retardation in America: An Historical Reader*, ed. S. Noll and J. Trent (New York, 2004), 281–299.

44. Alfred C. Kinsey, Wardell B. Pomeroy, and Clyde E. Martin, *Sexual Behavior in the Human Male* (Philadelphia: W. B. Saunders, 1948), 608.

45. For more about the importance of sexual agency and disability, see Wilkerson, "Disability." Wilkerson, along with other disability scholars, contends that the sex experts and other scholars fail to focus on female disabled sexuality and instead attend almost exclusively to male disabled sexuality, particularly that of the spinal cord injured. We have found, however, little historical analysis of paraplegic male sexuality. For more on this debate, see Anne Finger, "Claiming All of Our Bodies: Reproductive Rights and Disability," in *Test Tube Women: What Future for Motherhood?* ed. Ritta Arditti, Renate Duelli Klein, and Shelley Minden (London: Pandora, 1984), 281–297. Russell P. Shuttleworth has conducted interesting anthropological work on paraplegic men and sexuality. Shuttleworth, "The Search for Sexual Intimacy for Men with Cerebral Palsy," *Sexuality and Disability* 18 (December 1, 2000), 263–282. There are also some notable memoirist accounts of paraplegics and sexuality written by men with polio. See, e.g., Zola, *Missing Pieces*, 217–219; Lorenzo Milam, *Cripple Liberation Front Marching Band Blues* (San Diego: Mho & Mho, 1983).

46. While most impotence studies at the time had moved decidedly away from anatomical explanations, toward the psychological and endocrinal, early clinical scientists who treated paraplegics in VA hospitals returned to an older model for understanding sexual virility. For more on the history of impotence and how scientists studied it, see McLaren, *Impotence*. For work on "sex" hormones, see Nelly Oudshoorn, *Beyond the Natural Body: An Archeology of Sex Hormones* (London: Routledge, 1995); Chandak Sengoopta, *The*

Most Secret Quintessence of Life: Sex, Glands, and Hormones, 1850–1950 (Chicago: University of Chicago Press, 2006).

47. Bors, "Fertility," 392.

48. Talbot, "Sexual Function," 360.

49. Robert Moss, "Memo: To Paraplegics of the Korean War from Robert Moss, World War 2," *Paraplegia News* 5 (June 1951), 1, 8.

50. "Have You Been Thinking about Marriage?" *Paraplegia News* 10 (April 1956), 6.

51. Moss, "Memo," 8.

52. Judith Hover, "I Married a Paraplegic," *Paraplegia News* 10 (November 1956), 8–9.

53. The medical profession was not alone in this bias. In the pages of *Paraplegia News*, a magazine written and published by members of the PVA, birth announcements became front-page news. A typical announcement in *Paraplegia News* would provide the name, length, and weight of the baby and also include vital paraplegic statistics on the father, giving the date and place of the injury and the level at which the spine was wounded. See, e.g., "New Arrival," *Paraplegia News* 7 (April 1953), 1: "Mr. and Mrs. William Marquardt of Worthington OH announce arrival of Denis Marie who will take up her residents [*sic*] in OH. The father, a member of the PVA, is a service-connected quadriplegic."

54. Munro, Horne, and Paull, "Effect of Injury," 909.

55. McLaren makes a similar point, noting that "it was taken as a given in Western culture that sex was synonymous with intercourse, a man penetrating his partner. The implication of such a belief is that a man feared impotence, not so much because it might deprive him of pleasure, but because it would prevent him from providing proof that he could perform as a male should. Potency was long linked to maturity. . . . [The association between] sexual virility and youth is a relatively recent phenomenon." McLaren, *Impotence,* xiii.

56. Talbot, "Sexual Function," 360.

57. Bors, "Fertility," 392.

58. To the extent that they were studied, the same standard applied to paraplegic women at the time. Even if sexual arousal was briefly mentioned, most investigations of female paraplegic sexuality focused on reproduction and fertility, honing in on menstruation and childbearing. In 1975, E. R. Griffith and R. B. Trieschmann pointed out this problematic orientation, noting that "the literature on women with spinal cord injury deals primarily with the factors of hormonal function, fertility and delivery. Unfortunately, information is limited concerning issues which are relevant to the total sexual functioning of these women" and calling for further research. Griffith and Trieschmann, "Sexual Functioning in Women with Spinal Cord Injury," *Archives of Physical Medicine and Rehabilitation* 56 (1975), 18–21. For examples of the focus on fertility, see L. Guttman, "Cardiac Irregularities during Labor in Paraplegic Women," *Paraplegia* 3 (1965), 144–151; H. Goller and V. Paeslack, "Pregnancy Damage and Birth Complication in the Children of Paraplegic Women," *Paraplegia* 10 (1972), 213–217.

59. Bors, "Fertility," 392.

60. "Have You Been Thinking about Marriage?" 6.

61. Clifford R. Adams, *Preparing for Marriage: A Guide to Marital and Sexual Adjustment* (New York: Dutton, 1951), 20. Some of the other disabilities listed on the questionnaire included loss of speech, loss of one leg, loss of one arm, general permanent bad health, mental instability requiring long psychotherapy, incurable insanity, and incurable communicable disease.

62. Adams, *Preparing for Marriage,* 172.

63. Adams, *Preparing for Marriage,* 172.

64. "A P.V.A. Credo" *Paraplegia News* 4 (May 1950): 4.

65. McAdam, *Very Much Alive,* 85.

66. McAdam, *Very Much Alive,* 85.

67. McAdam, *Very Much Alive,* 86.

68. For more on this subject, see Carolyn Herbst Lewis, *Prescription for Heterosexuality: Sexual Citizenship in the Cold War Era* (Durham, NC: Duke University Press, 2010).

69. For one reader's enthusiastic response, see Frank G. MacAloon's letter, "Cartoon Denunciation Outlandish," *Paraplegia News* 4 (August 1950), 2.

70. The role that nurses play as mothers, wives, and sexual objects is crucial to understanding the history of sexuality for paraplegics. There is a large literature on the history of nursing (see Patricia D'Antonio, *American Nursing: A History of Knowledge, Authority, and the Meaning of Work* [Baltimore: Johns Hopkins University Press, 2010]; Julie Fairman and Patricia D'Antonio, "Reimagining Nursing's Place in the History of Clinical Practice," *Journal of the History of Medicine and Allied Sciences* 63 [2008], 435–446; Susan Reverby, *Ordered to Care: The Dilemma of American Nursing* [New York: Cambridge University Press, 1987]; among others) but little about nurses as sex objects. See Linker, *War's Waste,* 61–79; D. A. Nicholls and J. Cheek, "Physiotherapy and the Shadow of Prostitution," *Social Science and Medicine* 62 (2006), 2336–2348, 2339; Jane Marcus, "Corpus/Corps/Corps Writing the Body at War," in *Arms and the Woman: War, Gender and Literary Representation,* ed. Helen M. Cooper, Adrienne Auslander Munich, and Susan Merrill Squier (Durham, NC: Duke University Press, 1989), 124–167.

71. Woolsey described himself as a paraplegic with "complete flaccid paralysis below the waist." "Who's Who! Fred B. Woolsey—Cartoonist," *Paraplegia News* 4 (August 1950), 3.

72. See case study in text, for example. See also Munro, Horne, and Paull, "Effect of Injury," 909.

73. John Money, "Phantom Orgasm in the Dreams of Paraplegic Men and Women," *Archives of General Psychiatry* 3 (October 1960), 373–392.

74. "Cartoons Offend," *Paraplegia News* 4 (August 1950), 2. See also Herbert L. Kleinfield's criticism of the cartoons in the June 1950 issue of *Paraplegia News.*

75. Neuhaus, "Importance of Being Orgasmic," 460.

76. Oliver M. Butterfield, *Sex Life in Marriage* (New York: Emerson Books, 1937), 101, as quoted in Neuhaus, "Importance of Being Orgasmic," 457.

77. McAdam, *Very Much Alive,* 87.

78. Stanley Berger, "The Role of Impotence in the Concept of Self in Male Paraplegics" (PhD diss., Columbia University, 1951), 154.

79. Berger, "The Role of Impotence," 113.

80. Berger's comments about sexuality are particularly evocative in the context of the still-widespread Freudian notion that nonpenetrative sex acts were inherently infantile.

81. Elaine Tyler May, *Homeward Bound: American Families in the Cold War Era* (New York: Basic Books, 1990), 120; May, *Barren in the Promised Land: Childless Americans and the Pursuit of Happiness* (Cambridge, MA: Harvard University Press, 1997), 142.

82. McLaren, *Impotence,* xiv.

83. Foreman, in particular, spoke about how his time in the army engendered a "great sense of responsibility" as well as an attention to "the immense educational potential of films, the impact, both intellectual and emotional, that they had on people when properly

presented; the potential that they had for good or evil." Carl Foreman, interview by Joan and Robert Franklin, April 1959, transcript, Popular Arts Project, Columbia University Oral History Collection, New York City, 1674.

84. *Coming Home,* directed by Hal Ashby (1978; New York, 2002), DVD; *Born on the Fourth of July.*

85. Susan Wendell, *The Rejected Body: Feminist Philosophical Reflections on Disability* (New York, 1996), 25.

86. Siebers, *Disability Theory,* 142.

87. Hover, "I Married a Paraplegic," 9.

88. Milam and Nye, "Introduction," 3.

7

"A Blind Man's Homecoming"

MASCULINITY, DISABILITY, AND MALE CAREGIVING
IN FIRST WORLD WAR BRITAIN

Jessica Meyer

In an article titled "Nurses in War and Peace Times: Importance of Male Nurses,"
published in 1920, Lt. Col. E. M. Wilson, of the Navy and Army Male Nursing
Co-operation, was quoted as saying that British servicemen seriously disabled by
wounds incurred during the First World War "would prefer as nurse a male com-
rade who had served in the Great War to a civilian who had been in England the
whole of the past four years."[1] In identifying former military personnel as the preferred caregivers for war-disabled ex-servicemen, Wilson was making a number
of assumptions about the gendered nature of both war service and caregiving—
that war service, including military medical service, was an exclusively masculine
endeavor that took place overseas, creating a community of care based on mutual
experience.

These ideas were not, in some ways, hugely controversial. As Samuel Hynes
has shown, postwar British culture was defined by the tensions between those who
shared the experience of the war as overseas military service and those who did
not.[2] "About war, men who were there make absolute claims for their authority. . . .
war cannot be comprehended at second-hand."[3] Yet the assumption that the cultural authority of war experience was an exclusively male one was already being
challenged by the fact of women's overseas service in nursing and other caring
roles. As historians of First World War nursing have shown, the service of professional female nurses overseas as a formal part of the military medical hierarchy
was an important element of these women's claims for professional recognition[4]
and national honor.[5] For volunteer nurses such as Vera Brittain and Mary Borden,
their experience of caring for male bodies lay at the heart of their claims to be able
to bear witness to the horrors of war, although in ways that reinforced the gender distinctions between them and the men they cared for.[6] As Santanu Das has

demonstrated, in order to lay claim to the status of witness in the context of war, female nurses had to invoke their femininity as caregivers in defense of their right to "be there," within a sphere defined by both culture and military protocol as predominantly masculine.[7]

If the invocation of care as a female prerogative was central to female nurses' claims to their serving their country in war, then "The shattered male body is a central concern during and after the war years."[8] In exploring how women have interacted with these male bodies as providers of care, Das and other literary scholars have expanded our understanding of both war as a gendered experience and war's impact on gendered relationships. [9] It is, however, an analysis built on the presumption of bodily difference between the carer and the cared for. Yet, as Wilson's comments indicate, such difference was not the sole reality of care within the British military system during the war. Male caregiving played an important role throughout the conflict in ways that profoundly shaped the gendered understandings of the body of both the carer and the cared for.

While the manpower crisis that faced the British military throughout the war meant that, particularly from 1916, military medical caregiving was increasingly diluted by female professional nurses and volunteers, there remained throughout a corps of men who served in caring capacities. Some of these were themselves nonenlisted volunteers, including those who served with the 836 male Voluntary Aid Detachment (VAD) units that existed at the Armistice, and the conscientious objectors who served with the Friends' Ambulance Unit. These men served outside of the military hierarchy and disciplinary structure, under the aegis of the Joint War Committee of the British Red Cross and Order of St. John of Jerusalem.[10] The majority, however, were the men of the Royal Army Medical Corps (RAMC). These men included officers, who were required to hold a medical degree in order to obtain a commission in the unit, and the men of the ranks. These rankers undertook the clerical and dispensing duties, as well as the carrying, cleaning, and caring along the line of evacuation from regimental aid post (RAP) to home front military hospital.

From the RAP to the casualty clearing station, the furthest forward that female nurses were permitted to serve by the military medical authorities,[11] these men were the sole medical caregivers that wounded men encountered within the military evacuation structure. For these caregivers, the caring experience was dominated by encounters with the male body in extremis, a fact that defined their caring responses.[12] Yet for the stretcher bearers and tent orderlies of the Field Ambulances, who cleared the RAPs and formed the dressing stations where men were treated along the line of evacuation, the encounter with the any individual body, however damaged, was generally a fleeting one, with men moved down the line to a site where more complex treatment could be given. It was the men serving in casualty clearing stations and in the base and home hospitals whose encounters with the war-damaged male body were more extended. Even if the war-ravaged body was, by this time, at least partially tended,[13] these men also encountered the extreme damage that the violence of industrialized warfare could inflict, less in terms of rawness and quantity than in duration and intensity. A "Blighty" wound serious enough to involve evacuation back to Britain, although much longed for by men in the trenches, in reality often entailed damage of life-altering severity, including amputation, sensory impairment, paralysis, disfigurement, or a combination of these injuries.[14] Encounters with such disablement of the male body, and particularly the soldier body idealized in British wartime culture,[15] forced male caregivers to reflect on their own bodily experience. For RAMC orderlies serving in home hospitals, the gendered significance of such reflections and responses was made more acute by the fact that their own bodily integrity and consequent masculine status as a group was called into question throughout the war by their ambiguous position as uniformed servicemen in a noncombatant unit serving on the home front.

This chapter explores the responses of one such serviceman, Ward Muir, a lance-corporal with the RAMC(T) who served throughout the war at the 3rd London General Military Hospital, Wandsworth. A journalist in peacetime, Muir recorded his experiences in essays published first in journals and newspapers, including *The Spectator, The New Statesman, The Evening Standard,* and *The Daily Mail,* and then as two books, *Observations of an Orderly* (1917) and *The Happy Hospital* (1918), sold to raise funds for the hospital. In these essays, he records both his own lived experience of care provision and his observations of the patients he tended. In doing so, his writings explore a range of bodily frailties and impairments, both congenital and war-inflicted, which, on the one hand, served to distance the carer from the men he cared for, but also, on the other, served to unite caregiver and patient as servicemen in wartime. Muir's narrative draws on many of the ideas of witnessing through the body that Das identifies in female nurses' writings about care. In his focus on male caregiving bodies, his work also engages with the arguments of Ana Carden-Coyne and Deborah Cohen about the gendered power relationships of wartime caregiving.[16]

By analyzing the different narratives of male bodily experience of care in wartime that appear in Muir's writings, this chapter examines how male caregivers and war-disabled servicemen interacted to negotiate the complex transitions that men underwent from civilian to soldier and back again within the context of mass mobilization. It does so through the examination of two particular forms of the compromised male body that are central to Muir's narrative, the frail male caregiver and the wounded soldier patient. It also looks at the representations of these two types of men in *The Gazette of the 3rd London General,* the hospital journal that Muir founded and edited, which received contributions from other members of hospital staff as well as from patients. Finally, it examines in detail Muir's article "A Blind Man's Homecoming" to explore how the gendered caring relationship between these two bodies of men shaped the ability of men to transition between martial and civilian identities.

The Frail Orderly

We begin with the frail body of the male medical caregiver, a subject that runs throughout both Muir's writing and the articles and illustrations of *The Gazette*. The particular object of focus for both Muir and *The Gazette* was the figure of the medical orderly, the rankers of RAMC who, within the context of the home hospital served as "parlour-maid and waitress, . . . charwoman and messenger boy, bath-chairman, barber, bootblack, window cleaner, bath attendant, gardener, valet, washer-up and odd man all rolled into one."[17] Muir was deprecating about the status and labor of the orderly within wartime hierarchies. He wrote,

> The hospital orderly is not . . . puffed up with foolish illusions as to his place in the scheme of things. It is a humble place, and he knows it. His work is almost comically unromantic, painfully unpicturesque. Moreover—let us be frank—much of it is uninteresting, after the first novelty has worn off. Work in the wards has its compensations: here there is the human element. But only a portion of a unit such as ours can be detailed for ward work: the rest are either hewers of wood and drawers of water or else have their noses to a grindstone of clerical monotonousness beside which the ledger-keeping of a bank employee is a heaven of blissful excitements.[18]

The men who carried out such menial domestic labor in military home hospitals were the lowest rank within the RAMC. They were recruited on the basis not of their medical expertise but rather of their willingness and enthusiasm as volunteers. From the very beginning, their physical frailty was an integral part of their identity as servicemen, with many of them joining the noncombatant RAMC rather than combat units because their physique meant that they were unable to gain service in other branches of the military. J. B. Bennett, for example:

> With an office colleague . . . tried to enlist in the East Surrey Rifles and . . . failed the sight test (Astigmatism), having been caught out on the blind side of the hexagonal test chart despite memorising the visible faces. I had pocketed my normal spectacles. I appealed and obtained a second test without success. Nothing daunted, I persued [sic] my endeavours at recruiting centres in London for four wearying days and failed similar tests with the addition of height. In a last effort I went to the local Drill Hall following a recruiting "tip off" on Sat. 9th. September and succeeded with the 3rd East Anglian Field Ambulance . . . having evaded the sight test. The N.C.O. left me to answer a phone call in an adjoining room and forgetfully asked me if I had read the sight testing panel. My affirmative was accepted and so I passed the test that I never had.[19]

Muir himself, whose had poor eyesight and general lack of physical fitness appears to have debarred him from a combatant role, wrote that in joining the RAMC, "at last I had found a branch of the army which would accept me."[20] He would go on to share a hut with two recruits over sixty, while his unit "was kept up to strength by the drafting-in either of C3 recruits or of soldiers who, having been at the front and been wounded, or invalided back, were marked for home duty only."[21] These were men whose bodies were defined by infirmities as unsuitable for combat.

Yet to define home hospital orderlies throughout the war as solely the over-aged and unfit is, despite the implications of Figure 7.1, not entirely accurate. Younger, healthier RAMC servicemen served in this capacity, particularly in the early years of the war. Their service in home hospitals was, however, generally more temporary than that of men such as Muir, with regular drafts being "combed out" and sent for overseas service in base hospitals, casualty clearing stations and the tent units of field ambulances to replace the wounded men who were keeping the home hospitals up to strength. *The "Southern" Cross* noted in June 1916 that "fourteen officers ... three warrant officers, and one hundred and eighty-seven N.C.O.s and men have left the Hospital during the last few months."[22]

Nor were such drafts simply a matter of redeployment. Home hospitals were also used by the RAMC as training grounds for noncommissioned person-nel. Archie Whyte, a staff sergeant with the 3rd East Anglian Field Ambulance, was sent to the 1st Eastern General Hospital in Cambridge for a week's training

No. 4. The Youngest Lance-Corporal.

FIGURE 7.1 "Our Celebrities: No. 4. The Youngest Lance-Corporal," *The Gazette* [of the 3rd London General] (December 1915), 55.

just before Christmas 1914.[23] Emily Mayhew has suggested that the Cambridge Military Hospital at Aldershot, the first British home hospital to receive battlefield casualties, was the focus for training an increasingly professional stretcher bearer corps.[24] In fact, many of the territorial forces military hospitals that had been mobilized throughout the country on the outbreak of war served as training centers from RAMC personnel. In addition to the short courses run for men like Whyte, who, as a prewar territorial volunteer already had some first aid training, they also, as in the case of the 1st Southern General, Birmingham, provided longer term training for wartime volunteers who could then be drafted overseas. In the early years of the war, therefore, RAMC orderlies were only defined by their bodily frailty insofar as it barred them from combatant duties rather than overseas service.

As the manpower crisis deepened, however, the definition of the insufficiently fit combatant male body changed.[25] Recruitment to the RAMC itself was closed, with two related results. First, the combing out of men previously deemed unfit to make up casualty losses overseas meant that the training of new recruits in home hospitals became less and less necessary. The losses suffered by these units due to the drafting of men for overseas service was either absorbed in a reduction of staff or, increasingly, by the recruitment of women taking on roles formerly undertaken by men. In the case of the 1st Southern General, "Not only were men replaced by women, but the actual number of the male personnel was reduced, so that more work had to be done by those who remained. The trained Nursing Staff was also diluted by more V.A.D. Probationers."[26] Second, the combing out process altered the physical profile of the home hospital orderly. In 1918 Muir pointed out that

> The ward orderly is no Hercules. His ranks have been combed and combed until naught but the crocks remain: honest souls capable of trotting about on errands from dawn till dusk and of being useful in countless ways: their make-up a queer triad, one-third housemaid, one-third waiter and one-third valet: their physique so cranky they are apt, themselves to put in occasional periods as patients instead of as members of the staff.[27]

Male VAD units continued to be supplied by the Joint War Committee of the British Red Cross Society and Order of St. John of Jerusalem, which had responsibility from the War Office for supervising all voluntary medical aid to the British war effort. In their postwar report, however, the committee noted that "the standard of physical fitness for the Red Cross personnel . . . suffered relatively to the lowered standard of the Army" as, "on the passing of the Military Service Act the War Office allowed us to engage only men of low category."[28] Thus the men serving in home hospitals in the second half of the war, whether with the RAMC or as part of a VAD unit, can be said to be defined primarily by their lack of physical fitness for overseas service altogether, rather than solely for combatant roles.

Bodily frailty of different intensities was thus the defining feature of the home hospital orderly throughout the war. It defined not only his sphere of service but also his relationship with other members of the hospital community, as demonstrated in the cartoons of Stephen Bagot de la Bere, which appeared in the pages of the *Gazette*. In Figures 7.2, 7.3 and 7.4 the small figure of the "orderlim" is made insignificant by both the overbearing physicality of the matron and sergeant, figures of medical and military authority portrayed as masculine, and the elegant, attenuated length of the female nurse and "orderlette."[29] The doctors, commissioned officers of the RAMC,[30] are of such status that they have no physical representation in this series of cartoons at all.[31]

The Wounded Soldier

Indeed, the only figure in the pages of the *Gazette* whose physical body is more compromised than that of the male orderly is the male patient, at least the bedbound patient. These were men so physically helpless that they were reliant on the strength of others to be fed, washed, and dressed, something depicted as potentially humiliating.[32] As Ana Carden-Coyne has shown, the wounded male body in the hospital was an important site for the negotiation of power, both medical and gendered. The power of doctors and nurses to inflict pain on the disabled male body, and of the disabled man to subvert and resist such power, made hospitals

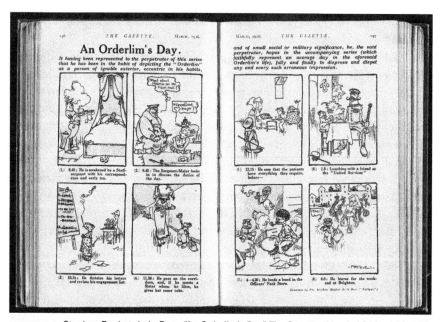

FIGURE 7.2 Stephen Baghot de la Bere, "An Orderlim's Day," *The Gazette* (March 1916), 146–147.

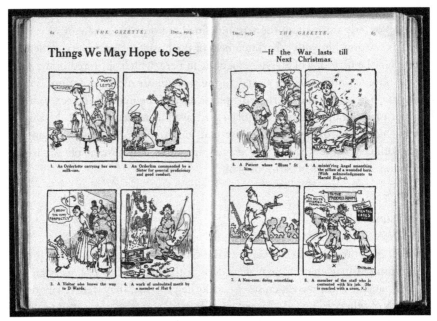

FIGURE 7.3 Stephen Bagnot de la Bere, "Things We May Hope to See—If the War Lasts till Next Christmas," *The Gazette* (December 1915), 62–63.

important sites of wartime sociability and coercion. These sites were powerfully shaped by gendered interactions, whether through the sexualizing of female medical staff or the admission of the limits of the masculinity of the male body in wartime.[33] The perceived powerlessness of the war-damaged male body was at the center of these struggles.

Male medical orderlies brought a particular perspective to gendered understandings of the hospitalized male body. Wielding neither the medical authority of doctors nor the cultural hegemony of nurses as caregivers, they struggled to even lay claim to the physical fitness of the healthy male body that might have given them some form of power in relation to their patients. As Muir pointed out, and as we have seen, orderlies were "not . . . able-bodied, even though muscular enough to stand [the] short physical effort" of unloading an ambulance convoy.[34] This point is reinforced by cartoons such as Figure 7.5, showing the care of men made possible only by the use of Heath Robinson–style contraptions. While images such as this emphasize the way in which the disabled body became part of a machine of care,[35] they equally present the male caregiver as insufficiently able to provide care without mechanical aids.

The orderly's awareness of the frailty of his own body thus profoundly influences Muir's depictions of war-disabled men. Much of his discourse follows contemporary cultural tropes, which assigned these men the socially acceptable role of the "cheerful cripple," with the emphasis placed firmly on their cheerful demeanor

FIGURE 7.4 R, B, Ogle, "Orderlette v, Orderlim," R. B. Ogle, *The Gazette* [of the 3rd London General Hospital] (May 1917), 224.

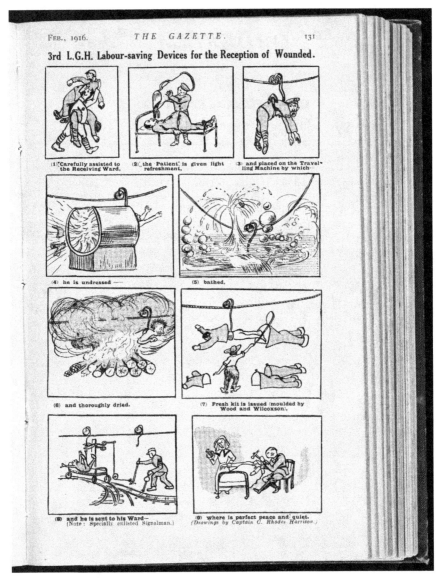

FIGURE 7.5 S.C. Rhodes Harrison, "3rd L.G.H. Labour-Saving Devices for the Reception of Wounded," *The Gazette* [of the 3rd London General Hospital] (February 1916), 131.

rather than their impaired bodies.[36] Patients from the Dardanelles, for instance, are described as

> Schoolboys—yes—with their "ragging" and their uproarious laughter and their intense interest in the tasty heating-up of odds and ends of left-over food: but what sights they had seen, what agony of hunger and thirst, pitiless

heat and pain, they had undergone and, by a miracle, survived! What blessed dispensation of nature is this, that mettlesome schoolboys, and not broken and prematurely-aged wrecks, emerged from the ordeal of suffering![37]

Much of Muir's focus is on men's recovery from the impairment of temporary wounds. He comments relatively infrequently on the more helpless "bed patients," as opposed to the walking patients who

> lent a hand [with the ward orderly's work]: I was good-naturedly ejected from the kitchen and larder by Jock, Wonk-Eye and others, who cut the bread-and-butter, laid the trays, filled the mugs of tea, made toast, cleaned knives, and boiled eggs to the accompaniment of a merry tumult of whistling, squabbling and chaff.[38]

Whatever the matter was with Wonk-Eye's eye, he could still labor cheerfully, implicitly, and more effectively than the male orderly. Similarly,

> The orderlette, en route for the Steward's Store or the Laundry, is often accompanied down the corridors by an obsequious gentleman in Blues, chivalrously eager to carry her tray or her bundle—even though he owns but one arm to do it with.[39]

By contrast, the male orderly's relationship with the orderlette was far more fractious, characterized by threatened masculinity rather than chivalry.[40] In the *Gazette* the orderlette is usually portrayed as a lazy, domineering figure, happy to allow others to do her work for her rather than one in need of masculine aid.

Despite the emphasis on the emotional and physical resilience of his patients, particularly those not confined to bed by their wounds, Muir nonetheless remains aware of the ways in which physical impairments could deprive wounded men of their sense of masculine self-worth. In writing of his care of bed patients, he notes that "any discomfort to which the orderly is exposed is negligible—an affair positively to blush for—compared with the sufferings and unavoidable physical humiliations of the patient."[41] The physical autonomy of the orderly, however limited it might be by both physical frailty and the demands of military discipline,[42] thus serves as some compensation for the male caregiver in relation to his bed-bound patient.

However, two groups of patients elicit from Muir an even more intense pity than the physically dependent bed patient. The first of these is the category of the facially disfigured soldier who, at the 3rd London General, were treated by a team led by Francis Derwent Wood, RA, in what became known as the Masks for Facial Disfigurement, or (more colloquially) the Tin Nose Department. Of these men Muir wrote, "I never felt any embarrassment in thus amicably confronting a patient, however deplorable his state, however humiliating his dependence on my services, until I came in contact with certain wounds of the face."[43] Unlike the other patients who appear in his essays, with these men Muir attempts to make the imaginative leap necessary to see the world through their newly impaired eyes:

> Suppose he is married, or engaged to be married . . . Could any woman come near that gargoyle without repugnance? His children . . . Why, a child would run screaming from such a sight. To be fled from by children! That must be a heavy cross for some souls to bear.[44]

The physical impairment of facial disfigurement is, in Muir's construction, far more disabling than the amputation of an arm, a loss that still allows men to enact appropriate masculine relations with women through chivalric displays. Facial injury, by contrast, has the potential to destroy the disabled man's domestic masculine identity as defined in relation to women by denying him proximity to them or to children due to his impaired state. Such wounds equally had the power to deny him the masculine identity of provider in the eyes of the State, with the Ministry of Pension awarding men with facially disfiguring wounds 100 percent pensions on the basis that disfigurement would automatically debar them from future employment.[45]

The second category of the war-disabled who elicited Muir's particular sympathy were the men of Block D, the blind, to whom he devotes two chapters of his collection *Observations of an Orderly*. These two chapters illustrate the competing narratives of impairment that we have already seen in Muir's representations of the disabled, with the chapter titled "From the D Block Wards" presenting blind patients exclusively in the guise of the "cheerful cripple." "As often as not, the loudest talk, the cheeriest chaff, the most spontaneous laughter emanate from the blue-clad stalwarts who have mustered from the 'D' Block wards," Muir writes.[46] He goes on to argue that, while

> The spectacle of men—particularly young men—who have given their sight for their country is, to most observers, a moving one[, i]t is the plain truth . . . that the blind men themselves are far from melancholy. One of the rowdiest characters we ever had in the hospital was totally blind. The blind men's wards are notoriously amongst the least sedate.[47]

He illustrates this assertion with an anecdote about the antics of a group of blind patients when they were taken by an orderly to a matinee in town. These include creating chaos on the Oxford Street tube escalators and the disappearance of two patients, one totally blind, one capable of discerning light from dark, in order to "seize this opportunity of seeing the sights of London."[48] The irony of this last escapade is not lost on any of the participants, including the reader, while Muir quotes the orderly who was escorting the party as declaring, "Never again . . . shall I jump at a matinee job if there are blind chaps in the party. They're the deuce."[49]

As Carden-Coyne has pointed out, the sort of behavior that Muir describes was an important outlet for patients, whatever their injury, whose lives in hospital were circumscribed by both military and medical discipline, giving them claims to agency that their impaired bodies and enforced treatment otherwise denied them.[50] Certainly, this interpretation is an important aspect of Muir's representation, which explicitly seeks to challenge the popular image of the blind man as the source of "Melancholy . . . reflections of the visitor who meets, for the first time, a promenading party of our blind patients."[51] In seeking to elicit laughter rather than pity from the behavior of these men, Muir is representing them as independent in both thought and action in spite of their disability. The laughter is thus at the expense not of the blind men but of the ineffective orderly attempting and failing to "exert . . . his (purely nominal) authority" over them.[52] Cheerful crippledom here, far from infantilizing the disabled man,[53] instead secures him, if only temporarily, status in the social hegemonies of wartime Britain, where the impaired ex-serviceman dominated the frail male medical orderly.[54]

"A Blind Man's Homecoming"

Yet the balance of power between these two groups was never solely one way, as Muir illustrates in the final chapter of *Observations of an Orderly*, "A Blind Man's Homecoming." In this chapter, he describes not the experience of another orderly but rather his own role as an escort to a blinded ex-serviceman traveling home from the hospital following his formal discharge from military service. Muir serves first as tour guide, arranging a detour past Buckingham Palace:

> at last I was able to inform Briggs that we were passing Buckingham Palace: I turned his head so that he looked straight towards that architectural phenomenon. It was, of course, invisible to him. No matter. He wished to be able to boast, to his wife, that he had seen (he used that verb) the house where the King lived.[55]

This episode echoes the escapades of the men of Block D's "seeing" the sights of London but, rather than a joke or act of rebellion asserting the blind man's autonomy from military and medical authority, Briggs's journey is an act of collaboration between patient and orderly. Muir is investing Briggs with information and an identity as a traveler and sightseer, which enhance his autonomy not in relation to the hospital and his former military identity but rather in relation to the home and his domestic civilian identity as husband.

When the pair reach Yorkshire, however, the partnership of guide and guided is reversed. Briggs

> would now act as my guide. . . . "First to the right. . . . Now we're goin' by a big watchmaker's-and-jeweller's . . . Now cross t' street . . . Now on th' corner over there by t' Sinnermer is we're we git our tram."
>
> The tram in due course appeared, and we boarded it. "Tha mun pay thrippence only, mind," he warned me when the conductor cam round. "It's

a rare long ride for thrippence." So it proved to be—through wildernesses which were half meadow and half slum, my cicerone at every hundred yards pointing out the notable features of the landscape. On our left I ought to see the so-and-so public house; on our right the football ground—I should know it by the grand-stand jutting above the palings; further on were brickworks; further still a factory which, my nose would have told me, even if Mr. Briggs had not, dealt with chemicals.[56]

In the role of guided, Muir again provides his companion with a sense of normalcy and agency that helps to counteract the emotional impairment that his disability has the power to inflict.[57] His actions allow Briggs to lay claim to his old civilian identity through his expertise as a native familiar with his surroundings.

When Brigg's home is finally reached, in his final act as caregiver, Muir serves as the bridge between these two identities that he has helped to foster, the wounded serviceman rich in experience gained in travel and the disabled civilian with the expertise of the native, and he acts as witness to this transition:

> I unhooked my arm from Briggs's and made as though to push him forward into the family group.
> "Nay!" said Briggs. "I mun take my top-coat off first."
> I helped him off with his coat. Not one of the three members of his family had either moved or spoken—beyond one faint murmur, not an actual word, in response to my "Here we are." But Briggs seemed to know that his folk were in the room with him, and he neither accosted them, expressed any curiosity about them, or betrayed any astonishment at their silence.
> When he had got his coat off I expected him to move forward into the room. A mistake. . . . Briggs put out his hand, felt for the cottage door, half closed it, felt for a nail on the inner side of it, and carefully hung his coat thereon.
> *Now* I could usher him into the waiting family circle.
> No. I was wrong.
> Briggs calmly divested himself of his jacket. He then felt for another door, a door which opened on to a stair leading to the upper storey. On a nail in this door he hung his jacket. And then, in his shirt-sleeves, he was ready. Shirt-sleeves were symbolical. He was home at last, and prepared to sit down with his people.[58]

The transformation, which began with the clothing of the disabled man in "reach-me-down garments which fitted him surprisingly" in place of his ill-fitting hospital blues,[59] concludes with the image of the shirt-sleeved man, no longer a soldier, wounded or otherwise, but a civilian within his family. Muir's eyes and arms have facilitated this transition, his frail body enabling the impaired body of the blind man to achieve agency, however short-lived such agency might, in reality, be.

Conclusion

Of all the bodies that inhabited the spaces of care that were wartime military hospitals, those of the war wounded and the medical orderly were among the most problematic. Subject to military and medical authority, compromised by wounds and physical frailty, both of these groups of men embodied challenged masculinities in the context of total war. Yet, as this chapter has argued, the relationships and interactions between these two groups enabled each to lay claim to dominant masculinities in different contexts. Disabled servicemen could demonstrate their heteronormative dominance through flirting with and offering aid to "orderlettes" in ways denied to the male medical orderlies. They were able to draw upon the authority of active war service, of being a "man who was there" to aid them in their self-construction as chivalric heroes.

By contrast, by adopting the persona of the cheerful cripple, wounded servicemen could render the male medical orderly's authority ineffective, even where the orderly's bodily integrity was a necessary aid to the serviceman's mobility. For the orderlies, this bodily integrity enabled them to fulfill their caregiving function, acting as arms, eyes, and ultimately bridges in the treacherous transition their patients made from wounded serviceman to disabled civilian. In doing so, they too gained the authority of the witness.

In their frailty and fragility as men, both orderlies and ex-servicemen posed challenges to highly gendered regimes of care in wartime Britain. While never able to fully challenge the social structures and cultural norms that defined them as insufficiently masculine in a society at war, their interactions nonetheless demonstrate the ways in which those norms could be queried, subverted, and even, on occasion, overcome by individuals. In doing so, both groups were able to reaffirm their status as men of and witnesses to war.

Notes

1. "Nurses in War and Peace Times: Importance of Male Nurses," *Streatham News*, November 8, 1920, RAMC 1922, Wellcome Library, London.

2. Samuel Hynes, *A War Imagined: The First World War and English Culture* (New York: Atheneum, 1991), 388.

3. Samuel Hynes, *The Soldiers' Tale: Bearing Witness to Modern War* (New York: Penguin Books, 1997), 1.

4. Christine Hallett, *Containing Trauma: Nursing Work in the First World War* (Manchester, UK: Manchester University Press, 2009), 198–201.

5. Alison S. Fell, "Afterword: Remembering the First World War Nurse in Britain and France," in *First World War Nursing: New Perspectives*, ed. Alison S. Fell and Christine E. Hallett (London: Routledge, 2013), 179.

6. Carol Acton and Jane Potter, *Working in a World of Hurt: Trauma and Resilience in the Narratives of Medical Personnel in Warzones* (Manchester, UK: Manchester University Press, 2015), 36–37.

7. Santanu Das, *Touch and Intimacy in First World War Literature* (Cambridge, UK: Cambridge University Press, 2005), 176–177.

8. Das, *Touch and Intimacy,* 178.

9. Margaret Higonnet, "Introduction," in *Nurses at the Front: Writing the Wounds of the Great War,* ed. Margaret Higonnet (Boston: Northeastern University Press, 2001), vii–xxx-viii; Jane Marcus, "Afterword: Corpus/Corps/Corpse: Writing the Body in/at War" in Helen Zenna Smith [Evadne Price], *Not So Quiet . . . Stepdaughters of War* (New York: Feminist Press, 1989), 241–300.

10. Male VAD units were established in 1909 as part of the British Red Cross and St. John of Jerusalem involvement in the medical training of the territorial forces. These units were mobilized for military service as part of the Territorial Army in 1914. The remaining units were made up of men who wished to volunteer but were not able to enlist as combatants due to age or infirmity. The Friends' Ambulance Unit, although set up as an independent voluntary organization in 1914, came under the authority of the Joint War Committee as part of an agreement between the military authorities, the British Red Cross Society, and the Order of St. John that the committee should authorize and supervise all voluntary medical aid to the British war effort. *Reports by the Joint War Committee and the Joint War Finance Committee of the British Red Cross and the Order of St. John of Jerusalem in England on Voluntary Aid Rendered to the Sick and Wounded at Home and Abroad and to British Prisoners of War, 1914–1919, with Appendices* (London: His Majesty's Stationary Office, 1921).

11. Major-General Sir W. G. Macpherson, *History of the Great War Based on Official Documents: Medical Services General History,* Vol. 2 (London: His Majesty's Stationary Office, 1923), 44.

12. Acton and Potter, *Working in a World of Hurt,* 42–45.

13. In the early months of the war, a base or even home hospital could receive a wounded man within a few hours of injury, often with wounds that had had little time to receive care and attention in the hurry to evacuate. As the war went on and the line of evacuation became more organized and sophisticated in the care it could offer, such cases were almost the exclusive preserve of the casualty clearing station. Mark Harrison, *The Medical War: British Military Medicine in the First World War* (Oxford: Oxford University Press, 2010), chapter 1.

14. Disease and psychological wounds also had the power to inflict long-term impairment, although often in ways less immediately visible in the body.

15. Joanna Bourke, *Dismembering the Male: Men's Bodies, Britain and the Great War* (London: Reaktion Books, 1996), 11.

16. Ana Carden-Coyne, *The Politics of Wounds: Military Patients and Medical Power in the First World War* (Oxford: Oxford University Press, 2014); Deborah Cohen, *The War Come Home: Disabled Veterans in Britain and Germany, 1914–1939* (Berkeley: University of California Press, 2001).

17. "A Nursing Orderly's Day," *Gazette of the 3rd London General Hospital,* November, 1915, RAMC/1312, Wellcome Library, London, 45.

18. Ward Muir, *Observations of an Orderly: Some Glimpses of Life and Work in an English War Hospital* (London: Simpkin, Marshall, Hamilton, Kent & Co., Ltd., 1917), 154.

19. J. B. Bennett, "Memories of Gallipoli, Aug 1915–December 1915 at Sulva Bay and Anzac," memoir, Liddle/WW1/GS/10, Liddle Collection, Special Collections, University of Leeds, 1–2.

20. Muir, *Observations of an Orderly*, 20.

21. Muir, *Observations of an Orderly*, 153.

22. *The "Southern" Cross: The Monthly Journal of the First Southern General, Birmingham* 1.6 (June 1916), Liddle/WW1/DF/GA/HOS/56, Liddle Collection, Special Collections, University of Leeds, 127.

23. A. L. G. Whyte, "Memoirs of the Great War, 1914–18," unpublished memoir, 1971, Liddle/WW1/GS/1728, Liddle Collection, Special Collections, University of Leeds, 11.

24. Emily Mayhew, *Wounded: From Battlefield to Blighty 1914–1918* (London: Bodley Head, 2013), 18–19.

25. J. M. Winter, *The Great War and the British People* (Basingstoke, UK: Macmillan, 1986), 50–64.

26. "History of the 1st Southern General Hospital," *The "Southern" Cross* 2.18 (June 1917), 139.

27. Ward Muir, *The Happy Hospital* (London: Simpkin, Marshall, Hamilton, Kent & Co., Ltd., 1918), 23.

28. *Reports by the Joint War Committee*, 94.

29. The "orderlette" was the dismissive name given by the *Gazette* to the female VADs assigned to the hospital to replace male orderlies combed out for overseas or combatant service. They were officially a mixture of nursing and "general service" VADs.

30. Ian R. Whitehead, *Doctors in the Great War* (London: Leo Cooper, 1999), 6–31.

31. As Carden-Coyne has shown, where doctors did appear in hospital cartoons, it was often as butchers or bullies, images often closely aligned to the masculinized figure of Matron. Carden-Coyne, *The Politics of Wounds,* 184, 279, 294.

32. Jeffrey S. Reznick, *Healing the Nation: Soldiers and the Culture of Caregiving in Britain During the Great War* (Manchester, UK: Manchester University Press, 2004), 83.

33. Carden-Coyne, *The Politics of Wounds,* 290, 329.

34. Muir, *Observations of an Orderly*, 152.

35. Carden-Coyne, *The Politics of Wounds,* 78–87.

36. Cohen, *The War Come Home*, 128–147.

37. Muir, *The Happy Hospital*, 29.

38. Muir, *The Happy Hospital.*, 29.

39. Muir, *The Happy Hospital*, 30.

40. For a discussion of the importance of chivalry to ideas of wartime masculinity, see Mark Girouard, *The Return to Camelot: Chivalry and the English Gentleman* (New Haven, CT: Yale University Press, 1981), and Michael Paris, *Warrior Nation: Images of War in British Popular Culture, 1850–2000* (London: Reaktion Books, 2000), 133.

41. Muir, *The Happy Hospital*, 103.

42. Muir, *Observations of an Orderly*, 150–151.

43. Muir, *The Happy Hospital*, 143.

44. Muir, *The Happy Hospital,* 145.

45. Bourke, *Dismembering the Male,* 66; Katherine Feo, "Invisibility: Memory, Masks and Masculinities in the Great War," *Journal of Design History* 20 (2007), 20. For a discussion of definitions of domestic masculinity as father and provider, see Jessica Meyer, *Men of War: Masculinity and the First World War in Britain* (Basingstoke, UK: Palgrave Macmillan, 2009), 6–7.

46. Muir, *Observations of an Orderly*, 79.

47. Muir, *Observations of an Orderly*, 81.

48. Muir, *Observations of an Orderly*, 88

49. Muir, *Observations of an Orderly*, 82.

50. Carden-Coyne, *The Politics of Wounds,* 223, 319–323.

51. Muir, *Observations of an Orderly*, 81. On constructions of blind ex-servicemen as objects of public pity, see Julie Anderson, "Stoics: Creating Identities at St Dunstan's 1914–1920" in *Men after War*, ed. Stephen McVeigh and Nicola Cooper (New York: Routledge, 2013), 81.

52. Muir, *Observations of an Orderly*, 84.

53. Seth Koven, "Remembering and Dismemberment: Crippled Children, Wounded Soldiers and the Great War in Britain," *American Historical Review* 99 (1994), 1189.

54. R. W. Connell, *Masculinities*, 2nd ed. (Cambridge, UK: Polity Press, 2005), 77.

55. Muir, *Observations of an Orderly*, 240–241.

56. Muir, *Observations of an Orderly,* 242–243.

57. Anderson, "Stoics," 88; Julie Anderson, "'Jumpy Stump': Amputation and Trauma in the First World War," *First World War Studies* 6 (2015), 16–17.

58. Muir, *Observations of an Orderly*, 246–248.

59. Reznick, *Healing the Nation,* 106–111.

PART III

Disabled Man as "Less than a Man"

8

Hysteria in the Male
IMAGES OF MASCULINITY IN
LATE-NINETEENTH-CENTURY FRANCE
Daniela S. Barberis

Hysteria is often presented as the "female malady" par excellence, among "the old-est described disorders in the history of medicine,"[1] with a long history that can allegedly be traced back to Greek or even earlier sources. This narrative, although it continues to be routinely repeated in historical treatments of the disease, is itself the product of a particular historical process—one that was essentially completed in the nineteenth century by medical authors who reified the category as peren-nial and thus natural. Helen King has traced the complicated history that led to the attribution of the identification of hysteria to Hippocrates.[2] In her account, a developing tradition of reading the Hippocratic corpus, concentrated around a set of early texts conventionally linked by subsequent writers, culminated in what she calls "the hysteria tradition" of the "suffocation of the womb" in the mid-sixteenth century. Nineteenth-century hysteria grafted itself onto this tradition, making Hippocrates its purported father. This canonical account presents hyste-ria (using the etymology of the term, from *ustera*, the Greek for "uterus," to give it self-evidence) as having been understood since antiquity as the "malady of the womb" and thus as a quintessentially feminine disease.

Important detail is added to this history by Sabine Arnaud[3] who examines how, by 1820, the term *hysteria* was firmly established and two approaches to the entity predominated: one saw it as a female malady, originating in the sexual organs; the other, less common, approach situated its origin in the brain or ner-vous system. These two divergent approaches also differed as to the possibility of male hysteria, the latter affirming it. Yet, until the late nineteenth-century, male hysterics remained rare—more a theoretical possibility than a commonly encoun-tered fact. Pierre Briquet's influential treatise of 1859, *Traité clinique et thérapeu-tique de l'hystérie,* famously estimated a ratio of 1 to 20 between male and female hysterics—of the 430 cases contained in his voluminous treatise, only 7 were men.[4] At the *fin-de-siècle*, however, especially in France, the diagnosis came to be widely applied through the work of Charcot and his students.

Before entering into the specifics of Charcot's medical conception of male hysteria, I close this historical introduction by noting that Charcot and his students were actively involved in projecting their version of hysteria into the past,[5] consolidating a narrative that made a variety of religious phenomena not previously associated with hysteria into manifestations of this nervous disease.[6] Furthermore, by emphasizing the canonical account of the "malady of the womb" and tracing the rare "precursors" to Charcot's neurological approach to hysteria, they could portray their *maître* as a heroic scientific figure fighting ingrained prejudices with the tools of positivistic objectivity and the history of hysteria as a history of the progressive uncovering of a stable, universal, timeless entity. Any treatment of Charcot, as Gauchet and Swain caution, must be wary of the mythology that surrounds this medical figure,[7] but we should also be wary of the conventional "historical" narrative of the disease category itself.

Jean-Martin Charcot (1825–1893), French professor of anatomical pathology, is considered one of the founders of neurology, responsible for the institutionalization of this discipline in France. From a modern scientific perspective, the importance of Charcot lies in his participation in the reorganization of the fields of knowledge concerning the nervous system, which resulted in a new division— our current one—between neurology, neuropsychology, psychiatry, experimental psychology, and, later, psychoanalysis. His contribution to this reorganization was based on the use of clinical skills and anatomical pathology—well-established medical methods at the time—to catalogue and define disease entities previously grouped together by resemblances in their symptomatology (e.g. paralysis, convulsions, etc.). Charcot's method was the anatomo-clinical method: he compared clinical observations with anatomo-pathological findings (postmortem). He applied this method to the study of hysteria, as he had done successfully with various other spinal and brain diseases.

In the beginning of the 1850s, when Charcot began his scientific career, the study of the diseases of the nervous system was undertaken mainly by anatomists and physiologists who obtained their results through animal experimentation.[8] Between 1860 and 1880, the relationship among clinical studies, anatomy, and physiology was completely transformed. During this period, the considerable development of the clinical studies of the diseases of the nervous system made them central to the understanding of the functioning of the human brain. Although Charcot did not engage in laboratory experimentation, he was thoroughly familiar with the cutting-edge science on the physiology and anatomy of the nervous system, not only through his reading but because he was in direct contact with researchers in the *sociétés savantes* (especially the *Société de biologie*, of which he was a founding member, but also the *Société d'anatomie,* of which he was president for a long time). Nonetheless, Charcot always privileged *la clinique*. In 1882, he quoted Claude Bernard, "that most illustrious physiologist," to state that while the anatomical and the physiological sciences were essential in medicine, they had to be subordinated to clinical study:

> "Pathology," said [Claude Bernard], "should not be subordinated to physiology. Quite the reverse. Set up first the medical problem that arises from the observation of a malady, and afterwards seek a physiological explanation. To act otherwise would be to risk overlooking the patient, and distorting the malady."[9]

In the first years of his tenure at the Salpêtrière hospital, Charcot's interests evolved from general medicine among the elderly to chronic illnesses affecting all ages. Two large and very loosely defined groups of patients were under Charcot's care: rheumatologic and neurologic. These two fields are considered distinct today, but in the nineteenth century they were seen as related. Working with these two groups, Charcot began to focus his attention on the spinal cord. In the mid-1870s, he started to apply this method to a higher level of the nervous system, the brain. Between 1862 and the mid-1870s, Charcot made the discoveries that established his reputation as the foremost neurologist of his time: the delineation of multiple sclerosis, of amyotrophic lateral sclerosis ("Charcot's disease"), and of locomotor ataxia, with its peculiar arthropathies ("Charcot's joints"), as well as his work on medullar and cerebral localizations. He had considerable success with this method in 1875–1876, when he proved, thanks to refined clinical observations and a precise anatomo-pathology, the role of certain parts of the cortex in movement, giving decisive arguments in favor of motor-cortical localizations in humans (it had been assumed that motor functions were restricted to the lower parts of the brain until then).

Charcot then extended the anatomo-pathological method to the domains of language and of memory, studying aphasia and related disturbances. He was thus led to a conception of the brain as composed of various autonomous areas, each of which has a precise function and whose lesion implies stable symptoms. He saw the areas as interconnected, but this interaction was less important for him than their localization. In continuing his study of diseases of the nervous system, Charcot then arrived at the "great number of morbid states, evidently having their seat in the nervous system, which leave in the dead body no material trace that can be discovered"[10]: the neuroses (*névrose*). These comprised epilepsy, hysteria, chorea, and other morbid states, but hysteria was seen as the most challenging because it was perceived as only an assemblage of odd incoherent phenomena inaccessible to analysis. Charcot was to bring order into this apparent chaos and to insist that hysteria has its laws. In his words: "nothing is left to chance, everything follows definite rules, always the same, whether the case is met with in private or hospital practice, in all countries, all times, all races, in short universally."[11]

Charcot's original model of hysteria was developed from the observation of female patients at the Salpêtrière, one of the major Paris hospitals and a hospice for elderly women, with over five thousand female patients. Charcot spent virtually his entire career at this institution, where he started as an intern in 1848[12] and slowly ascended the medical hierarchy.[13] Charcot did for the diseases of the nervous system what his colleague Paul Broca did for physical anthropology; he was successful in creating a center of international renown, supported by an institutional setting that included the latest technical innovations and a series of publications. Official recognition for the research backed by these innovations arrived in 1882, when the Chair of Clinical Diseases of the Nervous System was created for Charcot at the University of Paris. That same year, at Charcot's request, a new special ward opened at the Salpêtrière, a *Service des hommes*, a twenty-bed ward specifically reserved for men suffering from nervous disorders. Two years later this ward was enlarged to house fifty beds.[14] In this same year, the general wards of the *Service Charcot* at the Clinic for the Maladies of the Nervous System began to accept male patients, who usually presented chronic illness and stayed at the hospital for longer periods of time. Thus, by the first half of the 1880s, Charcot had assembled a significant patient pool for the study of diseases of the nervous system in the male; he published sixty-one case histories of male hysteria alone in the 1880s.[15]

Charcot's first article on hysteria was the case of a female patient, published in 1865 in *L'Union médicale*.[16] As noted, much of Charcot's work on neurological diseases developed through differential diagnosis of clinical symptoms (e.g., tremors in multiple sclerosis or in Parkinson's disease; epileptic vs. hysterical fits, etc.). This first phase of his studies on hysteria culminated in the description of a four-phase hysterical attack, an attack modeled on that of epilepsy, which he labeled hystero-epilepsy, *grande hystérie*, or *hysteria major*. The phases were as follows: (1) epileptoid (tonic seizures often preceded by an aura which rose from the hysterogenic points); (2) *grands mouvements* (contortions and acrobatic postures); (3) *attitudes passionnelles* (emotional gestures and verbalization; often reenacting a traumatic event); and (4) final delirium (dissolution of attack). Besides the attack, hysteria was characterized by the stigmata, or permanent symptoms, and by contractures or paralyses of any part of the body. The stigmata were of two kinds: hysterogenic points[17] and disturbances of sensibility. The latter could be of two kinds, anesthesias or hyperesthesias, that is, lowered or heightened sensibility. Hysterogenic points could be located in any area of the body and could be used, by simple pressure upon them, to provoke or stop an attack already underway. The other classical stigmata were hemi-anesthesias, a loss of sensibility that usually followed the midline of the body rather than anatomical features. Although this complete set of symptoms was rarely present in a single patient, this description was offered as a "type" encompassing the full set of possible symptoms.[18]

This was Charcot's first conceptualization of hysteria, and he continued to develop new models for the neurosis until the end of his life. Charcot moved from a model of hysteria that, although neurological, initially privileged the female, to a nongender-specific model. Charcot started to describe hysteria as a *diathesis*, a disease that is inscribed on the body as a hereditary potentiality that must nonetheless be activated by a trauma (emotional or physical). We find here the first hint of a psychological causation for hysteria, albeit firmly anchored in a material causation. Charcot argued that the traumatic event underwent a period of "unconscious mental elaboration" before manifesting as a symptom. This lag between trauma and symptom marked out hysteria from other possible diagnoses. Despite increasing discussion of psychic factors, Charcot never abandoned an essentially somatic frame of reference and continued to expect that a lesion for hysteria would eventually be found.

After 1880, Charcot began to study male hysteria and to experiment with a variety of therapeutic techniques. As an examination of the career trajectories of Charcot and of his classmate Alfred Vulpian shows, Charcot's lack of credentials in laboratory science was partially responsible for his slow ascension in the medical hierarchy. While Charcot eventually achieved great success through his clinical work, Vulpian, his classmate, early collaborator (they copublished many papers early in their careers) and later rival for faculty positions, had, thanks to his publications in experimental physiology, outdone his friend early on in the competition for a professorship and a more prestigious hospital appointment.[19] Charcot, according to most accounts, started this incursion into experimentation as part of a commission created by the president of the *Société de biologie*, Claude Bernard, to examine the work of another doctor, Victor Burq, on the influence of metals, electricity, and magnets on hysterical and neurological patients.[20] These experiments, which started in 1876, ultimately led to experimenting with hypnosis from 1878 onward. We can see here a shift from classic clinical observation in the wards to physiological experimentation in both wards and amphitheater. Charcot saw this as his entrée into the world of "laboratory" research. This led to the official recognition of his work on hypnosis by the Paris Academy of Science (1882) and to his becoming the recognized authority on the subject.

Charcot believed hypnosis comprised a series of nervous states[21] that needed to be carefully studied and whose full-fledged forms could be found only in hysterical patients. These states could be reduced to three main types: lethargy, catalepsy, and somnambulism.[22] He argued that they could be produced by strictly physical means and could be identified by special physiological signs. Charcot, thus, transformed hypnosis into an artificially induced phenomenon that followed regular, physiological laws and brought law and order to another formerly "chaotic" area of psychology. In addition, hypnosis made it possible to reproduce hysterical symptoms at will, being thus an ideal "experimental" research tool.

Charcot and his Salpêtrière school focused at first on the physical manifestations of hypnotism, the palpable signs of this state. They believed they were applying Claude Bernard's methods to psychology and that for the first time in the history of psychology they were practicing, in Charles Richet's words, "a psychological vivisection." Charcot and his student Paul Richer expressed themselves in the following terms on this subject:

> Between the normal functioning of the organism and the spontaneous troubles caused in it by disease, hypnotism becomes a road open to experimentation. The hypnotic state is an artificial or experimental nervous state, whose multiple manifestations appear or disappear according to the will of the observer and to the needs of his study. Considered in this fashion, hypnotism becomes a precious "mine" to be exploited either by physiologist and psychologist or by the physician.[23]

This way of presenting their work allowed them to identify themselves with the cultural prestige and authority of laboratory science.[24]

Charcot's work on hypnosis opened the way for development of the concept of traumatic hysteria. In his work on hypnosis with female patients, Charcot and his students reproduced or moved certain hysterical symptoms from one part of the body to another, or even made them disappear (this was modeled on the "transfer" of symptoms first discovered while experimenting with the application of metal plaques to the patient's skin). Charcot worked mostly in what he classified as the most basic, simplest phases of hypnosis: the lethargic and cataleptic states. The lethargic state was defined as a physiological state of deep sleep in which the body of the hypnotized person remained limp and the skin was analgesic. Its characteristic physical manifestation was "neuro-muscular hyperexcitability," through which this state was recognized and defined. This phenomenon occurred when a muscle was excited by pressing or rubbing lightly on the skin: a contraction of the underlying muscle took place immediately, as if an electric current had been applied to the muscle. If the excitement of the muscles was prolonged, they remained in a permanent contraction, which persisted after the subject was out of the hypnotic trance, becoming an "artificially induced" hysterical symptom.

Charcot considered the lethargic state as a state in which consciousness was entirely abolished because the higher mental functions of the brain were inactive. Only the spinal cord was "still alive;" in fact, it lived with increased intensity. Joseph Babinski, one of Charcot's favorite students, wrote that " neuro-muscular hyper-excitability has been considered [by the school of the Salpêtrière] as a reflex phenomenon whose center is in the spine . . . and whose starting point is in the peripheral excitation of the muscles."[25] These contractures were, therefore, conceived as reflex phenomena.

The cataleptic state was characterized by "cataleptic plasticity." The subject was immobilized like a statue. The limbs, however, were not stiff, and maintained for long periods of time any position they were pushed into. There was complete anesthesia, but the senses remained partially active. The cataleptic phase, considered as an intermediary between lethargy and somnambulism, was the "supreme degree of automatism." That is, in the state of catalepsy, the subject was supposed to be using nervous associations that through use had become unconscious, part of his or her organic memory. Charcot wrote:

> Here, as in the preceding phase [lethargic], there is mental inertia, but it is less profound, less absolute; it has become possible, indeed, to produce a sort of partial waking of the organ of the psychic faculties. Thus, one can call into existence an idea, or a group of ideas connected together by previous associations. But this group set in action will remain strictly limited. There will be no propagation, no diffusion of the communicated movement; all the rest will remain asleep. Consequently the idea, or group of ideas suggested, are met with in a state of isolation, free from the control of that large collection of personal ideas long accumulated and organized, which constitute the consciousness properly so-called, the *ego* [*moi*]. It is for this reason that the movements that represent the acts of unconscious cerebration externally are distinguished by their automatic and purely mechanical character. Then it is truly that we see before us the *human machine* [*l'homme machine*] in all its simplicity, dreamt of by De la Mettrie.[26]

The physical manifestations of each hypnotic state, being theoretically impossible to simulate, empirically demonstrated that the subject had, in fact, entered the state in question. If lethargy was a state in which only reflex medullar activity took place, patients could not pretend, for they were in a state where they had no control over their own actions. Everything was determined by the human physiological constitution. The same was true of catalepsy. "Secondary automatisms" were nervous associations made unconscious by habit, and they came into action in catalepsy. But this "unconscious" was no less organically determined that reflex action. In fact, subjects could not act in any other way, as their powers of inhibition were inert. They could only repeat actions that their bodies had performed thousands of time and that had become "engraved" in their nerve cells. Charcot thought that changes in the conditions of the muscles, variations in reflexes, and modifications of sensation were symptoms that could not be counterfeited. As he put it in 1877:

> A woman who retains a contractured limb for eight years is not a woman who is simulating; a woman who allows her arm to be pierced through [transpercer] without feeling anything is perfectly anesthetic; furthermore, the facts of absolute hemi-anesthesia are beyond all skepticism.[27]

There was a clear evolutionary crescendo in the conception of hypnotic stages or phases: from reflex, to automatism, to "semi-automatism;" from lethargy, to catalepsy, to somnambulism; from simple to complex; from organic to psychic; and from more organized to less organized. Charcot's work, thus, seemed to be "factually" demonstrating the existence of a continuum between conscious and absolutely unconscious states made of different degrees of consciousness, and, at the same time, to be displaying the hierarchy of function of the nervous system (spine, brain stem, cortex).

As mentioned earlier, Charcot's work on hypnotism opened the way for a more psychological conception of the development of hysterical symptoms. Charcot hypothesized that when hysterical patients underwent a traumatic event, whether physical or emotional, they tended to enter an alternate state of consciousness, similar to the lethargic state, during which their paralyses and contractures were developed through neuro-muscular hyperexcitability. Even if lightly struck on a part of the body, the special state of excitability would allow these small traumas to be converted into major paralyses and contractures. This helped explain the lack of proportion between the gravity of the traumatic event and the gravity of the hysterical symptom. Charcot was able to reproduce this process in his public lectures, thus demonstrating the plausibility of his theory, "making it visible," as it were and highlighting the absolute identity of the symptomatology obtained by completely different means (actual physical or emotional trauma, however minor, vs. hypnotic experimentation). This traumatic theory, as we will see, was further developed with the study of male hysterics.

The picture of hysteria that emerges from Charcot's collected works is, generally speaking, similar for male and female patients. In both sexes, the disorder was a hereditary-degenerative malady of the nervous system with an extensive symptomatology, a varying pattern of evolution, and a largely unfavorable prognosis. The overt symptoms might disappear, but the diathesis, revealed by the stigmata, rarely did, leaving the patients vulnerable to repeated symptom formation given any perturbing incident. Charcot often insisted on the essential equivalence of hysteria in the two sexes. The claim was controversial, and medical specialists were divided on this issue. As discussed earlier, a significant part of the nineteenth-century medical profession linked hysteria conceptually to the female reproductive organs. In offering a neurological etiology of the disease, Charcot challenged the existing gynecological models of the disorder, many of which advocated radical surgery as a cure: ovariotomies were the most up-to-date versions of this treatment, but hysterectomies were also common between 1875 and 1885.[28]

Throughout his writings on the subject, Charcot was concerned with establishing the reality and frequency of hysteria in the male, defining his theory in opposition to earlier, nonneurological models of the disorder. Thus, in 1888, he wrote:

> . . . words, and particularly words in medical nosography, mean nothing except as symbols. . . . Get yourself into the habit of thinking . . . that in itself the word hysteria signifies nothing, and little by little, you will get used to speaking of hysteria in men without thinking in the least of "the uterus."[29]

It was necessary to break with the history and etymology of the disease to accept male hysteria. In modernizing the male hysteria diagnosis, Charcot rejected a number of characterizations of the condition, which he presented as outdated stereotypes—for example: that the disorder was restricted to boys at the age of puberty, that it existed solely in the leisured upper classes of society, or that it occurred only in effeminate or homosexual men.

In his earliest published lectures on male hysteria, Charcot asked his audience repeatedly, "Hysteria thus exists in men?"[30] "Can hysteria develop in men?"[31] in order to affirm the equivalence of the condition in both sexes. This was obviously a strong argument in favor of a neurological causation for this disease, in opposition to a gynecological one. Although men lacked one of the common hysterogenic points present in women—"ovarie," an irritation of the ovary region that could provoke and stop attacks—they had equivalent areas in the testicles, especially if these manifested any abnormality. In some cases, Charcot and his students even argued that their male patients presented "pseudo-ovarian zones" in the area of the abdomen corresponding to the position of the ovaries in the female body, which could act as hysterogenic points.[32] Gauchet and Swain have suggested that there is a paradoxical aspect in this emphasis on ovarian and testicular signs of the disease while at the same time arguing for a neurological etiology,[33] but I disagree: the existence of these points helps Charcot explain how it was possible for a sexually based etiology to have been and still be persistently held, despite being incorrect— rendering his fellow medical practitioners' mistaken views comprehensible while serving to highlight Charcot's greater clinical acumen.

However, while similarities abound, Charcot's cases of male hysteria have characteristics that separate them, on average, from female hysteria. Charcot took pains to point out that *grande hystérie* in its most complete form was to be found in the male and that men presented all the typical stigmata of the disease. However, most cases of male hysteria were cases of "traumatic hysteria,"[34] mostly monosymp- tomatic, with extremely persistent symptoms. Over a third of his male patients exhibited no attack at all, and in the cases that presented the full-blown hysterical attack, the four phases were somewhat different in males. The most intense phases tended to be the first two, the epileptoid and the *grand mouvements*—the latter characterized by striking and stylized postures, such as the arched pelvis position (*opisthotonus*). These often required considerable muscular strength. Less preva- lent in the men was the third phase of *attitudes passionnelles*, characterized by the hallucinatory reenactment of emotional scenes from the patient's past, although a number of male patients did suffer violent hallucinations in which they were attacked by animals or humans during this phase. In male patients the range of emotions manifested in this phase was noticeably narrower and tended toward the sad, depressive end of the emotional spectrum. As Micale has pointed out, in a substantial number of cases (41 percent) this stage was absent altogether.[35]

Male cases were, in general, emotionally muted compared to the female cases. When comparing the general psychic state of the two sexes, Charcot pointed out that male hysterics do not present the capricious and volatile changes of humor and personality that are habitually present in female patients and often regarded as characteristic of hysterics. This characterization, however, was inaccurate, even for female patients. Charcot argued that although more male patients are depressed and melancholic, this could also be the case in female hysterics: *la donna è mobile*, but not always.

Yet hysteria was defined at the Salpêtrière as the illness of excess. Hysterical patients were almost never in a normal state: either their organs were too active or, on the contrary, their functions were diminished to the point of being seemingly suppressed. As Charcot's students wrote in 1879–1880:

> It is thus that the desire to eat can be exaggerated (bulimia) or practically null (abstinence), a persistent constipation will be followed by diarrhea, poly-uria will be followed by a more or less complete ischuria; that in an anes-thetic patient points will be found where the sensibility is considerably exalted (hyperaesthesia); it is thus, furthermore, that the depression of the intellectual faculties will follow their exaltation.[36]

These oscillations between extreme symptoms were explained by the sudden transference or withdrawal of nervous excitation from the corresponding part of the cerebral cortex. Contractures and paralyses of the limbs, of the larynx (depriv-ing them of speech), and of internal organs (depriving them of specific functions) appeared and disappeared frequently.

In men, the permanent symptoms of hysteria were particularly tenacious and resistant to treatment. After working with men, Charcot would qualify the image of the female hysteric as constantly changing:

> In the male, . . . the disease presents itself often as an affection remarkable for the permanence and tenacity of the symptoms that characterize it. In woman, on the contrary—and that is without a doubt what seems to make the crucial difference between the sexes for those who do not know the illness well in women—what is *thought* to be the characteristic trait of hysteria is its insta-bility, the mobility of its symptoms.[37]

This mobility was not an omnipresent characteristic, as those who, like Charcot, knew the ailment in depth were aware. Nevertheless, the contrast between sta-bility and instability as corresponding to male and female patients is roughly accurate.

The majority of Charcot's male patients were working-class men: masons, train engineers, bakers, locksmiths, factory workers. They were, that is, either laborers in the new, large-scale, mechanized industries or members of the tra-ditional artisanal class. The following are some examples of how they were described: "a vigorous man, a blacksmith of 35 years of age, married, and the father of several children"[38]; "Rig-, . . . a big man, strong and well-developed; he was for-merly a cooper and stood hard work without fatigue . . . has had nine children"[39]; "Gui . . ., age 27, working as a locksmith. . . . He has shown himself, in his pro-fession, skillful and intelligent. He has even obtained, several times, in locksmith competitions, medals for his work."[40] There is a noticeable emphasis on the capac-ity for hard work and the good work ethics of the patients before contracting their ailment. As Michèle Ouerd has highlighted, it was specifically the inability of these patients to *work* due to their nervous disabilities that defined them as sick in the eyes of their physicians and led to their diagnosis and hospitalization.[41] It has been widely recognized that masculinity became increasingly connected to work in the nineteenth century as the advent of heavy industry led to certain sectors being monopolized by men: mining, construction, railroads, and large machine factory work in particular.

Charcot's female patients were also mostly working class: seamstresses, washing-women, maids, and flower-sellers.[42] This was partly a result of the setting of his research: the Salpêtrière was a free municipal hospital that drew much of its population from the lower classes. Nonetheless, as a few printed cases indicate, such as those of the 17-year-old boy from Moscow and the 13-year-old from southern Russia,[43] individuals traveled from afar to consult with the world-famous neurologist, and Charcot does occasionally allude to his middle-class (if not to his bourgeois) patients.

Micale has argued that while Charcot does not seem to have made any conceptual cut between upper- and lower-class hysterical women, he used the diagnostic category of neurasthenia for upper-class patients in his private practice who presented symptoms very similar to those he diagnosed as male hysteria in his hospital patients. Neurasthenia was assumed to result, in a large number of cases, from intellectual overwork.[44] By labeling his private patients neurasthenics, Micale argues, Charcot associated them with a disease linked to the higher mental faculties (rather than to the lower, reflex and automatic ones) and to the stressful conditions of modern, civilized life. The diagnosis also had a more hopeful prognosis than that of hysteria and was less offensive to patients' sensibilities. Interestingly, Micale, who keeps careful count of a variety of characteristics of Salpêtrière male hysterics, fails to mention the existence of several cases of hystero-neurasthenia among Charcot's published cases. It could be argued that their number is not sufficiently significant, but certain of their characteristics seem to me worthy of attention, and I return to these cases later.

As was highlighted earlier, the diagnosis of male hysteria was controversial among segments of the medical profession. Charcot's construct conflicted not only with gynecological or obstetrical models of the disease (also espoused by some alienists) but also with other conceptions of traumatic nervous disease. Railway travel and accidents gave rise to what many surgeons considered as a novel spinal ailment. Further study led some to theorize that the brain, not the spine, was the source of this disorder. Eventually a mind-centered theory of the condition was developed.[45] These ailments were known as "railway spine" or "railway brain." Charcot rejected this purported new disease of the nervous system, reinterpreting these cases as male hysteria, in some cases combined with neurasthenia. Charcot also rejected the work of the German authors Oppenheim and Thomsen, who postulated a new special disease entity due to the shock received during train collisions. Through detailed clinical analysis, Charcot argued that all the traits found in these traumatic cases could also be found in similar cases of female hysteria and that, therefore, the claim to novelty in the male cases was spurious and due to inadequate observation and prejudices regarding hysteria. He noted that the effect of trauma, especially of the terror experienced during accidents that threatened the patients with very serious injury, operated in ways that had not yet been fully explored and produced symptoms often more severe than those due to an organic lesion.

Charcot then went on to develop a theory of traumatic hysteria, which he demonstrated, step by step, in the case studies of two male patients diagnosed with hysterical brachial monoplegia, Pin— and Porcz—. Pin—, age 18, a mason by trade, fell from a height of about 6.5 feet. He was unconscious for a few minutes and was then carried home, where he discovered some slight contusions, which did not interfere with the use of the affected parts. Two days later, he found that his upper extremity had become feeble and consulted a doctor, who diagnosed a paresis of all the movements of the left arm, with anesthesia of the limb. The motor paralysis of the left extremity became complete, and it was in this state that he entered the Salpêtrière, 10 months after the accident. Porcz—, a carriage driver age 25, fell off his carriage. He did not lose consciousness and was able to return to work almost immediately. He felt some pain in his arm but no bruising. Six days after the accident, he found on awakening that his right superior extremity was flaccid and incapable of all movement. The two cases are held to be virtually identical by Charcot, who writes: "Between the case of Pin— and that of Porcz— the presence of hysterogenic points in the former constitutes the sole difference; in all other respects they are identical."[46]

After describing the cases in great detail, Charcot considered therapy. Treatment would be more effective, he argued, if we could recognize, at least in part, the mechanism of the production of traumatic hysterical paralysis. "Evidently, this is a subject that would gain in clearness and precision if it could be submitted to experimental investigation."[47] And so it could; thanks to his work on "the science of hypnotic neuroses," he could now call upon the aid of experimentation. Returning to his earlier work on hypnosis, Charcot reviewed the now "notorious fact" that it was possible to originate by the method of suggestion an idea, or a coherent group of associated ideas, which "possess the individual, remain isolated, and manifest themselves by corresponding motor phenomena."[48] So, if the idea of paralysis was suggested, a real paralysis ensued, and one could see it manifest itself in the same way as that arising from a lesion to the cerebral substance. He then called in a female hysterical patient, Greuz—, who "has been subjected only four or five times to the influence of hypnotism," which meant no training was involved, and he proceeded to suggest to her verbally, under hypnosis, that her right hand was paralyzed. After a few minutes the patient developed a paralysis that was in all ways analogous to those of Pin— and Porcz—. Upon examination, the observers

. . . will at once recognize that the clinical characters are exactly those disclosed in our patient Pin— when he entered our wards, and which now exist in the case of Porcz—, with the sole difference, evidently of a secondary order, that in the latter motion and sensibility are preserved in the fingers.[49]

There is a further difference, however—a difference Charcot addresses in his next clinical lecture: the mode of production of the paralysis. The two male patients received a more or less violent blow to their shoulder; the hypnotized female received a suggestion[50] by speech. But Charcot was able to make this apparently important difference disappear. He caused Greuz—'s paralysis "*not now by means of a verbal injunction, but through an agency analogous to that which occasioned the monoplegia both in the case of Pin— and Porcz—, viz. a shock applied to the posterior part of the shoulder,* by sharply, yet not very forcibly, striking this region with the palm of the hand."[51] The paralysis thus obtained was in all ways identical to that of the male patients.

While the two men were not in a hypnotic sleep at the moment of their accidents (falls from a window and a carriage, respectively), nor later, when the paralysis was established (as we have seen, there was a time lag in both cases between accident and symptom formation), Charcot suggests that the nervous shock experienced at the moment of the accident can be considered equivalent "in a certain measure," in subjects predisposed such as Pin— and Porcz— to the cerebral condition that is produced in hysterics by hypnotism. Thus the blow to the shoulder received by the two male patients caused, as did the strike with the hand in the female patient, the idea of motor paralysis of the member. But because of the annihilation of the ego (*moi*) produced by the cataleptic state of hypnotism in one case and by the nervous shock in the two others, "that idea once installed in the brain takes sole possession and acquires sufficient domination to realize itself objectively in the form of paralysis. The sensation in question . . . in both the cases plays the part of a veritable suggestion."[52] After a short discussion of hysterical patients capable of receiving suggestions in a waking state (which further increases the analogy with the male cases), Charcot concluded his demonstration by stating "I do not believe that in any experimental physiologico-pathological research whatsoever it is possible to reproduce artificially with more fidelity an affection which one desires to study and investigate."[53] As in a classic laboratory experiment, Charcot was able to reproduce the disease entity he was studying, thus revealing the mechanism of its formation. He could make and unmake hysterical symptoms—and this seemed to demonstrate the validity of his neuro-psychological theory of their development. As Gilman has argued in relation to images of the hysteric, a basic assumption of the definition of a positivistic disease entity at the close of the nineteenth-century is that disease is real only if it is universal, and it is universal only if it can be seen and the act of seeing reproduced. "This latter axiom is rarely stated (except by the head of the Salpêtrière photographic service, Albert Londe), but it is assumed."[54]

We now return to the issue of predisposition raised by the case studies just examined. As mentioned earlier, Charcot believed there was a hysterical diathesis, a hereditary predisposition that had to be activated by an emotional or physical trauma. Charcot sought predisposing conditions both in the heredity and in the life story of each of his patients. Most of the male hysterics examined had tainted family trees or habits that weakened their constitution, such as alcoholism or sexual excesses (masturbation or "irresistible impulses towards women"). But even in cases where the men had been healthy and robust, with no bad habits or abnormal relatives, Charcot argued that the nervous shock could suppress the patient's will, judgment and mental spontaneity, as was the case in the hypnotic state. In case after case of traumatic hysteria, he highlighted the stupor that overtakes the patients after their accident, the mental depression and the depression of the will.[55] Rig—, for example, despite being intelligent and relatively well educated for his station, "cannot focus on anything and takes up and abandons five or six occupations almost at once."[56] Gil— remains in a "kind of stupor," which renders him incapable of working or even of reading with any continuity.[57] Greff— suffers from "great cerebral torpor: his memory is weakened . . . impossibility of concentrating his ideas."[58]

While mental depression was common to most male traumatic hysterics, some of their symptoms, as in the case of Greff— are attributed to neurasthenia. Charcot describes a specific kind of headache as a classic symptom of this state, a kind of "helmet" that compresses the front and back of the head: it is constant, permanent and is exacerbated by any effort on the part of the patient to "use his intelligence." This is often allied to digestive problems. Charcot writes:

> When we speak today of neurasthenia or male hysteria, it still seems that we almost exclusively have in mind the man of the privileged classes, sated by culture, exhausted by the abuse of pleasures, by business concerns or by an excess of intellectual labor. This is a prejudice I have often made an effort to combat, but no doubt it will be necessary to fight it for a long time still, for it appears far from being eradicated. It has been perfectly well established, however, that these same disorders, at least in cities, may be observed on a large scale among the proletarians, among those artisans less favored by fate, among those who know little other than physical labor.[59]

This claim brings upper- and lower-class men together in the similarity of their condition, rather than distinguishing between them. When discussing the case of V. . .lois, a former soldier and train conductor, Charcot addressed the issue of the different causation of neurasthenia in the two classes (nervous shock vs. intellectual depletion):

> Perhaps you may think, Messieurs, that the disorders produced by *nervous shock* in a robust man, who exercises the function of chief conductor, should differ in some way from those determined by analogous circumstances in a

cultivated man who lives on things of the mind [choses de l'esprit], in a doctor, for example. And yet, if you can believe it, Messieurs, I can set you right
on this matter by citing the example of one of my friends, a medical doctor,
who, as a result of a railway accident (collision of trains) of which he was
a victim in England, presented symptoms that were entirely comparable, at
least in their fundamental traits, to those which we have just described, and,
in consequence, for more than two years was absolutely incapable of exercising his profession.[60]

Earlier in the text, Charcot had highlighted the fact that very different causes produced the same result: "Here it wasn't intellectual effort or grief [chagrin] that
was involved; the disease was produced as a consequence of a nervous shock, of
a sudden disturbance and it is interesting to see the same result determined by
such *apparently* different causes."[61] Returning to the topic in a later lesson, Charcot
once again stated the equivalence of the neurasthenic symptoms acquired through
intellectual overwork, as for example in young students cramming for an exam,[62]
and those of male hystero-neurasthenics. The latter etiological factors acted slowly,
and nervous shock acted suddenly, but the results were entirely the same. Given a
hereditary predisposition the nervous depletion could be produced gradually (as
in intellectual overwork) or suddenly (as in a work-related accident). The "morbid species" stayed the same; what changed was the *agent provocateur*.[63] In conclusion, after comparing four cases of hystero-neurasthenia, Charcot wrote: "the
nosographic form remains stable while the occasional causes vary."[64] This conclusion is entirely consistent with his argument that although hypnotic suggestion
and trauma or nervous shock are not "the same" causally, they determine the exact
same morbid phenomena.

In a return to the case of Porcz—, Charcot, while discussing therapeutic
options for hystero-traumatic patients, writes:

> The patients are *generally more or less neurasthenic and anemic*, they eat little.
> Almost all of them, in other words, are weakened or in a mediocre state of
> health at the time when the hysterical phenomena, which we have been led to
> consider of mental or psychic origin, . . . develop.[65]

Given the evidence just offered, it is clear that the relationship between Charcot's
upper- and lower-class patients is more complex than it might initially appear.
While Charcot may have preferred to label his private male patients as neurasthenic, he also extended this categorization to his working-class patients and
even hypothesized that hystero-neurasthenics were frequently found in the population of hospitals and potentially among beggars and vagrants (i.e., men of
even lower social strata than the working-class patients thus far discussed). He
did admit that he had insufficient data for this hypothesis but nonetheless suggested "hystero-neurasthenia may be truly frequent among the *misérables*, those
in rags [loqueteux], those vagrants who frequent, in turn, prisons, flophouses and

poorhouses."[66] Of course, the fact that special pleading was necessary to make the case that both upper- and lower-class men suffered from neurasthenia and the added fact that most of the working-class cases were not pure cases of neurasthenia but combined cases of hystero-neurasthenia highlighted that a class difference was being, to some extent, undermined and potentially resisted. Nonetheless, in the same way that it can be argued that broadly "the account of hysteria that emerges from Charcot's collected writings is similar for male and female patients,"[67] the same can be said regarding class differences among male patients.

It could also be said that while Charcot avoided branding male hysterics as effeminate in one respect, since they were portrayed as big, strong, sexually active working men, he nevertheless conceptually feminized them by distinctly associating hysteria and hypnosis to the lower mental functions. Male and female hysterics were brought together by their closeness to "animality," their proximity to and therefore easier relapse into the lower mental functions. Closer to nature than upper-class men, hysterical men are closely linked to women, who have traditionally been linked to nature through the biological processes of childbearing.

Hysterical men thus lie between hysterical women and the ideal of the normal man. The stability typical of their symptoms draws them closer to the ideal of the Victorian bourgeois man, supposedly characterized by emotional stability, while hysteria and susceptibility to hypnosis brings them closer to women. That hysteria was regarded as a relapse to an inferior psychical state has not been given sufficient theoretical importance.

Pierre Janet, who obtained his medical degree with Charcot and eventually held the chair of psychology at the Collège de France, developed a theory of hysteria that argued that what lay at the center of the ailment was a splitting of consciousness that rested on an innate psychological weakness (*insuffisance psychologique*). Hysteria was, according to him, a *maladie par faiblesse* (disease due to weakness), and it developed most readily when an innately weak mind was submitted to influences that weakened it still further or was faced with heavy demands in relation to which its weakness stood out still more. Thus Janet regarded a particular form of congenital mental weakness as the disposition to hysteria; hysteria was, thus, almost a form of feeble-mindedness.[68]

As Millam and Nye recently argued, social constructions of masculinity function simultaneously as foils for femininity and as methods of differentiating between "kinds" of men.[69] Elite men, they note, tend to be treated as belonging to an unmarked social category. And yet, in making hysteria male, Charcot and his students were not only defining lower-class masculinity but also specifying their own gender characteristics and, in particular, their "scientific masculinity," the traits that legitimized their self-presentation, and Charcot's in particular, as heroic clinical observers and research scientists, boldly rejecting prejudices and spreading scientific objectivity.

By focusing on the nervous system as the origin of the disease, Charcot was led to see it as a unity: the disease is one, despite gendered and class presentations, because the nervous system is common to male and female. Hysteria manifests differently in the male and female body and in the upper- and lower-class male, but these differences are not nosographical but etiological and have to do with the different life conditions of the subjects. Working-class men, he tells us, have the same psychological constitution as men of the privileged classes,[70] but they are exposed more intensely to

> the perturbing consequences of painful moral emotions, to the anxiety attached to the difficulties of life, to the depressive influence of the exaggerated role of physical forces, etc.; not to mention the nervous shock produced by the great accidents to which they are particularly exposed or the professional intoxications whose pathological role is starting to be adequately appreciated only recently. One must not forget, furthermore, that nervous heredity is not the exclusive privilege of the great of this earth; it exercises its empire over the working class as it does elsewhere.[71]

Working-class women did not suffer accidents of the same kind, nor as often, because of their different working environments. Women were often exposed to sexual violence; several of Charcot's female patients reported rape or rape attempts by their employers, something entirely absent from the male cases. In the same way, working-class patients—or even more so, those of even lower social strata— might have a particularly tainted hereditary background (as exposure to adverse life conditions or intoxicants tended to exacerbate degenerative tendencies over time) and thus a higher tendency to hysteria, but the underlying disease was conceived as a stable, universal, and timeless entity and the differences between different types of patients as superficial or irrelevant. Charcot strove to identify the same disease entity underneath all the variations: what does not change is what counts as real. Beneath the bewildering variety of hysterical symptoms, he created order: a fixed entity. That this entity held together for about two decades—that fact became artifact—should not lead us to underestimate the accomplishment.

Notes

1. Mark S. Micale, *Hysterical Men: The Hidden History of Male Nervous Illness* (Cambridge, MA: Harvard University Press, 2008), 5. Almost identical statements can be found throughout the literature. For example: "Hysteria is one of the oldest disease entities in the canon of Western medicine. The Hippocratic school identified it in the fifth century BC. and gave it its graphic name, etymologically derived from the Greek for 'uterus' "; in Jan Goldstein, "The Hysteria Diagnosis and the Politics of Anticlericalism in late Nineteenth-Century France," *The Journal of Modern History* 54.2 (1982), 210. Another example: "Hysteria, both as a word and as a neurosis, carries with it unusually heavy cultural baggage. One of the oldest identified mental disorders . . . and named in ancient Greece by Hippocrates"; in Martha Noel Evans, *Fits and Starts: A Genealogy of Hysteria in Modern France* (Ithaca, NY: Cornell University Press, 1991), 1.

2. See Helen King's fascinating article, "Once upon a Text: Hysteria from Hippocrates," in *Hysteria Beyond Freud* in Sander Gilman et al., eds., (Berkeley: University of California Press, 1993). Not only which texts were selected but also how they were interpreted changed over time. Layers of history need to be peeled back to reveal the construction of the nineteenth-century entity.

3. Sabine Arnaud, *On Hysteria: The Invention of a Medical Category between 1670 & 1820* (Chicago: University of Chicago Press, 2015).

4. Micale, *Hysterical Men*, 96.

5. As Bruno Latour has argued, retrojecting a scientific fact into the past and making it "always already there" is part of the process of establishing a scientific fact. On the particular historicity of science, see Bruno Latour, "The Historicity of Things: Where Were Microbes before Pasteur?" in Bruno Latour, *Pandora's Hope: Essays on the Reality of Science Studies* (Cambridge, MA: Harvard University Press, 1999), 145–173.

6. The aesthetic and pathological reinterpretation of religious phenomena (possession, ecstasy, and miracle, most prominently) has been analyzed by Georges Didi-Huberman and P. Fédida in their reprint of Jean-Martin Charcot and Paul Richer's *Les démoniaques dans l'art* (Paris: Macula, 1984). See also Goldstein, "The Hysteria Diagnosis. . .," on the anticlerical agenda of Charcot's group.

7. Marcel Gauchet and Gladys Swain, *Le vrai Charcot: les chemins imprévus de l'inconscient* (Paris: Calmann-Lévy, 1997), 7, 15–17.

8. See Edwin Clark and L. S. Jacyna, *Nineteenth-Century Origins of Neuroscientific Concepts* (Berkeley: University of California Press, 1987).

9. Jean-Martin Charcot, *Clinical Lectures on Diseases of the Nervous System* (London: Tavistock/Routledge, 1991), 8. Jean-Martin Charcot, *Leçons sur les maladies du système nerveux faites à la Salpêtrière*, t. III, (hereafter LMSN) (Paris: Progrès Médical/Delahaye & E. Lecrosnier, 1887), 9. I am using the 1991 English translation but also giving the reference to the French original.

10. Charcot, *Clinical Lectures*, 12 and LMSN, 14. See note 9.

11. Charcot, *Clinical Lectures*, 13 and LMSN, 15.

12. Christopher Goetz, Michael Bonduelle, and Toby Gelfand, *Charcot: Constructing Neurology* (New York: Oxford University Press, 1995), 16.

13. As Swain points out, the Salpêtrière was not a very prestigious hospital when Charcot decided to develop his career there. The summit of the hierarchy was the Hôtel-Dieu, and some of Charcot's classmates, like Vulpian, quickly left the Salpêtrière for more prestigious institutions. Charcot, on the contrary, made the hospital he had chosen a prestigious institution in his chosen field. Gauchet and Swain, *Le vrai Charcot*, 23–24.

14. Mark S. Micale, "Charcot and the Idea of Hysteria in the Male: Gender, Mental Science, and Medical Diagnosis in Late Nineteenth-Century France," *Medical History* 34 (1990), 372.

15. Considering both published sources and manuscript materials at the Bibliothèque Charcot, information exists on over 90 male patients Charcot classified as hysterics. See Micale, *Hysterical Men*, 122–123.

16. Jean-Martin Charcot, "Sclérose des cordons latéraux de la moelle épinière chez une femme hystérique, atteinte de contracture permanente des quatre membres," *L'Union médicale* (mars-avril 1865), 451–457, 467–472.

17. It is significant that Charcot's hysterogenic points are analogous to the epileptogenic points detected experimentally by the physiologist Charles-Édouard Brown-Séquard in his guinea pigs, as Charcot explicitly states in *Oeuvres completes* (hereafter *OC*), IX, lesson 7, 281–282: "these are hysterogenic points analogous to the epileptogenic points in Brown-Séquard's guinea pig."

18. See Charcot's student's visual representation of all possibilities of the hysterical attack in table V in Paul Richer, *Études cliniques sur la grande hystérie ou hystero-épilepsie* (Paris: Delahaye & Lecrosnier, 1881). Also reproduced in Georges Didi-Huberman, *L'invention de l'hystérie: Charcot et Iconographie photographique de la Salpêtrière* (Paris: Macula, 1982), 114–115.

19. See Christopher Goetz, Michael Bonduelle, and Toby Gelfand, *Charcot: Constructing Neurology* (Oxford: Oxford University Press, 1995), 40–48, "The Failed Bid for a Professorship: 1866–1867," for a comparison of Charcot's trajectory to that of his close friend and colleague Vulpian.

20. See the work of Anne Harrington on this subject: "Metals and Magnets in Medicine: Hysteria, Hypnosis and Medical Culture in *fin-de-siècle* Paris," *Psychological Medicine* 18 (1988), 21–38, and "Hysteria, Hypnosis and the Lure of the Invisible: The Rise of Neo-Mesmerism in *fin-de-siècle* Psychiatry," in William F. Bynum, Roy Porter and Michael Shepherd, eds., *The Anatomy of Madness: Essays in the History of Psychiatry*, vol. III (London: Routledge, 1988), 226–246.

21. Charcot, *OC*, IX, 432: "C'est qu'en réalité l'hypnotisme comprend une longue série d'états nerveux très divers, différents les uns des autres, qu'il faut au préalable s'attacher, suivant l'exemple des nosographes, à bien délimiter et à bien définir."

22. Charcot, *OC*, IX, 435.

23. Charcot, *OC*, IX, 310.

24. George Weisz, *The Medical Mandarins: The French Academy of Medicine in the Nineteenth and Early Twentieth Centuries* (Oxford: Oxford University Press, 1995), 289.

25. Charcot, *OC*, IX, "Appendice," 526.

26. Charcot, LMSN, 337. The translation is from Charcot, *Clinical Lectures*, 290.

27. Charcot, *OC*, IX, 223.

28. Lawrence D. Longo, "The Rise and Fall of Battey's Operation: A Fashion in Surgery," *Bulletin of the History of Medicine* 53 (1979), 244–267.

29. Jean-Martin Charcot, *Leçons du mardi à la Salpêtrière. Policlinique 1888–1889* (hereafter LM) (Paris: Progrès médicale/Delahaye & Lecrosnier, 1888–1889), lesson 2, (October 30, 1888), 37.

30. Charcot, *OC*, III, 89.

31. Charcot, *OC*, III, 114.

32. Charcot, LM, lesson 19, pp. 454, 456; and Gilles de la Tourette, *Traité Clinique et thérapeutique de l'hystérie d'après l'enseignement de la Salpêtrière*, (Paris: Plon, Nourrit & Cie., 1891), vol. 1, 299–300.

33. Gauchet and Swain, *Le vrai Charcot*.

34. Charcot combined male hysteria and traumatic neurosis, not usually associated with hysteria, to create a new entity: traumatic male hysteria.

35. Micale, "Charcot and the Idea of Hysteria in the Male," 408.

36. Désiré-Magloire Bourneville and Paul Régnard, *Iconographie photographique de la Salpêtrière*, III (Paris: Progrès Médical/Delahaye & Lecrosnier, 1879–1880), 3.

37. Jean-Martin Charcot, *OC*, III, 252.

38. Charcot, *OC*, III, 93.

39. Charcot, *OC*, III, 257.

40. Charcot, *OC*, III, 269–70.

41. Michèle Ouerd (ed.), *Leçons sur l'hystérie virile* (Paris: Le Sycomore, 1984), Introduction, 21.

42. Goldstein, "The Hysteria Diagnosis. . . ."

43. Discussed in Charcot, *Clinical Lectures*, 77 and 80; LMSN, 89 and 92.

44. For a more detailed analysis of neurasthenia, see Francis George Gosling, *Before Freud: Neurasthenia and the American Medical Community* (Urbana: University of Illinois Press, 1987). For an analysis in terms of gender, see Elaine Showalter, "Hysteria, Feminism, and Gender," in Gilman et al., eds., *Hysteria Beyond Freud*, 294–298.

45. See Eric Michael Caplan, "Trains, Brains, and Sprains: Railway Spine and the Origins of Psychoneuroses," *Bulletin of the History of Medicine* 69 (1995), 387–419.

46. Charcot, *Clinical Lectures*, 286–7, LMSN, 333.

47. Charcot, *Clinical Lectures*, 289, LMSN, 336.

48. Charcot, *Clinical Lectures*, 289; LMSN 336.

49. Charcot, *Clinical Lectures*, 295, LMSN, 343.

50. In hypnotism, suggestion is the insinuation of a belief or impulse into the mind of a subject by words, gestures, or the like.

51. Charcot, *Clinical Lectures*, 304; LMSN, 354. Emphasis in original.

52. Charcot, *Clinical Lectures*, 305; LMSN, 355–356. I have restored the emphasis of the original French (not that of the English translation).

53. Charcot, *Clinical Lectures*, 307; LMSN, 358.

54. Gilman, "The Image of the Hysteric," in Gilman et al., eds., *Hysteria Beyond Freud*, 379.

55. For example, in the case of Gil. . ., Charcot, LMSN, 18th Lesson; Greff. . . LM, I, 12th lesson, after the accident "grande torpeur cérébrale"; Rig. . ., LMSN, 18th lesson; V. . .lois, LM I, 8th lesson, incapable of any prolonged "acte intellectuel."

56. Ouerd, *Leçons sur l'hystérie virile*, 44; Charcot, LMSN, 261.

57. Ouerd, *Leçons sur l'hystérie virile*, 47; Charcot, LMSN, 265.

58. Ouerd, *Leçons sur l'hystérie virile,* 209; Charcot, LM, 265.

59. Ouerd, *Leçons sur l'hystérie virile,* 201; Charcot, LM, 256.

60. Ouerd, *Leçons sur l'hystérie virile,* 188; Charcot, LM, 138–139.

61. Ouerd, *Leçons sur l'hystérie virile,* 186; Charcot, LM, 136, my emphasis.

62. Ouerd, *Leçons sur l'hystérie virile,* 205; Charcot, LM, 260.

63. Ouerd, *Leçons sur l'hystérie virile,* 213; Charcot, LM, 284.

64. Ouerd, *Leçons sur l'hystérie virile,* 226; Charcot, LM, 297.

65. Ouerd, *Leçons sur l'hystérie virile,* 154; Charcot, Jean-Martin Charcot, *Leçons du mardi: Policlinique 1887–1888,* (Paris: Progrès médicale/Delahaye & Lecrosnier, 1887–1888), 283.

66. Ouerd, *Leçons sur l'hystérie virile,* 214; Charcot, LM, 284–5.

67. Micale, *Hysterical Men*, 156.

68. Freud and Breuer would object to this characterization of hysterical women in their *Studies on Hysteria*, where they rejected both the theory that hysterics were hereditarily tainted and that they were of inferior intelligence.

69. Erika Lorraine Milam and Robert A. Nye, "An Introduction to *Scientific Masculinities*," *Scientific Masculinities, Osiris* 30 (2015), 1–14.

70. Ouerd, *Leçons sur l'hystérie virile,* 201. Charcot, LM, 256. Again, it is telling that he has to make that case (i.e., that the equivalence is not taken for granted by his audience).

71. Ouerd, *Leçons sur l'hystérie virile,* 201–202, Charcot, LM, 256.

9

Down and Out

AMERICAN MALE BEGGARS' PRESENTATIONS, 1860S–1930S

Robert Bogdan

I have been collecting historical photographs of people with disabilities since 1985 (Bogdan 1988, 2012, Bogdan and Marshall 1997).[1] I seek images at antique shops, flea markets, eBay, and postcard shows and peruse other venues to expand my collection.[2] My exploration has focused on photographs taken in the United States when photography became widely used in the 1860s, until the 1970s when the disability rights movement became a major force in the United States. In this chapter I examine the images I have collected to explore one genre of disability portraiture, begging cards that male mendicants used to raise money from the 1860s to the 1930s. The photo of the man in illustration Figure 9.1 is an example.

I am not the first to tackle the topic of the visual representation of people with disabilities. There have been important predecessors. Their work differs from mine along a number of dimensions. Most of these writers focus on a small number of images within a limited range of subject areas (Hevey 2006, Garland-Thomson 2004, Millet 2004). I have examined over a hundred examples of begging cards for this article. Some authors instruct us about whether particular images are positive or negative, whether they demean or in other ways malign people with disabilities, or whether they portray them in complimentary ways. (Haller 2010, Millet 2004, Hevey 1992, Norden 1994) I describe patterns of presentation the male beggars used in their solicitations rather than evaluate them by the criteria of contemporary standards. Others researchers develop classifications schemes of the various ways people with disabilities are depicted—"wondrous," "sentimental," "exotic," "realistic" (Garland-Thomson 2001). Scholars with a more abstract theoretical bent focus on how the images relate to aesthetics, ethics, race, class, gender, and other oppressed groups (Snyder et al. 2002, Garland-Thomson 2002, 2004, Siebers 2010, Sandell et al. 2010, Chivers and Markotic 2010). These approaches are concerned with broad and abstract cultural meanings and tend to use established theoretical

FIGURE 9.1 "Please Help the Blind" begging card, c. 1908. Photo postcard. Courtesy of the author.

lenses that most often do not capture the meanings of the images to those who produced them.[3] The study of images of people with disabilities should not stop with the pictures but should include the historical and cultural circumstances of those people who created and consumed them.[4] I attempt to do that in this chapter.

In the past, in many people's minds, begging went hand and hand with disabilities. People with incapacitations have always been overrepresented in the ranks of beggars, and among them male solicitors have significantly outnumbered their female counterparts.

Why were men so overrepresented among the ranks of beggars? During the period of our concern, men were more active in the public sphere. While men could freely linger on sidewalks, this practice was looked down upon for women. Thus men were more accepted when soliciting money in public. Second, women were more likely to receive charity from churches and other civic organizations then men, mitigating their need to solicit funds from strangers. Third, men were expected to fend for themselves, to be self-sufficient, while their female counterparts had more claim on dependence. Last, men were expected to be providers not only for themselves but for their families. This justified men soliciting money by any means necessary to fulfill their patriarchal duties.

In some communities so-called ugly laws prohibited disabled panhandlers from seeking alms. In other localities they were more or less given free rein (Schweik 2009).[5] Americans have always been distressed by people asking for a handout. That is true both of the concept of seeking alms and the face-to-face encounter it involves. Male beggars were a challenge to capitalism in that they divulged that many men were unable to find gainful regular employment under that economic system. Beggars were inconsistent with the American belief that men should have regular jobs and that they should not only work to provide for themselves but their families as well. Even though the beggar's physical act of soliciting often involved arduous effort and long hours in dangerous settings, most Americans did not think of panhandling as work; it was not seen as a legitimate vocation. These abstract considerations may have contributed to some potential patrons' visceral reactions to male beggars and resistance to contributing. Many citizens viewed all beggars as offensive, unworthy, hustlers, or some combination of these and other dismissive allegations. Men who engaged in begging were often cast as scroungers, sponges, freeloaders, bums, and moochers.

Begging on the street was more nerve-racking to the person who was asked to give than to the solicitors. People were not comfortable being approached for a handout by strange men, especially those with a demonstrable physical or mental anomaly (Goffman 1963). Out of fear, distain, or indifference or just to move on, many of those approached by beggars develop strategies designed to manage the encounter without forking over cash. Others were more sympathetic and dealt with those looking for a handout differently. They established rules for themselves about the interaction, criteria for whom to give to, under what conditions, and how much to give.

Beggars had their own ways of thinking about these encounters. Most beggars were experienced in confronting people. They had conventions to manage such meetings. Although some merely passively sat at their stations, others were more active. They sized up potential benefactors deciding who to approach and what tactics to use. They realized the discomfort they may cause. They were also aware of the strategies their patrons use to avoid them. Beggars developed tactics of manipulation to increase their chances to score.

Talking about beggars in the way I have, as manipulators, might offend some readers. I do not mean to single them out as schemers. All people present themselves in strategic ways, especially in vocational roles (Goffman 1959). To not acknowledge that men with disabilities manipulated the situation is paternalistic and denies them agency as well as their real connection to other human beings. Taking a wary approach does not mean that I do not believe many people who begged were needy and used what they received for real needs.

The cat and mouse game between beggars and their potential benefactors is an interaction that has a deeply rooted history in our culture. Male beggars' performance and scripts evolved in concert with American's values and expectations of male behavior. The patterns explored here have been handed down through the generations. These presentations are consistent with ideas about what is gender appropriate for men. Men learned how to beg. This is not to say that they all receive tutorials in an apprenticeship relationship with an experienced beggar. Some did, but most learned in indirect ways such as watching from a distance, hearing people talk about beggars, and developing a deep understanding of American norms and values and men's place in our society.

Begging Cards

For more than 150 years, male beggars with disabilities have used photographs and printed pictures derived from photos as part of their solicitation schemes. Although seldom used today, beggars selling or giving away likenesses of themselves—begging cards—-to potential marks was a regular begging practice a hundred years ago. Begging cards served solicitors as a way of making initial contact with people, engaging them in interaction, and pitching their case. Most often these images include captions or printed text on the card's back describing the beggar's circumstance and making a case for a donation, the plea. The image and the pitch reinforced each other.

Typically, the images and accompanying text were distributed face to face on the street and in other public places. An alternate approach was for the beggar to send his image through the mail requesting money be returned via post.

In this chapter I share some of the images male beggars on begging cards and the accompanying text to explore the embedded gendered messages. I cover the period from approximately the late 1860 to the 1930s. The beggar images remain similar throughout the period. The use of begging cards increased toward the end of the nineteenth century as photo and printing technology became more accessible. The number of men using begging cards dropped off in the 1920s and 1930s. This parallels the general decline of begging by men with disabilities and the rise of organized charities. Starting in the early decades of the twentieth century, formal charities opposed begging and campaigned to control and eliminate it (Schweik 2009, 41). In addition, agencies actively engaged in their own pictorial solicitations—charity fund drives.

The pictures I display here were produced for the beggars by local commercial photographers or by small printing companies who used photos to create plates to print these images. The beggar was an active participant in the production of the cards. The beggar, sometimes with a collaborator,[6] would present himself to a photographer and describe how he wanted to appear.[7] The resulting images represent roughly how the beggar wanted to be presented.

In some localities men with disabilities had a special claim to the role of beggar. Their physical or mental condition legitimated asking for a handout. Often men without a disability would feign impairment as a begging tactic (Schweik 2009, chapters 3, 5).[8] Some were so clever at their ruse that the deception is impossible to detect in their portraits. For the illustrations here I have no way of knowing whether the men depicted were frauds or authentic, that is, with real disablements. Whether they were genuine or impostor did not change the way the beggars appeared on their cards. Both shared the strategies and the form of presentation that would induce giving.

The issue of fraud is complicated. Just like men who were relatively healthy and unimpaired who faked disabilities, men with actual impairments fabricated stories about themselves and posed in deceptive ways. The latter exaggerated the nature and the extent of their condition or told lies about how they became disabled and about what they planned to do with the donations. They carried crutches and wore bandages and eye patches, as well as other accessories, when they were not needed. In one sense, all beggars shared a degree of fraud. It was the degree of deception that separated the liar from the deceitful.

Pity with a Twist

The role of the man in American society was to be self-sufficient, physically strong, capable, stoic, and the breadwinner of his family. Begging portraits present a picture that at first appears at odds with the idolized picture. A strong theme in the imagery of male beggars is of helplessness with a cry for pity.

The begging card of Harry T. Petry in Figure 9.2 is the personification of this approach to begging. Given the card's small size, 2½ by 4 ¼ inches, and the absence of an address to send funds to, Petry probably handed it out to passersby on the street.

Petry is sitting in a wheel chair in the picture. His face and posture convey gloom. The image effuses misfortune, or at least that is the conclusion that the message asks the viewer to draw: "Am Perfectly Helpless. My Legs Are Both Off Above The Knees And Have To Be Fed Like A Baby." As with most images of beggars, he appears well groomed and wears clean clothes. His attire is arranged to display his missing legs and his unusually formed arms. Petry's image is constructed to support the assertion at the bottom of the card: "This is the only way I have to make a living."

The text on the back of the card adds a subtle ambiguity to the helpless beggar approach: "Good Luck to the Purchaser of this Card . . . Please Give What You Wish." These words along with the earlier reference to "making a living" are significant because they embody a begging strategy, a twist in his presentation that makes begging more like an occupation. Note the use of the word "purchase." Normally "purchase" means a real exchange of goods or services for money. Petry also uses the word "give." Thus the card creates ambiguity regarding whether he is merchant or a panhandler.[9] To put it another way, the appeal for charity is finessed by the idea that the giver is receiving an object, his picture, in return. Further, his begging is cast in the language usually reserved for men who are employed in a regular job—"make a living."

..Harry T. Petry..

AM PERFECTLY HELPLESS.
MY LEGS ARE BOTH OFF ABOVE
THE KNEES AND HAVE TO
BE FED LIKE A BABY.

THIS IS THE ONLY WAY I
HAVE TO MAKE A LIVING

FIGURE 9.2 "Harry Petry. Am perfectly helpless," c. 1926. Printed postcard. Courtesy of the author.

Petry, in small print, on the back of his card, offers a poem that captures his misery.

"I was once happy, the same as you;
But now I'm a cripple and nothing can do.
I am compelled to ask strangers some assistance to give,
So please give me something—"Live and Let Live."
I pray God will reward you, my wants you will relieve,
And remember it is more blessed to give than receive."

Petry's verse adds another element to the exchange; he is giving away, or selling his poetry. To top it off, he offers a religious justification for giving; God will reward those who give to the less fortunate.

Petry's presentation embodies many aspects of the visual and verbal pity rhetoric that was a standard part of male begging cards. I examine some dimensions of these next.

Religion

Petry's reference to Christian charity is not unusual; religion is often evoked in male beggars' cards. In an early example, 1875, a carte de visit photograph, Nathan P. Van Luvanee assumes a sympathetic pose in his wooden wheel chair. He is touching a bible (see Figure 9.3).

The text printed on the back of the photograph is too long to include in its entirety here so I summarize the relevant parts. The text is not written by Van Luvanee; it is a testimonial allegedly by his pastor. We are told that Van Luvanee was born in 1848 and became a "helpless invalid" when he was fifteen years old. In 1871 he was "blessedly converted" to the Lord and at the time of the picture, 1873, was "constantly and sweetly resting in Jesus."

Some people were leery of beggars, suspecting that they were not what they claimed to be, impostors rather than afflicted.[10] Van Luvanee's approach was to deal with that concern directly by having a minister allegedly testify for him. Van Luvanee's message ends with the following backing: "I have known him for more than two years. He is a faithful and devoted Christian and a true follower of Jesus, whose blood cleanses from all sin." The choice of the minister to vouch for Van Luvanee was tactical. It is difficult to dismiss a minister as a liar. Further, it is beyond belief that Van Luvanee might have composed the statement himself, which he might well have done.

Male beggars made use of the charity sentiments embedded in Judeo-Christian text and tradition, "I am my brother's keeper." They quoted the bible regularly and, as with the case of Van Luvanee, called upon statements, both authentic and fabricated, by ministers and other church authorities to bolster their claims.

FIGURE 9.3 Nathan P. Van Luvanee. 1875, carta de visit. Courtesy of the author.

Family

We look at another assumed unhappy soul, A. Souslin, whose printed postcard begging card is in Figure 9.4. His back and neck brace is clearly visible in the picture. His address is given at the bottom, presumably so that people could mail in donations.

Souslin's card illustrates a number of additional begging strategies. He employs his family to evoke sympathy for his plight. Notice the stoic look on Mrs. Souslin's face and the child's somber gaze. Souslin takes on the persona of someone in distress. He evokes the male role as provider with phrase "Their Only Support." It has a double meaning; in his role of father, the male provider, Souslin was the sole support of his family, and now begging is the only way for them to survive.

The rest of the text in the Souslin card, reads:

"Neck broken October 23, 1906, while decorating new office building, N. C. R. Dayton, Ohio. Was stooped over in the act of removing rubbish, plank fell striking edgewise on the back of neck."

FIGURE 9.4 A. Souslin. "Their only support," c. 1908. Printed postcard. Courtesy of the author.

The specificity of the account adds detail and compelling credibility and to the narrative. The script introduces another theme prevalent in many begging cards: the beggar was a hard worker who was actively engaged in making a living, and now, due to no fault of his own, he cannot work—thus he is one of the deserving poor.

The last example illustrates that male beggars' appeals to potential donors often involved wife and children—giving to the beggar resulted in benefits to his family. Depictions of children with disabilities seeking funds for their own welfare are almost absent in begging cards, but children dominate the imagery in charity drives by philanthropic organizations that proliferate after the first third of the twentieth century.

Wonder of the World
NECK IS BROKEN

THEORDORE WILLIAM PETERS
Structural Union Iron Worker
Local No. 16; Baltimore, Md.

Tried to save a fellow-workingman's life and fell 350 feet into the St. Lawrence River, Quebec, Canada; ninety of his fellow-workmen were killed. His wife died from the shock, leaving five orphan children.

PLEASE BUY ONE OF MY CARDS.

FIGURE 9.5 Theordore Peters, c. 1914. Printed card. Courtesy of the author.

No Fault of Their Own

The next begging card is that of Theodore Peters (see Figure 9.5). His presentation is similar to Souslin's in that it emphasizes that he would work if he could and that resorting to begging is no fault of his own. Peters used "Human Wonder" in his presentation, but the meaning is decidedly different from its use in freak shows; Theodore Peters is presented as a hero.

According to the text Peters was a union iron worker who fell 350 feet into a river when he tried to save a coworker's life. Further, we are told, his wife died from shock after hearing about her husband's injuries. He was left with five children to support. The recipient of the begging card is asked: "Please buy one of my cards."

While in some of the begging cards there is no claim to prior employment, in more than half the man's physical disability is linked to employment accidents.

Not Licked Yet

The no fault of their own, down and out, and helpless presentation was extensively used by male beggars but, perhaps realizing the limitations of the depressing downbeat appeal, some beggars added a positive element to their plea. In the 1920s Mr. George Washington had a "keep your sunny side up" avowal (Figure 9.6).

The basics of the picture are the same as others we have examined. He looks cheerless, is clean and respectably dressed, and has a disability: a missing lower left leg and mangled right leg are prominently displayed. In the first sentence of the text he tells us of his plight: "40 Years Since I have Walked," but, in a turn of

40 Years Since I Have Walked
But Not Licked Yet: Anyone Can Quit

From the minute we are born
Until we ride in a hearse
No matter what ails us
It might be worse
"Keep smiling and Trying"

PRICE: WHAT YOU WISH TO GIVE
I THANK YOU

What you give for charity in health is gold
What you give in sickness is silver
What you give after death is lead

FIGURE 9.6 George Washington, c.1924. Printed card. Courtesy of the author.

tactic he tells us: "But Not Licked Yet: Anyone Can Quit" but not Washington. He goes on:

> From the minute we are born
> Until we ride in a hearse
> No matter what ails us
> It might be worse
> Keep smiling and Trying

Washington's overtly buoyant message is more directly positive than is typically on begging cards, but there many examples of handouts that use a less understated message of "not licked yet." This element supports male values of courage, never giving up while facing adversity.

Quasi Artists and Performers

One form of a less overt positive presentation were beggars who declared themselves to be artists or entertainers. In that role the man asking for a handout was not merely a panhandler; he was engaged in a productive activity, creating art or playing a musical instrument. The disability was central to the request for money, but the begging was accompanied by evidence of being productive.

Take, for example, the case of Daniel Rose, the man with a severely palsied body pictured in his home in Johnstown, Pennsylvania in Figure 9.7.[11] The image shows examples of his whittling. Rose distributed "The Expert Whittler" postcards

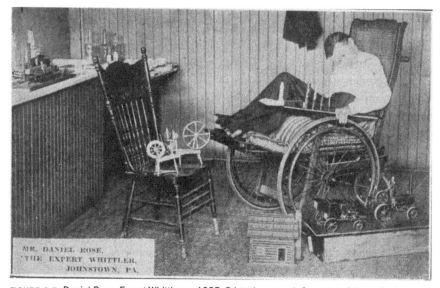

FIGURE 9.7 Daniel Rose, Expert Whittler. c. 1925. Printed postcard. Courtesy of the author.

through the mail as well as when people visited his home to see his carvings---miniature cars, houses, and other objects Rose created out of wood. The objects he allegedly created were special not because of their exceptional quality but because they were produced by a person with a demonstrable disability. The display and sale of pedestrian self-made objects showed that Rose and others who engaged in such crafts were trying, not just sitting around begging.

I have been rather dismissive and disparaging regarding Daniel Rose's whittling. In the second half of the twentieth century a form of art referred to as "outsider art" became popular and collectible and made headway in being accepted as part of the establishment art world (Fine 2004). Artwork by people with various physical and mental disabilities who had no formal art training, as well as work by those with unconventional lifestyles, found an audience and began selling for high prices. Some of these artists started as local oddities. They were "found" and championed by dealers and collectors and were lifted to the status of artist (Fine 2004). Although this transformation of beggar to artist is uncommon, it stands as a reminder that people do not necessarily remain in the same roles all their lives. Beggars become artists or move on to some other status. For most, begging was not a lifetime pursuit. Begging could be seasonal or just one of the many vocations a person participated in during his lifetime.

Musicians

In the studio portrait in Figure 9.1, a photo postcard of a blind beggar, provides another example of the mixing of begging and artist performance. The person pictured here distributed this card to pedestrians as he played his harmonica and dulcimer. Although the image seems bleak and the sign around his neck "Please Help the Blind" indicates he was a beggar, the fact that he also plays musical instruments puts him in another league of beggar—street performer.

Street entertainers solicit money just as beggars do. We do not know how talented the person in the illustration was, or the quality of his performances, but even if his playing was an assault to the ear, the fact that he was doing something in addition to asking for a handout put him in a different league of beggars. The beggar as performer was a more active role and was probably seen more favorably than, perhaps, that of just a run-of-the-mill beggar. Performance was a form of "not licked yet" and fit into the expectations for men to engage in work, not just idle begging.

On the Road

There is a genre of begging images that demonstrate that some male beggars with disabilities were willing to literally go the extra mile to enhance their fundraising success. Richard New, the "Legless Motor Cycle Rider," is a flamboyant example

(Figure 9.8). Originally from Akron, Ohio, Mr. New traveled about the country collecting money to support his roving lifestyle in a vehicle made especially for him. In the small insert on the postcard he distributed he is displaying his stumps where once there were legs. The lettering on the side of the cycle brags that he drove twice across the great American Desert, presumably the Great Basin Desert located primarily in Nevada. A portion of the text reveals that New made his expenses by selling photographs of himself and includes the phrase we have seen before, "Price. What you Choose."

Figure 9.9 is another postcard of a legless man who used pictures of himself to beg. Rather than getting about on a motorized vehicle, he employed a goat cart to accomplish his travel. The sign next to him reads: "Dear Friend, My name is John Rose driver of the only goat team in the world pulling 475 lbs. averaging 16 miles per day. I was crippled in a R. R. wreck 12 yrs. ago. Someone Help Me." By handing their begging cards to passersby, John Rose and Richard New solicited money as they traveled about the country.

Goats were not the only draft animal people with disabilities used to promote their solicitation. In one of the oldest images I have come across of beggars going the extra mile in pursuit of donations is that of Max Engel of Buffalo, New York. In 1890 after a railroad accident that left him legless, Engel hitched his dog, Carlo, to a handmade rig and set off begging.[12] Engel sold the likeness of himself in his travels. Stamped on the back of one that was taken in Buffalo is a message Engel composed stating that he had been on the road for five years and he was on his way to New York City. In the picture Engel is well dressed and is uses wooden blocks on his hands to increase his mobility (Figure 9.10).

FIGURE 9.8 Richard New, c. 1914. Printed postcard. Courtesy of the author.

FIGURE 9.9 John Rose with goat cart, c. 1915. Photo postcard. Courtesy of the author.

Fred Vaillancourt, shown in Figure 9.11, was a former railroad break man who also lost his legs in a train accident. He traveled about the country in a rig pulled by two dogs. Vaillancourt distributed a variety of photo postcards portraits in his travels. The image is one of eight different pictures I have seen of Vaillancourt and his dog team.

FIGURE 9.10 Max Engel and his dog Carlo, c. 1895. Cabinet card. Courtesy of the author.

FIGURE 9.11 Fred Vaillancourt, c.1907. Photo postcard. Courtesy of the author.

The begging strategy behind the travelers in these illustrations was to show that they were not mere slackers; they were men willing to go to great lengths, traveling about in their unusual rigs seeking alms. Given the number of postcards available today in the antique postcard market documenting beggars with disabilities touring in both motorized and animal driven carriages, it would seem that this method of solicitation was quite common and in line with expectations for men to be adventurous and creative in fending for themselves.

Veterans' Begging Cards

As far back as the Revolutionary War, veterans who were injured in service to their country received pensions and were some of the first people with disabilities to receive government services. Even so, some ex-soldiers who were mutilated chose begging as a method of support. The number of those who choose to beg with the assistance of photographic images was apparently small; I came across only six in my research.

The oldest begging card I found is of two Civil War amputees (Figure 9.12). One has a war medal pinned to his lapel; the other holds a gun. The veteran on the left displays a large American flag. The flag and the medal are part of the appeal of the solicitation. They remind the potential donor that these men served their country and should be reward with a contribution. At the bottom of the card is handwritten "25 cents," which suggests it was distributed as a begging card.

Another veteran begging card is of Captain Lewis Satterfield, who was wounded in World War I. On the card he flaunted his military service and appealed to people's patriotism in his solicitation. He is pictured in his uniform. On the back

FIGURE 9.12 Civil war veterans begging card, c. 1869. Carte de viste. Courtesy of the author.

is a poem about his war experience. In the text he presents himself as a "Disabled Veteran of World's War, making his was by the sale of a ballad."

One reason of the absence of male beggars emphasizing their military background in their solicitation might be that disabled veterans were one group that received services that was mandated by legislation and financed by the government. Another reason is that disabled veterans organized their own charities and raised funds under the banner of these organizations,

Beggar Merchants

Earlier I discussed how distributing images set up a quasi-exchange relationship that resulted in a more subtle form of begging. Images were not the only items beggars gave out or sold. Cards with printed prayers and inexpensive items such as pencils were offered to passersby. Milton Clewell, a man who claimed that he could not walk due to an injury to his spine, used the card in Figure 9.13 to solicit funds during the holiday season. He sent out his "Wishing you a Merry Christmas and a Happy New Year" card with a return envelope enclosed to encourage donations. Rather than give away an object of dubious value, he sent an inexpensive knife. The card states that he is selling the knife. The price was the familiar "What You Wish to Give." Note how, in addition to the selling ploy, Mr. Clewell notes a specific need he has: his wheelchair needs repair. An aspect of the picture that is unique in the begging cards I have seen is the presence of Clewell's dog, apparently a come-on to animal lovers. He reminds us: "Keep Smiling."

FIGURE 9.13 Milton Clewell, Merry Christmas card, c. 1924. Printed card. Courtesy of the author.

In the early 1930s Homer Minor of Plainview, Texas, used a tactic similar to Clewell's in soliciting funds. He mailed a box of engraved Christmas cards to potential donors asking that they either send a dollar or return the cards in a self-addressed stamped envelope. He waited a week and then sent a follow-up postcard asking if they had received the package and urging the recipient to send the money or the cards so that the his or her account could be settled. In the message he suggests that they buy more cards and sell them to others. Minor does not mention his disability in the text but on the address side of the card there is a picture of him sitting in a wheelchair with his proportionately small legs tucked in close to his body.

Besides offering marginal gifts, men with disabilities also offered real products, items sold in stores and available from other merchants. Some of these sellers with disability acted as any merchant would, but others promoted their wares by emphasizing their disability and suggesting that buying from them had added value—charity. Typically, they priced their items higher than other sellers, trading on the sympathy of the buyer as their promotional technique.

One of the earliest examples I found, c. 1875, was a photograph of L. D. Sine with a message in the back telling the reader that Mr. Sine had lost his sight in 1851 and soon after started his own business, "Gift Enterprises" (Figure 9.14). The message is not clear about what Mr. Sine is selling, but it encourages people to send for a circular with a full list items and prices. Interestingly the printed message on the back is in the third person, suggesting that another party might have been involved in the promotion of the business.

Another example of an ambiguous beggar card shows a man, L.W. Prettyman, the "Shut-in-Magazine Man" who appears to be actually selling a product: subscriptions to magazines (Figure 9.15). Though a real merchant, he is using pity and other begging strategies to improve his market position.

Prettyman's approach is that of an aggressive salesperson: "Yes, it's a fight—a fight against disease, pain, and COMPETITORS. In my condition the fight seems unusually hard. I must win, for I have to earn my own living. Will you help me win? Help me to succeed. You can by sending me each and every one of YOUR magazine and newspaper subscriptions." On the back of his postcard he notes that his subscription sales are "our only means of support, both mother and I."

I end this chapter with an image that illustrates the fuzzy line between begging and regular commerce in begging cards. Billy McGogan traveled around White Cloud, Minnesota, selling candy, popcorn, peanuts, cigars, and postcards. The postcards were of him sitting in his goat-drawn mobile store. In the picture he is shown nicely dressed in a straw hat in his favorite haunt, the railroad station where he would meet the trains and sell to travelers (Figure 9.16).

McGogan was an entrepreneurial beggar who had allegedly lost the use of his legs early in his life when he was shot by a local farmer while he attempted to steal chickens. A number of postcards show people with disabilities had the status of local characters; that is, they were widely known in a particular geographic area

FIGURE 9.14 L.D. Sine, "Gift Enterprises," c. 1869. Carte de visite. Courtesy of the author.

for their peculiar behavior and lifestyle. McGogan filled that role in his town and capitalized his notoriety in selling postcards and other goods.

Conclusion

Male beggars' presentations are rooted in century-old British laws that distinguish between the worthy poor and those not deserving charity (Katz 1990, 1996). According to this distinction, the worthy poor want to work, but they cannot fend for themselves. The unworthy are laggards, people who are too lazy to do the hard work of supporting themselves. We show pity for the worthy by providing charity and contempt for the unworthy by punishing them and requiring that they take

FIGURE 9.15 "L.W. Prettyman, Shut-in-Magazine man," c. 1920. Printed advertisement card. Courtesy of the author.

care of themselves. Men were particularly singled out for scrutiny under the doctrine of worthy. Male disabled beggars pitched their appeals knowing the distinction between worthy and unworthy and presented themselves as worthy.

The theme of pity is pervasive on the begging cards. This theme is often mediated with postures of the rugged individualism of American capitalism. Aspects

FIGURE 9.16 Billy McGogan, peanut vendor, c. 1910. Photo postcard. Courtesy of the author.

of beggars' presentations included posturing as salesmen or framing their begging as an exchange where the begging cards themselves were the commodities. Some men who begged traveled in the vehicles ranging from goat carts to specially rigged automobiles to claim independence. Disabled street performers sang, danced, and played musical instruments to earn their keep.

As the United State moved into the twentieth century, organized charities laid claim to being the respectable and wise collector and distributor of funds for the needy. Professional social workers came to guide charity organizations claiming that they could best separate the worthy from the unworthy, the truly needy from imposters, and tend to the destitute in ways that would lead them out of poverty. Social workers undermined the freelance beggars' appeal. It was more comfortable to give to an organized group in the business of charity than to deal with people who approached one in the street.

Depictions of men with disabilities on begging cards are only one stylized way people with disabilities were pictured. There were different conventions for souvenir photographs sold from the platform of freak shows, for fundraisers soliciting for charities (poster children), in art photography, in clinical textbooks, in advertising, in institutional propaganda, and others. There are also many examples of photos where the conventions of family and normal citizen trump disability visual rhetoric. These personal keepsakes were the types of photographs that were placed in family albums and other places of safe keeping. They bear witness to the fact that people with disabilities were not always pictured in ways where their difference was central to the composition and other aspects of disability rhetoric reigned.

As I have shown with begging portraits, the various ways of presenting disability in pictures need to be studied within the context in which they were produced. This approach also reminds us that men with disability were often actors in creating their own presentations.

Acknowledgments

This article is adapted from a chapter that appeared in Bogdan (2012) with permission of Syracuse University Press.

Notes

1. I collect both actual photographs as well as other printed images derived from photos.

2. Since I began collecting, I have been keenly aware that this type of material is scarce in traditional archival collections. I have also learned how such material can open new areas in the study of disability and popular culture.

3. Some of these writings favor postmodern and critical theories; my analysis is based on social constructionism and related works that pay attention to context, meaning and agency.

4. Norden's work (1994) on movie depictions of people with disabilities is the one example where the historical and cultural context of picture production is an important part of the analysis.

5. In the late nineteenth and early twentieth century, a number of cities adopted "unsightly beggar ordinances," also referred to as "ugly laws," to keep people with incapacities from asking for handouts in public. Some of these laws remained on the books until the second half of the twentieth century (Schweik 2009).

6. Some beggars were assisted by family members or associates including people who served as their managers.

7. There are two main types of images: ones printed on printing presses from plates made using original photographs and real photos printed from negatives directly on photographic paper. Because of the expense of making the initial print, the former were printed in large numbers. The real photos were usually done in smaller runs.

8. Early films often used a seeing person posing as a blind beggar as a source of humor. In one of the earliest, *Fake Beggar*, a man with a sign, "Help the Blind," quickly reaches down to pick up a coin from the floor that misses the cup. A similar routine has been present in films to the present day (Norden 1994, 14).

9. In some locations begging was illegal but peddling was not. This partly may explain some of the duel presentations.

10. See Norden (1994, chapter 1) for a discussion of disability fraud in early movies.

11. In an article that appeared in the magazine *Christian Monitor: A Monthly Magazine for the Home in June, 1926 (Vol. XVIII, No. 6)*. Rose is described as having a sever rheumatism.

12. For a discussion of disability and railroad workers see Williams-Searle (2001).

References

Bogdan, Robert. 1988. *Freak Show: Presenting Human Oddities for Amusement and Profit.* Chicago: University of Chicago Press.

Bogdan, Robert. 2012. *Picturing Disability: Beggar, Freak, Citizen, and Other Photographic Rhetoric.* Syracuse: New York: Syracuse University Press.

Bogdan, Robert, and Marshall A. 1997. "Views of the Asylum: Picture Postcard Depictions of Institutions for People with Mental Disorders in the Early 20th Century." *Visual Sociology* 12(1), 4–28.

Chivers, Sally, and Nicole Markotic. 2010. *The Problem Body: Projecting Disability on Film.* Columbus: Ohio State University Press.

Fine, Gary. 2004. *Everyday Genius: Self-Taught Art and the Culture of Authenticity.* Chicago: University of Chicago Press.

Garland-Thomson, Rosemarie. 2001. "Seeing the Disabled: Visual Rhetoric of Disability in Popular Culture." In Paul Longmore and Lauri Umansky, *The New Disability History.* New York: New York University Press, 335–375.

Garland-Thomson, Rosemarie. 2002. "The Politics of Staring: Visual Rhetorics of Disability in Popular Photography." In Brenda Snyder, Jo Brueggemann, and Rosemarie Garland-Thomson, eds., *Disability Studies: Enabling the Humanities.* New York: Modern Language Association, 56–73.

Garland-Thomson, Rosemarie. 2004. "Integrating Disability, Transforming Feminist Theory." In Bonnie Smith and Beth Hutchison, eds., *Gendering Disability*. New Brunswick, NJ: Rutgers University Press.

Goffman, Erving. 1959. *The Presentation of Self in Everyday Life*. Garden City, NY: Doubleday/Anchor.

Goffman, Erving. 1963. *Stigma*. Englewood Cliffs, NJ: Prentice Hall.

Haller, Beth 2010. *Representing Disability in an Ableist World*. Louisville, KY: Avocado Press.

Hevey, David. 1992. *The Creatures Time Forgot: Photography and Disability Imagery*. London: Routledge.

Hevey, David. 2006. "The Enfreakment of Photography." In Lennard Davis, ed., *The Disability Studies Reader,* 2nd ed. New York: Rutledge, 367–378.

Katz, Michael B. 1990. *The Undeserving Poor: From the War on Poverty to the War on Welfare*. New York: Pantheon.

Katz, Michael B. 1996. *In the Shadow of the Poorhouse: A Social History of Welfare in America*, 10th anniversary ed. New York: Basic Books.

Millett, Ann. 2004. "Exceeding the Frame." *Disability Studies Quarterly* 24(4). Retrieved at http://dsq-sds.org/article/view/881/1056

Norden, Martin. 1994. *Cinema of Isolation: A History of Physical Disability in the Movies*. New Brunswick, NJ: Rutgers University Press.

Sandell, Richard, Jocelyn Dodd, and Rosemarie Garland-Thomson. 2010. *Re-presenting Disability: Activism and Agency in the Museum*. New York: Routledge.

Schweik, Susan. 2009. *The Ugly Laws: Disability in Public*. New York: New York University Press.

Siebers, Tobin. 2010. *Disability Aesthetics*. Ann Arbor: University of Michigan Press.

Snyder, Brenda, Jo Brueggemann, and Rosemarie Garland-Thomson. 2002. *Disability Studies: Enabling the Humanities*. New York: Modern Language Association.

Williams-Searle. 2001. "Cold Charity: Manhood, Brotherhood and the Transformation of Disability, 1870–1900. In Paul K. Longmore and Lauri Umansky, eds., *The New Disability History*. New York: New York University Press.

10

Death on a Silver Platter

MASCULINITY, DISABILITIES, AND
THE NOXON MURDER TRIALS OF 1944

Ivy George and James W. Trent Jr.

Around six o'clock on the evening of September 22, 1943, John F. Noxon Jr., a prominent attorney in Pittsfield, Massachusetts, and a "crippled" polio survivor, telephoned Dr. George P. Hunt, his family's pediatrician, to come at once. Noxon's six-month-old son, Lawrence, had apparently entangled himself in wires and had received a terrible electrical shock. When the doctor arrived, he found the "mongoloid" baby dressed in a wet diaper, lying on a silver platter, and dead. A few days later authorities arrested "crippled" Noxon for the murder of "mongoloid" Lawrence. For the next five years, the citizens of Massachusetts and the nation followed in their newspapers the trials (there were two), verdict, death sentence, appeals, pardon, and parole in what many journalists called "the Noxon mercy killing."[1]

The significance of these events lies not only for the meaning of "mercy killing" for Americans just becoming aware of the horror of Nazi holocaust but also for the meaning of masculinity and disability (in this unique case, double disability) in war-time and postwar North America. The Noxon "mercy killing" suggests that at mid-century Americans were willing to acknowledge that there were some "lives not worth living." This willingness occurred despite late- and postwar popular and professional reaction against euthanasia, generated by events in Europe. As such, a postwar distinction emerged between proper and improper euthanasia. A peculiar kind of disability stratification, mediated by standards of disability manliness, made this distinction possible. A disabled man who was intelligent, resourceful, and well-to-do could remain within the parameters of proper disability and proper masculinity. However, a disabled man who lacked intelligence and who remained dependent and childlike could hardly assume or retain either such proper disability or masculinity. Thus social, economic, and political qualification of manly disability rendered some men within the boundaries of proper disability and masculinity and others outside such boundaries. With the Noxon mercy killing, the "proper" disabled man and "the other" could hardly have been more closely observed. One lived a life worth living; the other did not.

John F. Noxon Jr. had come from an established and leading family in Pittsfield. His father, also an attorney, had been the Berkshire County prosecutor during Noxon's youth. He attended Harvard University as an undergraduate and as a law student. His education in Cambridge had been interrupted by two important events: military service in Europe during the World War I where he was wounded by enemy fire and also exposed to mustard gas and, shortly after he returned from the war, polio. Although contracting polio had left him using leg braces and two wooden canes to aid in walking, the impairment neither prevented his professional achievements nor his May 1925 marriage to Margaret (Peggy) Swift, a Stanford University graduate and a member of another prominent Pittsfield family.[2]

Over the next eighteen years, Noxon developed a thriving corporate law practice, one so successful that he built what at the time was the largest residence in Pittsfield. As a good local citizen, he provided pro bono services to the local charity hospital. He enjoyed gardening and bowling. Peggy Noxon, like other upper-middle-class women of the time, was a homemaker, who participated in several cultural and women's organizations. The Noxons had a full-time maid and a part-time gardener. They attended what at the time was the leading and thoroughly upper-class St. Stephen's Episcopal Church. In 1928, their son, John F. Noxon III, was born. This son would go on to receive his PhD in physics from Harvard University. In 1972 he joined the Aeronomy Laboratory of the National Oceanic and Atmospheric Association as a senior scientist, having come from Harvard's Blue Hill Observatory, where he was an associate director.[3]

Nearly fifteen years after their first son's birth, the Noxons' second son, Lawrence Swift Noxon, was born on March 26, 1943. Given the several years between the births of their sons, one can imagine that Peggy Noxon's second pregnancy was not planned. From the parents' concerns about what appeared to be Lawrence's slow development, their local pediatrician, Dr. Hunt, referred the Noxons to Boston's Children's Hospital. There in August 1943 Dr. Richard M. Smith, a pediatric authority on "defective children," gave them the diagnosis of "incurable mongolism." As Smith would recall, he told the Noxons,

> Physically the children may proceed to adult size and activity, but their mental development remains permanently retarded. These children never attain economic or social independence. They require permanent supervision. They may learn to walk, to talk, to enjoy simple games or music, even to read a little, but do not advance beyond a mental age of 4 to 8 years. Such children usually die before reaching full maturity.[4]

Smith recommended that the Noxons place Lawrence in a residential institution, several of which had recently begun to admit "mentally defective" children less than one year old.

It was a month later that Dr. Hunt received the telephone call from John Noxon indicating that "something had happened to the baby." Earlier that same day, Peggy Noxon had taken Lawrence to Dr. Hunt's office for a Schick test and a vaccine against whooping cough. She arrived home with the baby at 4:00 that afternoon, and about an hour later she went to the garden to gather corn for the evening meal. She left Lawrence in John's care, while he remained in the house disassembling a radio in need of repair. When Dr. Hunt arrived at the Noxons' home, he found Lawrence dead with "a blistering area on the left forearm and what looked like a scratch on the right arm." Noxon told the doctor that he had placed Lawrence with a wet diaper on a silver platter while he had retrieved a screwdriver and pliers from his garage for his work on the radio. He later testified that he was out of the room for no more than three to five minutes. In his absence, Noxon informed Dr. Hunt, the baby must have tangled himself in the exposed wires of a frayed and nearly worn out extension cord that Noxon was using to repair the radio. From this information and given his observations, Dr. Hunt told the Noxons that, under the unusual circumstances of the baby's death, he would be required to inform the Pittsfield medical examiner, Dr. Albert V. England, who arrived shortly thereafter at the Noxons' residence. While there England questioned the Noxons, examined the burns on both of Lawrence's arms, and observed the condition of the extension cord. Within the hour, the baby's body was removed to a local funeral home.

The following morning Dr. England returned to the Noxons' residence. As he had the evening before, he questioned John Noxon about his actions before and shortly after the baby's death. Noxon recounted the same information as he had with the medical examiner the evening before, except for the addition of two matters. First, he explained that he had placed the child with his wet diaper on the tray in order not to stain the carpet, while also propping Lawrence's head and shoulders on a green pillow. Second, he indicated that he had burned the extension cord, along with the baby's diaper and shirt, in his basement incinerator shortly after Dr. England left the house the previous evening.

Later that same day, Noxon received two visits from police Chief John L. Sullivan. The first came shortly after Dr. England's call and after Sullivan had consulted with the doctor. With information from the medical examiner, Sullivan interviewed Noxon and his wife Peggy about the events of the previous evening. John Noxon recounted these events in much the same detail as he had for Dr. England. During the visit, Chief Sullivan and his police associates also took several objects from the Noxon home. A few hours after his first visit, Sullivan made a second call to the Noxon residence. On this occasion, he informed John Noxon that he had received some information that had made him suspect that Lawrence's death was intentional. First there was Dr. England's observation that the extension cord that had electrocuted Lawrence, but had now been destroyed by Noxon, had two clean cuts with exposed copper wires. It was not an old, frayed cord as Noxon had claimed. The doctor also doubted that the baby had the dexterity to grab and entangle himself in the extension cord. Even more suspicious, however, was information that Sullivan had learned from William A. Whittlesey, the president of the Berkshire County Savings Bank and an officer of the Western Massachusetts Electric Company. According to Whittlesey, a few weeks earlier Noxon had discussed with him newspaper reports of a women electrocuted by contact with a live wire. Why had Noxon been interested in this electrocution only a few weeks before the event of the previous day? Why had he asked Whittesey about the voltage it would take to kill a person? Noxon had no answer, but, nevertheless, denied any wrongdoing.

On Friday, September 24, Assistant Berkshire County District Attorney Valmore O. Cote invited John and Peggy Noxon to the Pittsfield police station where he interrogated them about the events of the death. The questioning was transcribed by stenographer Mary A. Bristol and continued for most of the day, only interrupted for the Noxons to attend Lawrence's funeral service that afternoon at St. Stephen's Church.[5] Under questioning, Peggy claimed that the baby could hold a rattle but could not shake it. When Cote asked Noxon to explain how Lawrence could have grabbed the cord and also twisted it around his arm so that the two live wires would come into contacts on his arm and body, Noxon replied,

> The only explanation I can see is that the baby in moving his arms pulled the wire over his chest and got his arm twisted in it. The Pittsfield Electric people were out, and I asked them if it could happen like that, and they said "yes." I described the wire to the Pittsfield Electric and they said the baby must have made contact with one wire under and one on top of his arm and that's where the electrical ground came in.[6]

Early in the morning on September 27, 1943, five days after the incident, Chief Sullivan, with a warrant in hand, entered the Noxons' home unannounced where he made a search of the residence. In the Noxons' bedroom he found scraps of paper in a wastebasket. Back at the police station after a police investigator reassembled them, the connected scraps revealed a document in John Noxon's handwriting that contained questions about Lawrence's death that Noxon anticipated receiving from local authorities, as well as his projected answers to those questions. At 10:30 later that same morning, Sullivan arrested Noxon in his law office and charged him with the murder of his son. At that point, Noxon refused to talk any longer with either the police or the district attorney's office. The next day Judge Charles L. Hibbard denied Noxon bail and ordered him confined to the Berkshire County jail.[7]

Nearly four months later on January 13, 1944, a Berkshire County grand jury indicted Noxon on the count of first-degree murder. Until this point, Noxon had received legal representation from his law partner, Michael L. Eisner, and a local criminal defense attorney, Walter J. Donovan. After the indictment was handed down, an especially important member joined the defense team, Joseph B. Ely, the former district attorney of the Hampden-Berkshire counties and, most significantly, a former governor (from 1931 to 1935) of the Commonwealth of Massachusetts. With Ely's prestige, the already regionally sensational murder was transformed into a state-wide dramatic trial and eventually into a national one as well. The presence of Ely on the defense team not only guaranteed greater prominence for the forthcoming trial but also insured that most of the political, class, religious, and social tensions and ironies in the western Massachusetts community of Pittsfield would reveal insights about civilian masculinity and disability in war-torn America.[8]

After a series of motions, the trial began on February 23, 1944, at the Berkshire Superior Court, presided over by Judge Abraham E. Pinanski. Representing the county was District Attorney Charles Rosario Alberti, a classmate of Noxon at the Harvard University Law School. The twelve jurors were men from several communities in the county. (All Massachusetts jurors at the time were men; women were legally prohibited from jury service.) Covering the trial for the *Boston Globe* was a veteran reporter, Dorothy G. Wayman, whom the paper had used on several occasions to cover sensational criminal trials. On March 9, after only eight days of testimony, Judge Pinanski declared a mistrial because one of the jurors had come down with what some reported to be the grippe, but others claimed was nervous exhaustion. In either case, because state's rules for juries at the time precluded the seating of alternate jurors, Pinanski was forced to end the trial and to schedule a new one that he set for the last day of May.[9]

The principal actors in the first trial, and the one to come in the spring, were in several ways remarkably alike but in other ways were quite different. Most obviously, they shared upper-middle-class economic positions—Noxon, Alberti, and Ely in their small western Massachusetts communities and Pinanski and Wayman from their positions in big-city eastern Massachusetts. Except for Dorothy Wayman, the others had all graduated from the Harvard Law School. Through the Great Depression and the war years each actor had hardly suffered; indeed, each had thrived. In short, they were well-to-do. Likewise, their social position matched their economic one. All actors were members of socially elite institutions—membership-only clubs, boards of charitable institutions, socially elite religious congregations, and private preparatory schools for their children. Like their elite economic and social positions, they were leaders in local, state, and even national politics. Ely, of course, was especially prominent, having been the Hampton-Berkshire district attorney and the state's governor, but the others too engaged in occasional political activities. Thus they shared a common elite position, a factor that no doubt contributed to the trials' local, regional, and national notoriety.

Yet there were differences. The most visible ones were the differences in their ethnic backgrounds and religious affiliations. Noxon was a Protestant Episcopalian, whose ancestry originated in England. He had married a woman of similar ancestry. Earlier generations of their families were well-known, highly respected, and founding members of Berkshire County. Like Noxon, Governor Ely came from an established Protestant family long ensconced in western Massachusetts politics and society. Abraham Pinanski, on the other hand, was Jewish and from Brookline, Massachusetts. His ancestry was Polish and, compared to Noxon and Ely, recently arrived. Like many Massachusetts judges of the time, he traveled throughout the state to preside at trials that involved capital offenses. Although western Massachusetts had a small Jewish population, Jews with the authority of a judge were unusual in Berkshire County. Finally, Pinanski, hailing from eastern Massachusetts, was a geographical outsider as well a religious one.

Prosecutor Charles Alberti was a Roman Catholic, whose family immigrated to the United States from Italy when Alberti was a young boy. In 1908, his father, a hod carrier, died. Working as a paper boy and a store clerk, Alberti graduated from high school and later from Williams College. Unlike the Noxons, the Albertis were neither well-to-do nor members of the old-guard Protestant founders of the county. Although Catholics made up large portions of Berkshire County's population, most of these residents were local factory workers, small business owners, and day laborers. They might be hard-working and even educated, but, like the Alberti family, they were Italian, Irish, or eastern European Catholics and, hence, not able to reside at the top of the region's social ladder. At best, they were, like Charles Alberti, merely nouveau riche.

Like Alberti, Dorothy Wayman was a Roman Catholic. But unlike the Pittsfield prosecutor, her journey to the Catholic faith had begun as a Protestant. In 1923, she found herself divorced and alone with three young sons. With grit and determination, she found work as a reporter and author in worlds ordinarily dominated by men. During the trials, Wayman would socialize with Judge Pinanski and Governor Ely, and she would become friends with the Noxons. She was never a Berkshire County blueblood, but as a respected *Boston Globe* reporter, she did not need to be.

Differences in ethnicity, religion, class, and status were compounded by differences in political affiliation. Judge Pinanski and District Attorney Alberti were Republicans, Noxon and Ely were Democrats, whereas Wayman managed to mute her political allegiance. Pinanski was appointed to the Superior Court in 1930 at the age of forty-two by reformist Governor Frank G. Allen, a Republican, who had defeated James Michael Curley in the Republican electoral sweep of 1928. During his two years in office and before his 1930 election defeat by Richard Ely, Allen also appointed, for the first time in the state's history, two women to judgeships. After Pinanski's death in 1949, his wife Viola Pinanski served as a Massachusetts delegate to the 1952 and 1956 Republican National Conventions.

If Pinanski was a rather conventional Republican, Richard Ely was a quite unconventional Democrat. At the end of the first of his two two-year terms in the governor's office, he supported Al Smith for presidential nomination in the

1932 Massachusetts primary, and at the nominating convention in Chicago he gave a rousing nominating speech for Smith. He only shifted his support to Franklin Roosevelt after the New York governor received the nomination after the fourth ballot. By the time he left the governor's office in 1936, Ely had come to distrust Roosevelt and what he saw as the growing "pink fringe of socialists and communists" coming from the Roosevelt administration. This distrust only heightened when Roosevelt indicated that he would run for a third term in 1940. In February 1944, just as he was about to start his courtroom defense of John Noxon, Ely announced that he would challenge Roosevelt for the Democratic presidential nomination. In both the Massachusetts primary, where voters cast ballots at a four-to-one ratio for Roosevelt over Ely, and at the Democratic convention, Ely's challenge went nowhere. Although neither Alberti nor Noxon was particularly active in party affairs beyond the local level, each was a member of a different political party—Alberti a Republican and Noxon a Democrat. Along with different social standing and religious traditions, their political party differences were not insignificant in the small communities of western Massachusetts.

The second trial began on May 31, the day announced by Judge Pinanski in March, and continued until the case went to the new jury on July 6. The trial progressed without interruption, except for an adjournment on the morning of that last day for trial attendees to go to local houses of worship to pray for success on what was D-day. Like the short-lived first trial, the second trial was fill with suspense, intrigue, and surprises, all of which Dorothy Wayman chronicled with flare in the *Globe* and that newspapers from across the country would draw from and print.[10] For example, Prosecutor Alberti introduced a life-size doll that resembled baby Lawrence, and he put into evidence samples of the baby's burned skin placed in small polymer containers (that still reside with other evidence, and apparently in perpetuity, in the Berkshire County Courthouse). Besides evidence, the jury and other trial participants toured the Noxon home. They also heard evidence that proved to be damning to Noxon's case.[11]

First, bank President William A. Whittlesey, who was also an officer of the Western Massachusetts Electric Company, testified that Noxon had discussed with him an article published in the Springfield newspaper on August 20, 1943, about a woman killed by an exposed electrical wire. Noxon asked him questions about the amount of voltage necessary to kill this woman. Two days later Noxon received the news from Dr. Smith at Boston Children's Hospital—what his pediatrician, Dr. Hunt, had suspected—that Lawrence had Down syndrome, and a month after that news, Lawrence received the electrical charge that would kill him.[12]

Second, later in the evening of the electrocution, Chief Sullivan testified that Noxon burned all of baby Lawrence's clothing, including his wet diaper, giving the appearance that he was destroying evidence. And third, there were the torn pages that the police found in a trash container in the Noxons' bedroom, clearly showing, when pieced back together, that Noxon was anticipating questions that the police would likely ask him, along with answers that he planned to give. The torn pages gave the appearance of calculations and deception. Testimony by Ida L. Royce, a salesperson at Kresge Five-and-Dime Store, added strength to the prosecution's case. Royce remembered that Noxon purchased a new extension cord in early September, thus calling into question his claim that the cord that Lawrence grabbed was old and frayed. Adding to the doubts cast by Royce, Joseph T. Walker, a forensic chemist and founding director of the Massachusetts State Police Chemical Laboratory, testified that he found microscopic copper residue from the extension cord not only on baby Lawrence's arm but also on the silver tray. The fragments, Walker testified, suggested that the cord had been cut and set in place. Finally, medical testimony claimed that six-month-old Lawrence was developmentally incapable of deliberately grabbing such a cord and placing it across his body. Given this testimony, logic would suggest, District Attorney Alberti argued, that the child's electrocution was no accident but a deliberate act planned and carried out by his father.[13]

From the questioning by Police Chief Sullivan shortly after his son's death until his own death in 1972, John Noxon never wavered in his claim of innocence. The evidence against him was entirely circumstantial. Although that evidence had a damning effect, Ely's skillful questioning of the prosecution's witnesses cast doubts. Noxon, after all, had claimed to Chief Sullivan that he had burned the extension cord and Lawrence's diaper and clothing not to conceal evidence but for two other reasons: first, to ensure that the extension never become a source of harm to others, and second, to destroy items that would bring back memories of the horrible accident. Likewise, Ely had forced Drs. Hunt and Smith to acknowledge that babies with "mongolism" had varying abilities, which suggested that neither physician could know for sure whether Lawrence was capable of grabbing the electrical cord and extending it across his body. Ely also reminded the jury that Whittlesey's testimony concerning his discussion with Noxon about the woman, who was electrocuted, was the discussion of a well-publicized incident that had been talked about by many residents of Pittsfield and Berkshire County. Noxon, Ely implied, was merely commenting and questioning about a matter many people at the time were discussing. And Ida Royce's memory of Noxon's purchase of an extension cord? According to Ely, dozens of such cords are sold daily. There was no way, even if Royce's memory was correct, that a reasonable person could determine if that particular cord was the same one involved in the baby's death. Finally, Noxon had another, if unacknowledged, thing going for him. Dorothy Wayman believed him to be innocent. Although her *Boston Globe* articles were balanced and fair, we know from her private writings that she believed Noxon not guilty of Lawrence's death and indeed felt that Noxon had been prosecuted by a cabal of local elites who resented Noxon's and his family's social position and private wealth.

On July 6, 1944, the case went to the twelve-man jury for deliberation. In four hours and forty-five minutes, the jury returned a verdict, finding Noxon guilty of first-degree murder. The next day Judge Pinanski sentenced Noxon to die in the state's electric chair, the mandatory penalty. In November he denied the defense's motion for a new trial, and in May 1945 the Massachusetts Supreme Judicial Court upheld the verdict. Things did not look good for John F. Noxon Jr.[14]

Nevertheless, Noxon had some things going for him. His wife, Peggy, had attended the trial faithfully, appearing petite, well dressed, and demure. When she spoke to reporters, and especially when she spoke with the *Globe's* Dorothy Wayman, she was always gracious and meek but affirming of her husband's innocence.[15] In turn, Wayman frequently used descriptions that favored Noxon and drew sympathy to what she saw as Noxon's plight. Some of this sympathy was directed at Noxon's disability. In every article written about the death of Lawrence and about the two trials, Wayman refers to Noxon as "crippled." And usually her "crippled" reference is to Noxon's manly triumph over this disability. Thus, he was a successful attorney, a devoted husband, a World War I veteran, a civic leader, and a true man despite being "crippled." About the baby Lawrence, on the other hand, Wayman always referred to him as the "mongoloid" or the "idiot," destined to be a helpless burden to his family and his community. Indeed, in her first diary entry as the first trial is beginning, she refers to Lawrence as Noxon's "idiot baby," thus rendering him unidimensionally disabled, the abject extreme of social powerlessness.[16]

As previously noted, Dorothy Wayman occupied an ambiguous social position as a Protestant turned Catholic, as a divorced mother and a news reporter in a largely male-dominated establishment, and as one who found herself operating in rarefied elite social circles. She understood the privilege of her position. It should come as no surprise that Wayman admired and sympathized with John Noxon whose success and status (despite being "crippled") exemplified the values that Wayman held as personal ideals.

Peggy Noxon also occupied a particular place in the social and group nexus of this case. The irony for Peggy was that Lawrence is her baby whom she had given birth to. References such as "mongoloid" (a biological reversal from Caucasian to the racial type of Mongols) and by extension "idiot baby" would have been serious affronts to Peggy's own humanity. Undoubtedly, as a Stanford University graduate, she was familiar with recent social history where scientists, philosophers, and physicians discussed Western ideas of progress through the lens of evolution. Ideas of natural and normal were used to justify social hierarchy on the basis of race, gender, class, and immigrant status.[17] Indeed, Langdon Down's initial description of "Mongolian idiots" in 1862 was a product of this idea of the evolutionary grounding of racial differentiation, racial hierarchy, and ultimately racial progress. The eugenics movement of the first half of the twentieth century only magnified this particular confluence of race and disability.[18]

Peggy and her infant son were caught in the cross-hairs of these debates. Like John, Peggy was also in possession of the right pedigree to occupy the upper rungs of the evolutionary ladder in the pristine social spaces of western Massachusetts society. Lawrence's "mongolism" upended all assurances of purity and perfection and must have thrust Peggy, both as a woman and a mother who produced an "abnormal" child, into a discomfiting space. Peggy Noxon's demeanor in court signified her gendered and class standing as the loyal wife of John Noxon, albeit the grief-stricken mother of Lawrence. In this she has no choice, as she was caught in what Marilyn Frye calls society's "double bind"—"situations in which options are reduced to a very few and all of them expose one to penalty, censure or deprivation."[19]

Finally, along with his wife's public demeanor and Wayman's sympathetic writings, Noxon had a third thing going for him, his politically influential attorney, former Massachusetts Governor Joseph B. Ely. Like Noxon, Ely was a Democrat. But as noted earlier, Ely was a peculiar Democrat, in that he was near-rabidly opposed to Franklin Roosevelt seeking a fourth four-year term in the upcoming November 1944 election. Despite his fall from grace at the national level, Ely was respected by Democrats in Massachusetts and was politically close to Massachusetts Governor Maurice J. Tobin, who on August 7, 1946, commuted Noxon's death sentence to life in prison. In Walpole State prison, "crippled" and now "lifer" John Noxon left death row and became a librarian in the prison's library.[20]

While he was running for the governor's office in 1930, Ely had become friends with Sara Rosenfeld Ehrmann, the most influential leader in the Massachusetts Council against the Death Penalty. During his two gubernatorial terms, Ely pardoned twelve men convicted of first-degree murder. He left the office in 1935 convinced that the death penalty only "leads to bargaining with guilty men." His efforts to end capital punishment, however, failed in the state house, where legislators remained skeptical of ending such punishment as they remained puzzled by his liberal use of his pardoning powers. Thus, Ely's efforts—both public and private efforts—were consistent with his previous position; nevertheless, they would have been futile had Noxon not been a part of the upper-class structure of western Massachusetts. Noxon's social position allowed Ely, for example, to request influential attorneys and political leaders throughout the state, and occasionally from outside the state, to send letters of support for Noxon's commutation to Governor Tobin.[21]

Later that same November, the Commonwealth elected a new governor, this time a Republican, Robert F. Bradford. Of a different political party from both Ely and Tobin, Bradford did not appear to be an official who would likely question the state's use of the death penalty. Bradford had come to governor's office after being the Middlesex County district attorney, where the public knew him as a vigilant and persistent prosecutor. So it surprised no one that on May 9, 1947, having been governor for only a few months, Bradford signed the execution order for Philip Bellino and Edward Gertson, each electrocuted a few hours later in the Massachusetts State Prison for the murder of nineteen-year-old Robert "Tex" Williams. The state's Supreme Judicial Court had denied the convicted defendants' appeal for a new trial, and the protests of the foes of the death penalty fell on the governor's deaf ears.[22]

Knowing that his influence was not as great as it had been with Tobin and quite aware that Bradford had no qualms about using the electric chair, Ely nevertheless filed a forty-page pardon petition with Governor Bradford's office. Ely had crafted the petition, carefully receiving signatures of support for the pardon from influential Democrats and Republicans alike. In December Ely had a private meeting with Bradford, but in April 1948 when Bradford vetoed a "mercy bill" to allow juries to recommend sentences of life for first-degree murder convictions, his confidence received a setback. Nevertheless, in December 1948, with a two-to-one majority recommendation of the state's three-person Executive Council Committee on Pardons, Governor Bradford commuted Noxon's sentence from life to six years, which made him eligible for immediate parole, with the stipulation that he live under parole supervision for the rest of his life. It is worth noting that the chair of the Council Committee on Pardons, Matthew W. Bullock, was the sole vote against pardoning. At the time, Bullock was one of the few African Americans in such an influential position. There can be little doubt that Bradford was willing to carry out the death penalty, especially if the convicted person was a member of the state's lower class (like Bellino and Gertson), and he had shown that he had little use for giving juries the authority to employ "mercy" in its capital-crime sentencing. His commutation of Noxon's sentence had less to do with justice or mercy than it did with class and disability.

On January 7, 1949, Noxon left prison. A week later he received permission from the parole board to move to Stoneham, Connecticut, where he lived, disbarred and never again practicing the law, until his death in 1972.[23]

Had Lawrence Noxon not died in 1943 under unusual and suspicious circumstances, John F. Noxon would likely have lived the remainder of his life as a successful corporate lawyer, who worked hard and, by the standards of Pittsfield, Massachusetts, was quite well off, who participated in several community institutions, who regularly attended his local Episcopal church, and who was not particularly political (despite a vague loyalty to the Democratic Party). His disability, polio—the same condition that his president, Franklin D. Roosevelt, lived with—would likely have been remembered as an impairment, over which Noxon triumphed. And baby Lawrence, like almost all children with Down syndrome at the time, would have been institutionalized, probably at the nearby Belchertown State School. But polio survivor John Noxon was tried for the killing—the brutal electrocution—of his six-month-old son. For that reason, in newspapers throughout Massachusetts and around the country, this convergence of "double disability" remained before a curious public. Added to this peculiar example of double disability, of course, were also matters of conflicting social arrangements in small-town America, arrangements that in the midst of a country in war and emerging from a distressing economic depression had national implications as well.

That Noxon contracted polio as an adult man meant that much of his sense of self had been formed prior to that event. His disability required an adjustment to a proper manly self-image formed by existing cultural, social, economic, and political experiences and realities. This adjustment was successful because Noxon had what Pierre Bourdieu called social capital, resources that he used to accommodate to his new "disabled" reality.[24] Although "crippled," he prevailed. He was able to court and marry Peggy. He had children, a law practice, and a big house, all markers of normalcy and success. Lawrence's birth was an interruption in this project of self-renovation. The child's presence hindered Noxon's rebuilding of self in two significant ways: Lawrence stood as John's full-blooded issue, a product of his biology and as a disabled child. In both instances, he was a dreadful reminder of John's failings as a male "struck down" by polio but further incapacitated with a weak-minded son who could not overcome his "feeblemindedness." This feeble mind had to be done away with. It is one thing to live as a proper man with a disability; it is quite another to encounter an offspring who is a reminder of his weakened, flawed, and less-than-manly self.

Embedded in the charges, trial, commutation, and parole are issues of class (Noxon was well to do), gender (Noxon was a successful man), religion (Noxon was a High-Church Protestant), and politics (Noxon was a Democrat). And all of these variables play into the events between 1943 and 1949. But Noxon was also a disabled polio survivor, one whose image of walking or standing with two canes was printed in newspapers across the nation. The image and words about him are embodied in the label, "crippled." In none of the several dozen articles about these events is there a failure to mention "crippled Noxon." What is unifying about the references to Noxon's disability is a mixture of pity and triumph. The pity is clearly linked to his impairment, but the triumph is just as clearly linked to his class, his masculinity, and his social status. A "crippled" man can triumph over his condition if he is a Harvard graduate and is married to a high-society wife, and if he attends an upper-class church and makes a success of himself in a lucrative profession. He is a real man, a triumph and an inspiration even if he kills his differently disabled child.

But should we be so harsh? The information that medical authorities provided to John and Peggy Noxon about their second son was the same information provided at the time to all parents with Down syndrome children. Lawrence Noxon was "doomed to a tragic life of hopeless mental deficiency."[25] With the Noxon murder trials, we have two disabilities, but one of them offers the possibility of pity and triumph, while the other offers no alternative to the pitiful. John Noxon became disabled as an adult man; by then he had been endowed with ample social capital to hold his own and achieve social and economic success. The world around him likely understood his disability as a tragedy and had ample sympathy for his condition. At all times John was able to defend himself. But baby Lawrence, being born with Down syndrome, was placed in a different caste automatically. Science and medicine, religion, philosophy, and social sciences contributed to Western understandings of the natural and the monstrous in order to organize society under industrial capitalism. People with Down syndrome were inferior and impediments to social and economic progress. They were effectively useless and seen as helpless and defenseless, with no social or economic potential. John Noxon could work with his brains, while Lawrence would have neither body nor mind to work with for the good of society. Thus, even disability, like class, gender, status, and power, is in this story stratified. And for those at the bottom end of the strata, the best outcome is "mercy killing." Although Noxon never waived from his claim of innocence, the rhetoric of the time—usually subtle and implied but at other times explicit—suggested that "crippled" Noxon had every right to kill "mongoloid" Lawrence. A triumphant disability represents a life worth living, a hopeless one does not.

Michael Kimmel draws on Erving Goffman's prototype of the "hegemonic" male as one who is

> young, married, urban, northern heterosexual, Protestant father of college education, fully employed, of good complexion, weight and height, and a recent record in sports. . . . Any male who fails to qualify in any one of these ways is likely to view himself . . . . as unworthy, incomplete, and inferior.

In light of this modern normative understanding of masculinity, one can see how John F. Noxon Jr. had achieved the status of "hegemonic" masculinity through his multiple accomplishments and ascriptions as a male, upper-class, white, war veteran and Harvard-educated Protestant lawyer of honorable pedigree. His setbacks as an adult "victim" of polio may have been psychologically and physically challenging. While it is possible that he was able to suppress and compensate for this disability with all the other social assets that he had previously acquired, it must be have been quite overwhelming and confusing to face what he probably perceived as a gross imperfection in the life of his infant male child. Could Lawrence have been a stark reminder and repudiation of his own masculine self? A self that was once able and now disabled? Did baby Lawrence present an affront to John Noxon in the way that he reflected his disability back to John? Did John, in turn, feel the desperate need to separate and disidentify from baby Lawrence? Did Lawrence's condition interrupt a prosperous future for both his father and his family?

The death of Lawrence Noxon, the subsequent trials of John Noxon in the courts and the media, and Peggy Noxon's role is a moving tale of the tenuous aspects of modern social hierarchy where the hegemonic white male occupies the top of the higher echelons of the society, while the bottom rungs are occupied by common populations of women and racial, religious, and sexual minorities—and the last and least of these are the disabled among them. Yet this hierarchy is not as hermetically sealed as one might presume. The central actors in this story were all in one way or the other slightly "off" in terms of their hegemonic profiles. As detailed previously, they were all similar in terms of class and gender and yet none of them fit the ideal type perfectly. They were divided by politics, religion, ethnicity, ancestral pedigree, gender, and physical ability. Each displays the impossibility of attaining the "hegemonic" prototype, perhaps even the inherently vapid nature of this ideal. In this sense, as Kimmel notes, "American masculinity is a relentless test"—a test that needs a clear and resolute "Other" to rally against. From baby Lawrence, Peggy Noxon, Dorothy Wayman, John Noxon, and all the other intermediate actors all the way to Governors Maurice Tobin and Robert F. Bradford played a role in service of this ideal.[26]

Notes

1. Dorothy G. Wayman, "Ill Juror Forces Noxon Trial Recess until Monday," *Boston Globe* (March 4, 1944), 1, 4. Wayman reports "scores of letters that arrive every day from around country to the judge and attorneys involved in the trial." Wayman calls it "a nationwide debate on the issues involved in the strange case of John F. Noxon."
Throughout the chapter we have used terms like "crippled," "mongoloid," "idiot," "mentally defective," and "feeble-minded" to reflect the labels of the period. We have placed these words in quotation marks because we recognize that, although they were commonly used words in the 1940s, they are currently offensive.
2. Frederick S. Mead, ed., *Harvard Military Record in the World War* (Boston: Harvard Alumni Association, 1921), 711; Donald B. Willard, "Noxon Held Without Bail, Denies Mercy Killing of Son," *Boston Globe* (September 29, 1943), 1, 12.
3. Eldon E. Ferguson, "Obituary of John F. Noxon [III]" *Physics Today* 38 (September 1985), 97. See also Henry S. Francis, "John Franklin Noxon, 1928–1985," *The American Alpine Journal* 28 (1985), 330.
4. "Noxon Pleads Innocent," *North Adams Transcript* (September 28, 1943), 3; Dorothy G. Wayman, "Noxon's Wife May Take Stand; Defendant's Story Told to Jury," *Boston Globe* (March 1, 1943), 1.
5. Donald B. Willard, "Noxon Denies Knowing How His Baby Died." *Boston Globe* (September 29, 1943), 1, 4.
6. Wayman. "Noxon's Wife May Take Stand; Defendant's Story Read to Jury," 4.
7. Willard, "Noxon Held without Bail, Denies Mercy Killing of Son," 1, 12.
8. "Joseph B. Ely Believes John Noxon Is Innocent," *Berkshire Eagle* (November 9, 1943), 1. It could not have been lost on Berkshire County old-timers that, when Ely was district attorney twenty-five years earlier, Mrs. Gladys Courvoisier Dunn, wife of Joseph Allan Dunn, a minor but locally well-known novelist, was tried for the pistol shooting of her two-year-old son, J. Allan Dunn Jr. Gladys Dunn was defended by John Franklin Noxon's father, who had previously been the county's district attorney.
9. Wayman, "Noxon 'Disappointed' Over Mistrial Ruling: New Trial, May 31," *Boston Globe* (March 10, 1944), 16.
10. Even the armed services newspaper, *Stars and Stripes*, covered the trials. See for example, "Guilty of Killing Son, an Imbecile—Lawyer to Appeal Verdict Carrying a Mandatory Death Penalty (John F. Noxon)" *Stars and Stripes* [London Edition] 4 (July 10, 1944), 3.
11. Wayman, "Murder Jury Studies Wiring at Noxon Home," *Boston Globe* (February 25, 1944), 1, 3.
12. "Noxon Reported to Have Discussed Home Accidents," *Berkshire County Eagle* (October 6, 1943), 19; "Court to Hear Bail Arguments for Noxon Today," *Boston Globe* (October 1, 1943), 12; "Noxon Told Chief 'No Matter How I Felt I Could Not Kill My Baby,'" *Berkshire Eagle* (June 9, 1944), 9, 13.

13. "Noxon Told Chief," 9, 13; "Opposing Counsel Battle as Noxon Trial Resumes," *Berkshire Eagle* [City Edition] (March 6, 1944), 1.

14. *Commonwealth v. John F. Noxon*, Supreme Judicial Court of Massachusetts. 319 Mass. 495; 66 N.E.2d 814; 1946 Mass. LEXIS 649, October 23, 1945, Argued; October 24, 1945, Argued May 10, 1946, Decided.

15. Willard, "Noxon Held Without Bail, Denies Mercy Killing of Son," 1, 12; and Wayman, "Noxon's Wife May Take Stand," *Boston Globe* (March 1, 1944), 1.

16. Wayman, "Diary," February 22, 1944, Holy Cross College, Wayman Papers, Series 1 File 2, Box 2, folder 3.

17. Douglas C. Baynton, "Disability and the Justification of Inequality in American History," *In the New Disability History*, edited by Paul K. Longmore and Lauri Umansky (New York: New York University Press, 2000), cited in Paula S. Rothenberg, *Race, Class, and Gender in the United States* (New York: Worth, 2014), 94.

18. David Wright, *Downs: The History of a Disability* (New York: Oxford University Press, 2011), 48–114; and James W. Trent Jr., *Inventing the Feeble Mind: A History of Intellectual Disability in the United States* (New York: Oxford University Press, 2016), 129–215.

19. Cynthia Eagle Russett has noted that "women and savages, together with idiots, criminals, and pathological monstrosities (those with congenital disabilities) were a constant source of anxiety to male intellectuals in the late nineteenth century." See her *Sexual Science: The Victorian Construction of Womanhood* (Cambridge, MA: Harvard University Press, 1989), 63. See also Marilyn Frye, "Oppression" in *The Politics of Reality: Essays in Feminist Theory*, cited in Paula S. Rothenberg, ed., *Race, Class, and Gender in the United States* (New York: Worth Publishers, 2014), 149–150.

20. "Noxon Declared Eligible for Parole Immediately," *Berkshire Evening Eagle* (August 8, 1946), 1.

21. Alan Rogers, *Murder and the Death Penalty in Massachusetts* (Amherst: University of Massachusetts Press, 2008), 347.

22. Rogers, *Murder and the Death Penalty,* 330–332.

23. "Noxon Released from Prison," *The New York Times* (January 8, 1949), 30; and Cornelius R. Owen, "Noxon Wins Parole, Free Friday," *Boston Globe* (January 7, 1949), 1, 6.

24. Pierre Bourdieu, "The Forms of Capital," in *Handbook of Theory and Research for the Sociology of Education*, John G. Richardson, ed. (New York: Greenwood Press, 1986), 241–260.

25. Jack Stone, "John Noxon's Change of Luck," *The American Weekly* (March 20, 1949), 18. See also Trent, *Inventing the Feeble Mind,* 111–114, 216–258.

26. Michael Kimmel, "Masculinity as Homophobia: Fear, Shame and Silence in the Construction of Gender Identity," in Rothenberg, ed., *Race, Class, and Gender in the United States,* 86–87.

PART IV

Men and Boys as "Supercrips"

11

Mythological Pedagogies, or Suicide Clubs as Eugenic Alibi

Kathleen M. Brian

According to all accounts—and there were at least two dozen[1]—the southwestern shore of Lake Michigan became the backdrop for a strange and remarkable spectacle in the summer of 1892. There, on the Saturday night of July 16, a corpse rested atop an 18-foot pyre while more than a dozen living men offered speeches, recitations, and a spattering of musical tributes. The corpse was clad in white; the living wore black. These men—that is, the journalists, lawyers, and physicians who had trekked more than thirty miles to pay homage—were members of the Whitechapel Club, a fraternal organization formed in the offices of the Chicago *Daily News* just three years prior and named for the section of London where Jack the Ripper had undertaken his lethal work. As this appellation and the dramatic immolation suggest, ritualistic engagement with (im)mortality was a crucial component of the group's distinctiveness.[2] Symposium invitations featured lively, reanimated skeletons, and members convened at a large table forged in the shape of a coffin.[3] They surrounded themselves with a noteworthy collection of human skulls taken from infamous crime scenes and donated by the Chicago police, or from deceased, diagnosed residents of the Cook County Insane Asylum, where club member Dr. John Spray had worked for more than a decade.[4] Unsurprisingly, neither women nor minors were granted access to said symposia—that is, *living* women and minors; the skull collection featured a goodly number of female remains.[5]

But who was the dead man who served as the vehicle through which these living men might enact their peculiarly morbid masculinity?[6] The only extant biographical account, like the tale of the immolation itself, was composed by the Whitechapelers and printed in the Chicago *Herald* the following morning: Morris Allen Collins was a native of Texas. He arrived in Chicago in 1886 amidst the dramatic furor that unfolded after the Haymarket Affair of May 4, in which a peaceable labor rally devolved into violent chaos when one among the gathered threw a dynamite bomb that killed seven members of the Chicago police force.[7] Albert Parsons, August Spies, Adolph Fischer, and George Engel, and Louis Lingg were ultimately sentenced to death for their alleged role in the events of that evening. While the bombing at the Haymarket provoked fury and terror across the nation, many found the state's swift and questionable retribution troubling. Two days before the scheduled execution, more than 40,000 residents of Chicago—including Collins, goes the Whitechapelers' narrative—put their names to a petition for clemency. Having lost that particular battle, however, Collins went to work first as a journalist for the Chicago edition of Joseph Buchanan's radical *Labor Enquirer*, then as a "common laborer," and then as a foreman.

At some point during 1888, Collins showed up in the newspapers yet again, this time advocating a rather remarkable labor reform tactic: establishing "death chambers" where the poor, weary, and "maimed" might painlessly kill themselves.[8] Such spaces would, the letter explained, "have a beneficial effect in two directions: it would afford an opportunity of escape for thousands of people whose lives [were] a nightmare of torture, and at the same time bring the horror of the situation home to that class of people which fatten[ed] and thrive[d] under the system." Collins himself was struck down by a Northwestern train in 1890, an accident that left him with severe neurological damage made manifest in regular seizures.[9] The incident, reported the Whitechapelers, was a turning point: from then until his completed suicide two years later, "his morbidness increased."[10]

Thus it was that an ensemble of generally white, nondisabled, professional men—at least one of whom openly advocated eugenic sterilization and at least one of whom held a position at a local insane asylum—gathered around an elephantine pyre built upon the Indiana dunes to trumpet the suicide of a white, disabled working man as a courageous act of resistance that the latter had himself promoted. But as word of the cremation circulated, it was neither Collins's unemployed status nor his neurological impairment that captured the public's fascination. The detail that consistently incited interest was the fact that, at the time of his death, Collins allegedly held the office of president of the Dallas Suicide Club—again, according to the Whitechapelers. The alleged Dallas assemblage was the lone Texas iteration of a much broader phenomenon that drew fascination, condemnation, and even approbation of the American press and its readership during the final decade of the nineteenth century. Between 1889 and 1903, newspapers across the United States alleged more than thirty active suicide clubs operating within the nation's geopolitical boundaries, from New York to California and more than a dozen states in between.[11] Though they differed in operational detail, each club consisted of (mostly) men who gathered (at least) once a year to drink, sing, and select one among them to die by his own hand.[12] These "astonishing societies" were first conceptualized by Scottish novelist Robert Louis Stevenson in a trilogy that was serialized in the *London Magazine* (1878) before being published in the United States as part of *New Arabian Nights* (1882).[13] Thirteen years later, the New York publishing house of George Munro's Sons pulled the trilogy from the longer short story collection and issued the first standalone American edition of *The Suicide Club*.[14] And, in the spring of 1889, American print culture exploded with the rumor that an actually existing "Robert Louis Stevenson suicide club" had been formed in Bridgeport, Connecticut.[15]

In this sense—and despite his fantastical position atop the pyre and the eventual status of local legend to which that pyre obtained—Collins occupied a place at the nexus of a more mundane but perhaps more revealing set of social, cultural, and political processes at the *fin de siècle*.[16] And yet, despite the vivacious public life of suicide clubs, historians have had virtually nothing to say about them.[17] Even accounts of the revelry of July 16, 1892, leave curiously unexamined the peculiar notation of Collins's presidency. Indeed, interest in the events of that evening tends to be subsumed within a more general interest in the Whitechapelers themselves. For some, the Whitechapel Club is representative of many such groups that sprung up among newspapermen during the period. As such, it reveals broader patterns of identity formation among male journalists who found themselves in an increasingly professionalized industry. In this telling, the pyre on the Indiana shore becomes evidence of what Alfred Lorenz has termed "newspapermen at leisure," an example of the homosocial attachments (here I extrapolate), subversive playfulness, and self-mythologizing that were crucial elements of newsroom masculinity of the 1890s.[18]

And yet, if we shift our gaze from the morbid masculinity of the Whitechapelers to the corpse itself, and to the suicide club over which it ostensibly once presided, the archival remnants leave us in uneasy uncertainty. For while certain elements can be corroborated—the fact of a death most emphatically and unequivocally— others stubbornly resist verification in any traditional sense of that term. There was a man. In the coroner's records, however, the only surviving trace of this man that I have yet been able to locate beyond the newspaper page, he is listed thus: M. A. Collins.[19] The full name of this man is not, as we might anticipate given his professed local notoriety, recorded. A man, Morris Allen or otherwise, did indeed die of a gunshot wound to the head in a Chicago boardinghouse in the summer of 1892.[20] Yet inconsistencies emerge regarding even this simple detail: while the official inquest dates the death to Saturday, July 9, the Whitechapelers' *Herald* article, carefully clipped and pasted into the club scrapbook, records instead the date of Friday, July 8.[21] The newspapers that reprinted the story by and large agreed with the Whitechapelers, though another offered a third option—June 28, a Tuesday.[22] And so, like an anonymous newspaperman in Galveston who characterized the events of July 16 as "mostly smoke," skepticism is the mood evoked by interfacing with the traces that remain.

We are left with little more than the proliferation of ambiguity—with silence, and with noise. Though less likely to occur when searching for white male citizen, scholars are far from unaccustomed to such encounters. On the contrary, a robust body of work has developed around these and kindred questions over the past two decades, led with particular vigor by postcolonial theorists and historians of Western imperialism who, interested in the myriad violences of imperial rule, have often meditated upon the archive itself in their attempts to think through epistemological and ontological questions of racialized knowing.[23] Historians of disability, though they have been less vocal in these debates, have also been forced to contend with the paradoxical coexistence of silence and noise in the archive. They, too, often seek historical subjects who do not appear in official indexes, whose remnants are scattered across multiple repositories, or who materialize only— or primarily—through the words of others.[24] In their efforts to ameliorate such moments of elision and ventriloquism, scholars have determinedly approached the past at a slant: they have researched creatively, expansively, and beyond the "official" archive[25]; collaborated with archivists and librarians to create and re-create repositories with disability and disabled people as nucleus[26]; deployed sophisticated theoretical frameworks to uncover the possibilities available to their subjects[27]; and brought a disability studies framework to bear on inveterate historical problems.[28] As this review suggests, the restoration of disabled people to dominant historical narratives, as well as the imperative to attend to disability as a revealing category of analysis, has been crucial for evidencing the significance of disability to scholars across temporal, geographical, and disciplinary distinctions. Historians of disability, that is, have long been concerned with what we might characterize broadly as projects of recovery and re-narration.

Such an approach offers terrifically tempting possibilities for the project at hand. In wrestling with these figures and the archival remains that now constitute them as (im)possible historical subjects, I have often caught myself thinking in just such a vein: what sort of subjects might I stitch together from, say, a naturalization record, a newspaper account, and a coroner's inquest? How might I prove that such clubs did or did not exist? And if they did exist, what did suicide club members mean by forming them? As men living in an historical epoch replete with proliferating technologies of state surveillance, perhaps these clubs functioned as covert spaces, unencumbered by the burdensome impingements of capitalism or the state, in which these men could play, revel, or—better yet— resist. Perhaps decisions to form suicide clubs and to choose death were, as the Whitechapelers touted, defiant mechanisms for opting out. To re-narrate these deaths as such seems, at least initially, to be a clear way forward. Indeed, this interpretation has held great salience for those who have been generous enough to hear and comment on these research findings as they accumulated.[29] Simply put, my audiences and I have been much tempted by what Saidiya Hartman has termed "the romance of resistance."[30]

Yet tethered as it is to questions of agency, resistance, and individual willfulness, this romance remains indebted to what we might call, after postcolonial theorists, the *ableist epistemes* of history. That is, the agentive, resistant, willful historical subject who intentionally *means to do* is always already coded as supremely masculine and supremely (cap)able; on the other hand, the same might be said of the historian, who plunders the archive in search of scraps with which to create coherent, ordered, rational narratives that can then be duly incorporated into that vast body of knowledge we know as "historiography." I am by no means the first to evince discomfort with hopeful ascriptions of intentionality[31], or with the collapse of the distinction between agency and resistance.[32] Nevertheless, it is well past time that such questions be framed and discussed as explicit dilemmas for those invested in the historical intersections of gender and disability. What follows, then, is a tentative effort at resisting the romance. I consider these categories as lived identities, and I analyze the gendered and ableist ways of knowing that were on such vivid display in popular narratives of suicide clubs: namely, death is preferable to wage-disabling difference; suicide makes sense in such instances. But I also seek to keep these categories at the fore as key nodes of power that underwrite much of historical methodology. As something of an opening gambit, I avoid constructing an historical narrative of suicide clubs or of Collins that is "coherent" in the traditional sense of that term. In the case of those whom historians may most want to know, I avoid ascribing agency, motive, or intent. I work to remain in the discomfort of not knowing. This chapter is thus also an effort to make strange our compulsion to know—an effort, of sorts, at an epistemology of uncertainty. What I do not know is entered alongside that which I may know, or that which I think I may even know for relative certainty.

For as figures who appear in the archive in almost entirely ventriloquized form, the men who may or may not have formed suicide clubs remind us of the ethical imperatives of lingering in uncertainty, of the need to practice what Lisa Lowe has called "history hesitant."[33] To avoid reinscribing the very violences that inaugurated their appearance in the archive, then, this chapter does not seek to restore these men as discreet, bounded, rational subjects. There are no efforts to parse their interiority or speculate on their motives. Indeed, the chapter works against such recuperation, though it does seek recuperation in another sense: to restore and pursue the uncertainty that marked the stories when they originally appeared, as well as the ultimate unknowability of the men who became the stories' main protagonists. Indeed, the chapter suggests that ambiguity and opacity were crucial elements of popular narratives of suicide clubs and that the corpses inhabiting them accomplished important cultural and political work. Tracking these corpses and the narratives that attached to, detached from, and reattached to them shows the profound power inherent in telling stories. The power to "mythify" entailed not only the bleeding out of biography and history but also the replenishing infusion of politically useful alternatives. In this particular case study, the hemorrhage was necessitated by the political urgency surrounding the labor question and by capitalist' need for a different story.[34] They needed a different "sense of life" that would reframe material realities, and they achieved this by ventriloquizing a handful of men who died by suicide.[35]

The (De)Composition of Victor Heisterhagen

The sound of the pistol shot, heard by Mrs. Kate Gregory and Napoleon Commette, issued from the cellar. When Gregory rushed toward the sound, she found Victor Heisterhagen slumped at the bottom of the stairs with a .32 caliber revolver in his hand and a gaping wound on the side of his head. He died within moments. It is not entirely clear how "police officials and Undertaker Bishop were notified" on that morning of February 3, 1887, how the body came to be "removed to Bishop's Morgue," or who officially declared the death a "deliberately contemplated" suicide. All three details, however, appeared in an article that materialized later that day in the Bridgeport *Evening Farmer,* known for its Democratic politics and its labor advocacy, which explained the incident through recourse to personal history.[36]

According to the unidentified author(s), the series of events culminating in suicide began, in the first place, with a very specific embodiment that, in this man's very specific context, became disabling: slowly decaying teeth.[37] Heisterhagen was a talented musician who had been particularly adept with wind instruments; indeed, his incorporation into the body politic depended upon it. In his naturalization application of 1876, it was noted that Heisterhagen had served in the US Army as one of the "music boys"—a route to citizenship that was acutely masculinized in the 1870s—and was therefore given the opportunity to renounce all allegiances to any but the US federal government, with particular reference to the emperor of Germany.[38] Less than a decade later, however, Heisterhagen's teeth were giving him trouble and he was, as a result, forced to contemplate alternative means of subsistence.[39] At some point in those same years—perhaps during 1882[40]—he also became estranged from his wife.

These convergences, the writers at the *Farmer* explained, compelled Heisterhagen to take up boarding at Gregory's place at 13 Gold Street and to open a saloon, a few doors down at 19 Gold Street, with the financial backing of Gregory herself. A savvy, entrepreneurial woman who seems to have mastered the masculine world of capitalist enterprise, Gregory had, the newspaper noted, provided a "not inconsequential portion of the capital."[41] The authors—extrapolating from we know not whether personal experience, hearsay, or the reports of Gregory and Commette—characterized Heisterhagen's new venture as a failure. "Business was bad," they wrote, "the place was strange to the majority of people, and the saloon didn't pay expenses." In the absence of financial or other records, there is no way to corroborate these and subsequent observations: that the situation "went from bad to worse," that Gregory often demanded repayment, or that Gregory's requests sent Heisterhagen to New Jersey in the ultimately unsatisfied hope that his brother would lend him the necessary amount.[42]

His teeth rotting, his marriage ruined, and his business failing, Heisterhagen opted for a .32 caliber revolver. To make this suicide make sense, in other words, the *Farmer* emphasized two elements of a mostly failed performance of nineteenth-century masculinity, both of which seem to have been inaugurated by disabling rot: Heisterhagen was as inept at heteronormative domesticity as he was at possessive individualism.[43] The *Farmer* coded the moment of death, however, as decidedly masculine. It was, according to the newspaper, intentionally undertaken ("proven by two letters found on his person"); decisively and swiftly enacted ("he had hardly snapped the catch of the door when a pistol shot was heard"); and aggressively, requisitely sanguinary ("blood rushing from a wound in the side of his head")—no passively feminine drowning or starvation here.[44] Distinguishing between the article's description of Heisterhagen and the article's description of suicide may remind us of the flexibility of gendered utterances, the uncanny ability of gender to attach even to nonsentient things. Alternatively, we may be tempted to interpret the masculine accents of the suicide as the newspapermen's attempt to allow an emasculated man to reclaim his manhood. The letters, found (somewhere, by someone) and reprinted in the *Farmer*, could certainly support such an interpretation. First, a note to Gregory in which Heisterhagen, it seems, ultimately sought to assert his dominance over her:

> KATY
> You dun et now is going to take me life and you are the fault of it good by
>   and may you have 10 times the trouble that I had
> VICTOR HEISTERHAGEN[45]

And, second, a request that he be buried in his army uniform, which he owned and which would thus allow for a final reclamation of self-sufficiency:

> If I am dad you put mi military Blonse on me that is the only ting i got not to put you in anny expense and see that all my relations find out that I am going.
>   VICTOR HEISTERHAGEN[46]

But I would like to do neither. Or, rather, I would like to go afield of such possibilities to consider how this body—interred at Park Cemetery three days later under the watchful gaze of "some 60 members" of the Bridgeport Lodge, No. 36, B.P.O. Elks—was resurrected in the name of an altogether different purpose.

For Heisterhagen's death by no means precipitated his disappearance from the archive. For the two years following his death, the Bridgeport city directories list him, ghostlike, as, "b[oar]ds. 13 Gold Street." Of perhaps greater interest to us, however, is that he—or some version of him—resurfaced in an 1890 story that claimed to expose the inner workings of "the Bridgeport Suicide club."[47] Penned by Fred C. Dayton, who formerly wrote for the Republican-leaning Chicago *Tribune* and whose suicide club story ran in the similarly Republican-leaning *North American and Daily Advertiser*, the article alleged that *Max* Heisterhagen was among the original members. Indeed, as Dayton told it, M. Heisterhagen's suicide followed directly on the heels of the uproarious, jovial founding of the club itself. It was at this inaugural meeting that M. Heisterhagen had "drawn death" with but a few rolls of the dice and, by the terms of the oath and constitution drawn up minutes before, was thus contractually bound to kill himself within the year.⁴⁸ In Dayton's rendering, upon taking his leave from his six companions, M. Heisterhagen

> went to his saloon on Gold street, unlocked the door, lit the gas, wrote a note, took a pistol from a drawer back of the bar and blew out his brains. The note was addressed to "my respected friends and fellow members of the suicide club," and the message was simply this: "I have kept my oath. I warn you to keep yours."

The only other details included in Dayton's description of Heisterhagen was his involvement in a *brass* band, the other members of which played at the funeral, for which, Dayton continued, the members of the suicide club had "contributed a magnificent floral offering which was to be the first of many of its kind."⁴⁹ The shifts are subtle. A morning suicide becomes one undertaken at evening. A musician particularly adept at wood instruments becomes one who played with a brass band. Two letters—one, resentful, to a lender, and another establishing funerary considerations—become a single, ominous note to members of a suicide club. The Elks members evaporate entirely.

Yet the biographical details that figured so prominently in the *Farmer*, and which Dayton eschewed, materialized elsewhere in the two years between the initial coverage and the later exposé—albeit selectively and attached to a different name. In the frenzied coverage of 1889, the year that witnessed the first allegations of a "real life" suicide club in Bridgeport, the particulars regarding the original "president" of the Bridgeport Suicide Club—whose name was variously recorded as Henry Jensen⁵⁰ and Henry Jansen⁵¹—were eerily similar to those of our actually existing Victor Heisterhagen. Ja/ensen was originally conjured in the *Farmer*, reappeared in diminished form in the *Evening World* two days later, received a more complete accounting in the Wichita *Daily Eagle* two days after that, and, finally, was afforded but a single line in Denver's *Rocky Mountain News*:

> Henry Jensen, the president of the Suicide Club, who kept a saloon on Gold street was the first member to kill himself.⁵²

> Henry Jensen, the President of the Suicide Club, put himself out of the world by his own hands two years ago.⁵³

> Henry Jansen, the president of the Suicide club, who kept a saloon on Gold street, was the first member to make way with himself. He put himself out of this world by his own hands about two years ago.⁵⁴

> Henry Jansen, the president, led off by taking poison.⁵⁵

Ja/ensen, if he ever existed, seems to have left no trace other than as the leader of the Bridgeport suicideites. As we have seen, however, Heisterhagen did indeed own a saloon at 19 Gold Street and did indeed lodge at Kate Gregory's nearby boardinghouse (13 Gold Street).⁵⁶ And, of course, his suicide was reported in the *Farmer* of April 1887—"about two years" and two months prior to the articles in which

Ja/ensen appeared.[57] And the suicide so carefully masculinized by the *Farmer* became, in the hands of these various newspaper men, something altogether different. He (gently) "put himself out of the world," or accomplished suicide by toxic substance—a mode of death that, as the Galveston *Daily News* succinctly put it, was an "effeminate [way] to die."[58]

Are these simply insignificant errors? Are they simply mishearings, miswritings, or misprintings? Perhaps. Or, if we are inclined to take seriously their accumulation, should we then see them as additional evidence of "newspaper men at leisure" (which seems to declare "boys will be boys," though in a more sophisticated register)? I would like to suggest something more portentously made; that is, I would like to suggest that the omissions, selective borrowings, and partial truths should alert us instead to a hemorrhage-in process. The task then becomes to determine what, exactly, was infused, how it did so, and to what ends.

Infusions, Inflections, and Other Urgent Doings

The journalistic furor of 1889 was precipitated by the death by gunshot of John Kienzy—or was it Kiewzry, Kiewzy, Kiewsey, Keezy, or Keensey?[59] Variable renderings aside (or, rather, duly noted), between April 22 and May 10, the news of this single fatality appeared in at least twelve separate articles. And while the *Farmer* originally published two separate articles (one announcing Kienzy's death[60] and one announcing a suicide club[61]), subsequent coverage collapsed the two, thereby turning what would otherwise have been a non-event at the national level—nothing more than one among scores of suicides in 1889—into something infinitely more.[62]

Seeming transparency was a crucial accouterment of these articles, accomplished in no small degree by attributions that inevitably situated the origin of the narrative elsewhere, at some distant location and with some other, similarly distant person. Juxtaposed and compared, however, we see that the New York *Evening World* not only occupied chronological pride of place (April 24) in terms of national coverage, but also claimed to be unveiling that which was "SPECIAL TO THE EVENING WORLD." the Pittsburgh *Dispatch*, verbatim the *World* article and published the same day, attributed its information to a "SPECIAL TELEGRAM," though from whom or where was left ambiguous.[63] When word surfaced in Kansas two days later, the *Wichita Daily Eagle* rightly ascribed the information to the Bridgeport *Evening Farmer* itself.[64] The report that appeared in Denver's *Rocky Mountain News* the following day was not an exact match for any previous article but rather borrowed snippets, here and there, from those that had preceded it. The byline, however, suggested New York City as the locus of knowledge, whether conveyed via telegram, correspondent, or some other, unnamed conduit.[65] And by the time the news had reached New Orleans, the *Daily Picayune* claimed for its authority a dispatch from Bridgeport, rather than the original article, but its content was verbatim an article from Chicago's *Daily Inter Ocean*, which in turn claimed to be a reprint from the Cincinnati *Enquirer*, which, in turn, was verbatim the original article of the *Evening World*.[66] That is, the more earnestly one attempts to name authorial origin—and then, perhaps, to establish motive, or to speculate on intent—the more secure the story becomes in its cacophonous bastardization.

Perhaps we should expect nothing less; at least, we need not be bothered by it.[67] Recalling that "myth is neither a lie nor a confession," this moment of acute uncertainty invites us to take stock of inflections as the story moved, and as each contributor offered his own subtle modulations. For each newspaperman who wrote about the Bridgeport club was, before he became a writer of myth, a reader of it. Barthes observes that the readers of myth—the "myth consumers"—are the ones who "reveal their essential function."[68] So, what might have been the essential function of the story of the Bridgeport Suicide Club once loosed by the *Farmer*? What might have been the salient details for the myth consumers of April 24 to May 10, 1889? Attempting to read ourselves into 1889, the following characterizations and turns of phrases present themselves forcefully, not least of all because they emerged not all at once, but, rather, accumulated slowly and incrementally over the period in question. Before considering their implications, I list them here in full, and in chronological order of appearance, with citations referencing their first occurrence:

- suicide[69]
- by ballot[70]
- Keenzy's saloon[71]
- William Meckl [or Weckl], a sign-painter[72]
- formed three years ago[73]
- consisted of five members[74]
- German[75]
- evidently insane men[76]
- a secret organization[77]
- recently returned from a European tour[78]
- what had been suspected, but not generally known[79]
- hopes to initiate new members into the order[80]
- fanatic club was organized by four fools[81]

German—Saloon—Sign-Painter—European Tour

The *Evening World* did nothing at all to register Kienzy's nativity on April 24. Within two days of that initial report, however, newspapermen in Wichita added a supplementary reference to an unnamed club member who was "a well known German resident of West Stratford." The following day, journalists in San Francisco, Helena, Los Angeles, and Denver dropped the reference to this unnamed club member but kept the German-ness: "Kienzy, a wealthy young German."[82] More than a century hence, a local historian notes that Kienzy was (German?) Swiss.[83] The newspapermen in Denver appended the first mention of Kienzy's connections abroad.[84]

The articles of 1889 thus abandoned local particularism—Alsatian, Prussian, Bohemian—for the more sweeping, ambiguous term "German."[85] The prismatic signifying power of the vague German-ness of Kienzy's corpse may have been the point: for readers in 1889, it was an invitation to briefly register any, all, or none of several associations at once. The term may have denoted an individual's émigré status; that is, the man or men in question may have lived in geopolitical territory that was, after 1871, under the sovereignty of the German Empire.[86] It may also have denoted, in more generic fashion, an individual's linguistic status as a speaker of the German language, or even an individual's racialization as a member of the Germanic race. This would have allowed for the inclusion of the individuals who had emigrated not from within the Second Reich but also from the Germanic lands and German speakers in the Austrian-Hungarian Empire and elsewhere across the continent.[87] More to the point may have been that the 1880s witnessed a high tide in immigration generally and German immigration specifically. Indeed, comparable numbers of the latter had not been seen since the 1850s. German émigrés would retain their status as the largest immigrant group in the United States until the era of the Great Depression. These numbers, combined with the economic depression of 1883–1885, whipped nativist sentiment to a frenzied pitch.[88] In addition to debates over religion and German-language education, the saloon—a site of German sociocultural distinctiveness—came under increasing attack by temperance advocates. Reformers urged the state, at various times and always with the amelioration of the "great curse of intemperance" in mind, to inaugurate a Sunday-closing requirement, higher licensing fees, and more concerted efforts to prosecute the sale of liquor to minors.[89] The notation of "German" in reports of the Bridgeport club thus indicated a specific brand of not-American-ness.

Taken alongside the generic German-ness of the corpse, that the Bridgeport Suicide Club was formed in a saloon encouraged a partial pivot, or, rather, the layering of an additional set of meanings to make this corpse and its compatriots even stranger and, indeed, more dangerous. For embedded somewhere in the midst of other, now familiar nativist concerns (crime, poverty, intemperance—a general failure or refusal to assimilate), were fears of radical politics, whether via socialist refugees of the failed 1848 Revolutions at midcentury or German anarchists in the 1880s.[90] "Saloon," that is, did not just place the "German" in a site of sociocultural distinctiveness.[91] It also, and perhaps more threateningly, placed the "German" in a space that was well known as a locus for the dissemination of anticapitalist ideologies—republican socialism, anarchism, or otherwise[92]—and for the development of concrete tactics for anticapitalist resistance.[93] The 1880s witnessed a fierce, unprecedented rise of both, and, as one contemporary disdainfully remarked, the "saloon-keepers with their low and contemptible resorts were the real bastille-keepers."[94] That the Bridgeport Suicide Club included Kienzy, the "wealthy" saloon-owner, and William Meckl, a "sign-painter," served as a stark reminder that labor organizers were increasingly uniting skilled, semiskilled, and unskilled workers alike: the Knights of Labor, for one, had approximately 100,000 individuals at the turn of the decade; by 1886, they could claim more than seven times that number.[95] This influx was, by and large, effected by what Richard Schneirov has called the "burgeoning army of semiskilled" workers.[96] Across the decade, in hundreds of lockouts, boycotts, and strikes, tens of thousands of workers sought to shake the very foundations of capitalist complacency.

Thus the corpse, already registered as foreign and as alien, now also registered as a subversive threat to both democracy and capitalism—or, better yet, capitalist democracy. This was a very specific kind of threat. Labor activity of the mid-1880s, as Richard Schneirov has argued, was distinct from earlier patterns of anticapitalist activity not only because it involved a marked number of semiskilled and unskilled workers but also because of its connections with trade unions, its organizational acumen, and its relative lack of crowd action.[97] Indeed, the trade union as a locus of organization had deep roots in sociopolitical traditions of German workers, and this influence is evidenced in the anticapitalist action of the 1880s.[98] No longer characterized by riots that became strikes, the tactics of this decade were tightly controlled and carefully planned: widespread boycotts, voluntary walkouts, and sympathy strikes, to name but a few. In discussions and preparations that lasted months, workers developed sophisticated strategies and created tightly knit networks that spanned artificial, geopolitical boundaries of state and nation.[99] The founding of the International Working People' Association (IWPA) in 1881 and the American Federation of Labor (AFL) in 1886 went, in part, to the purpose of maintaining these transnational networks. As the AFL termed it, they sought to create an "alliance of all national and international trade unions."[100] It would be but a small step for readers in Denver, a locus of labor radicalism, to wonder: What had Kienzy been up to on his recent European tour?[101]

Formed Three Years Ago—Consisted of Five Members

For readers of 1889, the invitation to inhabit, however briefly, an alternative temporality— "three years ago"—may have brought to mind this broad landscape of resistance, which has often been characterized as a "great upheaval."[102] German saloons, European tours, and sign-makers, lumped together and situated in the spring of 1886, in other words, could not help but register a quintessential moment in capital-labor conflict. And if the general tumult of this conflict in the first half of the decade failed to do so, another possible association—indeed, one that, like the founding of the AFL, fell squarely within the period of April 24 to May 10—would surely have not been missed: the Haymarket Affair of May 4.[103]

The most proximate effect of the dynamite bomb was indiscriminate shooting, perpetrated by the Chicago police officers who had, under the leadership of John Bonfield, unconstitutionally ordered the crowd to disperse. Ultimately, however, the events of that evening inaugurated a great, swift, and merciless Red scare: public meetings were suppressed, public processions banned, and more than two hundred arrests were made. Members of the IWPA—especially those connected to the radical *Alarm* and *Arbeiter-Zeitung*—were particularly vulnerable, as the final indictments and Haymarket trial made clear. The state was swift: by May 27, the grand jury had indicted thirty-one individuals, and by June 21, eight were officially charged: Albert Parsons, August Spies, Oscar Neebe, Louis Lingg, George Engel, Adolph Fischer, Michael Schwab, and Samuel Fielden. Of these eight, all but one were convicted and sentenced to death; of these seven, two requested and were granted a commutation. Five remained, four of whom were German-speaking émigrés.

From thirty-one to eight, from eight to seven, and, finally, from seven to five; or, the conspiracy was "formed three years ago" and the club "consisted of five members."[104] Though Louis Lingg famously managed to take his own life in the hours before the scheduled execution, the remaining four—Parsons, Spies, Fischer, and Engel—were hanged on November 11, 1887. Thus when newspapermen in San Francisco, Helena, and Los Angeles and strayed from "five" to report instead that "four" of the Bridgeport Suicide Club members had already died, they still wrote in the register of anarchism.[105]

Suicide—By Ballot

A battle for the memory of Haymarket was also otherwise afoot in 1889. As evidence of this, we might take note of the publication that year of two texts: *The Life of Albert Parsons*, self-published by Lucy Parsons, who was partner to the executed Albert Parsons and, like Kate Gregory, was a woman who figured prominently in masculine spheres[106]; and *Anarchy and Anarchists: A History of the Red Terror and the Social Revolution in America and Europe*, published by the more established F. J. Schulte & Co. and written by Michael Schaack, the Chicago police captain who spearheaded the persecution of radical thinkers in the weeks following the lethal incident in Haymarket Square. Anarchism was back in the news throughout the autumn and winter of 1888, when Schaack and Bonfield arrested three Bohemian anarchists and charged them with plotting Bonfield's demise.[107] The trial rekindled those old terrors, shaped and stoked by months of sensational media coverage of that other, earlier, more infamous trial of those held responsible for the dynamite bomb of 1886. And, certainly, L. Parsons and Schaack were as unwilling as newspapermen to let them fade away.

The Parsons were among the more colorful figures working, writing, and galvanizing on "the labor question." The pair met in Texas, where A. Parsons—like Morris Allen Collins—spent his childhood years after the death of his mother and father and where he joined the "Lone Star Grays," at the age of thirteen, during the

American Civil War.[108] Their interest in the amelioration of capitalism's negative impacts coincided with their earliest days in Chicago during the early 1870s.[109] The Parsons' articles, books, leaflets, and oratories evidence savvy intellects and fierce rhetorical styles. Indeed, their work simply reminds us of what historians have long known, namely, of the deadly and disabling nature of wage work during a period in which new technologies of production not only gradually replaced human labor but also required dangerous interfaces between body and machine.[110] By the 1890s two workers out of every hundred could anticipate becoming a casualty of these vicissitudes.[111] Though mining and railroad industries were particularly noteworthy in this regard, even mechanization in the less conspicuously dangerous telegraph, telephone, and textile industries presented novel, formidable threats.[112] Meanwhile, low wages and long hours resulted, too, in more mundane dilemmas of poor nutrition and high disease morbidity. It comes as no surprise, then, that the pastiche of texts L. Parsons collected into the *Life of Albert Parsons* approached disability not as inherent to the individual but, rather, as the inevitable result of "debasing, impoverishing, and enslaving industrial conditions."[113] A masterful work of alchemy, the text blended letters and speeches, historical narrative and positivist science, unflinching portraiture and political critique—all to convey the shape and structure of capitalism's death worlds."[114]

Surely this is what L. Parsons had in mind, though she used different rhetoric, in an 1884 leaflet that A. Parsons subsequently published in the *Alarm*, subsequently published, which described the "slow death" of the unemployed worker and that:[115]

> Next winter when the cold blasts are creeping through the rents in your seedy garments, when the frost is biting your feet through the holes in your worn-out shoes, and when all wretchedness seems to have centered in and upon you, when misery has marked you for her own and life has become a burden and existence a mockery, when you have walked the streets by day and slept upon hard boards by night, and at last determine by your own hand to take your life,—for you would rather go out into utter nothingness than to longer endure an existence which has become such a burden—so, perchance, you determine to dash yourself into the cold embrace of the lake rather than longer suffer thus. But halt—[116]

She did not follow "But halt," with hope. Even as she sought to "'slow' the act of suicide down," she also sought to mobilize the act as a site of nonnormative political resistance.[117] The ballot had failed—what then, was to be done?[118] L. Parsons was among the more well-known and outspoken advocates of suicide-by-dynamite. Or, more to the point, she was among the more outspoken advocates of suicide-by-dynamite in particular spatial locations: the terrain of capitalists. She did not call upon the "unemployed, the disinherited, and the miserable," to stay permanently the suicidal hand; rather, she called upon them to stay it only temporarily. "Stroll down to the homes of the rich," she urged. "Then let your tragedy be enacted *here*! . . . by the red glare bursting from the cannon's mouths."[119] In this way, then, the death of Louis Lingg could serve as an example: as the accused maker of the Haymarket bomb, Lingg was particularly notorious. After dynamite had ended the lives of several in Haymarket Square, Lingg used it, also, to become "his own executioner."[120] In a dramatic and widely circulated act of defiance that painted the walls of his jail cell with "clots of blood and dangling scraps of human flesh," he set fire to a dynamite bomb in his mouth.[121] Some thought he had used the candle in his cell, while still others conjectured that he must have used a cigar to light the fuse. Soon enough, newspapers across the nation and the world carried word of the suicide—and, in Chicago, it "was talked of on every corner, in every street car."[122] Die if you must, Lingg and L. Parsons seemed to urged, but do so with a purpose. During the trials and convictions that preceded Lingg's death, the counsel for the state submitted L. Parsons' leaflet to evidence the power of the "Haymarket Five" to stimulate workers to violence.

Yet there was much more at stake in the term "suicide" than this. For in the days, weeks, months, and years that followed the executions of 1887, a cross-class identification with the dead men coalesced, and it did so, in no small degree, upon the memory of these men as manly martyrs to the eight-hour day. So resonant and resilient has been this formulation that it seeped into New Left historiography of the 1960s and 1970s and has, in more recent decades, inspired historians to actively dismantle it.[123] Unlike much of this corpus, I am uninterested in proving or disproving the fact of conspiracy, or engaging in debates about whether the executions were lawfully brought to completion. But the power of martyrdom is revealing and was on fantastic display during the funeral procession: approximately two hundred thousand individuals either ambled with the dead or reverenced them by lining the streets. Some carried banners or signs that memorialized in the register of sacrificial manhood, a manliness that required "iron nerve and will" in the face of death. For while Lingg's was most clearly legible as suicide, his fellows, too, were remembered as going willfully to their deaths. Given the opportunity to beg the governor for commutation, had not Parsons, Spies, Fischer, and Engel refused?

It was this hermeneutics of suicide-as-manly-martyrdom against which Schaack, in perhaps the most elephantine treatment to date of the Haymarket affair and the subsequent trial, waged war. The tome occupied just under 700 pages. In the thirty-third chapter, we find Schaack's description of the final days in court, and, within that description, the following remarks:

SPIES: "Call your hangman!"
NEEBE: "I am sorry not to be hung with the rest of them."
LINGG: "I die happy on the gallows"— "Hang me for it!"
FIELDEN: "I freely give myself up."

These utterances[124] were embedded within the larger and longer denunciatory final speeches, which lingered on over the course of three October days.[125] But what was to be gained by Schack's inclusion of them? Did they not simply confirm and bolster the claims of those who supported the anarchists, who held them aloft and ornamented them with halos of martyrdom? Perhaps—yet they also alert us to what Jacques Derrida calls the "becoming-self-punishment of hetero-punishment" (151), to the symbolic re-placement of responsibility from state officials, who tied the noose and dropped the hatch, to the defendants themselves. Derrida's formulation emerges during a critical appraisal of Kant's distinction between internal and external punishments. For Derrida, the goal is to unsettle "naïve confidence" in distinctions between self and other, inside/outside, and so on. It would be a mistake, he insists, to suggest that execution is suicide, pure and simple.[126] Agreed; but Schaack knew nothing of Derrida, and, in Schaack's imaginative universe, such a collapse was necessary: "There is the ballot, free to every citizen, safe, satisfying, final. The men who try other methods are rushing to their own destruction."[127] And in the case of the Haymarket defendants, did they not beg for death?

Guilt, innocence—these are for me irrelevant. What interests me is the slipperiness of these concepts and the ongoing battle to contain them. The capacious signifying power of suicide is breathtaking. As I have argued elsewhere, the meaning of any suicide is profoundly dependent upon a vast array of factors: the status and intersecting identities of both the agent and the family and friends who (do or do not) survive, the mode of death and weapon of choice, and the political relevance of ascribed causation—all circumscribe the hermeneutics of this particular way of dying.[128] The traditional and reflexive tendency to characterize suicide as the most individual of actions belies this kaleidoscope of meanings; for, in 1889, when "the Bridgeport Suicide Club" was uttered in the context of not-Americanness, transnational networks of labor reform, anarchism, and dynamite bombs, suicide just as readily indicated class warfare.

Insane—Fanatic—Fools

Disability in its various guises has long served to circumscribe presence and participation in the American body politic, whether in the form of disenfranchisement, immigration restriction, removal from public spaces, or otherwise.[129] Indeed, such a label in the nineteenth century had also the significant effect of signaling the general incapacity of marginalized others, namely, the feminized and racialized.[130] The 1880s witnessed notable upticks in nativism and ableism. The move to characterize the men of the Bridgeport Suicide Club as insane, fanatics, and fools, then, conforms to inveterate scripts of which historians are already acutely aware. We may not even be surprised that subsequent coverage eagerly followed in this vein, referring to the men not just as insane, fools, and fanatics but also as "suicidal maniacs" who should be "immediately arrested and sent to an insane asylum" to safeguard the welfare of the general public.[131] As to the question of length of stay, a newspaperman from New Orleans suggested "permanent habitation."[132]

Such permanence is suggestive of alternative contemporary discourses, namely, the quickly consolidating field of eugenic science, which claimed criminality and disability as inherent, immutable characteristics in need of eradication. Within popular narratives of suicide clubs, however, there was no need for germ-plasms, hereditary defect, or other biological explanations; indeed, these newspapermen accomplished their aims with very little science at all.

What Had Been Suspected But Not Generally Known—Hopes to Initiate New Members

In Barthes's formulation, mythological speech is depoliticized yet highly political speech.[133] It reinscribes already existing dynamics of power and reinforces the ideological and institutional structures in which those dynamics are embedded by, quite simply, naturalizing them. Here we see mythological speech working toward analogous ends: they demanded not just complacency, but, rather, complacency tinged with vitriol. The open-ended nature of these clubs—that their doings were suspected but not generally known, that remaining members may or may not be able to successfully perpetuate the organization through the induction of new members—cultivated terror at its most unsettling and uncanny: the clubs were simultaneously known and not known, the members were both very, very dead and very, very live. They were and they were not, but, at any rate, they threatened.

The process of naturalization not only yoked disability to criminality; it also, crucially, naturalized violent utterances directed at certain subjects. It created a space in which it became possible to respond to the 1891 suicide of a German cabinet-maker with the headline, "The World Grows Better." It became possible for the newspapermen at the *North American and Daily Advertiser* to observe that this death inspired "hope that the pessimistic [perhaps read: nihilistically inclined to account for material realities] variety of man will be encouraged. As John Kop swung himself off in his cellar the world was minus one fool, and so much the better."[134]

The Bridgeport Suicide Club and its members were "no longer an example or a symbol" of the taken-for-granted right to advocate the eradication of abnormality; rather, they had become "the very presence" of it.[135]

Alibis and Commonsense

Though they sought a variety of outcomes, the ableist episteme under which each of these texts labored—capitalist, anticapitalist, or otherwise—is perhaps worth repeating: death is preferable to wage-disabling difference. Suicide makes sense in such instances. The *Farmer* article worked within this episteme to justify Heisterhagen's death; L. Parsons played upon it to bring attention to capitalist exploitation; and Collins's suicide letter, whether penned by the disabled Collins or the nondisabled members of the Whitechapel club, was mired in it as well. Whether to justify, to expose, or to accomplish something else altogether, these texts assumed and, in turn, perpetuated this lethal commonsense-ness. Indeed, the power of suicide club narratives to evoke venom coalesced, in part, because they told tales of suicide undertaken beyond this episteme. Evacuated of salient details, the narratives left readers with men who sought death for no "good" reason at all. This was on vivid display when newspapermen at the *North American and Daily Advertiser* conjoined their celebration of the beneficial death of John Kopp with further cogitations:

> It does not appear that the members were more unhappy than other people, nor that their lives were more burdened with misfortune. They wantonly bound themselves to die by their own hands. Of course, if they were unfit to live it was well enough to admit it, but in that case they out to have hired a cheep [sic] boat and rowed out into the deep waters of the Sound and scuttled the craft. Due considerations for the living should have constrained them to relieve society of the trouble of burying such persons. And they might have blessed the world by going off all in a bunch."[136]

This, then, was the context animating the corpse that the Whitechapelers reduced to ashes on the shores of Lake Michigan in the summer of 1892. Much more than newspapermen at leisure, a reconsideration of that pyre on the lakeshore recalls Elias Canetti's insight that "the moment of survival is the moment of power."[137] Like suicide clubs themselves, Morris Allen Collins may or may not have existed. He may or may not have been, said, or done what the Whitechapelers wrote that he was, said, or did. Yet, in the end, the ability to affirm or disprove any of these claims becomes irrelevant. What I am willing to say for certain, at least for now, is that Collins, as well as the cohort of corpses that populated narratives of suicide clubs, served as an alibi for a quickly consolidating eugenic impulse. As such, these corpses remind us that culture was not just a conduit for eugenic ideas nor a battleground upon which these ideas were debated.[138] Rather, it was a powerful site of mythmaking and emotional habituation that generated the conditions in which eugenic ideas and eugenic practices could thrive.

Notes

1. See, for example, "Gone into Thin Air," *Sunday Herald* (Chicago), July 17, 1892, as found in Wallace Rice, "Scrapbook on the Activities of the Whitechapel Club of Chicago, with accounts of the Cremation of Morris Allen Collins," n/d, 28–48, CHM; "Cremation of a Suicide," *Alexandria Gazette and Virginia Advertiser*, July 18, 1892; "A Suicide Incinerated," *Daily Independent* (Helena), July 18, 1892; "Weirdly Dramatic," *Daily Picayune* (New Orleans), July 18, 1892; "Morris Collins Cremated," *Evening World* (New York), July 18, 1892; "Collins Funeral Pyre," *Galveston Daily News*, July 18, 1892; "Collins Cremated," *Los*

Angeles Herald, July 18, 1892; "A Strange Ceremony," *Morning Oregonian* (Portland), July 18, 1892; "Incinerated on a Pyre," *Milwaukee Sentinel*, July 18, 1892; "Weird Funeral Ceremony," *Omaha Daily Bee*, July 18, 1892; "Cremation in Chicago," *Raleigh Morning News*, July 18, 1892; "Cremated," *The Record-Union* (Sacramento, CA), July 18, 1892; "Cremated a Suicide," *St. Paul Daily Globe*, July 18, 1892; "Human Sacrifice," *St. Paul Daily News*, July 18, 1892; "Cremation of a Suicide," *Washington Post*, July 18, 1892; "Cremated Collins," *Galveston Daily News*, July 19, 1892; "A Strangely Weird Scene," *Daily Tobacco Leaf-Chronicle* (Clarksville, TN), July 19, 1892; "Cremation of a Suicide," *News and Observer* (Raleigh), July 19, 1892; "Cremated by a Chicago Club," *Pittsburg Dispatch*, July 18, 1892; "Reduced to Ashes," *Salt Lake Herald*, July 19, 1892; "An Infamous Thing (Letter to the Editor)," *Daily Inter Ocean* (Chicago), July 20, 1892; "By the Sad Waves," *Lowell Journal* (Lowell, MI), July 20, 1892; "On a Funeral Pyre," *New Ulm Review* (Ulm, MN), July 20, 1892; "Incinerating a Suicide," *Austin Weekly Statesman* (Austin, TX), July 21, 1892; "A Remarkable Cremation," *Stark County Democrat* (Canton, OH), July 21, 1892; "Weird and Solemn," *Hickman Courier* (Hickman, KY), July 22, 1892; "Weird and Solemn," *Macon Beacon* (Macon, MS), July 23, 1892; "Weird and Solemn," *Ohio Democrat* (Logan), July 23, 1892; and "A Chicago Cremation," *Washington Bee* (Washington, DC), July 23, 1892.

2. Christa Shusko has analyzed the Whitechapelers' use of atheological practices in the development of unconventional religious identities. See Christa Shusko, "Alcohol Consumption, Transgression, and Death," in *Dying to Eat: Cross-Cultural Perspectives on Food in Death, Dying and Afterlives*, Candi K. Cann, ed. (Louisville: University Press of Kentucky, 2017); "The cremation of . . ." *Galveston Daily News*, July 25, 1892.

3. An example of an 1892 Whitechapel invitation can be found in "Whitechapel Club: Miscellaneous Pamphlets," folder 1F38SP W58, Chicago History Museum, Chicago (hereafter CHM).

4. Henry M. Hurd, William F. Drewry, Richard Dewey, Charles W. Pilgrim, G. Alder Blumer, and T. J. W. Burgess, *The Institutional Care of the Insane in the United States and Canada*, Vol. 2 (Baltimore: Johns Hopkins University Press, 1916), 294.

5. Wallace Rice, "Scrapbook on the Activities of the Whitechapel Club of Chicago, with accounts of the Cremation of Morris Allen Collins," n.d., CHM.

6. I here align myself with Judith Butler, who argues that what we know as "gender" emerges from repetitive acts over the course of a person's life—beginning, according to Butler, in the womb and before sentience. These last elements are what distinguish Butler's formulation from the more dramaturgical framework of identity formation advanced most significantly by Erving Goffman. Judith Butler, "Performative Acts and Gender Constitution: An Essay in Phenomenology and Feminist Theory," *Theatre Journal* 40.4 (December, 1988), 519–531.

7. On the Haymarket Affair, see D. Roediger and F. Rosemont, eds., *Haymarket Scrapbook* (Oakland, CA: AK Press, 2012); Carl Smith, *Urban Disorder and the Shape of Belief: The Great Chicago Fire, the Haymarket Bomb, and the Model Town of Pullman* (Chicago: University of Chicago Press, 1996), 101–176; James Green, *Death in the Haymarket: A Story of Chicago, the First Labor Movement and the Bombing that Divided Gilded Age America* (New York: Anchor Books, 2007); Timothy Messer-Kruse, *The Trial of the Haymarket Anarchists: Terrorism and Justice in the Gilded Age* (Chicago: University of Illinois Press, 2012); Timothy Messer-Kruse, *The Haymarket Conspiracy: Transatlantic Anarchist Networks* (Chicago: University of Illinois Press, 2012); and Bruce Nelson, *Beyond*

the Martyrs: A Social History of Chicago's Anarchists, 1870–1900 (New Brunswick, NJ: Rutgers University Press, 1988). On Chicago labor politics more generally, see Richard Schneirov, *Labor and Urban Politics: Class Conflict and the Origins of Modern Liberalism in Chicago, 1864–97* (Chicago: University of Illinois Press, 1998); Richard Schneirov, Shelton Stromquist, and Nick Salvatore, eds., *The Pullman Strike and the Crisis of the 1890s: Essays on Labor and Politics* (Chicago: University of Illinois Press, 1999); and Thomas Guglielmo, *White on Arrival: Italians, Race, Color, and Power in Chicago, 1890-1945* (New York: Oxford University Press, 2003), 129–145. For histories of the working classes and labor politics beyond Chicago, see Leon Fink, *In Search of the Working Class: Essays in American Labor History and Political Culture* (Urbana and Chicago: University of Illinois Press, 1994); Leon Fink, ed., *Workers across the Americas: The Transnational Turn in Labor History* (New York: Oxford University Press, 2011); David Thomas Brundage, *The Making of Western Labor Radicalism: Denver's Organized Workers, 1878–1905* (Chicago and Urbana: University of Illinois Press, 1994); and Dorothee Schneider, *Trade Unions and Community: The German Working Class in New York City, 1870–1900* (Urbana and Chicago: University of Illinois Press, 1994).

    8. "Wholesale Suicide," *Pittsburgh Dispatch*, March 22, 1890. The full text of the suicide letter can also be found in Rice, "Scrapbook on the Activities," 31–32, CHM.

    9. Rice, "Scrapbook on the Activities," 25–27, CHM.

    10. Rice, "Scrapbook on the Activities," 25–27, CHM.

    11. At least two served as local branches of a single international club in New York City and Salt Lake City. "HIGH MAN KILLS HIMSELF," *Daily Inter Ocean* (Chicago), October 14, 1892. The southeastern states were largely unaffected by the phenomenon, with only New Orleans newspapers claiming a local club. "The Suicide Club," *Daily Picayune* (New Orleans), August 2, 1895.

    12. "SUICIDE CLUB. The Most Remarkable Organization Ever Heard Of," *Rocky Mountain News* (Denver), April 8, 1890. Several women's clubs were also alleged. See "A NEW SUICIDE CLUB. Several Young People of Michigan Carry Out a Reckless Compact," *Morning Oregonian* (Portland), December 24, 1891; "A SUICIDE CLUB. Fate Has Demanded the Death of Six Since Last March," *Morning Oregonian*, June 10, 1895; "NUMBER THREE. Another Member of a Suicide Club Composed of Women Goes to Death," *Denver Evening Post*, September 2, 1897; and "A Probable Cause," *Broad Axe* (Chicago), December 26, 1903.

    13. A British edition of *New Arabian Nights* also appeared in 1882. See Robert Louis Stevenson, *New Arabian Nights* (London: Chatto & Windus, 1882). Scribner's published its version five years later. See Robert Louis Stevenson, *New Arabian Nights* (New York: Charles Scribner's Sons, 1887).

    14. Robert Louis Stevenson, *The Suicide Club* (New York: George Munro's Sons, 1895). The trilogy first appeared as a discreet text in France. Robert Louis Stevenson, *Suicide-Club*, translated from the French by Louis Despreaux (Paris: Calmann Lévy, 1885). A German translation appeared in 1896, the same year that Charles Scribner's Sons issued a second American edition. See Robert Louis Stevenson, *Der Selbstmordklub*, translated from the German by Fritz Bergen and Max Pannwitz (Stuttgart: Franckh, 1896); Robert Louis Stevenson, *The Suicide Club* (New York: Charles Scribner's Sons, 1896).

    15. "A Suicide Club," *Rocky Mountain News* (Denver), April 27, 1889.

    16. Chicago papers marked the anniversary the following summer, and, in the hands of *Tribune* journalists and editors, the ritualistic happenings of July 16, 1892, eventually became the stuff of local legend. See "A Coffin Dance," *Morning Call* (San Francisco), June 10, 1893;

"With Robe and Hood," *Daily Inter Ocean*, July 16, 1893; "Celebration of a Cremation," *Chicago Daily Tribune*, July 17, 1893; "A Mysterious Vigil," *Chicago Daily Tribune*, April 26, 1896; and "Indiana Dunes Strewn with Bones and Wreckage," *Chicago Daily Tribune*, July 29, 1900. Charles H. Dennis, who had served the *Tribune* in multiple capacities at the time of Collins's death and who served as boss to many of the Whitechapelers, published a thirty-six-part series about the club—including the 1892 cremation—that ran from July 27 to September 5, 1936, with the title "Whitechapel Nights." The Chicago History Museum maintains a copy of some installments. See "Miscellaneous Pamphlets," folder qF38SP.W58, CHM.

17. Other than in the work of regional historian Michael Bielawa, I have been unable to locate discussion of suicide clubbing in any historical accounts of this period. Michael Bielawa, *Wicked Bridgeport* (Charleston, SC: History Press, 2012), 60–68. The only scholarship on the phenomenon is the small corpus of critical works on Stevenson's story, which does not historicize suicide clubbing. The term does appear in several short works and reviews as a euphemism for the military and its technologies. Timothy Boon, "Making the Modern World," *History Today* 51.8 (August 2001), 38–45, where the mention comes in the inlay on page 44 dealing with submarine technology; Sik Alan Daso, "Operation LUSTY," *Aerospace Power Journal* 16.1 (Spring 2002), 28–40, where the mention comes on 29; and Dik Daso, "Origins of Airpower," *Airpower Journal* 11.3 (Fall 1997), 94–113, where the mention comes on 102.

18. Alfred Lawrence Lorenz, "The Whitechapel Club: Defining Chicago Newspapermen in the 1890s," *American Journalism* 15.1 (Winter 1998), 83–102, 84. Lorenz thus places the Whitechapelers into broader conversations about journalistic "cultures of professionalism" brought into our purview through work such as Michael Schudson's *Discovering the News: A Social History of American Newspapers* (New York: Basic Books, 1978), esp. 68–70; Larzer Ziff, *The American 1890s* (New York: Viking, 1966), 165; and, of course, Burton Bledstein, *The Culture of Professionalism* (New York: W.W. Norton, 1976).

19. I have conducted searches in census and other vital records drawn from all locations at which the Whitechapel narrative places Collins: Aberdeen and Dallas, Texas; New Orleans; St. Louis; and Chicago—to no avail.

20. "Inquest No. 10601, upon the body of M.A. Collins," July 9, 1892, Illinois Regional Archival Depository, Chicago (hereafter IRAD).

21. "Inquest No. 10601," IRAD; Rice, "Scrapbook on the Activities," 48, CHM.

22. "Weirdly Dramatic," *Daily Picayune*, July 18, 1892.

23. Though this body of work is far too robust to represent holistically here, several key points of entry are Ann Laura Stoler, *Along the Archival Grain: Epistemic Anxieties and Colonial Common Sense* (Princeton, NJ: Princeton University Press, 2009); Ann Laura Stoler, ed., *Imperial Debris: On Ruins and Ruination* (Durham, NC: Duke University Press, 2013; Saidiya Hartman, *Lose Your Mother: A Journey Along the Atlantic Slave Route* (New York: Farrar, Straus, and Giroux, 2007) and "Venus in Two Acts," *Small Axe* 12.2 (June 2008), 1–14. For a multiplicity of important voices on questions of the archive, see *Social Text 125*, "Recovery, Slavery, and the Archive," 33.4 (December 2015); *Radical History Review* 120, "Queer Archives: Historical Unravelings" (Fall 2014); and *Radical History Review* 122 "Queer Archives: Intimate Tracings" (Summer 2015). Much of this scholarship exists at the nexus of several recent trends: the emergence of memory studies; the latest archival turn; the ever-urgent interventions of queer theory and critical race theory; reinvigorated interest in the imperial and the transnational following the ongoing events of 2001; and,

finally, calls to bring the state "back in," advanced with particular vigor in the US context by scholars of American Political Development.

24. Susan Burch and Michael Rembis, "Re-membering the Past: Reflections on Disability Histories," in *Disability Histories*, Susan Burch and Michael Rembis, eds. (Urbana, Chicago, and Springfield: University of Illinois Press, 2014), 4–5.

25. See, for example, Susan Burch, "Disorderly Pasts: Kinship, Diagnoses, and Remembering in American Indian-U.S. Histories," *Journal of Social History* (2016), 1–24. See also Robert Bogdan's piece in this volume, as well as Bogdan, Martin Elks, and James A. Knoll, *Picturing Disability: Beggar, Freak, Citizen and Other Photographic Rhetoric* (Syracuse, NY: Syracuse University Press, 2012), both of which are based on primary source material gathered from flea markets, antique shops, eBay, and similar venues.

26. Susan Burch and Michael Rembis, eds., *Disability Histories* (Urbana, Chicago, and Springfield: University of Illinois Press, 2014), 13, n.14–15. See also the Living Archives on Eugenics in Western Canada at http://eugenicsarchive.ca.

27. See, as an example of one of the more compelling and sophisticated efforts in this vein, Ellen Samuels, "Examining Millie and McKoy: Where Enslavement and Enfreakment Meet," *Signs* 37.1 (Autumn 2011), 53–81.

28. See, for example, Douglas C. Baynton, *Defectives in the Land: Disability and Immigration in the Age of Eugenics* (Chicago: University of Chicago Press, 2016); John M. Kinder, *Paying with Their Bodies: American War and the Problem of the Disabled Veteran* (Chicago: University of Chicago Press, 2015); and the *Bulletin of the History of Medicine* 87.4 (Winter, 2013), in which Catherine Kudlick, Beth Linker, Julie Livingston, and Daniel J. Wilson, reflect on the potentially fruitful intersections between medical and disability histories.

29. I presented this work under the rubric of "Morbid Masculinities" on December 5, 2013, at the Scholars Colloquium of the George Washington University's Department of American Studies (Washington, DC); and on January 3, 2014, at the annual meeting of the American Historical Association (Washington, DC).

30. Hartman, "Venus in Two Acts," 9.

31. David A. Gerber, "Forming a Transnational Narrative: New Perspectives on European Migration to the United States," *The History Teacher* 35.1 (November, 2001), 61–78; see esp. 65–66.

32. The most compelling and cogent argument against this collapse remains, to my mind, Walter Johnson's "On Agency," *Journal of Social History* 37.1 (Fall 2003), 113–124.

33. Lisa Lowe, "History Hesitant," *Social Text* 33.4 (December 2015), 85–107.

34. Barthes, *Mythologies*, 134.

35. Didier Fassin, "Another Politics of Life is Possible," *Theory, Culture & Society* 26.5 (2009), 44–60, 49. In his distinction between the biological and the biographical, Fassin's "sense of life" constitutes the latter.

36. Ann Stoler helpfully distinguishes "between what was 'unwritten' because it could go without saying and 'everyone knew it', what was unwritten because it could not yet be articulated, and what was unwritten because it could not be said." In the case of the omissions cited here, it seems to be most clearly a case of the thing unwritten because it could go without saying. Stoler, *Along the Archival Grain*, 3.

37. "A Bullet Ends His Troubles," *Evening Farmer* (Bridgeport, CT), February 3, 1887.

38. "Index to Petitions for Naturalizations Filed in Federal, State, and Local Courts in New York City, 1792–1906," Record Group 21, "Records of District Courts of the United

States, 1685–2009," National Archives and Records Administration, Washington, DC. The *Evening Farmer* noted more specifically that Heisterhagen was "an Alsatian," an émigré from the bitterly contested Alsace region, which came under the sovereignty of the German Empire in 1871, at the conclusion of the Franco-Prussian War. On the causes and outcomes of the Franco-Prussian War, see Michael Howard, *The Franco-Prussian War: The German Invasion of France, 1870–1871* (New York: Routledge, 2001); and Geoffrey Wawro, *The Franco-Prussian War: The German Conquest of France, 1870-1871* (New York: Cambridge University Press, 2003).

39. "A Bullet Ends His Troubles," *Evening Farmer*, February 3, 1887.

40. The Bridgeport City Directory of 1882 places Heisterhagen at his wife Sophia's long-term address at 451 Pembroke, while the next year he is listed at Gregory's boarding house at 13 Gold Street. See "U.S. City Directories, 1822–1995: [database online]. Provo, UT: Ancestry.com.

Operations, Inc., 2011, which were digitized from the holdings of the Connecticut State Library in Hartford according to a communication to the author from Maria Paxi, August 5, 2016.

41. "A Bullet Ends His Troubles."

42. "A Bullet Ends His Troubles."

43. For a compelling analysis of disability, race, and possessive individualism in a nineteenth-century context, see Cynthia Wu, *Chang and Eng Reconnected: The Original Siamese Twins in American Culture* (Philadelphia: Temple University Press, 2012), esp. 1–35. See also Amy Dru Stanley, "'The Right to Possess All the Faculties that God Has Given': Possessive Individualism, Slave Women, and Abolitionist Thought," in *Moral Problems in American Life: New Perspectives on Cultural History*, eds. Karen Halttunen and Lewis Perry (Ithaca, NY: Cornell University Press, 1998); and C. B. McPherson, *The Political Theory of Possessive Individualism: Hobbes to Locke* (New York: Oxford University Press, 1962).

44. "A Bullet Ends His Troubles."

45. "A Bullet Ends His Troubles."

46. "A Bullet Ends His Troubles."

47. Fred C. Dayton, "ONE VICTIM A YEAR," *North American and Daily Advertiser* (Philadelphia), April 18, 1890. Dayton began his career as a newspaperman in Rockford, Illinois, worked for the Chicago *Times* between 1874 and 1880, and worked as night editor for the Chicago *Tribune* from 1880 to 1884. From 1885 to 1888, he worked for the St. Paul, Minnesota, *Globe* before relocating to New York. "OBITUARY. Fred C. Dayton," *American Stationer*, September 13, 1894, 460; and "OBITUARY. Fred C. Dayton," *Inland Printer* 14 (October 1894-March 1895), 73.

48. Dayton, "ONE VICTIM A YEAR."

49. Dayton, "ONE VICTIM A YEAR."

50. "Bridgeport's Suicide Club: Only One Member left—Will He Vote Himself to Death?" *New York Evening World*, April 24, 1889.

51. "A SUICIDE CLUB," *Wichita Daily Eagle*, April 26, 1889.

52. "ONLY ONE IS LEFT," *Bridgeport Evening Farmer*, April 22, 1889.

53. "Bridgeport's Suicide Club."

54. "A SUICIDE CLUB."

55. "A Suicide Club," *Rocky Mountain News*, April 27, 1889.

56. "A Bullet Ends His Troubles."

57. "A Bullet Ends His Troubles."

58. "SUICIDE CLUB," *Galveston Daily News*, June 19, 1891.

59. See, respectively, "JOHN KIENZY COMMITS SUICIDE. HE SHOOTS HIMSELF AT HIS HOME TO-DAY WHILE MENTALLY UNBALANCED," *Bridgeport Evening Farmer*, April 22, 1889; "A Suicide Club," *Helena Independent*, April 27, 1889; "Suicide Club," *Daily Evening Bulletin*, April 27, 1889; "A Suicide Club," *Rocky Mountain News*, April 27, 1889; "Bridgeport's Suicide Club"; "News in Brief," *Evening Bulletin*, April 26, 1889; "The Suicide Club," *Daily Inter Ocean*, April 28, 1889.

60. "JOHN KIENZY COMMITS SUICIDE."

61. "ONLY ONE IS LEFT."

62. "Bridgeport's Suicide Club"; "A Suicide Club," *Pittsburg Dispatch*, April 25, 1889; "News in Brief," *Evening Bulletin* (Maysville, KY), April 26, 1889; "A SUICIDE CLUB," *Wichita Daily Eagle*, April 26, 1889; "Suicide Club," *Daily Evening Bulletin*, April 27, 1889; "A Suicide Club," *Helena Independent*, April 27, 1889, as reprinted from the *Daily Evening Bulletin*; "Suicide Club," *Daily Herald* (Los Angeles), April 27, 1889, as reprinted from the *Helena Independent*, which was, in turn, reprinted from the *Daily Evening Bulletin*; "A Suicide Club," *Rocky Mountain News*, April 27, 1889; "The Suicide Club," *Daily Inter Ocean*, April 28, 1889, as reprinted from the Cincinnati *Enquirer*; "A Suicide Club," *Daily Picayune*, April 29, 1889; and "But One Member. . ." *Weekly Register-Call* (Central City, CO), May 10, 1889.

63. "A Suicide Club," *Pittsburg Dispatch*, April 25, 1889.

64. "A SUICIDE CLUB," claimed to be taken from "JOHN KIENZY COMMITS SUICIDE."

65. "A Suicide Club," *Rocky Mountain News*, April 27, 1889.

66. "A Suicide Club," *Daily Picayune*, April 29, 1889.

67. Though I will here confess that earnest frustration accompanied my earnest attempts to name authorial origin.

68. Barthes, *Mythologies*, 128.

69. "Bridgeport's Suicide Club."

70. "Bridgeport's Suicide Club."

71. "Bridgeport's Suicide Club."

72. "Bridgeport's Suicide Club."

73. "Bridgeport's Suicide Club."

74. "Bridgeport's Suicide Club."

75. "A SUICIDE CLUB," *Wichita Daily Eagle*, April 26, 1889.

76. "A SUICIDE CLUB," *Wichita Daily Eagle*, April 26, 1889.

77. "Suicide Club," *Daily Evening Bulletin*, April 27, 1889.

78. "A Suicide Club," *Rocky Mountain News*, April 27, 1889.

79. "A Suicide Club," *Rocky Mountain News*, April 27, 1889.

80. "The Suicide Club," *Daily Inter Ocean*, April 28, 1889.

81. "But One Member. . ." *Weekly Register-Call*, May 10, 1889.

82. "Suicide Club," *Daily Evening Bulletin*, April 27, 1889; "A Suicide Club," *Helena Independent*, April 27, 1889; "Suicide Club," Los Angeles *Daily Herald*, April 27, 1889; "A Suicide Club," *Rocky Mountain News*, April 27, 1889.

83. Michael J. Bielawa, *Wicked Bridgeport* (Charleston, SC: The History Press, 2011), 61.

84. "A Suicide Club," *Rocky Mountain News*, April 27, 1889.

85. On the role of ethnic particularism among New York's organized workers, see Schneider, *Trade Unions and Community*, 177–208.

86. The territorial breadth of Second German Empire emerged from the German Wars of Unification, fought between 1864 and 1871. For a consideration of this period that places the German Wars of Unification in a comparative, transnational context, see Stig Förster and Jorg Nagler, eds., *On the Road to Total War: The American Civil War and the German Wars of Unification, 1861–1871* (New York and Cambridge, UK: Cambridge University Press, 1997).

87. On the German-language lands beyond the German Empire, see David Blackbourn, *Localism, Landscape, and the Ambiguities of Place: German-Speaking Central Europe, 1860–1930* (Toronto: University of Toronto Press, 2007). For a discussion of European "races" as distinct from the concept of "ethnicity" that emerged later in the twentieth century, see David R. Roediger, *Working toward Whiteness: How America's Immigrants Became White; the Strange Journey from Ellis Island to the Suburbs* (New York: Basic Books, 2005). Though German émigrés have not been privileged in the field of whiteness studies, for whom the Irish and émigrés from southern and eastern Europe have been crucial case studies, see Matthew Frye Jacobson, *Whiteness of a Different Color: European Immigrants and the Alchemy of Race* (Cambridge, MA: Harvard University Press, 1999), esp. 39–90.

88. John Higham, *Strangers in the Land 1860–1925* (New Brunswick, NJ: Rutgers University Press, 2002 [1955]),

89. Schneirov, *Labor and Urban Politics*, 163–166. The "curse of intemperance" appeared in a great many places over the course of the century, but this author pulled this particular passage from A. B. Richmond, *Intemperance and Crime: Leaves from the Diary of an Old Lawyer* (Meadville, PA: Meadville, 1883), 69.

90. Paul Scheffer, *Immigrant Nations* (New York: Polity, 2011). On nineteenth-century patterns of German immigration, see John Hawgood, *The Tragedy of German-America: The Germans in the United States of America during the Nineteenth Century and After* (New York: G.P. Putnam's Sons, 1940). On the periodic emergence of nativist sentiment, see Higham, *Strangers in the Land*.

91. Schneirov, *Labor and Urban Politics*, 163–166. The "curse of intemperance" appeared in a great many places over the course of the century, but this author pulled this particular passage from A. B. Richmond, *Intemperance and Crime: Leaves from the Diary of an Old Lawyer* (Meadville, PA: Meadville, 1883), 69.

92. On the divergences and continuities between these economic and sociopolitical commitments, see Schneirov, *Labor and Urban Politics*, 173–179; Bernard Moss, "Republican Socialism and the Making of the Working Class," *Comparative Studies in Society and History* 35.2 (1993), 390–413, and Timothy Messer-Kruse, *The Haymarket Conspiracy*. In part, Messer-Kruse critiques what he sees as a collapse of distinctions between multiple branches of socialist thought, a tendency that he attributes to revisionist histories of the Haymarket affair, which emerged with New Left scholars. Indeed, one need only return to the a classic to be reminded of these several divergences: see Karl Marx and Friedrich Engels, "III. Socialist and Communist Literature," in *The Communist Manifesto*, Samuel H. Beer, ed (Arlington Heights, IL: AHM Publishing, 1955), 33–46.

93. Schneirov, *Labor and Urban Politics*, 101–102, 112; Jon Kingsdale, "'The Poor Man's Club': Social Functions of the Urban Working-Class Saloon," in *The American Man*, Elizabeth H. Pleck and Joseph H. Pleck, eds. (Englewood Cliffs, NJ: Prentice-Hall, 1980), 255–284. Kyle Anthony, "'To Hesitate Is Cowardly': Radicalism and American Manhood, 1870–1920" (PhD diss. University of Kansas, 2011), 72–73.

94. Michael J. Schaak, *Anarchy and Anarchists: A History of the Red Terror and the Social Revolution in America and Europe. Communism, Socialism, and Nihilism in Doctrine and in Deed. The Chicago Haymarket Conspiracy, and the Detection and Trial of the Conspirators* (Chicago: F.J. Schulte & company, 1889), 216–217. As noted later in this article, Schaak spearheaded the persecution of radical thinkers in the weeks following the Haymarket Affair of May 4, 1889.

95. Schneirov, *Labor and Urban Politics*, 183, 184, 70–76, 195–99.

96. Ibid., 184, 199.

97. Ibid., *Labor and Urban Politics*, 205.

98. Schneider, *Trade Unions and Community*, 43.

99. More than a decade ago, David Gerber offered a compelling argument for the relevance of transnational frameworks for immigration history. See Gerber, "Forming a Transnational Narrative," as well as the book project that drew on this framework, *Authors of Their Lives: The Personal Correspondence of British Immigrants to North America in the Nineteenth Century* (New York: New York University Press, 2008). On transnational labor alliances, see Messer-Kruse, *The Haymarket Conspiracy*; Leon Fink, ed. *Workers across the Americas: The Transnational Turn in Labor History* (New York: Oxford University Press, 2011); and Schneider, *Trade Unions and Community*, 42–44. Additionally, and more a more concerted on transnational anarchist alliances, see Travis Tomchuck, *Transnational Radicals: Italian Anarchists in Canada and the U.S., 1915–1940* (Lansing: Michigan State University Press, 2015).

100. Philip S. Foner, *History of the Labor Movement in the United States*, Vol. 2 (New York: International Publishers, 1955), 141.

101. David Thomas Brundage, *The Making of Western Labor Radicalism: Denver's Organized Workers, 1878–1905* (Chicago and Urbana: University of Illinois Press, 1994).

102. Schneirov, *Labor and Urban Politics*, 183; Selig Perlman, *A History of Trade Unionism in the United States* (New York: Macmillan, 1922), 81–105.

103. On the Haymarket Affair, see Roediger and Rosemont, eds., *Haymarket Scrapbook* (Chicago: Charles H. Kerr, 1986); Carl Smith, *Urban Disorder and the Shape of Belief: The Great Chicago Fire, the Haymarket Bomb, and the Model Town of Pullman* (Chicago: University of Chicago Press, 1996), 101–176; James Green, *Death in the Haymarket: A Story of Chicago, the First Labor Movement and the Bombing that Divided Gilded Age America* (New York: Anchor Books, 2007); Timothy Messer-Kruse, *The Trial of the Haymarket Anarchists: Terrorism and Justice in the Gilded Age* (Chicago: University of Illinois Press, 2012); Messer-Kruse, *The Haymarket Conspiracy*; and Bruce Nelson, *Beyond the Martyrs: A Social History of Chicago's Anarchists, 1870–1900* (New Brunswick, NJ: Rutgers University Press, 1988).

104. "Bridgeport's Suicide Club."

105. "Suicide Club," *Daily Evening Bulletin*, April 27, 1889; "A Suicide Club," *Helena Independent*, April 27, 1889; "Suicide Club," *Daily Herald*, April 27, 1889.

106. Though Lucy and Albert claimed to be married, there is no evidence to suggest that the relationship was ever made official before the eyes of the state. Some attribute this to antimiscegenation laws, as contemporaries and historians alike have attributed African American, Native American, and Mexican identities to Lucy. Some sources suggest that she was enslaved in because she lived with a former slave before she met Albert Parsons. Lucy's strategic changeability has had a great impact on scholarly debates over her memory. See Robin D. G. Kelley, *Freedom Dreams: The Black Radical Imagination* (New York: Beacon

Press, 2003), 41–42; Keith Rosenthal, "Lucy Parsons: 'More Dangerous than a Thousand Rioters,'" *Links International Journal of Socialist Renewal* (2011).

107. Schneirov, *Labor and Urban Politics*, 277–278.

108. Lucy Parsons, *The Life of Albert Parsons* (Chicago: published privately by the author, 1889), 7.

109. Parsons, *The Life of Albert Parsons*, 9–10.

110. John Fabian Witt, *The Accidental Republic: Crippled Workingmen, Destitute Widows, and the Remaking of American Law* (Cambridge, MA: Harvard University Press, 2004), esp. 2–3, 24–33.

111. Witt, *The Accidental Republic*, 3.

112. Witt, *The Accidental Republic*, 26–27.

113. Parsons, *Life of Albert Parsons*, 18.

114. Achille Mbembe, "Necropolitics," translated by Libby Meintjes, *Public Culture* 15.1 (2003), 11–40, 40.

115. Lauren Berlant, "Slow Death (Sovereignty, Obesity, Lateral Agency)," *Critical Inquiry* 33 (2007), 754–80.

116. Lucy E. Parsons, "To Tramps," *Alarm*, October 4, 1884.

117. Jasbir Puar, "Coda: The Cost of Getting Better: Suicide, Sensation, Switchpoints," *GLQ* 18.1 (2011), 149–158, 152. This recalls, too, Mbembe's formulation, in which he argues that "under conditions of necropower, the lines between resistance and suicide, sacrifice and redemption, martyrdom and freedom are blurred." *Necropolitics*, 39–40.

118. Parsons, *Life of Albert Parsons*, xix–xx. As Timothy Messer-Kruse details, the advocacy of violence emerged in the late 1870s. *The Haymarket Conspiracy*, esp. 69–136.

119. Lucy Parsons, "To Tramps," *Alarm*, October 4, 1884.

120. "HIS OWN EXECUTIONER," *Daily Inter Ocean*, November 11, 1887.

121. "Six Hours of Agony," *Atchison Daily Globe* (Kansas), November 11, 1887.

122. "HIS OWN EXECUTIONER."

123. See, for example, Nelson, *Beyond the Martyrs*; Schneirov, *Labor and Urban Politics*, 199–204; and Messer-Kruse, *The Haymarket Conspiracy*, 5, 8, 188.

124. Schaack, *Anarchy and Anarchists*, 592, 594, 596, 600.

125. Schaack, *Anarchy and Anarchists*, 605–606.

126. Jacques Derrida, "Death Penalties." *For What Tomorrow . . . A Dialogue* (Stanford, CA: Stanford University Press, 2004), 139–165.

127. Schaack, *Anarchy and Anarchists*, 26–27.

128. Kathleen Brian, "Indians, Negroes, and Mental Aberrations: Racing Suicide in the Antebellum Press," paper presented at the Society for Disability Studies, June 2012; Kathleen Brian, "Where Ends Meet: Suicide and Eugenics in America," *Process*, Organization of American Historians, www.processhistory.org/suicide-sympathy-and-the-making-of-american-eugenics.

129. See, respectively, Rabia Belt, *Ballots for Bullets? Disabled Veterans and the Right to Vote*, 69; Stan. L. Rev. (2017); Baynton, *Defectives in the Land*; Penny Richards, "Points of Entry: Disability and the Historical Geography of Immigration," *Disability Studies Quarterly* 24.3 (2004); Susan M. Schweik, *The Ugly Laws: Disability in Public* (New York: New York University Press, 2009); Alison Carey, *On the Margins of Citizenship: Intellectual Disability and Civil Rights in Twentieth-Century America* (Philadelphia: Temple University Press, 2009); Nancy J. Hirschmann and Beth Linker, eds., *Civil Disabilities: Citizenship,*

Membership, and Belonging (Philadelphia: University of Pennsylvania Press 2015); Susan M. Schweik, "Disability and the Normal Body of the (Native) Citizen," *Social Research* 78.2 (Summer 2011), 417–442.

130. Douglas C. Baynton, "Disability in History," *Perspectives* 44 (November 2006), 5–7.

131. "A telegram from Bridgeport . . ." *Morning Oregonian*, October 21, 1890.

132. "I see that . . ." *Daily Picayune*, July 21, 1895.

133. Barthes, *Mythologies*, 142.

134. "THE WORLD GROWS BETTER," *North American and Daily Advertiser*, November 11, 1891.

135. Barthes, *Mythologies*, 127.

136. "THE WORLD GROWS BETTER."

137. Elias Canetti, *Crowds and Power* (New York: Farrar, Straus and Giroux, 1984), 227.

138. I associate the former position with work done by such as Mark Haller and Daniel Kevles, while I associate the latter with the powerful insights of Martin Pernick. See, respectively, Mark Haller, *Eugenics: Hereditarian Attitudes in American Thought* (New Brunswick, NJ: Rutgers University Press, 1963); Daniel Kevles, *In the Name of Eugenics: Genetics and the Use of Human Heredity* (Berkeley: University of California Press, 1985); and Martin Pernick, *The Black Stork: Eugenics and the Death of "Defective" Babies in American Medicine and Motion Pictures since 1915* (New York: Oxford University Press, 1996).

12

Making Useful Men

THE ROMAN ROSELL INSTITUTE AND ASYLUM FOR THE BLIND, 1933–1950

Rebecca Ellis

Wealthy businessman and Spanish immigrant Roman Rosell died in 1933. In his will, he stipulated that the majority of his wealth be used to create an asylum or institute for blind men of Argentine or Spanish nationality. He hoped that the institute would, "provide them [blind men] at least some skills that permit them to be self-sufficient."[1] The provisions in Rosell's will created the Instituto e Asilo para los Ciegos "Román Rosell" (Román Rosell Institute and Asylum for the Blind; IACRR). Under the leadership of his widow, Petronila Herrera Tedín Uriburu, the IACRR opened in 1940 and joined the pantheon of institutions for the blind already in the city created by blind activists in Argentina. Twenty years earlier, these organizations emerged to take control over the expansion of services to the blind after a series of public scandals and chaos at Instituto Nacional para Ciegos (National Institute for the Blind; INC) caused public officials and sighted advocates to abandon the blind cause.[2] During the ensuing decades blind leadership focused the bulk of their energies around the task of creating dignified employment for the blind, especially blind men. Blind leaders agreed that despite disagreements over the meaning of dignified masculine labor, the goal of social services for the blind was to generate independent blind men capable of serving as head of households in their own homes. Roman Rosell's previously cited statement seemed to support these blind leaders' aspirations. In reality, the programs at the IACRR represented a conservative resurgence in sighted organizing for the blind, which rejected the blind leaders' goals to promote the blind male head of house. In its place the administrators at the IACRR imagined that the highest ideal for blind men was a semi-dependent form of cultured middle-class bachelorhood. Reading, writing, and musical training were supposed to help residents achieve this intellectual independence. As a result of the emphasis on limited intellectual independence as an ideal, the IACRR did not initially commit to the workshop program designed to provide manual labor skills that in theory should have allowed their students to earn a living outside of the institute.

Formal education of the blind in Argentina began in the late nineteenth century and was funded by sighted liberal reformers in the private sector. These sighted liberals sought to emulate the programs for the blind in northern European countries by prohibiting blind individuals from serving as administrators and teachers in the new institutions. However, despite their best efforts, sighted experts on blind education in the United States and Europe refused to relocate to Argentina. Consequentially, it was a blind Italian immigrant, Francisco Gatti, who opened the first private school for the blind in 1901. Gatti's school remained the only option for the blind until 1908 when Congress nationalized it after a long period of political disinterest in blind issues. From the outset, the national institute was fraught by mismanagement and internal conflict that culminated in a student strike in 1917. The strike, though sensational in its moment, arrested public interest in blind education for the next several years. Then, in 1924, a group of blind leaders and their sighted partners founded the Biblioteca Argentino para Ciegos (Argentine Library for the Blind; BAC). The BAC became a crucial advocate for the blind in Buenos Aires and spearheaded a new wave of interest in social services for the blind.

Throughout the 1920s, blind leaders at the BAC embarked on aggressive propaganda campaigns to demonstrate that the blind were an especially deserving population and that with the right resources they could readily be converted from social and economic "dead weights" to useful citizens. The BAC generated a propaganda program focused on cultural and intellectual productions by the blind. The program was designed to assure patrons that the blind did not represent a threat to the intellectual health of the nation. In an era increasingly defined by eugenic theories that questioned the place of the "unfit" in society it was critical that the blind represent a disabled population who did not threaten the hereditary body of the nation. In the 1920s and 1930s, the blind community was able to parlay social anxieties about individuals with mental illness, intellectual disability, and communicable diseases into support for their cause. The BAC organized a variety of musical concerts, public readings, and poetry presentations to highlight the intellectual and cultural achievements of the educated blind. Blind performances helped convince potential patrons of blind institutions that their support would encourage the conversion of a safe but unfortunate population into useful citizens.

The term "useful citizen" became a ubiquitous phrase to describe the goals of social services for the blind in the Buenos Aires press. However, there was a deep divide between blind leadership about who constituted the blind population to be made useful and how to accomplish those goals. The BAC supported the development of programs and social services that were open to both men and women, but economic and political chaos beginning in 1930 led many blind leaders to reassess the goals and focus of organizing for the blind. By the time of Roman Rosell's bequest, most blind leaders had shifted their rhetoric to focus on the problems of male blindness and male labor. However, this new focus generated deep rifts over the meaning of dignified labor and masculinity in the organized blind community. The community was divided roughly to the left and right of the political center in Argentina. On the left, leaders tended to view dignified labor in terms of equality with sighted workers. For a job to be dignified it had to be in a field in which sighted workers also performed and the blind worker had to earn equal wages to the sighted worker. Theoretically, equal wages would then allow blind workers to perform the role of male head of house. On the right, the act of providing for a family itself was the crucial component that defined work as dignified for blind men. The key point of controversy that revealed the tensions between these definitions was over street side cigarette stands. Groups to the left equated these stands with begging and denounced cigarette selling as a humiliating compromise for blind men. Organizations on the right actively worked to create cigarette vending as a protected job market that only blind men could perform. They reasoned that it was one of the few areas that blind men could easily acquire a decent living to provide for their families.

In their rhetoric the IACRR appeared to sympathize closely with the more conservative institutions operated by blind leaders in Buenos Aires. In reality, the IACRR was born from a very different tradition of organizing for the blind. Conservative blind leaders emerged out of several decades of blind political activism that asserted the right of the blind to self-determination in their own lives. The IACRR grew out of a tradition of paternalistic charity at the heart of late-nineteenth-century liberal reform movements. The 1930s witnessed a resurgence of these forms of paternalism as conservatives in power sought to resolve the "social question" that plagued class and labor relations in the country. After decades of labor unrest and steady immigration conservatives began to believe that addressing the issues of the lower classes was crucial to establishing peace in the cities.[3] However, by the 1930s the social infrastructure of Argentina was overstretched, particularly in the city of Buenos Aires. While conservative lawmakers recognized the need to expand services, they preferred to do so by expanding the system of subsidies to private organizations rather than building public institutions. The key importance of subsidies was that they allowed the government to utilize organizations controlled by groups within the elite that were considered unsuitable as administrators in the public sphere, namely elite women.[4] One of the most important organizations in Buenos Aires that benefitted from this approach was the Sociedad de Beneficencia de la Capital (Capital City Beneficence Society; SBC), created in 1823 to serve the women and children of Buenos Aires. By the 1930s, the number of institutions under the control of the SBC was vast and covered nearly every area of social services, but those institutions were still rigidly limited to women and children. The SBC's members refused to provide services to adult males even in emergency situations.

Argentine politicians were content to allow elite women to control and contain the lives of lower class women and children with relatively low interference. Lower class men, however, were seen as the principal economic resource of the nation and politicians were less willing to entrust social services for men in the hands of women, regardless of social class. As such Rosell's will should have presented a problem because it stipulated that Rosell's wife, Petronila, was to act as the executor of the foundation connected to the IACRR as well as the institution itself. Additionally, the SBC was named as the final inheritor of the foundation and institution and would gain control when the executors could no long fulfill their duties.[5] The exclusively female authority at the new institution should have presented a problem for both public entities and the SBC. However, blind men were not categorized as vital economic resources by governmental authorities. In contrast, political and social professionals discussed blind men in the same language as they discussed children. They needed to be guided, molded, and formed into an appropriately useful population. As scholars of Argentina highlight, class and occupation were crucial to concepts of masculine adulthood, and therefore untrained blind males were readily understood in the same context as children or adolescents regardless of their age.[6] Just as in the case of childhood education, political actors agreed to permit women to act as authority figure in institutions for the blind no matter the nature of the institution or the age or gender of the residents.[7]

The most compelling evidence that demonstrates the bending of gender norms in the case of blind men is the SBC's reaction to the role stipulated for them in the Rosell will. When the SBC received word in 1935 that it had been named in the Rosell bequest, members held several meetings to discuss incorporating a wholly masculine institution in light of the legal stipulation that they were an organization exclusively for women and children. To resolve the issue, SBC lawyers evoked the first clause of the decree reinstituting the society in 1852 after its forced hiatus during the administration of Juan Manuel de Rosas. The final sentence of its charter allowed the SBC to modify its mandate as circumstances changed and as long as the SBC determined that such a change was needed and appropriate.[8] This addendum to the charter allowed the society some flexibility in determining the nature of its services. However, the only other time the clause had been used to incorporate new services was 1884 when the SBC arranged to open a classroom for the blind in its Asilo de Huerfanos (Orphan's Asylum). Most of the classroom's first students were young men in their late teens and twenties that the SBC could not shift to other organizations. The classroom for the blind served as a mechanism for the organization to find a way to deal with young men whose disability made it difficult to remove them from institutional care in the same manner as their sighted counterparts.[9]

At the core of sighted reformers' understanding of blindness was the question of dependency. In the case of female-run institutions for blind men, dependency was both an important component in the construction of social position of institutional authorities and a measure of the capacities of the blind. Petronila used the supposed dependency of the blind in her institution to justify her position of authority over the male bodies supposedly under her care. Through rituals of performance, primarily conducted by the blind students, she demonstrated her importance to modernization projects that would make dependent "childlike" populations independent. Newspaper accounts that covered the institute's progress and goals lauded the IACRR's mission of turning "useless" boys into productive men but were rarely concerned with the actual age of institutional residents. One clipping described the opening of the IACRR in the following glowing terms: "One institute more that can bring the light of knowledge to boys disinherited from physical light so that tomorrow they will be useful men to themselves and to society under conditions identical to that of their peers in the world in which they live."[10] Unlike blind leaders, Petronila not only saw the capacity for independence as bounded by the residents' limited capacity for sight but needed that to be true to maintain authority over the predominately adult male bodies in her institute. Consequentially, sighted administrators, teachers, and caretakers emphasized equality with the sited or self-reliance but believed that their task was to shift the residents from a state of complete dependence to a level of semi-independence. In doing so, they believed society as a whole benefitted from their project because it reduced, though did not eliminate, the burden of caring individuals who otherwise "leached" off their families and society.[11] This narrow definition of independence structured what was taught in the school, the skills learned in the workshops, and the labor performed by the sighted at the IACRR.

Educating the Blind at the IACRR

The initial problems posed by the stipulations in Rosell's will that placed women in charge of men created a lag in the development of the proposed institution. For her part, Petronila was not in a hurry to begin construction and allowed several years to lapse before setting any plans in motion. A year after her husband's will was published she remarried a noted ophthalmologist and only then departed for Europe and the United States on a grand tour to research institutes for the blind. Her descriptions of her travels suggested that she was more interested in the buildings than in the blind. She described for the SBC leaders the exact layout of marble in the hallways, the location of the founder's statue, and the cleanliness of the bathrooms. The report contained comparatively few details regarding the blind individuals she met, the educational practices, or the goals of the institutions she toured. For Petronila, the institution was about cementing a social legacy and accessing a particular form of class authority dominated by Argentine women.

After Petronila's return from abroad the process of constructing the IACRR did not accelerate. Construction of the institute lasted another six years, and it was not until 1939 that Petronila was finally ready to begin recruitment. When she began to solicit applicants, she expected a residential population consisting of young boys, ages six to fourteen, from the capital city and its surroundings.[12] Petronila's correspondence with the SBC indicated that she was relatively confident that she would easily locate applicants. In the intervening years between her first husband's death and her efforts to open the institute, however, blind leaders dramatically extended the number and variety of services for the blind in the province of Buenos Aires. In addition to the INC, education and reeducation programs for the blind included several Braille classes and a number of specialized vocational programs, none of which required that students live at the respective institutions. Consequently, Petronila received few applications from children in the city. By 1940, she solicited the aid of the SBC's Comisión de Visitaciones a los Pobres (Visitation Commission for the Poor), but even this failed to generate residents. After it became clear that she would not find applicants in Buenos Aires, Petronila widened her search to the provinces. After two years of soliciting applications, she finally generated fifty prospective students through a combination of radio campaigns, newspaper advertisements, and direct requests to provincial governments. The students were significantly older than the organization initially anticipated. Though the highest enrollment of children under the age of ten occurred in the first two years of operation, by 1947 only sixteen out of sixty-eight students were under the age of sixteen and at least two were over the age of fifty. Consequently, when the IACRR opened its doors in 1941, young men, not boys, occupied most of the dormitories on the seven-hectare complex.[13]

The teachers hired by Petronila were disconcerted by the lack of school-aged boys at the institute. In 1947, the director of the primary school lamented that,

> As in previous years, the number of grade school age students remained relatively low. This can principally be attributed to parents who, due to incomprehension or ignorance, keep their blind children away from centers where they would receive an adequate education for their condition.[14]

The frustration of those in charge at the institute did not translate into major transformations in the initial plan of organization. The directors found that most of the candidates were illiterate and enrolled them in the primary school as initially planned. Over two-thirds of the enrollees were in one of the four first-grade classrooms, whose primary objective was to teach reading and writing using the Braille system.[15] Enrolling all the residents into the primary school created massive age disparities in the classrooms. In first grade section A, the students' ages ranged from ten to fifty with the median age being twenty-two.[16] No attempt was made on the part of school directors to group the three first grades by relative age, even though they consistently noted that one of the challenges they faced in the classroom was the disparity in the students' ages.[17]

For sighted administrators and educators at the institute, blindness created a permanent childhood only disrupted by the intervention of education.

Dependency was the antithesis of masculine adulthood. Because blind residents were on some level dependent on others, teachers and administrators could treat them as children rather than as fully realized male adults. Adult male identity was defined largely by the ability to work and the type of work conducted. Blind leadership in Argentina utilized anxiety over blindness and work accidents to push for resources for blind adults, arguing that through reeducation programs men blinded later in life could be made useful or "whole" again. Unlike these injured working-class individuals, the majority of the new entrants to the IACRR, were adults who lost their sight in childhood, but because there were few programs for the blind in the provinces, they reached adulthood without receiving a formal education. The fact that the men at the institute needed to pass through this fundamental act of being a child, attending primary school, deepened the association of blindness with childhood made by administrators and educators at the IACRR.

Educators hired by Petronila were not trained to work with the blind and came to see blind education as one fraught with pathology. Blind students, they argued, were prone to several psychological problems that prevented them from succeeding.[18] The teachers' central concern regarded what they believed was the residents' psychological propensity toward negativity and low self-esteem. These problems led blind individuals to be passive and diminished their motivation to adjust to new circumstances. These were the most problematic of several traits known as *cieguismos* (blind characteristics or tics) that the staff desired to train out of the residents.[19] According to Argentine experts, eradicating cieguismos required specialized training at colleges focused on the education of specific populations with specialized needs. However, the professors working at the primary school were novices in special education and were hired prior to the creation of a normal school for educators of the blind. At the beginning and end of every semester, teachers were instructed to complete psychological evaluations of each student using a form constructed by the lead medical physician. Teachers used these forms to identify problems and devise strategies for eradicating those problems in the hope that residents would learn faster and with more confidence.

Teachers at the institute were heavily influenced by the growing popularity of Freud in Argentina. They began to utilize Freudian theory to understand the cieguismos that they believed interfered with their students' learning. They noted their students' tendency toward inferiority complexes, negativity, and their subconscious terror of making errors.[20] In some ways, the supposed problems of the blind reflected the sighted staff's imagination of what being blind might be like and were perhaps as much personal responses of the sighted to blindness as they were cognitive issues of blind individuals. Educators perceived blindness as an inferior state of existence that created self-pity, depression, and esteem issues. They assumed that students who achieved a healthy acceptance of their condition would demonstrate gratefulness to those who had lifted them out of their low mental state. This led one teacher to state that some healthy students "comprehend their social situation as blind persons, the notable work realized for their benefit by the Asylum-Institute, they are sincerely grateful and they contribute, to the best of their abilities, to fulfill the hopes that they have deposited in them."[21] The goal of the staff was to elevate all their students to the same psychological stability as these more "grateful" students.

Like their peers in public schools, the staff emphasized physical education and reading as the key mechanisms for improving student mental health. While in sighted schools physical education emphasized strength and agility for males, at the IACRR physical education emphasized movement, spatial orientation, and physical control in an effort to build confidence. In 1942, the physical education instructor, Armendo Mario Monti, boasted that his training had given the students the confidence to not only move about the school but to run in it.[22] Running was important in an era that increasingly prized male physicality as part of an effort to improve the strength of the national population.[23] However, while physical education in public schools was central to the project to create an Argentine population that was physically separate and superior to its peers, at the IACRR the emphasis was on helping students assimilate with the sighted population. To that end professors were concerned with Professor Monti's ability to rid their students of the physical tics they also referred to as cieguismos.[24] Physical cieguismos included balancing the body in a direction other than upright, pressing the fingers or hands to the eyes or face, rapid turns in place followed by small jumps, and tilting the head to one side. The staff saw these tics as detrimental to social integration because they seemed to signal a lack of control over the physical body. Physical control over the body was crucial to prove the eugenic fitness of the blind.[25] Physical education not only provided the confidence to move through space, therefore; it also was integral to ensuring that blind students' movements allowed them to assimilate in sighted society.

Reading and writing skills were the intellectual and cultural equivalents to the physical project to develop proper posture and movement in IACRR residents. Since its invention in the mid-nineteenth century, Braille was the greatest historical shift in the education of the blind. Learning Braille was equated with the acquisition of culture, modernity, and communication. Reading and writing in Braille, like literacy in general, were seen as significant acts of independence.[26] For men, literacy could also equate to class mobility. In early-twentieth-century Argentina, literate men moved into clerical jobs that in Europe and the Americas were increasingly occupied by women.[27] From those professional positions arose a cadre of early-twentieth-century male writers who conveyed a form of masculinity rooted in intellectuality and culture. Most of the blind male leaders in Buenos Aires were also authors, poets, musicians, or librarians. Literacy and its accompanying trades had provided the most stable and visible employ for the blind in the city. For administrators at the IACRR, literacy was not only an avenue for blind men to gain entrance into the middle class, but literate residents required less attention from professors, shop teachers, and caretakers. By 1947, all professors at the music conservatory and some at the workshops began to make knowledge of Braille a prerequisite for entrance into their higher-level classes.[28] This signified a cultured and intelligent reduction in the dependency of the blind on the sighted and was something that appealed not only to administrators but to their donors and patrons as well.

If education created a form of cultured independence prized by the middle and upper classes, then the daily rhythms at the IACRR constructed on the principles of uniformity, routine, and subordination offset the school's attempts to create a sense of confidence and independence in residents. All residents wore uniforms, ate the same meals, were attended by a caretaker, and adhered to the same schedule. Inhabitants could not leave the institution without permission and even then they were required to be accompanied by a member of the staff.[29] Blind residents performed few of the labors that sustained their domestic lives. The IACRR's definition of independence did not include self-sufficiency. Meals were prepared for the students by a kitchen staff. An in-house staff of seamstresses made their clothes. Their sheets and uniforms were cleaned, dried, disinfected, and ironed by a large group of laborers in the laundry facilities. The hallways, eating quarters, and common rooms were all kept clean by crews of maintenance personal managed by the institute's labor supervisor.[30] Outdoors, the grounds, a small cohort of pigs and cows, and garden areas were also maintained by hired labor.[31] Unlike other institutions in Argentina that placed high significance on daily chores like laundry or cleaning, the residents at the IACRR were not expected to perform any domestic tasks.

Within the IACRR there was a strict hierarchy of authority stretching from Director Petronila at the top to the manual laborers at the bottom. The students and residents of the institute were situated above the day laborers. Administrators believed that students needed special protection from those below them in the hierarchy. All people in educated, middle-class positions such as administrators, professors, medical personnel, and caretakers were assumed to protect students' interests. There were no regulations governing their interactions with residents. The employee handbook was very clear, however, about the relationship between manual laborers and the residents of the institute. This sector of the IACRR's labor force was admonished in the employee handbook to "Maintain the highest respect for the students, residents, educational and auxiliary personnel, observing in all their acts the necessary correctness."[32] Further, manual laborers were not to be "depositors" or keepers of residents' money or personal effects. They could not accept tips, nor maintain relationships of any kind with the students and residents. The asylum's administrators possibly feared that contact between the two groups might generate attempts to subvert the institute's authority over the residents. For the first five years of the institute's existence, the majority of the students were from rural areas in the provinces, a fact that generated concern regarding their lack of culture and rough mannerisms. Administrators likely worried that relationships between the two groups might perpetuate the wrong cultural traits, open the students to fraud, or allow them to gain extra institutional benefits that would endanger hierarchical balance. Hence, workers could not accept tips from the students, presumably for performing extra services for individual residents.

Culture and Musical Performance

The question of student dependence/independence was bound together with the idea of cultured masculinity and blindness. Since the late nineteenth century the word "culture" was used to discuss the relative success of programs for the blind. Both blind leaders and sighted activists believed that instilling "culture" in young blind men would alleviate the persistent poverty of blindness. For blind leaders, the pursuit of culture meant creating a vibrant community of blind artists, poets, journalists, musicians, and authors who would produce original contributions to the cultural heritage of the nation. For sighted administrators like Petronila, culture also meant musical and literary production, but they were less interested in original production and more interested in blind reproduction of cultural classics. In part, there was a comparative element to emphasizing the classics. By reproducing well-known musical productions, blind performers "proved" to sighted audiences that they could perform as well as or better than sighted performers. This reinforced the importance of the institute to the public good and boosted the social capital of institutional administrators. In her case, Petronila needed to show that as a female administrator of a male institution she could transform the supposedly inert and unrefined lives of blind men into lives of activity and culture, thus proving herself and her institute as essential assets to modernizing projects in Argentina. To that end, Petronila extended invitations to ceremonies during which the residents of the IACRR performed for a crowd of illustrious guests. The most important of these rituals took place annually at the closure of classes. During the ceremony students demonstrated the skills they had acquired during the year. Music, particularly classical music, was the centerpiece of these celebrations and was the aspect most equated with the notion of culture. Musical performance was the highest example of progress that could be exhibited and therefore the most effective form of performance.

Music's key role as a form of publicity and the perception that the blind were musically gifted meant that musical education held a distorted place in the institute's program of development. Across Argentina, musical training for the blind was a strictly masculine pursuit. With one exception, Argentine institutions for the blind did not allow women to pursue a musical education.[33] Students who turned their musical training into successful careers enjoyed the highest earning potential and became very public examples of the work done at institutes for the blind. The IACRR was willing to spend exorbitant amounts of money and political capital on the acquisition of instruments such as an organ imported from Germany.[34] Petronila justified the purchase of the organ, arguing that it was a clear favorite among the blind, though only two students learned to play the instrument in the five years following its acquisition. By 1940, other institutions for the blind around the globe could no longer justify disproportionate expense on music programs.[35] The advent of recorded music decreased the ability of musicians to earn a wage as it increasingly replaced live musicians. Instructors at the IACRR began to acknowledge that even good students were unlikely to enter musical occupations and began to recommend that the institute limit the enrollment of students in the conservatory to only the most gifted.[36] The directors never acquiesced to this request, insisting that because musical performance was integral to the perpetuation of the institute's social position, musical education would remain at the heart of curriculum. A description from a 1945 article about the IACRR was a powerful illustration of the symbolic place of music in the public perception of the purpose of blind education. Toward the end of the article the anonymous author stated in reference to watching students play at the conservatory:

> And our frantic city, our egotistical city, our city that appears to only do for the winners, it can turn its gaze now and then to contemplate those that do not see, to those that do not know of colors or light, to those that are ignorant of the infinite subtleties of form, to those Destiny has deprived from seeing the sky and the light and the stars, to all them for whom the world has lost the marvelous charm of chromatic passage. The blind had been left grave and sad. Now they smile. And they play. There they have received the quota of happiness to which they have a right, as children, as human beings.[37]

Cottage Industry and Workshops at the IACRR

Music's role as an important form of propaganda for the IACRR could not alter the reality that it was only a viable avenue of employment for the most gifted of the students, and the IACCR was at least theoretically committed to teaching students a paid vocation. For most residents, this meant training in a series of workshop crafts. At its inauguration, the plan for the primary school, the musical conservatory, and the daily routines of the asylum were set and only minimally changed over the next five years. The workshops, however, were initially in disarray. In February, five months before the opening ceremonies and two months after students began arriving, *El Mundo* (The World) reported that the workshops would teach basket-making, cabinet-making, bookbinding, and weaving. Only one of those workshops, bookbinding, was incorporated into the final schedule of workshops in the opening year.[38] Five months later, a report of the opening ceremonies by *La Prensa* (The Press) reflected a more accurate description of the workshops incorporated into the institute: whickering, bookbinding, paintbrush and fine brush-making, carpentry, and mattress stuffing.[39] The serious confusion over the direction of the workshops was further reflected in the first annual report published in 1942, which stated that the workshops began operating too late in the year to provide a detailed account of their production or plan. Compared to the primary school and the musical conservatory, the organization of the workshops was severely neglected in the first year of the institute's existence.

The delayed implementation of the workshops reflected several issues at the institute. First, administrators expected the first class to be school age and therefore likely delayed preparation of the workshops to allow students time to age into them. Additionally, planning the workshops required more extensive research and preparation than other institutional components. To plan the primary school and musical conservatory administrators simply adapted the curriculum in use at the INC. They hired teachers from the local normal schools and established professors of music. This was not as possible in the workshops. By the 1940s, the manual production of goods like brushes and brooms was rare due to the intensification of import substitution policies and the increasing industrial manufacture of daily goods. Finding sighted instructors with basic knowledge of increasingly rarified workshop skills and enough experience to adapt specialized manual labor skills to their blind students was less straightforward than hiring primary school teachers. Finally, elite administrators demonstrated far less enthusiasm for the workshops. In her own reports, Petronila rarely mentioned the workshops, and few discussions referenced the goals of the workshop structure. On the contrary, newspapers and magazine articles tended to latch onto the workshops as the most important element of the institute, glorifying them as a means of making the blind man useful. Consequentially, between 1941 and 1943 the workshops took on an experimental nature and shifted significantly based on assumptions about the students' capacity, economic trends, and the structural needs of the institute.

The workshops began operations with six different sections: whickering, fine brush and paintbrush making, broom-making, carpentry, mattress stuffing, and bookbinding. The first three activities were the most popular. The popular workshops produced goods that were more frequently sold outside of the institution in bulk quantities. This was an advantage for students because they could collect a greater amount of money from the sale of these items. Students earned 10 percent of every item sold after the cost of materials was deducted. Outside the institute the goods could be sold for significantly higher prices, especially when marketed as handcrafts whose sale supported a charitable cause.[40] Goods like paintbrushes and baskets, for example, earned a premium when marketed as hand produced by the blind and then sold to upper-class individuals at specialized sales. When the IACRR purchased goods from the workshops it did so only slightly above cost, meaning that every good produced for the benefit of the IACRR significantly reduced the amount earned by the student who produced it.[41].

For students working in the carpentry and bookbinding sections, the institution's practice of purchasing at cost was a significant disadvantage. In 1943, the top earning carpenter made 53 pesos while the top-earning student in fine brushes made 256 pesos.[42] Carpentry projects tended to be for the benefit of the institute. These students made tables, chairs, stools, and so on, and their work was more time consuming than brush-making; it required greater care and skill and some assistance from a sighted worker at the finishing stage. The same held true for bookbinding, which predominately bound the Braille books produced by the professors and students for use in the IACRR library. For a time, the IACRR benefitted from these workshops because they reduced the institute's need to purchase furnishings and books at retail prices. In 1943 alone, the carpentry workshop spent almost the entire year producing articles for use in the institute. The residents sat at carpentry students' tables and the staff climbed their stools to reach high places. Additionally, the labor of bookbinding students significantly reduced the number of books purchased from the BAC, allowing for the expansion of the IACRR library. However, in 1943 the workshop's director challenged the efficacy of these two specialties. In his annual report for 1943 the director recommending closing the workshops as they both represented professions that would never be dominated by the blind. Students, he argued, were unlikely to use skills learned in these workshops because they would have to compete with the sighted. This was in fact the goal of blind leaders on the left who urged institutions for the blind to open more workshops that put the blind in direct competition with the sighted. Under the rubric of these blind leaders, competition with the sighted added to the dignity and desirability of a workshop skill. The opposite held true at the IACRR, and in reality the skills learned in the workshop were relatively unimportant when the cost of the workshop to the institution was factored in. Due to the rising cost of materials and a decline in the institution's need for the goods produced, these workshops were no longer profitable. The IACRR could obtain most of the goods produced in the carpentry shop at prices lower than the cost of the raw material, which continued to rise through the 1940s.[43] In bookbinding, by 1943 the IACRR had established a working relationship with the BAC that allowed students to check out as many books as they desired from the BAC's collection. This reduced the pressure on the institute to build up a library of its own. Carpentry and bookbinding were closed at the moment they began to represent a drain on finances and were no longer an advantage to the institution.

For residents of the IACRR, the highest earning potential lay in the workshops that produced bulk goods for sale outside the institute. However, the piecework structure of the pay scale meant, even in the highest earning workshops, student earnings ranged widely. For example, earnings among brush makers varied between 43 centavos and 246 pesos. The pay mechanisms of the institute created a disparity of earnings between the students. After five years of labor, some residents were owed almost 750 pesos while the vast majority maintained between 100 and 200 pesos in their accounts.[44] Few of the students earned enough at the institute to support themselves even minimally outside of it. The average yearly earnings from the workshops ranged from 12 (bookbinding) to 60 pesos (brushes), though the pay of a few top earners skewed these averages.

The divide between the top earners and the bottom deepened in 1944 when directors at the institute decided to cut personnel costs by reducing the number of paid assistants in the workshops. The sighted assistants were replaced by the top blind students in each workshop as part of their "prize" for excelling in their field. In monetary terms the prize amounted to 46 pesos for the year, a fraction of what the school paid in wages to the sighted assistants. Additional personnel costs were saved by having students at the lower end of the earning scale take over duties such as cleaning the shops or collecting pig hair for the brushes. These students were paid just a few pesos a year for this labor, which would otherwise be done by hired workers for a few pesos a week.

The workshop system was supposedly at the heart of the institute's efforts to turn useless blind boys into useful blind men. However, the manual trades chosen by the institute were generally considered to be women's work in the world of blind education. In a detailed accounting of standard workshops for the blind given at the World Conference on Work for the Blind in 1931, S. W. Starling, general superintendent and secretary for the Birmingham Royal Institution for the Blind in England, identified all but two, carpentry and bookbinding, of the trades chosen by the IACRR as women's work. After those two workshops were removed in 1943, they were replaced by mechanical weaving, another area historically considered women's work. The addition of weaving introduced the first and only female instructor to the institute. In an era of intensely gendered rhetoric and strict institutional division of sexes, the willingness to train men for women's work is telling. The skills learned in the workshops were not meant to be portable to sighted male industries. Skills such as whickering, brush-making, and broom-making were intended to provide skills for cottage or home-based industries that would allow individuals to earn a supporting wage through the sale of handicrafts. As stated, the putting out system was one of the few arenas where women dominated in Argentina. Blind hand crafts were construed in similar ways to women's production of clothing. The sale of workshop crafts was intended to lessen the financial burden on a blind individual's family or institution. The work structure of the institute assumed the perpetual dependency of residents. Most men at the institute were designated for vocational training as opposed to musical training. This meant that at the IACRR most men were trained in feminine labors that were unlikely to lead to the full independence that Petronila and administrators associated with masculine adulthood. As a result, residents could be discussed in child-like terminology, stripped of gendered characteristics that would place Petronila in the untenable situation of presiding over a social institution for adult males. The ongoing dependency of the IACRR residents insured the position of its female director and its future as an all-male institution administered by an organization historically committed to social service for women and children.

Conclusions

Missing from this narrative of the IACRR are the stories of the residents and the day laborers and private concerns of the teachers and administrators. The records of the SBC cannot tell us how they perceived their place at the institute or what they hoped to gain from their time there. What can be said is that they worked within a set of externally imposed expectations rooted in specific notions about the capacity of the blind to work and live independently. Administrators of the institute did not envision a future for the residents in which they worked in the formal labor economy, married, or raised children. As they saw it, their role was to take men who existed in a near infantile state of dependency and provide them with enough skills to alleviate their caretakers' burdens, much like adolescents. Therefore, blind residents were trained in cottage industries in a piecework structure, work commonly considered as supplemental to formal labor wages. Because administrators did not envision that residents would someday marry and care for dependents, they did not feel constrained by gendered divisions of labor. The absence of the potential of fatherhood or spousal relations in the residents' future removed the need to prepare them for masculine industries that would allow them to provide for a family. Instead caretakers, teachers, and administrators focused on infusing them with culture, education, and self-confidence that would allow them to accept their "lesser" role in the social structure through a kind of cultured bachelorhood.

Publicly, the IACRR emphasized its cultural projects to justify not only its existence in the pantheon of social service programs but also the unusual arrangement of authority within the institute. Very few institutions had female directors that oversaw adult men. Petronila relied on musical and intellectual performance to reinforce her place at the head of the IARR and to build social capital for herself in the elite circles. After 1946, the effectiveness of the IACRR as a social placeholder for its elite director diminished.[45] The elevation of Juan Domingo Perón to power shifted the provision of social services by elite private organizations to centralized governmental control of those services within rhetoric of social justice. In 1952, Perón requested that his portrait be produced in relief so that the blind could see his face. In doing so, Perón signaled the personalism that marked the provision of social services during his years in power.[46]

Notes

1. *Para proporcionarse así algunos medios de vida que les permita bastarse a sí mismos.* Letter from Doña Petronila Elisa Herrera de Rosell to Doña Elisa Alvear de Bosch, May 11, 1935, Archivo General de la Nación (AGN), Sociedad de Beneficencia, Colección de la Administración Central, Asilo Román Rosell, 1935–1950, legajo 84.

2. For a more detailed discussion, see Rebecca Ellis, "Basically Intelligent:" The Blind, Intelligence, and Gender in Argentina, 1880–1939" (PhD diss., University of New Mexico, 2016), 181–220.

3. Mariano Ben Plotkin, *Mañana Es San Perón: A Cultural History of Perón's Argentina*, Latin American Silhouettes (Wilmington, NC: Scholarly Resources, 2002); and Sandra McGee Deutsch, *The Argentine Right: Its History and Intellectual Origins, 1910 to the Present*, Latin American Silhouettes (Wilmington, NC: SR Books, 1993).

4. Susana Belmartino, *La atención médica Argentina en el siglo XX: Instituciones y procesos* (Buenos Aires: Siglo Veintiuno Editores Argentina, 2005).

5. The records of the IACRR housed in the society's collection therefore represent only that which Petronila and her staff chose to share. As a result, the collection consists largely of legal issues, yearly reports, and social invitations. Documentation from the late 1940s, following the dissolution of the SBC, was exclusively legal in nature, because Petronila continued to utilize society lawyers after the organization began to transition to governmental control.

6. Natalia Milanesio, "Gender and Generation: The University Reform Movement in Argentina, 1918," *Journal of Social History* 39.2 (Winter 2005), 505–529; Pablo Ben, "Plebeian Masculinity and Sexual Comedy in Buenos Aires, 1880–1930," *Journal of the History of Sexuality* 16.3 (2007), 436–458; and Eduardo P. Archetti, "Multiple Masculinities: The Worlds of Tango and Football in Argentina," in *Sex and Sexuality in Latin America*, Daniel Balderston and Donna J. Guy, eds. (New York: New York University Press, 1997), 200–216.

7. In 1908 Congress demoted Francisco Gatti, the blind founder and director of the institution that they nationalized to create the INC, and promoted the woman who had served as the head of the women's section at the original institute to the directorship.

8. *A seguir con sus objetos y bajo los mismos reglamentos que reían, sin perjuicio de extenderse aquellos y de modificarse estos, todo lo cual tendrá lugar oportunamente a propuesto de la misma.* Letter from Elisa Alvear de Bosch to Don Carlos Saavedra Lomas, December 12, 1935, AGN, Sociedad de Beneficencia, Colección de la Administración Central, Asilo Román Rosell, legajo 84.

9. The original plan had been to create a school for all the blind children of Buenos Aires that would function as a separate institution. This plan was altered when none of the sighted professionals on blindness in Europe and the United States proved willing to move to Argentina and serve as the director for the institute. In the end the SBC hired a blind teacher and converted the proposed school into a small classroom that exclusively trained orphans at the asylum. Ellis, "Basically Intelligent," 32–69.

10. *Un instituto más que podrá llevar la luz del saber a los niños desheredados de la luz física para que pueden ser mañana hombres útiles a si mismos y a la sociedad en idénticas condiciones que sus semejantes dentro del mundo en que actúen.* "Se inauguro en marzo el Asilo e Instituto para Ciegos 'Román Rosell,'" publication unknown, July 13, 1941, AGN, Sociedad de Beneficencia, Colección de la Administración Central, Asilo Román Rosell, legajo 84.

11. "Quedo inaugurado ayer el Asilo e Instituto para Ciegos R. Rosell," *La Nación*, July 13, 1941, Sociedad de Beneficencia, Colección de la Administración Central, Asilo Román Rosell, legajo 84.

12. Preliminary entrance forms, initial purchases for the library, and early architectural reports clearly indicated that the proprietors of the new institute prepared for an initial student body comprised of children.

13. "Alumnos promovidos-curso escolar, 1941," AGN, Sociedad de Beneficencia, Collection de la Administración Central, Asilo Román Rosell, legajo 84.

14. *Como en años anteriores, el número de alumnos en edad escolar ha sido relativamente bajo. Esto se debe, principalmente, a que muchos padres, por incomprensión o ignorancia, mantienen a sus hijos ciegos alejados de los centros donde podrían recibir una educación adecuada a su condición.* "Memoria de la Escuela Primaria Instituto y Asilo Román Rosell,

1947," AGN, Sociedad de Beneficencia, Colección de la Administración Central, Asilo Román Rosell, legajo 84.

15. Of the four first-grade sections three were labeled "inferior" and the fourth "superior." During 1941 the school also included a preparatory, second, and third grade. The third-grade classroom was reserved for students who were literate before their loss of sight. The school eventually expanded to include fourth, fifth, and sixth grades by 1944. A seventh level was added in 1945 supposedly for the sixth-grade class who wanted to continue their education. The reality is that the school could not certify the students' sixth-grade certificates due to a battle with various ministries over the qualifications of the faculty and therefore had to keep the students in classes until that issue was resolved. All indications point to a period of several years before that issue was resolved.

16. "Alumnos promovidos, 1941," AGN, Sociedad de Beneficencia, Colección de la Administración Central, Asilo Román Rosell, legajo 84.

17. Inferior Class A's ages were: 10, 17, 26, 20, 24, 38, 50, 22; Inferior Class B: 14, 15, 13, 14, 27; Inferior Class C: 18, 18, 16, 17, 20, 37, 35; ages could potentially have been grouped in three sections ranging from 10 to 16, 17 to 22, and 24 to 50.

18. Frances A. Koestler, *The Unseen Minority: A Social History of Blindness in America* (New York: David McKay, 1976); Simon Hayoe, *God, Money, and Politics: English Attitudes to Blindness and Touch, from the Enlightenment to Integration* (Charlotte, NC: Information Age, 2008); Zina Weygand, *The Blind in French Society from the Middle Ages to the century of Louis Braille* (Stanford, CA: Stanford University Press, 2009); and G. A. Phillips, *The Blind in British Society: Charity, State, and Community, 1780–1930* (Hampshire, UK: Ashgate, 2004).

19. "Memoria de la Escuela Primaria del Instituto e Asilo Román Rosell, 1944," AGN, Sociedad de Beneficencia, Colección de la Administración Central, Asilo Román Rosell, legajo 84.

20. In Argentina, Freudian theory was fairly malleable and used across the political spectrum to explain individual and social problems. For more on Freud in Argentina, see Mariano Ben Plotkin, *Freud in the Pampas: The Emergence and Development of a Psychoanalytic Culture in Argentina* (Stanford, CA: Stanford University Press, 2001).

21. *Unos comprenden su situación como no-videntes, la obra notable que realiza en su beneficio el Asilo-Instituto, la agradecen sinceramente y contribuyen, en la medida de sus fuerzas, a colmar las esperanzas que en ellos se han depositado.* "Memoria, 1944."

22. "Memoria, 1942" and "Memoria, 1944."

23. Diego Armus, *The Ailing City: Health Tuberculosis and Culture in Buenos Aires, 1870–1950* (Durham, NC: Duke University Press, 2011), 276–306.

24. Armus, *Ailing City*.

25. For a substantial discussion on physical health and social theories, see Marisa Miranda and Gustavo Vallejo, eds., *Una historia de la eugenesia: Argentina y las redes biopolíticas internacionales, 1912–1945* (Buenos Aires: Editorial Biblos, 2012); Armus, *Ailing City*; and Julia Rodriguez, *Civilizing Argentina: Science, Medicine and the Modern State* (Chapel Hill: North Carolina University Press, 2006).

26. William G. Acree, *Everyday Reading: Print Culture and Collective Identity in the Río De La Plata, 1780–1910* (Nashville, TN: Vanderbilt University Press, 2011), EBSCOhost.

27. Paul Jordan, *The Author in the Office: Narrative Writing in Twentieth-Century Argentina and Uruguay* (Rochester, NY: Tamesis, 2006).

28. By 1947, the first generation of students passed through sixth grade and the professors could expect a reasonable number of students to have decent knowledge of Braille. "Libro 1, Acto 1," AGN, Sociedad de Beneficencia, Colección de la Administración Central, Asilo Román Rosell, legajo 84.

29. "Reglamento General de la Fundación Román Rosell y de su Instituto e Asilo," AGN, Sociedad de Beneficencia, Colección de la Administración Central, Asilo Román Rosell, legajo 84.

30. The used word for labor supervisor was *mayordomo*, "Reglamento General."

31. There was some indication that the school intended some of the outdoor tasks to be performed by students, but in the first five years of the IACRR it did not implement that plan.

32. *A guardar el mayor respeto a los alumnos o asilado y al personal docente y auxiliar observando en todos sus actos la debida corrección.* "Reglamento de Fundación Román Rosell."

33. The Francisco Gatti Institution for the Blind of Both Sexes trained girls to play musical instruments between 1900 and 1908.

34. The acquisition of the organ is a prime example of the power relationship between Petronila and the SBC. After concluding that only an imported organ would suffice, Petronila contacted the SBC and requested that they intervene with the Ministry of National Finances to permit her to circumvent paying importation taxes on the organ. The Ministry complied without hesitation. Letter to Doña Rosa Saen Peña de Saavedra Lamas from Doña Patronila Elisa Herrera de Tedín Uriburu, July 6, 1939, AGN, Sociedad de Beneficencia, Colección de la Administración Central, Asilo Román Rosell, legajo 84; and Letter to Dr. Pedro Groppo from Rosa Saen Peña de Saavedra Lamas, July 7, 1939, AGN, Sociedad de Beneficencia, Colección de la Administración Central, Asilo Román Rosell, legajo 84.

35. Robert B. Irwin, *World Conference on Work for the Blind* (New York: American Foundation for the Blind, 1932), 155–156 and 383–384.

36. "Libro 1, Acto 1."

37. *Y nuestra ciudad frenética, nuestra ciudad egoísta, nuestra ciudad para contemplar a los quien no ven, a los que no saben de colores ni de luces, a los que ignoran la sutilezas infinitas de la forma, a los que el Destino los a privado de ver el cielo y la luz y las estrellas, a todo aquellos para quienes el mundo ha perdido el maravillosa encanto cromático de paisaje. Los ciegos han dejado de ser graves y tristes. Ahora sonríen. Y juegan. Allí han recibido la cuata de alegría que tenían derecho, como niños, como seres humanos.* "Un Oasis de Luz Para Ciegos: El Instituto e Asilo Román Rosell en San Isidro." *Revista Duperial* (January 1945), 16, in AGN, Sociedad de Beneficencia, Colección de la Administración Central, Asilo Román Rosell, legajo 84.

38. "Terminose la Obra del Instituto Asilo para Ciegos, "Román Rosell," *El Mundo*, February 4, 1941, AGN, Sociedad de Beneficencia, Colección de la Administración Central, Asilo Román Rosell, legajo 84.

39. The list failed to mention broom-making, which was possibly a last-minute addition to the workshops. "Esta tarde se inauguro en San Isidro el Instituto para Ciegos Román Rosell," *La Prensa*, July 12, 1941, in AGN, Sociedad de Beneficencia, Colección de la Administración Central, Asilo Román Rosell, legajo 84.

40. "Memoria de los Talleres del Instituto e Asilo Román Rosell, 1946," AGN, Sociedad de Beneficencia, Colección de la Administración Central, Asilo Román Rosell, legajo 84.

41. "Memoria de los Talleres del Instituto e Asilo Román Rosell, 1943," AGN, Sociedad de Beneficencia, Colección de la Administración Central, Asilo Román Rosell, legajo 84.

42. Top earners in other sections: mattresses, 96.52; brooms, 108.67; books, 36.00; and wickering, 41.48. "Memoria de los Talleres, 1943."

43. "Memoria, 1944;" "Memoria, 1944;" "Memoria, 1945;" "Memoria, 1946;" and "Memoria, 1947."

44. There is no indication that students could access these accounts while they resided at Román Rosell. Students' pay was directly deposited based on the report of the director of the workshops and oversight was in the hands of the institute's fiscal department. "Cuentas Particulares, 1946," AGN, Sociedad de Beneficencia, Colección de la Administración Central, Asilo Román Rosell, legajo 84.

45. In 1946, under the government of Juan Domingo Perón, the Sociedad de Beneficencia was dissolved and the Fundación Eva Perón, run by the president's wife, inherited its institutions.

46. "Argentina Moves to Let Blind 'See' Peron's Face," *Chicago Daily Tribune*, July 10, 1952: 1.

13

Weeping and Bad Hair

THE BODILY SUFFERING OF EARLY CHRISTIAN HELL AS A THREAT TO MASCULINITY

Meghan Henning

Early Christian Hell, Early Christian Bodies, Punishment, and "Disability" Now and Then

Lennard J. Davis has argued that disability studies can play a critical role in contemporary identity politics because disability "is an identity that interrogates and can help transform the very idea of identity. Disability, by the unstable nature of its category, asks us to redefine the very nature of identity and of 'belonging' to an identity group."[1] As Davis contends, disability forces us to rethink not only our cultural construction of disability as such but also late-twentieth-century identity politics as a whole, challenging the notion that "identity" always equates to an exclusive group with a particular set of political concerns.[2] Davis concludes that the future of disability studies lies in a cultural paradigm shift that escapes the dichotomy of normal–abnormal and a "concept of the subject, of character and personality, that derives its strength from knowledge of where identity has been but more where it is going."[3] Davis here issues a challenge that forces us to think seriously about the way that we do work as scholars of disability studies, as disability rights activists, and as participants in a fading cultural episteme. I begin here with Davis's challenge because as a historian of early Christianity who works on disability and gender, it is easy to find oneself enmeshed in the identity politics of the twentieth century as they are read back upon antiquity. And yet even as we take to heart Davis's call for us to lean into a future beyond this "paradigm shift," our work here is part of the ongoing effort to attend to the intersection between multiple identity categories. In this way, we hope to contribute to the knowledge "of where identity has been," specifically focusing on the history of scholarship of early Christianity and the history of gender and the body in antiquity.

This chapter uses the conceptions of gendered bodily suffering found in the ancient medical corpus (Hippocrates, Galen and inscriptions), martyrdom literature, and the Roman judicial rhetoric of punitive suffering to read apocalyptic depictions of bodily suffering as "effeminizing" punishments, which in turn utilize masculinity and bodily normativity to police behavior, equating early Christian ethical norms with masculinity and bodily "health." First, we situate our study within the history of early Christianity, explaining the historical relevance of the bodies we find in hell, and provide an overview of the relevant primary texts within the early Christian apocalypses. Next, we highlight the different types of bodies that are found in those early Christian apocalypses, including the hanging punishments, the weeping of the saints and sinners, and the frightening hair of the punishing angels. After looking at the range of bodies that we find in the early Christian apocalypses, we consider the intersection between suffering bodies and gender in antiquity. This section treats briefly the way in which Christians are interacting with Greek and Roman notions of the body in these texts and the relevant theoretical works on gender and bodily suffering in the ancient world. Finally, we apply the theoretical reflections and historical evidence that we have synthesized thus far to selected images of the body from the early Christian apocalypses. In this final section of the paper we show how masculinity and ancient notions of bodily normativity worked in concert to mark sin in early Christian hell, in turn creating an ancient Christian culture of bodily normativity. As we will see, these early Christian texts expanded the existing frameworks of bodily suffering as a disciplinary performance, focusing on the nonnormative body as a punitive spectacle and pedagogical object. The conclusions of the chapter offer directions for thinking about the intersections of gender, bodily suffering, and disability in hell and ancient Christianity at large.

Why Hell? Bodily Suffering, Ethical Norms, and the Early Christian Apocalypses

In many ways hell, and in particular the hell of the early Christian apocalypses, might seem like an odd choice for an investigation about masculinity and disability in antiquity. We could have looked to any number of places in the corpus of ancient Christian literature to find suffering bodies that tell us something about the intersection between gender, the body, and early Christian ethics. In fact, much of the scholarly reflection upon these subjects has analyzed the fascinating depictions of martyrs, whose suffering is valorized,[4] or the slave bodies whose physical torment is directly correlated to their social marginalization.[5] As these studies have demonstrated, gender and bodily suffering are inextricably linked in the ancient world. The ancient Christian bodies of martyrs and slaves represented public performances of Greek and Roman gender expectations, enacting, re-enacting, and in some cases reworking what defines an ideal "body."[6] Here, we hope to build upon these studies and broaden our understanding of ancient Christian conceptions of bodily suffering and gender, expanding the conversation beyond redemptive suffering and the "real bodies" of the martyrs to include the "imagined bodies" in hell. Despite the resurgence of interest in apocalyptic literature in the past twenty years, there has been very little research on the depiction of the suffering body in these texts,[7] either because they depict imaginary spaces that are removed from "real bodies" or because they occur in apocryphal books, which much of Jewish and Christian tradition views as peripheral literature.[8] As historians of antiquity who study gender,[9] the body,[10] disability,[11] and apocalyptic literature[12] have shown, however, the distance between "imagined bodies" and "real bodies" is short indeed.

Yet we are not simply turning to the hell of the early Christian apocalypses because they represent "understudied" literature when it comes to questions of masculinity and the body. Rather, these apocalypses that describe hell in vivid and grotesque detail are an important object of study because of the influence that they had on ancient Christian discussions about ethics. Augustine of Hippo (354–430 CE), a theologian and bishop in North Africa, was leery of the hell of the early Christian apocalypses because he believed that their vision of punishment was too lenient, offering a temporary respite for the damned.[13] His concern that sinners not be provided a way out demonstrates the high value he saw in visions of the afterlife.[14] Augustine believed that the torment of hell was a powerful motivator for his audience, and he was keen to keep it that way. As Peter Brown has argued, "[Augustine] gave his questioners little room to maneuver. He frequently warned them that there was no easy way by which hardened or negligent sinners might enter heaven."[15]

But when we open our gaze to depictions of the afterlife beyond Augustine and his interlocutors, or trace the reception history of the apocalypses Augustine engaged (which Brown does not do),[16] we see that it is not simply Augustine's reaction to the variables of history that codified Christian ideas about damnation. John Chrysostom (347–407 CE), theologian and archbishop of Constantinople, quips "If only it were possible to preach like this always and continually speak about Hell . . . I know what I say is painful, but I cannot tell you how great a benefit it contains," revealing a prioritization of teaching about hell that seems to be more about pedagogy and ethics than economics.[17] The descriptions of hell's torments often carried some explicit instruction regarding one's earthly behavior, punishing specific individual sins for the benefit of hell's onlookers, with the set of sins and punishments changing in each hell to suit the context of the audience and author. The catechetical function of images of punitive bodily suffering seems to have been widely accepted, making its way into early Christian Good Friday liturgies, a practice that continued well into the fifth century CE.[18] Even after falling into disuse in liturgy, these apocalyptic tours of hell continued to capture the imagination, inviting Dante, a key medieval reader of the Apocalypse of Paul, to reimagine hell's torments for a new generation of readers in his *Inferno*.[19] As Piero Camporesi has observed, Dante's hell transformed the ancient vision of hell as a vast "region" into a "project of architectural engineering" that reflected "the Italian urban landscape of the age of the city-states."[20] Through Dante's wide readership and cultural impact these "painful cities" and the bodies that inhabit them have had an influence on our contemporary understandings of suffering bodies.[21]

Because of its wide readership in antiquity and its later influence on Dante, the Apocalypse of Paul is one of the two most important Christian depictions of hell. Likely written around 400 CE,[22] the Apocalypse of Paul marks an important shift in the tours of hell, focusing on the punishments of sinners within the Christian community who fail to live out the ethical norms and expectations of their assigned social or political role.[23] In addition to the impression it made on Dante, the Apocalypse of Paul also represented what Anthony Hilhorst has called a "living text," whose many versions in at least nine languages "captivated the Christian imagination for over a millennium."[24] In addition to the Apocalypse of Paul, the Apocalypse of Peter also played a crucial role in the development of early Christian imaginations of the afterlife. The Apocalypse of Peter was likely written during the second century CE and was the basis for many of the later tours of hell, including the Apocalypse of Paul.[25] We also find Christian visions of hell in some of the apocalypses that are typically grouped as Jewish texts like the Apocalypse of Zephaniah, or 2 Enoch.[26] Although these texts may have originated as Jewish apocalypses, their preservation by Christians has resulted in depictions of the afterlife that look much like the Christian ones that developed around the same time. Finally, we also find scenes of eternal torment in hell outside of the apocalyptic genre, as in the Acts of Thomas, which contains a young woman relating her journey to hell to the apostle Thomas after she has been caught in adultery, murdered, and brought back to life by the apostle.[27]

The Torments of Hell: A Disciplinary Regime or Bodies Beyond Control?

The specific torments and types of bodies we find in these early Christian hellscapes are wide ranging and tailored to the specific sins that are being punished. In many cases we find the sinners who are punished in hell weeping uncontrollably, lamenting their fate in a way that is visible to the tourists who find them there.[28] The righteous onlookers in these tours of hell also weep, depicting hell as a space that evokes this outward emotional response from every body, regardless of its ethical status.[29] Some of the bodies that we find in early Christian tours of hell are undergoing a torment that fits the ancient standard of *lex talionis*, the idea that the punishment should "fit the crime" in measure and intensity. These "measure for measure punishments," as they are also called, sometimes involve hanging by the offending body part, immersion in fire up to the offending body part, asphyxiation, or tantalization.[30]

For instance, in the Apoc. Pet. 7, we find those who have committed a sin of speech hanging by their tongues in the place of eternal fire: "Then will men and women come to the place prepared for them. By their tongues with which they have blasphemed the way of righteousness will they be hung up. There is spread out for them unquenchable fire." This is the first punishment that Peter sees after all of the general punishments of the "evil creatures and sinners" on the Day of Judgment (described in Apoc. Pet. 6), here making an explicit connection between the sin of blasphemy and the punishment of hanging by the tongue, the body part "with which they" sinned. Not only do these punishments follow the ancient legal standard of *lex talionis*, but they also recall the real torture that ancient persons experienced as a part of the ancient judicial process.[31] Thus the concept of hell as a prison with "adamantine bars" was a metaphor that linked the early Christian reflections on judgment and eternal punishment to the familiar juridical and disciplinary spaces of the Roman world.[32]

In addition to mirroring contemporary ideas about punitive suffering from the Roman judicial context, the punishments of early Christian hell also mirror the bodily suffering of persons with disabilities. Blindness is a punishment in the Apocalypse of Peter 12, the Apocalypse of Paul 40, and the Apocalypse of Zephaniah 10. In the Apocalypse of Zephaniah this image of bodily disability is invoked as a consequence of an intellectual sin:

> And also I saw some blind ones crying out. And I was amazed when I saw all these works of God. I said "Who are these?" He said to me, "These are the catechumens who heard the word of God, but they were not perfected in the work which they heard." And I said to him, "Then do they not have repentance here?" He said, "Yes," I said "How long?" He said to me, "Until the day when the Lord will judge." (Apoc. Zeph. 10)

In the Apoc. Zeph. 10, the blind bodies of the unperfected catechumens are not merely a metaphor for misunderstanding, as in other ancient texts.[33] Instead, blindness is a punishment that is exacted on real bodies.[34] Likewise, in other places in the early Christian apocalypses we find sinners with lacerated or amputated limbs, mirroring the large number of ancient persons who lived without the use of one of their limbs.[35] But beyond simply mirroring the familiar bodies of the disabled in the real world, the bodies of those who are punished in hell accomplish something else. By threatening disability as a punishment, the bodies that we find in hell intensify and reinforce the ancient idea that bodily difference was a punishment for sin. In the Apoc. Paul 39, for instance, Paul finds those who harmed widows and the poor "with lacerated hands and feet (*or* with hands and feet cut off) and naked in a place of ice and snow, and worms consumed them."[36]

Still other bodies that we find in hell challenge ancient concepts of bodily normativity in ways that might seem strange to the contemporary reader as mechanisms of torture.[37] As in the previous example, there are several texts that describe unceasing consumption by worms (Acts of Thom. 56, Apoc. Pet. 9, Apoc. Paul 39, 42), chattering teeth (Apoc. Paul 42), and the description of the ugly angels who carry off the souls of the ungodly that frighten Zephaniah with their "eyes that were mixed with blood" and "hair that was loose like the hair of women" (Apoc. Zeph. 4.4–5). Bodies that are eaten by worms, teeth that chatter, and the unkempt hair of a punishing angel might seem undesirable to the contemporary reader but do not seem to be on par with the hanging punishments or immersion in a river of fire. As Martha Himmelfarb rightly cautions, each of these punishments "has its own history," and Himmelfarb's work tracing the history of each of these distinctive punishments is still foundational in that regard.[38] What we hope to add here is an awareness of the way that those distinctive punishments were likely interpreted by early and late antique Christians once they were assembled together into the early Christian hellscapes of the apocalypses. In order to understand how each of these different images would constitute punitive suffering for an ancient audience, we need to gain a clearer concept of the way in which suffering bodies intersected with ancient concepts of gender and the body.

Gender and Bodily Suffering in the Ancient World: Medicine, Judicial Punishment, and Martyrdom

As we might expect, ancient concepts of the body operated on a hierarchical understanding of gender, in which the superior body was the male body.[39] Men's bodies were characterized as strong, hot, dry, and compact, or impervious to penetration, whereas women had bodies that were weak, cold, moist, and porous. One of the most frequently cited works on gender and the body, Thomas Laqueur's *Making Sex*, contends that ancient thinkers operated on a "one-sex" model, in which gender was not a binary but a continuum.[40] Laqueur primarily bases this theory on Aristotle's assertion that women are incomplete males whose bodies have simply never reached the level of heat, dryness, or solidity that characterize masculinity.[41] After starting with Aristotle, Laqueur reads Galen's medical treatises as manuals designed to protect and preserve masculinity by maintaining heat, dryness, and compactness, so that male bodies do not become cold, moist, or porous.[42] The major asset of Laqueur's work is that it offers an explanatory model of the ancient body that is sufficiently different from our contemporary model but simple enough to apply broadly to other ancient literature.[43] As a result, Laqueur's one-sex model has been extremely influential among scholars of early Christianity as a way to explain early Christian ideas about bodies that achieve salvation or glorification by becoming "more male."[44]

Nevertheless, Helen King and others have demonstrated that "claims for the dominance of the 'one-sex' model fail to account for the complexity of the classical world."[45] In particular, reading more widely into the works of Galen or the Hippocratic corpus reveals that a more complex "two-sex" concept of the body was operative in antiquity and late antiquity. The Hippocratic corpus sees woman not as an incomplete male but as a radically different, inferior body.[46] And even for Aristotle and Galen, the fundamental "perfection" or "completeness" of the male body lies not in the physical form of genitalia but in its heat and dryness.[47] One of the major ideas that Laqueur's emphasis on the one-sex model obscures is the importance of blood flow for both Hippocratic and Aristotelian concepts of gender.[48] Leslie Dean-Jones argues, "Menstrual blood is the linchpin of both the Hippocratic and the Aristotelian theories on how women differed from men. Whether a woman was healthy, diseased, pregnant, or nursing, in Classical Greece her body was defined in terms of blood-hydraulics."[49]

In both the medical literature and Aristotle's one-sex model, the female body is inferior to the male body, and that inferiority is integrally linked to the flow of blood. The female body is naturally cooler than the male, which equates to poor blood flow and greater susceptibility to imbalance (and thus disease and bodily suffering) than the male body. The centrality of blood flow influences the entire economy of the body, extending to "every part of the flesh: men are firm and hard, women are wet and spongy. In terms of the texture of their bodies as a whole, men are like woven cloth, women are like fleece."[50] While these outward signifiers seem to posit a simple mechanism for identifying, caring for, and preserving male bodies, the outward signs of gender were understood to reflect a more complicated economy of the body.[51] In some ways this understanding of gender allowed for bodies to change, performing the ideal of the impervious male body to a greater or lesser extent, and, at the same time, it relied upon the hierarchical dualism in which "men and women were perceived as 'opposites' in a very real manner."[52]

As we turn to thinking about masculinity and the suffering body in early Christianity, we attempt to keep this nuanced understanding of gender and the ancient body at the forefront. Much of the recent scholarship on masculinity in early Christianity has demonstrated that early Christian literature does reflect and engage in the ongoing struggle to attain and preserve that ideal male body, however diverse the ancient understanding of male might have been.[53] On the whole, the suffering body represented a failure to attain normative masculinity. But in a culture that used punitive suffering to reinforce those bodily norms and "make men" out of women and slaves, the suffering body is a complicated site that simultaneously symbolizes power and powerlessness. Chris L. de Wet argues that John Chrysostom's preaching on slavery reflects this tension:

> To Chrysostom, Christian identity was founded in being scourged, not flinging the whip. Public and spectacularly violent punishment reflected the degradation of Roman society—a society founded on the brutality of slavery. The harsh punishment of slaves further destabilized masculinity, hence Chrysostom's strict measures to regulate and redistribute the means of punishment.[54]

Like the suffering imposed upon the Christian slave, the suffering bodies we find in early Christian hell were part of the culture of surveillance, the pervasive power of domination meant to ensure productivity and good behavior.[55]

As we observed at the outset, disability and cultural expressions of bodily difference often confound categories, so that bodies that are marked as "other" expose the operative bodily norms. And so, it is through the suffering bodies of ancient Christian hell that we are able to examine the intersection between masculinity and bodily normativity in early Christianity.

We can see these concepts of gendered bodily suffering at work in the descriptions of the bodies that we find in judicial and martyrdom literature. In the Roman world, martyrdom and judicial punishment served as a kind of public spectacle, a violent performance of imperial power.[56] Here, as in the early Christian depictions of hell, the body is used as a tableau for representing the punitive consequences for particular action or inaction, expressing these consequences in ways that were intended to deter any body in the empire.[57] The early Christian martyrdom accounts certainly played with this framework and resisted the narrative of the empire through their vindication of the martyrs as bodies that suffered righteously. Yet, even in acts of textual resistance those accounts participated in performances of gendered bodily suffering, placing the suffering body on display and drawing attention to the complex ways in which it participated in the ancient gender economy.[58]

The spectacle of violence in the judicial context is perhaps the most important for our own study of punitive bodily suffering. As Brent D. Shaw has argued, the fear of being involved in a public display of physical torture was "embedded in the conscience of the ordinary people" in antiquity. For early Christians, Shaw argues, this fear became manifest in the belief in a "final court," an idea that came to look more and more like the judicial proceedings of the Roman world as the early Church Fathers interpreted New Testament notions of divine judgment.[59] Just as the Roman punishments served as theatrically staged events that provided public entertainment and incited fear, the Christian visions of eternal torment were crafted to provide their own kind of haunting spectacle.[60] Likewise, David Frankfurter examines eroticized voyeurism across "Roman spectacle culture," including martyrdom and apocalyptic eschatology. Here, Frankfurter argues that in early Christian depictions of hell "the graphic scenes of the suffering of the unrighteous also provided audiences with a safely set-off context for fantasizing aggression."[61] Whereas martyrdom literature sanctifies the violence by villainizing the Roman as aggressor, the apocalyptic judgment scenes are justified as "appropriate" punishments for the sinful victims.[62] Within each context gender and bodily suffering act as props in the punitive spectacle, helping to draw the audience's eye to particularly horrifying or confounding elements of the drama.

Masculinity and Marking Sin: Hell's Torments as Effeminizing Punishments

As already mentioned, many of hell's inhabitants weep, including both the righteous and unrighteous. In the Apocalypse of Peter 3, Peter sees the separation of the righteous and the sinners on the last day. Those who see the spectacle of punishment are moved to tears as they see the sinners weeping in sorrow:

> We saw how the sinners wept in great distress and sorrow, until all who saw it with their eyes wept, whether righteous, or angels or himself also. And I asked him and said, "Lord, allow me to speak thy word concerning these sinners: 'It were better for them that they had not been created.'" And the Saviour answered and said "O Peter, why speakest thou thus, 'that to not have been created were better for them?'" Thou resistest God. Thou wouldest not have more compassion than he for his image, for he has created them and has brought them forth when they were not. And since thou hast seen the lamentation which sinners shall encounter in the last days, therefore thy heart is saddened; but I will show thee their works in which they have sinned against the Most High.

At the sight of the sinners weeping in hell the Saviour and Peter are both moved to tears. Throughout this passage the narrator and the Saviour interpret these tears as a sign of sadness. More than simply sadness, in the context of the ancient court weeping was one of the signs of guilt, alongside other gestures of subservience and bodily weakness such as blushing and sweating.[63] Playing upon the culturally prevalent fears of judicial torture, these tears were likely part of an attempt to emotionally move the audience, inciting the fear of divine judgment and encouraging repentance.[64] But in addition to inviting the audience to weep and repent their own sins, these weeping bodies represent compromised male bodies that are overcome with emotion in a characteristically female way.[65] And in martyrdom narratives the weeping of a family member could serve as an effeminate foil for the martyr's own performance of the strong, unmoving, masculine ideal.[66] In the Apocalypse of Peter, then, early Christian hell is depicted as a space in which everybody weeps and thus a space in which normative masculine bodies are made more effeminate.

Another way in which the normative masculine body is compromised in hell is through bodily torment. Through these tortures the bodies of the sinful are marked as both abnormal and female, so that the nonnormative female body becomes the signifier of punishment. In many ways the types of bodily punishments one finds in hell mirror the judicial punishments of the Roman world. Those who had judicial nightmares might fear imprisonment, hanging, beheading, being thrown to wild beasts, crucifixion, or burning alive.[67] Of these punishments, all but crucifixion occur in the early Christian visions of hell, while hanging, wild beasts, and burning figure highly as mechanisms of torture. In the Apocalypse of Peter 9, those who bore false testimony against the martyrs have their lips cut off as "fire enters into their mouths and their entrails," and the rich are cast upon a stone pillar of fire to suffer unceasing torment.[68] In the Apocalypse of Paul 31–37 Paul sees a variety of sinners, all immersed in the river of fire with the fire reaching up to different places on their bodies. The deacon who ate up the offerings and committed fornication is seen wading up to his knees in fire: "And his hands were stretched out and bloody, and worms came out of his mouth and from his nostrils and he was groaning and weeping and crying" (Apoc. Paul 36). Similarly, in Acts of Thomas 56, those who have committed adultery are in a pit welling up with mire and worms.

In each of these passages fire and worms penetrate the suffering bodies of the damned. In some cases, another form of bodily deformity accompanies this, and in other cases the bodies of the sinners are literally enveloped or consumed by fire or worms. The sinful body is abnormal, dysfunctional, weak, penetrable, porous, and leaky. In short, the unrighteous have become disabled and female in hell.

In addition to the emasculated bodies of the unrighteous, hell also contains angelic bodies that are also depicted as abnormal. There are different groups of angels in hell, most of whom carry out the punishments or serve as administrators, or guards. The Apocalypse of Zephaniah describes the ugly angels who carried off the souls of the ungodly: "Their eyes were mixed with blood. Their hair was loose like the hair of women, and fiery scourges were in their hands. When I saw them I was afraid."[69] The eyes mixed with blood and the effeminate hair of these ungodly angels is a horrifying sight to Zephaniah. Eyes mixed with blood would signal a sick or abnormal body to the ancient audience and might also play upon prevalent theories of vision that associated the health of the eyes with ethical conduct.[70] Loose hair is explicitly identified in this text as an undesirable female trait, as is a common trope in the ancient world, perhaps made more horrifying by virtue of the fact that it is found upon punishing angels who are expected to project strength and masculinity.[71] Despite the fact that modern thinking of the afterlife imagines souls moving about as distinct from bodies, this passage reinforces that ideas about the body still held sway in conceiving the afterlife. And while we might assume that gender does not play a large role in defining the spaces of the afterlife, it is obvious here that even the angels, who do not have an earthly body, are still defined by the ancient standards of bodily normativity and masculinity.[72]

Perhaps the most germane example for thinking about issues of masculinity and disability is one of the less obvious in terms of how it emasculates the sinner. In the Apocalypse of Paul 42, Paul sees those who deny the resurrection in a place of extreme cold and snow that will never become warm:

> And I looked from the north towards the west and I saw there the worm that never rests, and in that place there was gnashing of teeth. Now the worm was a cubit in size and it had two heads. And I saw there men and women in the cold and gnashing of teeth.

Here the text combines the eternal punishment tropes of gnashing of teeth and the worm that never dies with a third element: extreme cold.[73] Remember that in ancient medicine women's bodies were thought to be colder and have poorer blood flow, making them more susceptible to bodily dysfunction or illness. In the Apoc. Paul 42 those who deny the resurrection are exposed to extreme cold, literally making their bodies function like those of women so that they exhibit female traits like the loss of bodily control. Here in the early Christian imagination of hell the loss of control of one's body is not simply a metaphor for sin; it becomes a part of the judicial mechanism for policing sin, implicitly reinforcing the scaffolding of gendered notions of the body.

Conclusion: Ableism, Ethics, and the Mechanics of Masculinity in Early Christian Hell

After our brief journey through early Christian hell, it might be tempting to exonerate ourselves, celebrating the differences between the ancient punitive model of justice and our own world, hopefully looking for all of the ways in which Davis's paradigm shift beyond the dichotomy of normal/abnormal is already afoot. And yet, Davis reminds us that if we are to truly move beyond identity politics we have to do so with eyes wide open, taking stock of the ways in which our own identity politics are bound up in not only Western notions of democracy and "rights-based" approaches to advocacy but also conceptions of the body that are grounded to some extent in the same hierarchies and binaries of the ancient world. And with this in mind we take seriously the ancient technologies of the body and judicial rhetoric that are, to be sure, distinct from our own but also not totally remote.

In the early Christian apocalypses, it is abundantly clear that punishment was important to early Christians. The punishments themselves deformed, dismembered, and emasculated those who were punished, using the cultural fear of one's body becoming female and abnormal as a mechanism for deterring unethical behavior. Apart from reinforcing ethical norms, even the saints who were observing the punishments and the angels who carried out the punishments were othered and made less male by gazing upon sinners in torment. There is something about the very place of punishment itself that challenges the normative male body. In this way, gender categories and bodily normativity are used in the apocalypses not only to imagine future punishment but to further ostracize the other. As a spectacle that was intended to draw in audiences and emotionally move them, early Christian hell did not simply trade upon Greek and Roman cultural conceptions of the perfect male body. The hell of the early Christian apocalypses engendered their own discourse of bodily conformity that had a wide-reaching influence, equating the strong, impervious, hard, dry, hot, self-controlled, male body with ethical superiority.

Notes

* A previous version of this paper was read at the Annual Meeting for the Society of Biblical Literature, in November, 2016. I am grateful to J. Albert Harrill for sharing his pre-publication work with me, and for the criticism and direction of the editors of this volume

that helped me to make my argument stronger. Any remaining errors are my own. Thanks also go to Harold Van Broekhoven, who remains a steadfast mentor and friend-even when my own path takes me to strange places like hell.

1. Lennard J. Davis, "Identity Politics, Disability, and Culture," in *Handbook of Disability Studies,* Gary L. Albrecht, Katherine D. Seelman, and Michael Bury, eds. (Thousand Oaks: Sage, 2001), 535–545, 544, discusses the way in which the representation of disability and identity politics are intertwined, forecasting a cultural paradigm shift in the way we think not only about disability but identity politics as well.

2. As Davis, "Identity Politics, Disability and Culture," 536–537, notes, this is one of the reasons that he identity community in the United States has been slow to recognize disability, because "disability is seen in some sense as 'spoiling' the neatness of categories of oppression, or victim and victimizer."

3. Davis, "Identity Politics, Disability and Culture," 544.

4. Judith Perkins, *The Suffering Self: Pain and Narrative Representation in the Early Christian Era* (New York: Routledge, 1995); Elizabeth Castelli, *Martyrdom and Memory: Early Christian Culture Making* (New York: Columbia University Press, 2004); Stephanie L. Cobb, *Dying to be Men: Gender and Language in Early Martyr Texts* (New York: Columbia University Press, 2008); Candida R. Moss, *Ancient Christian Martyrdom: Diverse Practices, Theologies and Traditions* (New Haven, CT: Yale University Press, 2012).

5. Mathew, Kuefler, *The Manly Eunuch: Masculinity, Gender Ambiguity, and Christian Ideology in Late Antiquity* (Chicago: University of Chicago Press, 2001); J. Albert Harrill, *Slaves in the New Testament: Literary, Social, and Moral Dimensions* (Minneapolis: Fortress Press, 2006); Bernadette J., Brooten, with Jacqueline L. Hazelton, ed. *Beyond Slavery: Overcoming Its Religious and Sexual Legacies* (New York: Palgrave Macmillan, 2010), Jennifer Glancy, *Corporeal Knowledge: Early Christian Bodies* (Oxford: Oxford University Press, 2010); J. Albert Harrill, "'Exegetical Torture' in Early Christian Bibilical Interpretation: The Case of Origen of Alexandria," *Biblical Interpretation* 25 (2017) 39–57.

6. Castelli, *Martyrdom and Memory,* 33–68, 104–133, discusses martyrdom as both performance and spectacle and the relationship of these performances to societal gender norms, reminding readers that the bodies of the martyrs "produced meaning."; Cobb, *Dying to be Men*, 92–123, analyzes the extent to which the female martyrs performed masculinity and femininity; Candida R. Moss, "Blood Ties: Martyrdom, Motherhood, and Family in the Passion of Perpetua and Felicity," in *Women and Gender in Ancient Religions: Interdisciplinary Approaches*, Stephen P. Ahearne-Kroll, Paul A. Holloway, and James A. Kellhoffer, eds. (Tübingen: Mohr-Siebeck, 2010), 189–205, esp. 197, 198–204, connects the conversations about gender performance in the martyrdom Acta to scholarship on family and gender roles, arguing for the need to be attentive to the way that early Christians were attempting to modify existing models of family or produce novel ones through these performances.

7. Although there has not much attention to the role of the body in these texts, there have been many important works on the historical development of the genre of the "tour of hell" and concept of early Christian hell. See especially Martha Himmelfarb, *Tours of Hell: An Apocalyptic Form in Jewish and Christian Literature* (Philadelphia: University of Pennsylvania Press, 1983); Richard Bauckham, *The Fate of the Dead: Studies on the Jewish and Christian Apocalypses* (Leiden: Brill, 1998); Jan N. Bremmer, *The Rise and Fall of the Afterlife: The 1995 Read-Tuckwell Lectures at the University of Bristol* (New York: Routledge,

2002); Tobias Nicklas et al. eds., *Other Worlds and Their Relation to this World* (Boston: Brill, 2010).

8. For recent scholarship challenging the definition and use of the apocrypha see Tobias Nicklas, Semiotik – Intertextualität – Apokryphität: Eine Annäherung an den Begriff "christlicher Apokryphen," *Apocrypha* 17 (2006), 55–78; François Bovon, "Besides the Canonical and the Apocryphal Books, the Presence of a Third Category: The Books Useful for the Soul," *HTR* 105 (2012), 125–137; Tobias Nicklas, "Christian Apocrypha and the Development of the Christian Canon," *Early Christianity* 5 (2014), 220–240.

9. Christl M. Maier, *Daughter Zion, Mother Zion: Gender, Space, and the Sacred in Ancient Israel* (Minneapolis: Fortress, 2008) studies the interrelationship gender, space, and the metaphorical language of the city personified in the Hebrew Bible. Maier, 22–25, draws upon Paula M. Cooey, *Religious Imagination and the Body: A Feminist Analysis* (New York: Oxford University Press, 1994), and situates historical critical readings of Zion amidst the theoretical tension between "the body as material reality," and "the body as sociocultural artifact." Her conclusions preserve this tension, urging readers to eschew simple readings of gendered metaphors that would disconnect discursive practices about the body from actual bodies. Describing the body of Daughter Zion in Lamentations, Maier argues "Her broken body is a *site* of destruction that simultaneously represents the loss of the city space (*perceived space*), the collapse of the traditional Zion theology (*conceived space*), and the painful survival of a few inhabitants (*lived space*)" (214).

10. J. Albert Harrill, *Slaves in the New Testament: Literary, Social, and Moral Dimensions* (Minneapolis: Fortress, 2006), 2ff. for discussion about the way in which Christian texts "promote the literary imagination about slaves and the ideology of mastery." See also Jennifer Glancy, *Corporeal Knowledge*, 131–156, for the argument that early Christian slave-holding practices created a culture of bodily control, influencing early Christian ideology. Glancy argues that this has been overlooked in the history of scholarship because "the identification of slaves as bodies has historically interfered with the ability of scholars, more interested in the life of the soul, to acknowledge the impact of slavery on the structures and beliefs of early Christianity" (156).

11. As David T. Mitchell and Sharon L. Snyder, "Representation and its Discontents: The Uneasy Home of Disability in Literature and Film," in *Handbook of Disability Studies*, Gary L. Albrecht, Katherine D. Seelman, and Michael Bury, eds. (Thousand Oaks, CA: SAGE, 2001), 195–218, show, even a derisive or comedic representation of disability in literature or film can tell us something about cultural attitudes toward "real" disabled bodies and even play a role in disability rights advocacy as "transgressive resignifications."

12. As Adela Yarbro Collins, *Crisis and Catharsis: The Power of the Apocalypse* (Philadelphia: Westminster, 1984), 160, argues, the book of Revelation used "symbols and artful plots" to make "feelings which were probably latent, vague, complex, and ambiguous explicit, conscious, and simple." Collins suggests that by evoking emotions the imagery of the apocalypse was intended to have a cathartic effect on the real bodies of the audience. And as Greg Carey, *Ultimate Things: An Introduction to Jewish and Christian Apocalyptic Literature* (St. Louis: Chalice, 2005), 147–178, notes, several of the Jewish apocalypses are written as a response to the tragedy of the destruction of the Jerusalem Temple in 70 CE, using the imaginary spaces of the apocalypse to make sense out of a new, devastating, spatial reality.

13. See Augustine *Civ.* 21.17–27 and Apoc. Pet. 14.1. Richard Bauckham in *The Fate of the Dead*, 147–159, argues that Augustine's interlocutors were represented in the text of the Apocalypse of Peter.

14. See Meghan R. Henning, *Educating Early Christians through the Rhetoric of Hell: "Weeping and Gnashing of Teeth" as Paideia in Matthew and the Early Church* (Tübingen: Mohr Siebeck, 2014), 181–182; Peter Brown, *The Ransom of the Soul: Afterlife and Wealth in Early Western Christianity* (Cambridge, MA: Harvard University Press, 2015) 61–65, 79–82.

15. Brown, *The Ransom of the Soul*, 63, depicts Augustine as resistant to imaginations of the afterlife that allowed clemency for those that could attain it through economic means.

16. Despite Augustine's North African context, the popularity of the tours of hell in late antique Africa, and Augustine's direct engagement with those texts, Brown, *The Ransom of the Soul*, 57–82, 83–114, does not include the Apocalypse of Peter, or the critical scholarship on the apocalypses, or their ancient readership in his discussion. Although Brown, 113–114, 139–141 does discuss the Visio Pauli, he classifies this as a "post-imperial phenomenon" and does not engage any of the critical scholarship on early Christian apocalypses here. What is more, when Brown, *The Ransom of the Soul*, 63–65, does discuss Augustine's interlocutors in the debate about the afterlife, he completely ignores the hypothesis proposed by Richard Bauckham in *The Fate of the Dead*, 147–159.

17. John Chrysostom, *Laz.* 2.3.

18. Sozomen, *Hist. eccl.* 7.19.9, details the practice of some Palestinian churches, which read the Apocalypse of Peter every year on Good Friday, while fasting in memory of the Passion.

19. For discussion of the thematic similarities between Dante's *Divine Comedy* and the Apocalypse of Paul, see Tamás Adamik, "The Apocalypse of Paul and Fantastic Literature," in *The Visio Pauli and the Gnostic Apocalypse of Paul,* Jan N. Bremmer and István Czachesz, eds. (Leuven: Peeters, 2007), 144–157.

20. Piero Camporesi, *The Fear of Hell: Images of Damnation and Salvation in Early Modern Europe,* trans. Lucinda Byatt (University Park: Pennsylvania State University Press, 1991), 10–11.

21. See Katheryn Gin Lum, *Damned Nation: Hell in America from the Revolution to Reconstruction* (Oxford: Oxford University Press, 2014), for discussion of the influence of preaching about damnation in the United States from the Revolution to post–Civil War reflections.

22. The Apocalypse of Paul was likely written around 400 CE, since Augustine cited it in 416 CE (*Tract. Ev. Jo.* 98.8). For a summary of the argument supporting this date, see Bremmer, "Tours of Hell: Greek, Roman, Jewish and Early Christian," in *Topographie des Jenseits: Studien zur Geschichte des Todes in Kaiserzeit und Spätantike,* Walter Ameling, ed. (Stuttgart: Franz Steiner Verlag, 2011), 13–34. Unless otherwise noted, the English translations of the Apocalypse of Paul are from Hugo Duensing and Aurelio de Santos Otero, "Apocalypse of Paul," in *New Testament Apocrypha,* Wilhelm Schneemelcher and Edgar Hennecke, eds., R. Wilson, trans. (Louisville, KY: Westminster John Knox, 1991). The Latin is available in Theodore Silverstein and A. Hilhorst, eds., *Apocalypse of Paul: A New Critical Edition of Three Long Latin Versions* (Genève: P. Cramer, 1997).

23. As Jan N. Bremmer, "Christian Hell: From the Apocalypse of Peter to the Apocalypse of Paul," *Numen* 56 (2009), 307–314, describes, the Apocalypse of Paul marks the shift from using hell to separate Christians from outsiders in the earlier apocalypses, toward demarcating doctrinal boundaries within the community.

24. Anthony Hilhorst, "The Apocalypse of Paul: Previous History and Afterlife," in *The Visio Pauli and the Gnostic Apocalypse of Paul,* Jan N. Bremmer and István Czachesz, eds.

(Leuven: Peeters, 2007), 1–21, 3–4, describes the way that the traditions of the Apocalypse of Paul represent its inheritance of earlier traditions and its influence on later thinkers, beginning with St. Patrick's use of the traditions that we also find in the Apocalypse of Paul. As Adamik, "The Apocalypse of Paul and Fantastic Literature," 156–157, notes, the Apoc. Paul had multidirectional influence in late ancient and medieval Christianity, mediated by Gregory the Great: "in the later centuries the ApPl exercised both a direct influence and an indirect one through Gregory's Dialogues."

25. Although some scholars, like Richard Bauckham, "The Apocalypse of Peter: A Jewish Christian Apocalypse from the Time of Bar Kokhba," in *The Fate of the Dead: Studies in Jewish and Christian Apocalypses* (Leiden: Brill, 1998), 160–258, have argued for a very early second-century date, arguing that the "liar" of Apoc. Pet. 2.10 is Bar Kokhba; this hypothesis is based upon the problematic association of apocalyptic literature with official persecution. For critiques of the early dating of the Apoc. Pet., see Eibert Tigchelaar, "Is the Liar Bar Kokhba? Considering the Date and Provenance of the Greek (Ethiopic) Apocalypse of Peter," in *The Apocalypse of Peter,* Jan N. Bremmer and István Czachesz, eds. (Leuven: Peeters, 2003), 63–77; Peter Van Minnen, "The Greek Apocalypse of Peter," in *The Apocalypse of Peter,* 29. Unless otherwise noted, English translations of the Apocalypse of Peter are from C. Detlef G. Müller, "Apocalypse of Peter," in *New Testament Apocrypha,* 625–638.

26. Second Enoch is thought to have been written between 30–70 CE by an Alexandrian Jew, influenced by the Hellenized Judaism of his day. Translations of 2 Enoch are available in F. I. Andersen, "2 Enoch," in *Old Testament Pseudepigrapha,* James H Charlesworth, ed., 2 vols. (Garden City, NY: Doubleday, 1983), 2:103–167. The Apocalypse of Zephaniah is roughly contemporaneous with 2 Enoch, dated between 100 BCE–70 CE. The English translations cited are from O. S. Wintermute, "Apocalypse of Zephaniah," in *Old Testament Pseudepigrapha,* 1:508–515.

27. Acts Thom. 6.51–61. Unless otherwise noted, English translations of the Acts of Thomas are from Han J. W. Drijvers, "Acts of Thomas," in *New Testament Apocrypha,* 322–411.

28. In Apoc. Pet. 3, the "sinners" weep "in great distress and sorrow" as they are separated from the righteous on the Day of Judgment and in Apoc. Paul 38, those who committed adultery are weeping over their eternal fate.

29. In Apoc. Pet. 3, the righteous onlookers, the angels, and Peter also weep at the sight of the "sinners" who weep, mirroring the desired emotional response of the readers, who are intended to repent. Likewise, in Apoc. Paul 43, both the righteous and the unrighteous weep at the torments, and in both textual versions of 2 Enoch 40:12, Enoch weeps at the sight of punishment. See Henning, *Educating Early Christians,* 186–188, for a discussion of the rhetorical function of the "weeping."

30. See 68–105 for a summary of the various kinds of measure for measure punishments that occur in the apocalyptic tours of hell, including charts that summarize the correlation between specific sins and punishments.

31. Himmelfarb, *Tours of Hell,* 75–78; Patrick Gray, "Abortion, Infanticide, and the Social Rhetoric of the Apocalypse of Peter," *JECS* 9 (2001), 313–37; István Czachesz, "Torture in Hell and Reality. The *Visio Pauli,*" in *The Visio Pauli and the Gnostic Apocalypse of Paul,* Jan N. Bremmer and István Czachesz, eds. (Leuven: Peeters, 2007), 130–143.

32. The image of hades or hell as a prison was very prevalent in the ancient world. Examples of this motif include but are not limited to Virgil's depiction of Tartarus' screeching

gate that is protected by columns of solid adamantine (*Aen.* 6.550–560), Plutarch, *Sera* 564F–565F in which Erinys imprisons souls who are "past all healing," the "gates of Hades" in Matt 16, the adamantine bars of hell in Apoc. Pet. 4, and the "prison of the underworld" in Apoc. Paul 18.

33. There are countless examples of this theme in ancient literature. A particularly salient example is recorded in an inscription from the Asclepion at Epidaurus, in which a woman named Ambrosia who was blind in one eye ridicules the cures at the sanctuary and is only healed after she repents by offering a silver pig at the sanctuary as a memorial of her ignorance. See stele A4 in Lynn R. LiDonnici, *The Epidaurian Miracle Inscriptions: Text, Translation, and Commentary* (Atlanta: Scholars, 1995). For a succinct summary of other ancient texts that link blindness and ignorance see Chad Hartsock, *Sight and Blindness in Luke-Acts: The Use of Physical Features in Characterization* (Leiden: Brill, 2008), 73–81.

34. Meghan Henning, "Metaphorical, Punitive, and Pedagogical Blindness in Hell," *Studia Patristica* (forthcoming 2017), discusses the way in which hell's punishments in Apoc. Pet., Apoc. Zeph., and Apoc. Paul intensify and codify the culturally available concepts of blindness as a punishment for sin. Elsewhere in Apoc. Zeph. 10, the reader learns that bodies in hell are very much like real bodies on earth: "And I saw others with their hair on them. I said, 'Then there is hair and body in this place?' He said, 'Yes, the Lord gives body and hair to them as he desires.'"

35. As Candida R. Moss, "The Righteous Amputees: Salvation and the Sinful Body in Mark 9," lecture at Yale Divinity School, September 25, 2014, has noted, amputation was not as anomalous in the ancient world as it is in our own.

36. For other instances of limb amputation or laceration see Apoc. Pet. 9; Apoc. Pet. 11; and Apoc. Paul 40.

37. The different kinds of suffering bodies that we survey here are by no means exhaustive, for the most part leaving out the body of the tourist, the angelic bodies, or the heavenly bodies due to the constraints of time and space.

38. Himmelfarb, *Tours of Hell*, 82.

39. As Rebecca Flemming, *Medicine and the Making of Roman Women: Gender, Nature, and Authority from Celsus to Galen* (Oxford: Oxford University Press, 2000), 119, argues, this is distinct from contemporary gender hierarchies in the functional way that Aristotle conceived of gender: "It is not so much that the female is inferior as that the inferior is female."

40. Thomas W. Laqueur, *Making Sex: Body and Gender from the Greeks to Freud* (Cambridge, MA: Harvard University Press, 1992), 25–62.

41. Laqueur, *Making Sex*, 28, "But he [Aristotle] also insisted that the distinguishing characteristic of maleness was immaterial, and as a naturalist, chipped away at the organic distinctions between the sexes so that what emerges is an account in which one flesh could be ranked, ordered, and distinguished as particular circumstances required." (cf. Aristotle *Historia animalium*, 1.9.491b26ff and 4.8.1–3 and *Economics*, 2.3.1343b25-1344a8).

42. Laqueur, *Making Sex*, 25–30, 52–62, cf. Galen *On the Usefulness of the Parts of the Body*, 2.628–32.

43. In her corrective to Laqueur, Helen King, *The One-Sex Body on Trial: The Classical and Early Modern Evidence* (New York: Ashgate, 2013), 13–15, cites the simplicity and accessibility of Laqueur's argument as part of the reason for its influence across disciplines. King also notes that Laqueur's own initial position was more nuanced than those who

appropriated it, and his own later arguments: "I agree with an assertion found in the preface to *Making Sex*, one which is at odds with Laqueur's subsequent work and its reception; in his words, 'the startling conclusions that a two-sex and a one-sex model [have] always been available to those who thought about difference'" (8).

44. Dale B. Martin, *The Corinthian Body* (New Haven, CT: Yale University Press, 1995), 32–33, explains Hippocrates and Galen through the lens of Aristotle and Laqueur, "Much of Galen's hygienic and therapeutic method reads like a training manual designed to maintain the right degree of heat, dryness, and compactness for the masculinization of the young man's body and to keep it from slipping down the precarious slope to femininity"; and again, Dale B. Martin, *Sex and the Single Savior* (Louisville, KY: Westminster John Knox, 2006), 84, introduces the one-sex model, arguing that "In this system, any change that would be construed as salvific must be understood as a movement higher on the spectral hierarchy. Thus, women may experience salvation as a movement upward into masculinity, but men who experience a movement downward into femininity (and both kinds of movement are noted in ancient texts) are not understood by that to experience an improvement in state or status." Martin's work on the body and gender and the body in early Christianity was highly influential, maximizing the impact of Laqueur's thinking on the subdiscipline. See for instance, the work of Stephanie L. Cobb, *Dying to be Men: Gender and Language in Early Martyr Texts* (New York: Columbia University Press, 2008). Notable exceptions to this trend include Chris L. de Wet, *Preaching Bondage: John Chrysostom and the Discourse of Slavery in Early Christianity* (Oakland: University of California Press, 2015); and Kuefler, *The Manly Eunuch*, 304, n.5.

45. King, *The One-Sex Body on Trial*, 25; See also Flemming, *Medicine and the Making of Roman Women*, 357–358.

46. King, *The One-Sex Body on Trial*, 44, notes that this error of Laqueur's is in part because of his partial reading of the Hippocratic corpus, ignoring the *Gynaikeia* treatises that demonstrate a "two-sex" understanding of the body.

47. *The One-Sex Body on Trial*, 44–45, citing Hippocrates *Diseases of Women* 1.62 and 1.1, summarizes "Women are like unprocessed fleece, men like a closely woven garment, and if someone were to put fleece and garment in the same damp place for the same length of time, it is the fleece that would draw up more moisture."

48. King, *The One-Sex Body on Trial*, 46, argues contra Laqueur, *Making Sex*, 35, 37, and 105, "Not being aware of the *Gynaikeia* tradition, Laqueur plays down the pre-modern importance of menstruation in defining what it is to be female, replacing this with his focus on inside/outside organs."

49. Dean-Jones, *Women's Bodies in Classical Greek Science*, 225.

50. King, *The One-Sex Body on Trial*, 48, citing Hippocrates *Diseases of Women* 1.1. See also, Meghan Henning, "Paralysis and Sexuality in Medical Literature and the *Acts of Peter*," *Journal of Late Antiquity*. 8.2 (2015), 306–321, for further discussion of the intersection between blood flow and gender in antiquity and late antiquity.

51. Flemming, *Medicine and the Making of Roman Women*, 369–370. See also Teresa M. Shaw, *The Burden of the Flesh: Fasting and Sexuality in Early Christianity* (Minneapolis: Fortress Press, 1998), 64–78, who discusses the ways in which ancient medical texts reflected broader cultural ideas about gender and the body.

52. Kuefler, *The Manly Eunuch*, 20.

53. See Maud W. Gleason, *Making Men: Sophists and Self-Presentation in Ancient Rome* (Princeton, NJ: Princeton University Press, 1995), 160–162, on the way in which that ideal

was somewhat malleable especially over time. Chris de Wet, *Preaching Bondage*, 174–183, describes the way that the different ideals of Roman masculinity, or "masculinities," shaped slaveholding discourse.

54. de Wet, *Preaching Bondage*, 218.

55. de Wet, *Preaching Bondage*, 199, argues that the Christic panopticon collapses the divine and the master, and thus robs the slave of his last bit of agency: "although Chrysostom sees this move as giving the slave agency, the Christic panopticon and the interiorization of surveillance rob the slave of the last strand of agency he or she may have had in psychological or spiritual terms, increasing the slave's carceral state and creating a powerful spiritual carcerality with no means of escape."

56. Castelli, *Martyrdom and Memory*, 33–68, 104–133; David Frankfurter, "Martyrology and the Prurient Gaze," *JECS* 17.2 (2009), 215–245, 238–240.

57. Brent D. Shaw, "Judicial Nightmares and Christian Memory," *JECS* 11.4 (2003), 533–563, 535.

58. As David Frankfurter, "Martyrology and the Prurient Gaze," 228, has argued the sado-erotic themes of the martyrdom accounts are "far more complex imaginative experiences than simply tableaux for male misogyny." See also Elizabeth Castelli, "Visions and Voyeurism: Holy Women and the Politics of Sight in Early Christianity," *Protocol of the Colloquy of the Center for Hermeneutical Studies* n.s. 2 (1995), 1–20; Harrill, *Slaves in the New Testament*, 157–163; Moss, "Blood Ties," 198–204.

59. Shaw, "Judicial Nightmares and Christian Memory," 556, states that "The relationship between the Christian and his or her God came to be configured as a judicial one." Shaw cites Tertullian and Ambrose as prime examples of church Fathers who employed the *topos* of the judicial nightmare in their own descriptions of divine judgment.

60. The pedagogical value of these spectacles of torture is part of what contributes to the positive view of punishment in early Christian thought. Harrill, "Exegetical Torture and Truth," 56, argues that Origen's "sanctification of violence extends to a positive view of punishment generally." Harrill connects the metaphorical language of dissecting a text to the real bodies of the household slaves of Origen's readers. As Harrill argues, this is a "live metaphor." For these early Christian masters, torture of the slave body was often punitive, and pedagogical for the onlookers as well as for the slave himself.

61. Frankfurter, "Martyrology and the Prurient Gaze," 238–239.

62. Frankfurter, "Martyrology and the Prurient Gaze, 239.

63. Shaw, "Judicial Nightmares and Christian Memory," 544, argues that the body language of "blushing, sweating, shuffling, bowing, scraping, and weeping" was widely recognized as a behavioral symptom of guilt, elicited by judicial rituals.

64. Shaw, "Judicial Nightmares and Christian Memory," 539, notes that the judicial process was designed to "induce fear" so that those watching would become "mentally overwhelmed." See also, Henning, *Educating Early Christians*, 186–188.

65. This is one way in which early Christian hell parallels the Greek and Roman depictions of Hades, in which we also find tearful scenes between loved ones (Odysseus weeps with compassion at the sight of his unburied friend Elpenor *Od.*11.55, and Anchises is overcome with tears when he sees his son Virgil *Aeneid* 6.688–689).

66. Cobb, *Dying to Be Men*, 100–102, argues that Perpetua, for example, is masculinized through the effusive displays of her father. By way of contrast to her father's leaky, effeminate body, Perpetua's own emotional distance and silence is a model of masculine self-control.

67. Shaw, "Judicial Nightmares and Christian Memory," 537, cf. Artemidorus *Oneirocritica* 1.40, 2.49–54.

68. Himmelfarb, *Tours of Hell*, 108–110 describes the way that fire imagery made its way into visions of hell, largely because of fire's association with earthly places of punishment. Compare the phallic pillar of fire in Apoc. Pet. 9 with the observations of Frankfurter, "Martyrology and the Prurient Gaze," 224, who notes that the sado-erotic phallic imagery of the sword was commonplace in female martyrdoms.

69. Contrast the horrifying hair of this passage with the heavenly hair of Elijah in Apoc. Pet. 15: "like the rainbow in the water was his hair."

70. See Polemo 1.1.158 F quoted in Gleason, *Making Men*, 62, who describes the importance of straight eyelids and unmoving pupils for conveying masculinity. If these traits are absent Polemo says "you may be sure that this is the profile of someone who is really feminine, even though you might find him among real men." For a thorough discussion of the philosophical theories of vision in the ancient world, the prominence of the "extramission" theory of vision in which the eye was thought to emit light, and the influence of these theories upon Second Temple Jewish and early Christian literature, see Candida R. Moss, "Blurred Vision and Ethical Confusion: The Rhetorical Function of Matthew 6:22–23," *Catholic Biblical Quarterly* 73 (2011), 757–776.

71. There are a plethora of ancient sources that describe long hair as a feminine and, thus, undesirable trait. Most notable in the early Christian context are Paul's discussion of head coverings (1 Cor 11:2–16) and the exegetical tradition that follows him (Tertullian *De virginibus velandis;* and Acts Thomas 56, in which women who do not wear head coverings are hung by their hair), the locusts of Rev 9:8–9 which have "hair like a woman," and Perpetua's request for a hairpin because it was unfitting for a martyr to die with disorderly hair (*Martyrdom of Perpetua* 20.4–5). As Maria Doerfler, "'Hair!': Remnants of Ascetic Exegesis in Augustine of Hippo's *De Opere Monacharum,*" *JECS* 22.1 (2014), 79–111, 101, n. 72, has noted, there was also a "polyvalence of hair in late ancient discourses," as evidenced in the writings of Clement of Alexandria who was able to criticize Romans for their ornate hair in the same breath that he praises the "barbarians" who whore long hair without adornment (*Pedagogue* 3.3 [PG 8.589B]).

72. This is a different view of angels than the one we find in Tertullian, *De virg. vel.* 10, who argues that the celibacy of male asceticism places one in an "angelic state."

73. The worm that never dies is found in Isaiah 66: 24. The gnashing of teeth as a reference to emotional distress is found throughout the LXX: Job 16:9; Ps 34:16; 36:12; 111:10; Lam 2:16. "Weeping and gnashing of teeth" is used in Matt 8:12; 13:42, 50; 22:13; 24:51; 25:30, Luke 13:28a, and in *Sib. Or.* 8.231. The persistent use of this phrase in Matthew influenced the early Christian apocalypses in which we find different interpretations of those who weep and gnash their teeth in the places of eternal punishment. Although in Matthew, this phrase is often connected with Gehenna and fiery punishment, not cold. See Henning, *Educating Early Christians*, 162–173, 186–192.

14

Porgy and Dubose

Susan Schweik

Look through any selection of reviews of George Gershwin's *Porgy and Bess* (1935) and you will find material regarding disability. After all, the principal character, Porgy, is a "cripple." Critics can hardly avoid mentioning Porgy's disabled status. Some go further, getting metaphorical mileage out of Porgy and the famous goat cart that he drives through Catfish Row in Charleston, South Carolina. As one writes,

> Though Gershwin was not, like his Porgy, a physical cripple, he was a psychological cripple: an archetypical White Negro, a poor boy who made good, a Jew who knew about spiritual isolation. . . . Through these hazards he preserved, like Porgy, an innocence which shines through the radiant "Summertime" lullaby.[1]

Something must always be made of Porgy's disability in the reviews, but often, as in this case, the "physical cripple" vanishes at the very moment he is invoked, inducing a "crisis" of ableist relations.[2] Such crises go hand in hand, as this volume shows, with crises of gender relations, in this case of masculinity.

This critic's psychological emphasis on Gershwin, in which Porgy emerges as a kind of stand-in (or kneel-in) for the composer's class and ethnic conflict, obscures—for a start—the original creator of Porgy, white Charleston writer DuBose Heyward. Heyward wrote the novel *Porgy* in 1925, co-wrote (with his wife Dorothy) the play version that premiered two years later, and himself wrote the lyrics to the radiant "Summertime" when he and George and Ira Gershwin collaborated on the musical version of the Porgy drama. The "psychological cripple" analysis also obscures the person upon whom Heyward's Porgy was based: Samuel Smalls, a black disabled man who begged on the streets of Charleston for some time in the years leading up to the mid-1920s. Behind Porgy lies "Goat Sammy" Smalls, whose story, now entangled with the fictive Porgy's, fuels a thriving commercial tourist industry in Charleston today. This essay concerns the Porgification of Samuel Smalls, a case study of the terms by which people like Samuel Smalls have (and have not) been taken up into the realm of representation.[3] To the question asked by the first Porgy, Todd Duncan, upon first hearing George Gershwin play "Summertime" ("Well, this is so beautiful. Where did this man get this from?"), a question echoed by critics like Richard Crawford ("Where Did Porgy and Bess Come From?"), my answer will be that far more than we have recognized it came from strains of American disability culture and from grapplings with the relation of disability to masculinity.[4]

The Porgy figure emerges first in Heyward's novel as seen from the exterior perspective of an impressed passerby, a beggar "equipped by a beneficent providence for a career of mendicancy" by the "totally inadequate nether extremities" that he was born with, "quick to touch the eye, and touch the ready sympathy." Africanized and orientalized, Porgy is "black with the almost purple blackness of unadulterated Congo blood"; "there was," the narrator muses, "something Eastern and mystic about the intense introspection of his look." As the text shifts to focalization from Porgy's point of view, he is constituted by two features, smoldering and waiting-for-ness: "he was waiting, waiting with the concentrated intensity of a burning-glass."

> He would sit there in the cool of the early hours and look across the narrow thoroughfare into the green freshness of Jasper Square. . . . Then, when the morning advanced, and the sun poured its semi-tropical heat between the twin rows of brick, to lie impounded there, like a stagnant pool of flame, he would experience a pleasant atavistic calm, and would doze lightly under the terrific heat, as only a full-blooded negro can. Toward afternoon a slender blue shadow would commence to grow about him that would broaden with great rapidity, cool the baking flags, and turn the tide of customers' home before his empty cup. But Porgy loved best the late afternoons, when the street was quiet again.[5]

What Porgy waits for is never exactly specified, though the plot to follow offers multiple possibilities: evening, gambling, change, love, flames, agency, mobility, manhood. Here, though, initially, plot reduces to the simplest passage of time, the sun's movement and how it feels. The primitivist racial fantasy in the passage, crudely apparent in the rhetoric of atavism, of "unadulterated Congo blood," and in the representation of Porgy's insensitivity to heat, his natural indolence and blunted senses, marks what Porgy feels as the experiences of an other. But the scene cannot be reduced entirely to that; Porgy's body in the sun is rendered as nearer, more familiar, less sensationalized, more internalized. While Porgy waits, in his waiting, *Porgy* imagines a phenomenology of begging. In an era characterized by hostile depictions of "unsightly beggars," this is an atypical representation. The inspiration for it came from Samuel Smalls.

The Beggar with the Goat Cart

> And into my life drove a beggar in a goat cart. I did not then know
> that he had come to stay . . . I assumed the novel would be about white
> people, because—well, most novels are.
>
> DOROTHY HEYWARD, *ON FIRST READING THE MSS.*
> *OF* PORGY, *IN HER "PORGY'S GOAT"*[6]

> And into my life drove a crippled Negro beggar in a Goat-cart. But
> from that day on I seem to have lived in Porgy's shadow.
>
> DOROTHY HEYWARD, *IN HER UNPUBLISHED DRAFT OF THIS PIECE*[7]

What we know of Smalls we know because of Porgy. Trying to track down
Porgy's model Goat-Cart Sammy, who had disappeared from the streets of
Charleston, became a project (first for the Heywards and later for reporters and
scholars) that began as soon as Heyward completed his novel and extended
into the early 1960s. With the exception of one newspaper article that predated
Heywood's novel, the texts that tell Smalls's history are already Porgified; Smalls's
story is always backstory for the Gershwin and Heyward plot. And so we must
read with caution in an attempt to glean details about Smalls. The city newspaper
articles with titles like "Remember 'Porgy'?" offer sparse and sometimes conflicting information. Some facts are clear: Samuel Smalls was one of 27 children of
Mrs. Elvira Gibbs. He was born into the Gullah culture of James Island and moved
mainland to Charleston at age 15.

Images (frequently contradictory) of Smalls's body circulate through the
reportage, to be worried and puzzled over. His body, unlike Porgy's, is a problem,
eventually a problem to be contained but initially a problem to be interpreted. One
reporter's account quotes the husband of Elvira Gibbs, John Gibbs, on the nature
of Smalls's impairment: " 'No sir', said John, 'he just didn't have no legs or feet. He
had what you might call little images of feet.' " In the same article, published in
1951, Elvira "said that Porgy [*sic*] was born with his deformity . . . he also had a
partially useless right arm and hand." But other reporters in the early 1950s found
family members who insisted that Smalls was not "born crippled" but had a "fever"
that paralyzed his legs when he was ten. And Elvira Gibbs is quoted by another
reporter, in 1959, in ways that contradict her earlier reported testimony: "Sam was
cripple. He fell when he wuz li'l chile. About five years ole. Had feet but no able to
walk."[8] Whatever the reasons for these discrepancies, all these narratives share a
deep investment both in determining the cause of impairment and in the significance of the distinction between congenital and acquired.[9]

In most of these articles, Samuel Small's body signifies two ways: from the
waist down incapacity, from the waist up strength. "Sam could get around right

lively when he had a mind to it," says his mother's husband. "See that fence there? He could jump over that in a hurry. He just used his good hand." One reporter describes him as "a heavyset, powerful negro whose legs were shrunken." "He was a strong fellow except for his legs," an acquaintance says in an interview. A Mrs. Edward King told a reporter in 1951 that "Porgy" had once been employed as a day-laborer in her bean patch, producing this bit of Porgiana:

> Beginning at one end of a row, apparently devoid of all definite means of locomotion except his dwarfed, inadequate pedal extremities, a misfortune of birth, the indomitable Porgy, moving with astonishing rapidity down a row of bean-poles, despite his lack of legs, gathered the ripening bean-pods as fast as other bean-pickers on two legs.[10]

Inevitably, because Smalls's story is a begging story, his prodigious upper body strength indicts him as someone who could "work for a living" but does not. Samuel Smalls's mendicancy, unlike his fictional counterpart's, signifies criminal deviance; his body is a "brutalized body," a form of outlaw hypermasculinity.[11]

With Smalls's strength, in these biographical accounts, goes animality—an animality paradoxically both heightened and comically mitigated by the goat he travels with.[12] Like other disabled people who traveled in this way, Charleston's goat Sammy took on goatness when he used a goat cart as a mobility aid. Much is made in the biographies of the goat's smell, which transfers onto Smalls. "He had lost both his legs," wrote Hervey Allen of Smalls (but calling him "Porgy") "and drove about in a little cart only a few inches high, behind an olfactorily memorable goat."[13] "The Charleston beggar and his smelly goat": this is the capstone reference to Samuel Smalls in Hollis Alpert's exhaustive 1990 study of *Porgy and Bess*, and Alpert comments earlier that "if anything stood out about him," it was the acrid goat smell.[14]

The newspaper articles on Smalls's life done by reporters in the 1950s at the height of the *Porgy and Bess* revival cover only a few more details, particularly concerning the criminal activities that brought him to the attention of DuBose Heyward. These are fleshed out slightly in the self-interested, untrustworthy testimony of Heyward's wife and collaborator Dorothy Heyward, whose "Anyone Here Know Porgy: Real Life Hunt for Goat Sammy Retold" recounted an investigation by Henry Church into Smalls's history, stressing Porgy's fictionality (for good reason, given the reporters' tendency to call Samuel Smalls "Porgy" with no self-consciousness whatsoever) by emphasizing his unlikeness to "Sammy." (Dorothy would also attempt to transfer Smalls's relation to another fictional character entirely, calling Goat Sammy "a local Hadj," after the beggar/trickster character in the Broadway musical *Kismet*, in which a song about Baghdad includes lyrics like "Our princes more aristocratic / Our beggars more distinctly aromatic.")[15] The title of Dorothy's essay (and its alternate version "Anybody Hyuh Know Porgy") reveals the paradoxical and conflicted nature of this project; a work designed to prove Porgy's difference from Samuel Smalls takes its title from a passage within Heyward's novel in which a beneficent white lawyer seeks Porgy out in order to help him—hence reinscribing the very association between Sammy and Porgy that Dorothy was attempting to undo.[16]

Yet undo it she felt she must, for Samuel Smalls's mother was attempting to claim a share of the profits of Porgification.[17] In a private letter in 1959 Dorothy wrote to Thomas Stoney, a cousin of DuBose and former district attorney and Mayor of Charleston:

> Charleston seems quite set on believing that "Porgy" is a true story while it is, of course, pure fiction—except for being about a goat cart beggar. Porgy was an honest, faithful Negro while, as you remember, Sammy Smalls was not.[18]

For Dorothy Heyward and Thomas Stoney, Smalls was comic but also sick and degenerate, falling short of being a menace to society only because of his physical incapacity.

According to Dorothy, complaints about Smalls's begging rarely produced police action, "not, I fear, because of compassion for the afflicted. They found the care of a helpless cripple . . . too great a nuisance to endure."[19] But Smalls's criminal record extended well beyond citations for begging. At various points he shot at two women, one named Sally Singleton, whom he apparently hit, and one named Maggie Barnes. The woman he later married, whom Dorothy calls "Normie" but who may have been named Naomi, told Henry Church that Smalls shot at Barnes not as a crime of passion but in retaliation for theft, a detail soon lost as Smalls as well as Dorothy came into Porgy's shadow.

Thomas Stoney produced for Dorothy an informal deposition on his dealings with Smalls in the court case regarding Sally Singleton:

> In the June 1923 term of the Court of General Sessions, I hailed Smalls before Judge R.W. Meminger, on an indictment for aggravated assault and battery with intent to kill, and with carrying a concealed weapon.
> Two bailiffs gingerly carried in the defendant and placed him in the prisoner's dock, and the trial commenced. . . . The sole comment of the prisoner was that he admitted to the charge of aggravated assault but that the woman and not he had done the aggravating.

Stoney quotes the judge's decision in the case:

> I herewith sentence you to serve one year at hard labor in the State penitentiary. [Here Dorothy Heyward has added a handwritten addendum: "or upon the public works of Charleston County."] BUT because of your physical handicap, and the fact that your jailers and not you would be punished if I so delivered you upon their hands, I am going to again inflict you upon the public and suspend your sentence during the period of your good behavior. BUT—!

And then Stoney provides his own commentary on the scene:

> The terror of that thundered final word of warning sent Sammy's eyes rolling back until only the whites of them were visible, and the bailiffs carried him out and delivered him into the arms of the waiting Negroes in the corridor.

Rumor has it that Sammy held high carnival that night, perched on the top of a pool table, and his admiring disciples waited in line for the privilege of rolling a turn of the dice with this special pet of the Fates, against whom not even the dread Law of the white man was effective.

Dorothy Heyward adds her own note about Smalls's later appearance in court on the second assault charge: "Once again Sammy was given a suspended sentence, and surely once again"—she is so sure!—"he held high carnival."

Stoney's testimony pits Smalls's in-court minstrel show antics and his beyond-the-law carnivalesque against the sputtering ambivalence of the judge, whose legal discourse reduces itself to two primal antithetical "BUT ... BUT"s. Who wins? Ostensibly Sammy, whose disability permits—is—incorrigibility. But Thomas Stoney's story renders Sammy not only as untouched by law but as an untouchable. He may party in the short run, but in the long run his body still does hard discursive labor, performing the humiliated eye-rolling terror that the white law needed to see.

> And in fact Smalls' life in the wake of his two assault cases was no party. His sister is quoted by a Charleston reporter saying that after Smalls was arrested for the attack on Maggie Barnes, he "fell sick of de jail-house fever and gone off to a island" (James Island). His wife ("Normie"?) is said to have nursed him when he was dying there.[20]

When all was said and done, something like jailhouse fever, not pool hall partying, was what Samuel Smalls had to expect.[21]

Other versions offer different explanations of what happened in the end to Samuel Smalls. A handwritten note by Dorothy Heyward records that when Smalls was arrested for assaulting Barnes "the late James Allen, who had succeeded Thomas P. Stoney as solicitor, recognizing the signs of tuberculosis in the little prisoner, nol prossed the case, which had been scheduled for the June, 1924, term of Court."[22] Smalls's mother told a reporter that after his release from jail "his spinal condition grew worse and he died," probably within the year, so that he would have been dead by the time DuBose Heyward's *Porgy* was published in 1925.[23]

At some point, most critical treatments of *Porgy and Bess* trot out the story of DuBose Heyward's encounter with Samuel Smalls. The story of the meeting has two parts. The first consists of interaction on the street. Here is Dorothy Heyward's version of it, published in 1957 over three decades after *Porgy* and over twenty years after the premiere of *Porgy and Bess*:

> DuBose Heyward had known the Goat-Cart Beggar for as many years as he could remember, and he had known him exactly as other Charlestonians knew him—which was by sight, nothing more. ... DuBose thought of the beggar as a poor creature who existed, rather than lived, an unfortunate who needed help so that he might go dragging on through his dull, monotonous days.[24]

In a draft chapter of the manuscript of her autobiography, Dorothy elaborates even more bluntly: "For various reasons he [DuBose] thought of the beggar as possibly mentally deficient—a sort of vegetable who merely existed."[25]

The second encounter between DuBose and Sam is transformative and textual. In the morning local newspaper in the early 1920s, Heyward reads a news story:

> Samuel Smalls, who is a cripple and is familiar to King Street, with his goat and cart, was held for the June term of Court of Sessions on an aggravated assault charge. It is alleged that on Saturday night he attempted to shoot Maggie Barnes at number four Romney Street. His shots went wide of the mark. Smalls was up on a similar charge some months ago and was given a suspended sentence. Smalls had attempted to escape in his wagon and was run down and captured by the police patrol.[26]

In all accounts, Heyward responds strongly to this story. Something about the plot catches attention. Dorothy Heyward gives two versions of what this might be.

One comic explanation involves the chase scene. Smalls catches the eye because he drives a goat cart while black:

> It is strictly against the law in Charleston, South Carolina, to shoot women, but for a beggar to shoot at, and miss, a woman of highly questionable integrity is not really news. Sammy made news—not the headlines but an obscure back-page paragraph—not because of his involvement in an unsavory backalley fracas, but because his method of resisting arrest was unusual.[27]

DuBose Heyward's own rendition of this scene in the novel seems both to embrace and to abjure the humorous interpretation Dorothy forwarded. Attributed to others, phrased ambiguously in the form of a question, the mockery here is partly disclaimed, but nonetheless made available:

> To many, the scene which ensued . . . stands out as an exquisitely humorous episode. . . . To those, in the eyes of whom the negro is wholly humorous, per se, there was not the omission of a single conventional and readily recognizable stage property.
>
> For after all, what could have been funnier than an entirely serious race between a negro in a dilapidated goat-cart, and the municipality's shiny new patrol wagon, fully officered and clanging its bell for the crowds to hear as it came. (153)

The second more serious account of what caught DuBose's eye dominates the critical tradition. Dorothy puts it like this:

> And then he read, in his morning newspaper, the account of the shooting of Maggie Barnes. And into this brief story DuBose read passion, frustration, despair. He was filled with amazement that inside this passive silent figure, eternally and docilely moving on, there lived a man with emotions so strong, so violent, that they had twice driven him to attempt to kill.[28]

A common version of this pivotal moment, in which Dubose's "merely exist-ing" Goat-Cart Sammy suddenly, volcanically, gets a life is summed up in Hollis Alpert's 1990 *The Life and Times of Porgy and Bess*: " 'Just think of that old wreck having enough manhood to do a thing like that,' " Heyward said to his sister, and he clipped out the item and put it in his wallet."[29] The objectified, abject "old wreck" takes on manhood and thereby acquires tragic subjectivity. "To Smalls I make acknowledgement of my obligation," wrote DuBose Heyward.

> From contemplation of his real, and deeply moving, tragedy, sprang Porgy, a creature of my imagination . . . upon whom, being my own creation, I could impose my own . . . conception of a summer of aspiration, devotion, and heartbreak across the color wall.[30]

Crip Like Me

The bulk of critical cultural studies of Porgy and his poor black Catfish Row com-munity have focused their energies on the "color wall" and Heyward's compli-cated claim to have "contemplated" and "imposed" across it. Heyward would at one point, using a musical image that presaged the importance of music in the Porgy history, figure himself as up against that wall, out of breath: "What was the quality," he pondered, "in a spiritual sung in the secrecy of some back room that brought the chance listener up short against the outer wall with a contraction of the solar plexus?"[31]

Early reviewers of Heyward's *Porgy* and a long tradition of later (often white) critics imagined Heyward (and, later, Gershwin as well) not as up short against the outer color wall but effortlessly crossed-over to the inside of the other side. "About the story of this colored cripple," wrote Hervey Allen, "Mr. Heyward wove his plot. It was more than a fine narrative. It was the actual life of the colored race, seen through clear eyes."[32] African American response to the Porgy texts has most often been sharply negative, a line of critique brilliantly summarized in Arthur Knight's analysis of black jazz renditions and demolitions of *Porgy and Bess*.[33] In his article for *Ebony* "Why Negroes Don't Like 'Porgy and Bess' " (1959), Ezra Bell described the latest version of the opera: "same old kettle of catfish."[34] The famous dismissal misattributed to Duke Ellington—"It is time to debunk Gershwin's lampblack negroisms"—inaugurated a strong tradition of resistance to the fan-tasies of crossing and erasing something called a "color wall" that dominate many of the white-authored reviews.[35] This critical tradition importantly indicts the "Porgification" of black poverty, that is, the orientalization of black poverty into the sentimentalized figure of the crippled beggar with a heart. Porgification reveals itself as the social process through which enlightened liberals unburdened themselves of responsibilities for social inequalities through the fetishizing of the black beggar.[36]

Imagining Porgy entails relation to other interconnected imaginary walls and crossings too—the "class wall," for instance, or the wall dividing workers from beggars, and, of course, the wall that divides those who are "crippled" and those who are not. In fact, both Porgy and Heywood experience what Fiona Kumari Campbell refers to as "outsider-insidedness," a positionality involving intense ambivalence, subjugated knowledges, and, not surprisingly, dis/orientation.[37] Is it time to debunk the "lampblack ableisms" of the *Porgy* novel and its later outgrowth *Porgy and Bess*? An answer to this question requires a closer look at DuBose Heyward. Being at the outer wall involves, for Heyward, a bodily experience: wind knocked out of him, solar plexus contracting. What about Heyward's body, then? Where did he stand in relation to what we might call the dis/ability wall?

If walls there must be, in the matter of disability DuBose Heyward seems more on Samuel Smalls's side than across any imagined divide. In his early biography, his close friend Hervey Allen makes a brief mention of Heyward "recuperating from an illness."[38] Later biographers write more bluntly. James Hutchisson's *DuBose Heyward* (2000) describes the Charleston boy DuBose as "a sickly child" in "a sickly place." Then

> [w]hen he was eighteen he contracted polio, a devastating condition at that time in the South, for none of the physicians there had yet witnessed it. It was thus some time before Heyward was diagnosed, through the serendipitous intercession of a northern cousin who paid for his treatment at a Philadelphia hospital. The disease left its mark on him permanently with weakened shoulder and arm muscles, a thin, fragile torso and tendency to fall prey to other illnesses. The atrophying of Heyward's muscles also sometimes gave him a cadaverous look. . . . Moreover, he later developed painful arthritis in his hands. At its worst, the condition made his fingers bunch downward into a shape resembling a crab's claw. Writing was often physically painful for him.
>
> After recovering from the polio, Heyward was struck down by a typhoid epidemic. . . . He was invalided for eighteen months. . . . Then in 1906, by bizarre bad luck, Heyward was hit with pleurisy and had to undergo another lengthy rest cure. That time, he left the humid Charleston air for the deserts of Arizona, where he spent nearly two years recuperating on a combined sanitarium and work farm.[39]

"His right arm never came back to normal," writes Hollis Alpert, "and he would have serious bouts of illness throughout his lifetime."[40]

"It would be too easy to equate the author's sympathy with Porgy with his own physical weaknesses," Alpert writes of DuBose Heyward. Yes, but the statement forecloses any exploration of the social situation of disability in *Porgy*. And indeed it would be too easy to ignore the complex disability dynamics at work in the production of the Porgy texts. Not only *Porgy* but Heyward's work more generally needs to be addressed as an early twentieth-century body of disability writing.

Heyward wrote his own experience into a variety of texts, some published, most unpublished.[41] James Hutchisson has pointed out that Heyward's unpublished stories set in sanitariums or western rest-cure venues revolve around crises of masculinity. Their titles illustrate the point: "Be a Man." "A Man's Job." "Making a Man of Rayburn." In these tales, Hutchisson writes, "undertones of irony and wistfulness alternate, suggesting that Heyward felt mingled contempt and envy at the masculine culture that excluded him."[42] The most interesting of the stories for our purposes is "The Mayfield Miracle," a fictional representation of the experience of physical rehabilitation in a men's hospital ward.

Mayfield's white narrator tells the story of his white friend "Eyes" Fayne, whose "love of the beautiful had transcended everything else in the life of this slim sensitive lad. . . . It was in the play of physical perfection that Fayne found his greatest delight." Best of all Fayne loves his own "lithe graceful physique," which is no sooner mentioned than mutilated when the "vast munitions factory" where he and the narrator work blows up. Waking in "the bright sunlit ward of the Mayfield Sanatorium," the narrator, himself injured but three weeks away from "home-cured," beholds the more badly injured Fayne in the next bed. Fayne cannot walk. Or rather, he cannot walk well enough—for him, or for the other men in the boorish masculine rehab culture of the ward:

> Fayne was the victim of one of these hideous scientific miracles by which with terrible ingenuity a human wreck is patched into a semblance of humanity. Fascinated, I followed the figure with my eyes as it swayed forward in what was all too obviously a ghastly caricature of one of the modern dancing steps. Imagine with me, if you can, the effect of the wild incongruity! It was as though one had gone to the bier of a loved friend and found the face covered by a grinning mask. Quickly I lifted my eyes to the face—"God! He did not know!"

When one of the "rough men" jeers at him, "Bravo, Maurice, now come back with a tango," Fayne crumples under the weight of combined homophobia and ableism:

> Slowly his face dropped until his limbs came into his range of vision, and then quietly, like a child, he collapsed in his tracks. . . . "They laughed . . . Listen! As God is my witness, I will never walk another step. . . . I shall get away to some quiet country place where . . . the sunshine and the sky won't stare."

Heyward's personal experience of rehab life—its condescensions, its invasions of privacy, its complex peer culture, its pressures to perform—and his general personal experience of disability give this otherwise strained tale moments of startling realist effect. Much of the plot, for instance, centers on problems of physical access and mobility. The men in the ward are brought upstairs for recreation, to watch an inane "performance by a troupe of trained dogs, cats and birds" meant to veil "the ugly business-like underwrappings of the institution." The story describes at surprising length, long before the Americans with Disability Act, the slow inadequate workings of a tiny, creaky elevator that hauls them up one at a time to the top floor.

All of this is in the service of the story's melodramatic climax. When the floors below catch on fire and the men are trapped, Fayne alone realizes it, in time to distract the others and prevent panic by improvising an ironic performance of a mock "cure." First he speaks: "Think of it! A man goes through life with the wish to dance always in his heart . . . but no, Fate has made him a drudge—his freedom is impossible. Then one day Fate . . . sends him reeling, broken and crushed into the hands of our marvelous physicians." Then he calms the crowd and rivets their attention by walking across the stage, "at the price of an agony that is beyond the power of men to conceive, who would judge only by physical pain." His distractions buy enough time for the fire brigade to lay a bridge to a nearby roof, and everyone is safely evacuated. The story's end finds Fayne in the arms of rehab nurse "Miss Stoddard," her eyes "wide and starry," offering both maternal comfort and the promise of "greater gifts of womanhood that were his as well" and calling him her hero. Having proved his crippled manhood, Fayne gets the girl. The girl's first name is—well, Bess. Bess, you is my eroticized nurse now. Or rather: Miss Bess Stoddard, you *are*, in standard English.

Miss Stoddard is originally called Big Bess. Initially "heavy and plain," she transforms as she gathers "the limp form in a close mothering embrace," with a look that lights "her plain face into a thing of beauty." In the context of representing a largely unmarked white culture (Fayne is at one point explicitly called "a slim white figure"), "The Mayfield Miracle" establishes, years before *Porgy*, a Bess function of which the Bess of "Porgy and" constitutes only one version: unattractive woman all lit up and changed by relation to good disabled man.

In Heyward's novel *Porgy*, unlike later staged versions, Bess as we first encounter her is "unpleasant to look upon . . . An ugly scar marked her left cheek, and the acid of utter degradation had etched hard lines about her mouth." Drunk, drug addicted, literally lying in the dust in her initial appearance, she, as much or more than Porgy, plays the role of the unsightly impaired person in the text. Only later, domestic life with Porgy and adoptive mothering (after a hurricane that plays some of the same function that the fire plays in "Mayfield") transform her: "a new-born element in the woman . . . rendered the scarred visage incandescent." Heyward's misspelled notes on *Porgy* describe "Bess's development . . . as follows": "She fills out, and the look of deg[r]adation leaves her face somewhat, the scar is now scarcely noticible."[43]

In theatrical versions, too, Bess glows and cleans up after she connects to Porgy. But stage and film Besses have been pretty much unanimously glamorous from the start—a phenomenon to which DuBose Heyward made mild objection. "The Bess of my novel had been a tragic, gaunt figure," Heyward wrote about the casting of the first dramatic version of *Porgy* in 1927. But "the part was given to Evelyn Ellis, young, slender and immediately noticeable for a certain radiant charm. . . . We found this painful at first."[44] An unscarred Bess fit more easily into the recognizable performance tradition of black female unbridled sexual appeal. Dorothy Dandridge's portrayal in the 1959 film version of *Porgy and Bess* epitomizes this casting tradition. "As Catfish Row's torrid Bess," writes Donald Bogle,

Dandridge "put her star qualities on brilliant display. Designer Irene Sharaff's long tight skirt and dark wide-brim hat made Dandridge a stunning creation . . . Costar Sidney Poitier [playing Porgy] was literally dwarfed."[45] This kind of interpretation put Porgy into his disabled place and Bess as far away from it as possible. The unscarred, sexy first-scene Besses of theater and film mean a turn away from the structure of mutual vulnerability and mutual anomaly between the disabled man and the marred woman that undergirded Heyward's "Mayfield" and the Porgy novel.

Writing Porgy

Putting Fayne's "boy gets Bess" plot into Porgy's black-and-beggar face let Heyward write disability differently, playing its anxieties and fantasies faster and looser, mobilizing figures of "colored life" sometimes to underscore, sometimes to undercut the givens of (white, genteel) disabled manhood that got worked, too close to home, into his "Mayfield Miracle." In some cases, such as the mirrored Bess stories, the resemblances between "Mayfield" and "Porgy" illuminate some of Heyward's stakes in disability representation. In other cases, the imagined primitive expressiveness and authenticity of Porgy's Gullah culture allowed for exploration of what remains buried and blocked in white Mayfield's drab ward. I make no apologies for the racist aspects of Porgy. "[I]t was part of a racist ideology," as David Krasner writes in a related context, "and must be seen as such, contributing to a mendacious epistemology of racial identity."[46] But I do want to suggest that Heyward's efforts to undo mendacious epistemologies of *disability* identity also play a part in this plot, complicating without mitigating the racist work it does.

For Heyward, Porgy could do "raw," "natural" disability, in contrast to the effete style of social impairment assigned to Fayne.[47] Hence, for instance, Porgy in the theatrical versions articulates bluntly what Fayne cannot say—"When Gawd make cripple, he mean him to be lonely. Nighttime, daytime, he got to travel that lonesome road"—and Porgy's plot moves beyond these sentences with greater force and also more complexity.[48] Porgy develops a deep relationship with Bess across time, and Porgy's story also grapples with threats to that relationship in ways that Fayne's trite marriage plot avoids. When Porgy's Bess leaves him—bereft and lonely in the novel, off to fight to get her back in the play and opera—many explanations, none entirely adequate, can be supplied for her behavior. As Kenneth Tynan put it (with a dose of unconscious ableism) in his review of the Leontyne Price 1953 production of Porgy and Bess, "We never know why Bess takes to the virginal Porgy, except that she is a good girl, nor why she deserts him for Sportin' Life, except that she is a bad girl."[49] Primitivism supplied one partial answer to this conundrum: Bess abandons Porgy because she is a black "girl"; black women do that, they are promiscuous, debased. Primitivism also may have allowed for an exploration of a potentially difficult issue for a white disabled man, the pressures

of a culture that assumes he is meant to be lonely on his ongoing intimate relationships, particularly with partners identified as nondisabled. Bess's looseness
permits the novel to engage the fear that Bess leaves Porgy because she is a nondisabled "girl." At least one reviewer, with no explicit basis or encouragement from
any Porgy text, remarks of Porgy that he is a man "in love with a desirable woman
who needs his affection but also wants the pleasure he cannot give her."[50]

I do not have space here to explore all the ways in which recasting his experiences into Porgy's, writing disability in blackface, offered Heyward a safe space for
exploring the social dynamics of crippling abjection precisely because it also provided a compelling way to affirm disabled masculinity (a phrase often understood
in his culture and in mine as oxymoronic).[51] "Now you is a cripple's woman," Porgy
says to Bess in the initial draft of the libretto that emerged from Heyward's novel;
the primitivist space of Catfish Row permitted exploration of a full range of meanings attached to the idea of the "cripple's woman," from anxiety to empowerment.[52]

W. E. B. Dubois argued in 1926 that Heyward wrote "beautifully of the black
Charleston underworld" but could not "do a similar thing for the white people
of Charleston," for if he did, whites would "drum him out of town." The only way
Heyward could "tell the truth of pitiful human degradation," Du Bois wrote, was
"to tell it of colored people."[53] The only way Heyward could tell much about his
experience of impairment was to tell it "of colored people." What he told, though,
was not finally a tale of pity and degradation but a tale that countered those supposed home truths regarding disability.

In scene after scene, for instance, disability in *Porgy* consists of blocked movement, inadequate or absent helpers, unreachable spaces. At the heart of the novel
is the problem of access. Here is one example: To a great extent, the plot revolves
around the consequences (direct and collateral) of the white legal system for its
black (and particularly its black disabled) characters. Early on, the police jail Porgy's
friend, the old "honey man" Peter who drives him to and forth from his begging spot
each day, as a murder witness, precipitating a serious crisis of mobility, dwelt on at
some length in the text. Without help, unable to leave home, Porgy finally evolves an
inventive solution: his goat cart. Finding the goat and building the cart as a mobility
aid restores Porgy's basic ability to survive by begging as well as something more
ineffable and profound: his right, self-claimed, to move abroad in the land.[54] Though
the goat cart, described as a mock-heroic "chariot," is undoubtedly supposed to be
humorous (as Dorothy Heyward insisted; her essay "Porgy's Goat," about the perils
of training goats for the stage productions, truly is funny), it should not (only) be
taken lightly. After devising his cart, Porgy, writes Dubose Heyward, "had become
a 'character.' " "Character," that is, in at least two senses: Porgy becomes markedly
eccentric, the butt of tolerant and condescending humor, but he also becomes fully
invested with attributes necessary for a leading character, a particular subjectivity
and particular ways of moving, and from this his story ensues.

Porgy in performance is too vast a topic for me to take up in this chapter.
The black disabled beggar's textual body, as it is performed and recorded and

publicized, is an oscillating assemblage, ragtag, cut and paste, a poster here, a review here, jazz here, TV there, novel here, opera there, Broadway here, Charleston there, all combined unstably to produce American Porgy.[55] I conclude with just two examples, one to exemplify further how disability representation is watered down in the majority of Porgy performances and the other to suggest one way in which Hayward's explorations of disability and masculinity still linger. The first involves that cart.

Like the casting of Bess, the handling of the goat cart in the early theatrical versions of Porgy's story weakens the disability politics of the original novel. In *Porgy* the play and in *Porgy and Bess* Porgy's goat cart is a given from the start; he enters with goat in scene one and exits with it at the finale. But in *Porgy* the novel, Porgy's idea to build himself a means of transport is "a radical change," a "new emancipation," a real pivot midway through the plot. Before the cart, Porgy responds to a woman who says "Porgy ain't gots much leg, but he sho got sense" with "Sense do berry well; but he can't lift no weight . . . Sense gots power tuh take a t'ing atter yuh gits dere . . . But he nebber puts bittle in a belly what can't leabe he restin' place." By building his cart, as Bess notices, Porgy acquires agency. In short, as the novel puts it memorably, Porgy "gots goat."[56]

As the process of Porgification got goat and continued through the Harlem Renaissance, the 1930s, and the Cold War, and as the figure based on Samuel Smalls took on new enacted forms first in the dramatic version of *Porgy* and then in sequential productions of *Porgy and Bess*, the contradictions Porgy worked to reconcile remained in play. Let us consider one final example, a question of how Porgification gets musically *scored*.[57]

In DuBose Heyward's novel, Porgy ends up desolate after Bess abandons him. The first dramatic adaptation, upon which *Porgy and Bess* was based, has a different conclusion, first proposed by Dorothy Heyward, in which Porgy goes off in search of Bess, providing no certainty about the outcome of his quest but leaving no doubt about his ability to act on his desires. "I'm on My Way," Porgy sings "with religious fervor" in the opera, in a melody that converts the initial minor notes that precede the opening "Summertime" into a major key.[58] This finale was not meant, exactly, to be happy; Dorothy objected strenuously to the Trevor Nunn version in which a cured Porgy throws away his crutches, arguing that Porgy needed to remain "pathetic" to the end.[59] For Porgy's initial makers, the disabled beggar could not entirely throw off his blues. They designed the stage ending to mitigate but not eliminate entirely the bleak implications of the novel's last line, in which Porgy, now an old, bent, destroyed man, sits with his goat "alone in an irony of morning sunlight" (158).

Porgy's irony is sharpest here, when it is named; but let us look more closely at *Porgy and Bess*'s radiant "Summertime" to see how ironies of disability attend even that most lyric moment at the dawn of the score. Here I return to where I started, with the reviewer who called George Gershwin a "psychological cripple: an archetypical White Negro, a poor boy who made good, a Jew who knew about spiritual isolation. . . . Through these hazards he preserved, like Porgy, an innocence which shines through the radiant 'Summertime' lullaby." If, as Andrea Most and Jonathan Gill, among others, have argued, the "Yiddish blackface" of *Porgy and Bess* became a way in part for Gershwin to "explore Jewishness," it also offered Heyward a chance to explore disability; in the combination, Porgy's innocent tunes produce the sweet aura of what Most calls the assimilation effect.[60] But they also work up what I would call "inclusion effects," in which disability is met with and surrounded by the sweet aura of "emotional response and communal celebration" that Most argues marks musical comedies. In such a production, far afield from the world of Brecht's *Threepenny Opera*, the unsightly beggar gets his opera, one in which alienation effects have no place. Still, the exclusion effects of disability leave their mark even here.

Critics often attribute the inspiration for "Summertime" to the equivalent lullaby sung near the outset of the Heywards' stage play, Clara's "Hush, li'l baby, don' yo' cry./Fadder an' mudder born to die" (7). Since the baby's parents, Clara and Jake, are both destined to die before the final curtain, this version of lullaby is bitterly ironic; the undertow of melancholy in "Summertime," hinted at in the melody's echoes of "Sometimes I Feel Like a Motherless Child," is far subtler.[61] Though the idea for a lullaby undoubtedly emerged from Clara's version in the Heywards' play, these lyrics have deep hidden roots in other moments in DuBose Heyward's novel, in passages that extend beyond the generalized threat of mortality to deal more specifically with the social consequences of disablement (not that those two issues are entirely separable).

The direct antecedent for the evocative, grammatically distinctive "Summertime, and the living is easy" structure, for instance, is this line from *Porgy*: "June, and the cotton season was over" (45). Both lines plunge directly into an immediate temporal moment, an immersion reinforced by the minimal action that ensues after each "and": living easy, season ceased. But despite their similarities, these are two very different moments. What follows "June, and" in the novel is precisely *not* easy for Porgy. "The long, hot days, so conducive to indolence, brought a new phase of life," the passage continues. As a result, the outdoor community life of Catfish Row, the dice-gaming and conversation, diminishes, leaving Porgy in isolation: "Men came in earlier in the evenings, and spent more time with the women. Porgy sat alone in his doorway." In the rest of the scene, Porgy openly shows anguish at his social exclusion.

Then Bess arrives, and the pleasure of hiatus, "summertime," seems actually to be granted to Porgy. But before long Bess meets up again with his threatening rival Crown. And here the second textual link to the "Summertime" lyrics occurs. "Now 'member wut I tells yuh," Crown says as he reasserts his claim on Bess.

> "Yuh kin stay wid de cripple til' de cotton come. Den I comin' . . . Den soon de cotton will be comin' in fas', an' libbin will be easy. Yuh gits dat?"
>   For a moment she looked into the narrow, menacing eyes, then nodded. (100–101)

In this abusive anti-lullaby, nothing is easy for Bess, or for Porgy. Crown's "living is easy" fantasy is just that, a fantasy, and one dependent, violently and impossibly, upon purging "de cripple." The menace here—coercion masking as gratification—leaves its trace in the lyric "Summertime." Its transfer into the scene of lullaby renders to the infant that which is infantile and yet that which forms the basis of all social dynamics of exclusion: satisfaction-seeking, loss, lack, fear of deprivation, longing, need. The haunted lyrics of "Summertime," in which "de cripple" (and for that matter, the question of manhood) gets left behind, constitute DuBose Heyward's most deflected and secretive, and perhaps in a way his greatest, example of disability writing.

Notes

1. Wilfred Mellers, *Music in a New Found Land: Themes and Developments in the History of American Music* (Boston: Faber and Faber, 1987), 392, 397.

2. Fiona Kumari Campbell, *Contours of Ableism: The Production of Disability and Abledness* (Basingstoke, UK: Palgrave Macmillan, 2009). I am grateful to Campbell for her invaluable help throughout this chapter. All errors, of course, are my own.

3. These terms inevitably involve both race and disability (as well as gender). The terms are popular and scholarly. "Too much critical work in African American Studies posits the African American body politic in an ableist (read non-disabled) fashion," Chris Bell observed, bringing attention to one aspect of this dynamic. "Introduction: Doing Representational Detective Work," in Christopher M. Bell, *Blackness and Disability: Critical Examinations and Cultural Interventions* (East Lansing: Michigan State University Press, 2011), 1–3.

4. "Todd Duncan: From an Interview by Robert Wyatt (1990)," in Robert Wyatt and John Andrew Johnson, *The George Gershwin Reader* (New York: Oxford, 2004), 222; Richard Crawford, "Where Did Porgy and Bess Come From?" *Journal of Interdisciplinary History* 36.4 (2006), 697–734.

5. Dubose Heyward, *Porgy* (1925; rpt. University Press of Mississippi, 2001), 18–19.

6. Dorothy Heyward, "Porgy's Goat," *Harper's Magazine* (December 1957), 3.

7. In the Dorothy Heyward papers, South Carolina Historical Society, Charleston.

8. Clippings in the Dubose Heyward papers at the South Carolina Historical Society, Charleston.

9. This is a modern preoccupation, one that tends to assign a scale of moral culpability to impairment. But the legacy of slavery points to a different possible sentiment in response to the nexus of disabled/black. Dea Boster argues that the acculturation into or adoption of disability allowed new means for enslaved people in negotiating power with their "owners." Paradoxically, the diminished disabled body enabled bondspeople to achieve a certain degree of control. That said, the disabled black body (like Porgy's or Small's) was often seen as *characterologically* suspect, automatically accused of feigning or self-inflicting impairment. Dea H. Boster, "'I Made Up My Mind to Act Dumb': Displays of Disability and Slave Resistance in the Antebellum American South," in Jeffrey Brune and Daniel Wilson, eds., *Disability and Passing* (Philadelphia: Temple University Press, 2013), 71–98, 72.

10. John Bennett, "Porgy at Least Once Worked for a Living," *News and Courier* clipping, n.d. (1951), in the DuBose Heyward papers.

11. Cassandra Jackson, "Visualizing Slavery: Photographs and the Disabled Subject in the Art of Carrie Mae Weems," in Christopher M. Bell, ed., *Blackness and Disability: Critical Examinations and Cultural Interventions* (East Lansing: Michigan State University Press, 2011), 31–46, especially 36–37.

12. Space does not allow for the teasing out of the theme of animality. I have noted elsewhere that punishment is twofold: the subject is punished for animality and punished by relegation to animality. Susan M. Schweik, *The Ugly Laws: Disability in Public* (New York: New York University Press, 2009), 100. Compare the recent, version of this theme captured, in a different cultural context, in Indra Sinha's fictional character "Animal," a nineteen-year-old man who walks on all four limbs in the Indian city of Khaufpur and battles scams and plots in a subterranean world of street culture. *Animal's People* (London, Simon & Schuster, 2007).

13. Hervey Allen, *DuBose Heyward* (New York: George H. Duran, 1973), 13.

14. Hollis Alpert, *The Life and Times of Porgy and Bess: The Story of an American Classic* (New York: Knopf, 1990), 331, 19.

15. Dorothy Heyward, "Anybody Hyuh Know Porgy?," typescript in the Dorothy Heyward papers.

16. Heyward, *Porgy*, 51.

17. When a Charleston reporter asked Samuel Smalls's mother, three decades after her son's death, whether she had "benefited at all from the money her son's life has made for others," she did not respond, like Gershwin's singing Porgy, that nothing was plenty for her. "No suh," she is quoted as saying. "Ah don' get nothing. But I sho do need it." "Porgy's Mother Still Alive," Perkins titled his article, prompting a nervous desire on the part of the widowed Dorothy to distinguish between Goat Sammy and her husband's creation Porgy. On the complex interactions that ensued, see Thomas P. Waring, letter to Dorothy Heyward, July 8, 1959, in the Dorothy Heyward papers.

18. Dorothy Heyward, letter to Thomas P. Stoney (July 17, 1959), in the Dorothy Heyward Papers.

19. Dorothy Heyward, "The Goat-Cart Beggar of King Street," unpublished manuscript in the Dorothy Heyward papers.

20. Dorothy Heyward, "Anyone Here Know Porgy? Real Life Hunt for Goat Sammy Retold," *News and Courier*, July 26, 1957.

21. Bryan Wagner's work on black culture and the police power is pertinent in thinking about this originary moment in a story of Smalls's arrest; the lineage between Samuel Smalls and Porgy's various novelistic, stage and musical (operatic, jazz, Broadway) avatars—not a "black tradition" but a "lampblack" tradition—is nonetheless "predicated," as Wagner puts it, "not upon the ceremonial continuity of cultural tradition but rather upon the tradition's negative relation to law." "Disarmed and Dangerous: The Strange Career of Bras-Coupe," *Representations* 92.1 (2005), 142.

22. Heyward, "Anybody Hyuh Know Porgy?"

23. Otis Perkins, "Porgy's Mother Still Alive, Unaware of Fame Which She Gave 'Goat Sammy,'" *News and Courier* (July 23 1959).

24. Heyward, "Porgy's Goat," 3.

25. Heyward, "Porgy," in "Notes on the Life of DuBose Heyward," unpublished manuscript in the Dorothy Heyward papers.

26. Frank Durham, *Dubose Heyward: The Man Who Wrote Porgy* (Columbia: University of South Carolina Pres, 1954), 47.

27. Heyward, "The Goat-Cart Beggar of King Street," 1.

28. Heyward, "The Goat-Cart Beggar of King Street," 3.

29. Alpert, *Life and Times of Porgy and Bess,* 17. See also Durham, *Dubose Heyward,* 47; William H. Slavick, *DuBose Heyward* (Boston: Twayne, 1981), 60.

30. DuBose Heyward, *Porgy,* 11–12.

31. Quoted in James M. Hutchisson, *DuBose Heyward: A Charleston Gentleman and the World of Porgy and Bess* (Jackson: University Press of Mississippi, 2000), 54.

32. Allen, *DuBose Heyward,* 12–13.

33. Arthur Knight, "It Ain't Necessarily So That It Ain't Necessarily So: African American Recordings of Porgy and Bess as Film and Cultural Criticism," in *Soundtrack Available: Essays on Film and Popular Music* (Durham, NC: Duke University Press, 2001), 319–347. See also Richard Crawford, "It Ain't Necessarily Soul," *Yearbook for Inter-American Musical Research,* Vol. VIII (Austin: University of Texas, 1972), 17–38.

34. Ezra Bell, "Why Negroes Don't Like 'Porgy and Bess,'" *Ebony* (October 1955), 51.

35. Quoted in Robert Garland, "Negroes are Critical of Porgy and Bess," *New York World Telegram,* January 16, 1934, 14. These words are actually those of Ellington's interviewer Edward Morrow. Ellington's own analysis was more complicated. See Mark Tuker, ed. *The Duke Ellington Reader* (New York: Oxford University Press, 1995), 116–117.

36. I am indebted to Curtis Marez and anonymous reviewers at *American Quarterly* for this clear, sharp formulation.

37. Fiona Kumari Campbell, "Crippin' the Flâneur: Cosmopolitanism, and the Landscapes of Difference," *Journal of Social Inclusion* 1.1 (2010), 75, 79.

38. Allen, *DuBose Heyward,* 10.

39. Hutchisson, *DuBose Heyward,* 11–12.

40. Alpert, *Life and Times of Porgy and Bess,* 22.

41. See, for instance, the post-polio poem "Weariness," in his *Skylines and Horizons* (New York: Macmillan, 1924).

42. Hutchisson, *DuBose Heyward,* 12.

43. DuBose Heyward, "Notes on Porgy," in the DuBose Heyward papers.

44. Durham, *Dubose Heyward,* 109.

45. Donald Bogle, *Toms, Coons, Mulattoes, Mammies and Bucks: An Interpretive History of Blacks in American Films* (New York: Continuum, 2002), 174.

46. David Krasner, *A Beautiful Pageant: African American Theatre, Drama and Performance in the Harlem Renaissance 1910–1927* (New York: Palgrave Macmillan, 2002), 62.

47. On primitivism in related contexts see Krasner, *Beautiful Pageant.*

48. Only the first of these two sentences is uttered by Porgy in the Heywards' play; the second "nighttime, daytime" line, with its echoes of other lyrics ("Morningtime and eveningtime and summertime and wintertime") was added after Gershwin's first draft of the Porgy and Bess score. Deena Rosenberg, *Fascinating Rhythm: The Collaboration of George and Ira Gershwin* (New York: Dutton, 1991), 284.

49. Quoted in Alpert, *Life and Times of Porgy and Bess,* 177.

50. Wanda Hale, "Porgy and Bess: A Screen Classic," *New York Daily News,* June 25, 1959, 68.

51. We know that Heywood fervently believed in portraying black "authenticity" as a vehicle for increased recognition of black contributions to Southern social life, despite the

challenge involved, in his words, of "attempting an interpretation of the inner life of an alien people." That may have been the case with the colorline, but no matter how much Heywood struggled with internalized ableism and disability alienation, disability was far from alien for him. Ray Allen, "An American Folk Opera? Triangulating Folkness, Blackness, and Americans in Gershwin, and Heywood's *Porgy and Bess*," *Journal of American Folklore*, 117.465 (2004), 245–261, 253; Du Bose Heywood, "Introduction," in DuBose Heywood and Dorothy Heywood, *Porgy: A Play in Four Acts* (Garden City: Doubleday, 1928), ix–xxi, xii.

52. First draft of Porgy and Bess libretto, Scene 2, line 9.

53. W. E. B. DuBois, "Criteria of Negro Art," *Crisis* 32.6 (October 1926), 297.

54. I am invoking the legal theorist of disability Jacobus Ten Broek's phrase in his "The Right to Live in the World: The Disabled and the Law of Torts," *California Law Review* (1966), 841–919. Note that the life of Samuel Smalls is in this respect faithfully reproduced in Porgy; in representations of Smalls, the cart becomes a modality of subversion of both impairment and normalcy. Smalls's resistance to docility is reported by Sarah Dowling, one of his contemporaries: "Oh, Lawd, you'd see [Sam] just going along, just a –singing, a body in a cart with two wheels . . . he would spring out that wagon and spring in that door, and the goat would stay there all day. You could always tell when he was there-when that goat was out there in the Long Alley" Kendra Hamilton, "Goat Cart Sam a.k.a. Porgy, an Icon of a Sanitized South," *Southern Cultures*, 5.3 (1999), 40.

55. I comment here on just one example, since it is recent and received a great deal of press: The American Repertory Theater's staging of *Porgy and Bess* in 2011. Here Porgy, played by Norm Lewis, is transmogrified into an upright hero. Instead of being comfortable with disability, being the uppity crip-cart-man, this Porgy dreams of being cured and is driven to overcome his disability. This turn erases Porgy's deliberative capacity and reinscribes what Fiona Kumari Campbell identifies as ableist normativity; here to be a "real man" one must become "abled-up." See Russell Shuttleworth, Nikki Wedgwood, and Nathan Wilson, "The Dilemma of Disabled Masculinity," *Men and Masculinities*, 15.2 (2010), 174–194. The theater's hermeneutical betrayal of Heywood's characterization of Porgy renders Porgy's once empowering dis/technology of the cart as a theatrical inconvenience. "Norm Lewis noted that the cane has given Porgy strength, while the cart rendered him weak. He also referenced the design team's needs, stating that a cart 'would not work on this type of stage,' which, with its raised platform, would have been inaccessible to cart (if not goat)." The solace in ableism here is extremely problematic. See Stephanie Jensen-Moulton, "Porgy's Cane: Mediating Disability in ART's Porgy and Bess *American Music Review* 41.1 (Fall 2011).

56. *Porgy*, 48.

57. On this subject, Raymond Knapp offers an excellent concentrated intersectional analysis of the role music plays in *Porgy and Bess*'s cultural work in the race/disability nexus. "Waitin' for the Light to Shine: Musicals and Disability," in Blake Howe, Stephanie Jensen-Moulton, Neil Lerner and Joseph Straus, eds., *The Oxford Handbook of Music and Disability Studies* (New York: Oxford University Press, 2016), 816–817.

58. See Rosenberg, *Fascinating Rhythm*, 307–308.

59. Rodney Greenberg, *George Gershwin* (London: Phaidon Press, 1998), 189.

60. Andrea Most, *Making Americans: Jews and the Broadway Musical* (Cambridge, MA: Harvard University Press, 2004); Jonathan Gill, "It Is Necessarily So: The Yiddish Blackface of Porgy and Bess," in Jay Bochner and Justin D. Edwards, eds., *American Modernism Across the Arts* (New York: Peter Lang, 1999).

61. On the echo of "Sometimes I Feel" see Rosenberg, *Fascinating Rhythm*, 281. The conjunction of "Summertime" and "Sometimes" is a standard one in analysis of the opera; see also Samuel A. Floyd Jr., *Black Music in the Harlem Renaissance* (New York: Greenwood Press, 1990), 22, and Jeffrey Melnick, *A Right to Sing the Blues* (Cambridge, MA: Harvard University Press, 1999). Jack Gottlieb finds hints also of lullaby from southern Russia and argues that the melody "may be an amalgamation of Jewish- and Black-based components." He notes that Gershwin told a friend he worried that the song sounded "too Yiddish." Gottlieb, *Funny, It Doesn't Sound Jewish* (Albany: State University of New York Press, 2004), 42–43.

15

Masculinity and Disability
ERNEST HEMINGWAY, THE MAN, THE GIRL,
AND THE GENIUS

Carolyn Slaughter

Ernest Hemingway was a girl in a boy's body. His mother, Grace Hall Hemingway, wrote "summer girl" in her scrapbook alongside a photograph of her son a month before his second birthday. She often dressed Ernest in girls' clothing and decided that he and his sister, Marcelline, were girl-twins—even though Marcelline was eighteen months older and, since she and her brother had skinny-dipped from an early age, neither could have missed the anatomical differences. Their mother took her fantasy of her children's twin-hood to some lengths: she kept Marcelline out of school for a year so they could both be in the same grade. She insisted they behave as if they were two parts of a whole: sometimes their hair was long and curly, sometimes cropped, at other times Hemingway was dressed in girly clothes with short hair, sometimes the other way round. Grace would give her "twins" identical tea sets and air rifles. They slept in the same twin white cribs, had the same dolls, and were made, as Marcelline writes in her memoir, *At the Hemingways*, "to feel like twins by having everything alike."[1]

Grace's theft of her son's sexual integrity and her intrusion into and control of his life created deep sexual splits and insecurities that were to affect him for the rest of his life. It drove him to live out a caricature of masculinity and tipped him into deep, dark depressions, obsessive compulsions and fantasies, and an intense preoccupation with war, guns, brawling and boxing, crime, booze, women, big-game hunting, deep-sea fishing, bullfighting, suicide, and death. He liked to kill—wild animals and enemy combatants—and he killed plenty. Hemingway's outer life was a desperate performance of physical excellence, courage, and endurance. Over the years, it led to the creation of a sprawling mythology he helped to create and was obliged to prove. His life was an attempt to live up to his public image of macho adventurer and reckless sensation seeker, a man obsessed with danger and violence. Beneath all the bravado lurked dark fears and even darker secrets.

Hemingway's posthumous novel, *The Garden of Eden* (1986), revealed for the first time the secret side of a man struggling with vulnerable splits in his psyche, as well as defenses designed to protect his androgynous fantasies and interest in fetish and sexual transformation. He was plagued all his life by constant sexual arousal linked to associations developed in early childhood. The revelations in this sensational novel brought a more nuanced understanding of the struggle and anguish Hemingway endured around issues relating to his masculine gender, identity, and self-image. He did not seem to know who he really was, and in his novels he created heroic and tragic fictional characters in search of a true self. As Edmund Wilson famously wrote about *Green Hills of Africa* (1935):

> For reasons which I cannot attempt to explain, something dreadful seems to happen to Hemingway as soon as he begins to write in the first person. In his fiction . . . the conflicting elements of his nature . . . are externalized and objectified and the result is an art that is severe and intense, deeply serious. But as soon as he speaks in his own person, he seems to lose all his capacity for self-criticism and is likely to become fatuous or maudlin.[2]

In his early letters, as in his later fiction and nonfiction, Hemingway does not easily use "I" or "you." From Paris he writes to his boyhood friends in fraternal terms invoking a brotherhood of heroic men. In these letters he refers to both himself and a friend as simply a "male": "Bring a male up to date." His first wife, Hadley, was close to being another male. She was outdoorsy, strong, capable, and a good sport. He refers to her as "the best guy on a trip you ever saw" and is said to fish "not with the usual feminine simulation of interest but like one of the men." For Hemingway, anyone who lacked physical excellence had no authenticity, neither in his world nor his fiction. Without manly action there was nothing and no one, no I, no self, just a hollow man.

As a small boy/girl how could Ernest manage these splits in his identity and sexuality except by trying to piece the broken pieces together? He did this by trying to merge with someone else as the only way to find wholeness and peace. As an infant, Ernest had slept in his mother's bed and felt part of her maternal warmth and closeness. Later, as a small boy, he was, according to his mother, happy to sit and sew with her and might have liked the attention he received from pleasing her by being of her sex and being her girl. The other side of him fought her authority over his sexuality with great vehemence and throughout his life he hated her with a passion that never let up. He was also deadly afraid of women—unable to free himself from the dark mother who continued to haunt his life and fuel his fiction. From an early age he referred to his mother as "that bitch" and often used "bitch" as a verb. In a letter to Fitzgerald, he writes: "We are all bitched from the start and you especially have to be hurt like hell before you can write seriously."[3]

Hemingway wrote about his mother constantly, killing her off in stories, humiliating and hurting her as he had been hurt. As a boy he slapped his mother and acted out shooting her. He played a game of shooting his sister, too, making her fall down dead whenever he could. Later, he used words to slash and maim and was well-known for his killer letters. Everywhere we look there is evidence of Hemingway's love of killing, of death, murder, self-murder, and annihilation. Stuck in the middle of his mother's wish to castrate him while also encouraging him to be the "little man," Ernest as a boy began to spin into confusion and insecurity, shouting out "'fraid of nothing" at the top of his voice as a defense against mounting fears about who he was. Because he wore the same clothes as his sister, he was afraid Santa Clause would not know he was a boy, nor could he be sure anyone would really believe he was a boy. This appalling doubt carried over into his adult life and was compensated for with hypermanly behavior and excessive violence.

Ernest continued the androgynous life started by his mother by developing dual sexual identities and ambiguities in his fiction: his characters played out both roles, flipping between male and female as he himself had learned to do as a child. He understood and wrote about these conflicts with a depth of observation and candor that he was unable to extend to himself. His profound understanding of complex characters and their vulnerabilities, and the tenderness with which he writes about his character's feminine feelings are beautifully portrayed in his fiction. This dual perspective made it possible for Hemingway to give us a unique take on feminine yearning and identity without ever having to reveal such feelings as his own. In many ways, he remained a boy, arrested at a point of development that was transsexual and fluid. Much of Hemingway's life and writing has been simplified into proof of his misogyny, and yet something deeper and older kept returning him to that twinned childhood with his sister. Recurrent transsexual fantasies of what it would be like to become a woman acquire a frightening intensity in books like *A Farewell to Arms*, *The Garden of Eden* and *The Last Good Country*. Hemingway's vulnerabilities rise up in *The Nick Adams Stories* and allow for a moving and beautiful description of a boy who has been betrayed by his girl: "In the morning there was a big wind blowing and the waves were running high up on the beach and he was awake for a long time before he remembered that his heart was broken."[4]

As Ernest grew up, the confusion, shame, and despair of deep conflicts began to explode into dark and violent rages, which could be sparked by tiny infractions on his masculinity. He would savagely beat up anyone who suggested he might be unmanly or impotent, and his competitive urges were so extreme that he would humiliate and physically demolish rivals and fellow writers—particularly those less able to defend themselves against his bulky body and massive shoulders. His hidden life darkened all his relationships: his portrayal of men in his books were often used to lampoon and humiliate his friends; in his fiction and nonfiction he used real names and presented deadly accurate and nasty portraits that publicly exposed the weaknesses of his fellow writers. He did all this brilliantly and with no remorse. His homophobia ran high.

His deepest traumas were played out in his unconscious life, in black sweats, insomnia, dreams, and waking nightmares. The boy afraid of the dark remained that way as a man. Later he tried to attribute his inability to sleep to traumatic wartime experiences and memories, but in his early fiction fear emerges in *The Nick Adams Stories* in a way that feels personal and close: "He was always a little frightened of the woods at night . . . He was not afraid of anything definite as yet. But he was getting very afraid. Then suddenly he was afraid of dying."[5] To complicate things further, Ernest, when permitted to be a boy by his mother, was held to the highest standards of manliness, courage, and gallantry. Grace had named him for her father, Ernest Hall, "the finest purest noblest man I have ever known."[6]

Hemingway's father—aware of his son's dilemma and himself living a life of humiliation and subjugation under the control of his wife—took up the cause of helping his son follow the path of a boy. Clarence Hemingway, "Ed," was a physician and a sportsman who took his family to live in Oak Park, Illinois, just outside Chicago, in the early years of the twentieth century. Ernest was born here in 1899 and in 1917 left for a newspaper job in Kansas City. Clarence Hemingway loved camping and being out in the woods, and every summer he made sure that he and Ernest were able to get away from Oak Park and the women. When the two of them took off for hunting and fishing trips in Windemere, Dr. Hemingway taught his son how to handle himself, eat what he killed, and do things correctly in the woods and rivers. The boy quickly picked up his father's skills and knowledge in a way that became part of his own character. These times of boyhood freedom began when Ernest was barely three years old, when he apparently knew how to handle a fishing rod and a gun. And his mother, constantly bewildering, encouraged these opportunities for him to prove he was a "little man." She writes in her scrapbook that

> Ernest Miller at 2 years 11 months went fishing with two men—his father and Mr. Glofelty. He caught the biggest fish of the crowd. He knows when he gets a bite and lands them all himself. He shoots well with his gun and loads and cocks it himself.[7]

This seems a tad precocious for a boy not yet three and makes one wonder if Hemingway's lifelong tendency to embellish his triumphs may have been learned in the lap of his mother.

Ernest formed a strong kinship and respect for his father in these early years when they were much in one another's company, and for the rest of his life certain times of the year or particular parts of the country would remind him of his father and bring the early days back to him, as in this fragment from *Fathers and Sons*:

> His father came back to him in the fall of the year, or in the early spring when there had been jacksnipe on the prairie, or when he saw shocks of corn, or when he saw a lake . . . or when he saw or heard wild geese, or in a duck blind,

remembering the time an eagle dropped through the whirling snow ... His father was with him, suddenly, in deserted orchards and in the newly-plowed fields, in thickets, on small hills or when going through dead grass.[8]

Ernest's love of landscape and nature came from this time with his father and can be seen in much of Hemingway's writing: he takes us deep into forests and rivers, mountains and sea, where we actually feel and smell the places where he has been, his love of it, the precision of his vision, the sensuous brilliance of his world. Later, growing up, Ernest was to lose respect for the father who had inspired some of his most exquisite writing. Dr. Hemingway was complex and confusing for a boy—tormented by wild explosions of rage and deep depressions that no one around him understood. He was a strict and deeply religious man, excessive in his punishments: Ernest, after being beaten by his father, was made to kneel and ask the Lord for forgiveness. The contempt and anger he felt about his father's subservience toward his wife was increased by frequent and harsh discipline. His father's wild swings between depression and frenzy must have created anxiety and dread in the son, who shared many of these characteristics himself. And yet as a small boy an abiding love for his father remained: In Esquire in 1935, Hemingway wrote, "And when I look back at the shooting I am a great admirer of my father ... He was a beautiful shot, one of the fastest I have ever seen." These remarks, rather chillingly, were made some time after Clarence Hemingway's suicide in 1928: a shot to the head—a foreshadowing of Ernest's own suicide in 1961.

In all this gender turbulence, confusion, and violence, we should not forget Marcelline's early influence on her brother. She had the advantage of passing as a tomboy while Earnest had no such option as he dutifully played the part of his sister's sister. How did she contribute to his excessive competitive streak, which, in later life, often led to dirty tricks, ugly scenes, Semitic insults, literary stabbings, and acts of vengeance, not to mention his cheating and pathological tendency to lie and embellish his experiences—which went so far as to include his war-time experiences and injuries.

Kenneth Lynn, in his magnificent biography *Hemingway*, takes a penetrating psychoanalytic view of Hemingway's intensely competitive relationship with Marcelline. He wonders: "Did the infant boy take pride in the equipment that set him apart from Marcelline? Or did the sight of her smoothness make him think that she'd suffered some sort of dreadful accident which might soon befall him as well? Or were pride and fear intermingled in his turbulent imagination?"[9] Marcelline had many advantages over her younger brother: she was handsome, a good and sturdy walker, and she could easily outwrestle her brother. She was also taller, smarter, and more studious than he, more vocal, more of a smart-ass, and of course a whole eighteen months older. Earnest was deeply competitive with his sister, and he never liked her. He had a tendency to refer to her as "a bitch complete with handles" and held a lasting grudge against her that grew and developed with time. For Marcelline, a brother who was constantly trying to make her fall down dead could hardly be thought of with much affection.

Ursula was the sister Ernest loved; she was younger and his favorite, and it is she who comes up as an androgynous and incestuous love object in his fiction, most explicitly in "The Last Good Country." In this story, part of the *Nick Adams Stories*, Ursula is named Littless, and one of Littless's dreams is to set up a family of her own with her brother as her husband. Of the two lovers Littless is the more assertive, "I want to be your common-law wife. We'll have a couple of children while I'm a minor. Then you [will] have to marry me." Littless also has an interest in androgyny: she wears boy's clothes and wants to cut her hair short. And, after cutting off her hair, she says: "Now I'm your sister but I'm a boy."[10] There's no way of telling whether Hemingway's relationship with his sister was incestuous, but they certainly grew up in a household without boundaries, where sexuality was a strange, confusing, and moveable feast. We do know that when Hemingway came back from the war in 1919, he told the critic, Arthur Mizener: "my [seventeen-year-old] sister Ura . . . would sleep with me so that I would not be lonely in the night."[11]

Psychoanalysts have excavated Hemingway's life and work meticulously: analyzing and cataloging his mental illnesses, symptoms, writing, marriages, and relationships. The result is a full-bore diagnostic list, including a long range of symptoms: Oedipal complex, bipolar disorder, narcissistic personality disorder, alcoholism, psychosis, delusions and paranoia, impotence, chronic death wish, gender identity issues, self-image issues, latent homosexuality, spousal abuse, physical and emotional abuse. Running along these mental afflictions is a list of self-destructive behaviors that came with the disabilities. He was accident-prone: he shot himself in the head and in both legs; his war wounds were real if exaggerated; his death wish was powerful enough to bring mirrors down on his head; he was injured a dozen times in plane and car crashes; he damaged his knees and broke ribs and almost killed himself in hunting accidents and expeditions in dangerous places.

He was constantly running off to war as a correspondent and getting as close as he could to the front lines. And yet, there are also witnesses to his bravery under fire or his way of putting his own life at risk to help someone else—but surely these were death wishes too? Few could discount his real courage in situations where he found himself in tremendous pain, even of his own making. And still he lived, too afraid to die in any way that would remove the hero epitaph from his obituary or reveal him as a man who, like his father, had taken "the coward's way out."

How could a single individual manage so many serious mental afflictions as well as physical injuries that caused life-long pain and, in the latter part of his life, serious illnesses? How did he get up each morning to write descriptions of human sexuality, longing, and suffering, and how could he manage to illuminate personal relationships without ever risking emotional surrender in himself? His most profound disability might perhaps have been his disconnection from himself and others. His deepest desire was to dissolve with another in a way that did not require him to be a separate, individual person. In *A Farewell to Arms*, he is at his most precise: "There isn't me. I'm you."

And then there are the suicides. Suicide, like mental illness and incest, runs in families and down the generations, as the Hemingway tragedies so starkly reveal. There were six suicides in the Hemingway family over four generations: Ernest's father killed himself with an ancient Civil War revolver he had inherited from his father at the latter's death two years before, a clean—perhaps beautiful?—shot to the head. Ernest's younger brother, Leicester—who found his father's dead body in all its gory horror—was further disturbed by Ernest's suicide. Leicester committed suicide in the same way—a single shot to the head. Ursula, Hemingway's beloved sister, distraught after Ernest's death, and hearing she had cancer, promptly swallowed enough prescription pills to kill herself. Hemingway's youngest son, Gregory, died from heart failure in 2001, in a jail cell, after being picked up in the street for walking about naked. Hemingway's granddaughter, Margaux, killed herself by drug overdose in a Paris hotel room in 1966.

A sad addition to Gregory's story: he was the youngest son and the one most deeply disappointing to his father. He was also the son most emotionally disturbed by Hemingway's behavior. Gregory was encouraged to drink before he was five and soon became an alcoholic. He also developed a serious drug problem that landed him in jail on several occasions. He had seven nervous breakdowns and underwent ninety-seven shock treatments. He was transsexual and later had a sex change operation and changed his name to Gloria. All these aspects of Gregory revolted his father, even though, or perhaps because, he shared many of the same disturbances himself.

Shame and humiliation were emotional triggers in the Hemingway suicides. These emotions link to depression and self-loathing and can be acted out in violent and self-destructive ways. Hemingway's father and many of his children and grandchildren suffered from bipolar disorder, which included high levels of emotional disturbance fueled by alcohol and rage. All his life, Ernest was to project the humiliation and emotional abuse he had had to endure from his mother onto women and men alike. He tried to control and force his women into a version of himself, with no right to a life or a sex of their own. He was also extremely emotionally dependent. He made sure a new wife was in the bag before he got rid of the old one. It was unbearable for him to be alone, but he could not keep a woman or make her happy and, in the end, the intensity with which he began each love affair soon descended into hatred and contempt, terrible fights and ugly scenes. And every time he abandoned a wife he was filled with remorse and guilt and felt a dark and deep sense of failure. His wives went on to rat on him and spoke of his sexual inadequacy and, as time passed, others began to question his virility, too, moving him deeper into rage and despair.

His relationships with men followed the same disruptive pattern. His male friends: F. Scott Fitzgerald, Ezra Pound, Edmund Wilson, James Joyce, John Dos

Passos, and many of the luminaries of the Paris years, at first received his wonderful friendship, even his respect and admiration, but all too soon he began his scalding attacks on their writing and behavior, as he shamelessly exposed their secrets both in private and in public while lampooning them in clearly recognizable portraits in his novels. Everyone who knew Hemingway seems to have put up with a great deal of ugly behavior from him—he punched people in the face, knocked men unconscious—and often limped back drunk, in tears, saying he could never forgive himself, making excuses and lame gestures of contrition—usually to protect himself from loss, which he could not take, of any kind, good or bad.

His consumption of alcohol increased his pugnacity and violence. Some of his friends and drinking buddies liked to imagine Hemingway was a happy drunk, enjoying himself by out-drinking anyone he could. Kenneth Lynn wrote:

> Hemingway as he entered the bar had been induced by the booze he had been tapping into in all likelihood since dawn and the drink he took for the road was but the prelude to the wine he would drink at dinner and the nightcaps afterwards.[12]

Meanwhile, his friendships were crashing all around him, and his godawful ways had cost him most if not all the easy, creative friendships he had first made in Paris in the glory years of the 1920s. In these sexually exuberant years after the end of the war when sexual inversion was visible and uncensored—drag queens, men loving men, women loving women—it was a time when lesbians like Gertrude Stein, Alice Toklas, Sylvia Beach, and many others were influencing as well as directing artistic life and publishing banned books like *Ulysses*. This was a time when Hemingway could both come out in print with his own sexual inversions and also make the laxity of the historical moment work to his advantage. He spent much of his time hanging out with the rich and famous. He feared being alone but created isolation by behaving very badly and showing no accountability. Jeffrey Kottler, in *Divine Madness*, gives us a quote by Don Stewart, a writer and friend of Hemingway's:

> The minute he began to love you or the minute he began to have some sort of obligation to you of love or friendship that is when he had to kill you. Then you were too close to something he was protecting. One-by-one, he knocked off the best friendships he ever had.[13]

In spite of all his competitive and spiteful literary tournaments, Hemingway, of all his competitors, was the writer most able to put a strong, true voice to the sexual turmoil of the lost generation after World War I. He was also the soldier-poet who would make the Great War vivid and unforgettable to anyone who reads *A Farewell to Arms, For Whom the Bell Tolls,* and *To Have and Have Not.* When we include his front-line dispatches, his Greco-Turkish war correspondence, his journalism on the Spanish Civil War and the French occupation of Germany—not to mention his participation in blood sports, his deep-sea fishing, his hard drinking, hard fighting, and hard loving—it is impossible to discount his profound effect on his time. And for all his disabilities, he was able to put himself at the forefront of a generation of writers—who, without benefit of his material, his exceptionalism and plain simple genius—could not match him in ambition or in his capacity to produce a body of work more beautiful and harrowing than any other writer of his generation. He was going to cement his reputation as the greatest living writer even if it killed him.

And yet, if it is impossible to call him a coward, it is also impossible to see him as a man of integrity and honor. What Hemingway's hypermanliness tried so desperately to conceal was his greatest fear that at any moment he would be found out—and yet what sheer guts to pitch his shivering self and all his mighty gifts against that terrifying truth. There were many, though, who decided that this huge manly edifice concealed a fake. Archibald MacLeish, in a letter supposedly defending Hemingway, writes: "By some psychoanalytic hocus-pocus, the literary impotent have come to believe that: "Mr. Hemingway's artistic virility . . . proceeds from the fact that Mr. Hemingway believes himself unvirile."[14]

Women were quickly onto him. Zelda Fitzgerald called him "phony as a rubber check." She decided that though he came across as all male, no man could be "as male as all that." She also grew more and more convinced that there was something ambiguous about her husband's relationship with Hemingway and came to the conclusion that they were lovers. Fitzgerald responded to her smear in a letter: "The nearest I ever came to leaving you was when you told me I was a fairy in the Rue Palatine."[15]

An interesting piece of information about this relationship is provided by Hemingway in *A Moveable Feast,* where, on first impression, Fitzgerald, as himself, is described as both boyish and girlish:

> Scott was a man then who looked like a boy with a face between handsome and pretty. He had very fair wavy hair, a high forehead, excited and friendly eyes and a delicate long-lipped Irish mouth that, on a girl, would have been the mouth of a beauty. His chin was well built and he had good ears and a handsome, almost beautiful, unmarked nose. This should not have added up to a pretty face, but that came from the coloring, the very fair hair and the mouth. The mouth worried you until you knew him and then it worried you more.[16]

Fitzgerald, after reading a draft of *The Sun Also Rises*—a novel that involves a war hero with a war wound that made him impotent—made an astute observation that there was something veiled about the novel and cites the main character's emasculating groin injury, his war wound, as being a cover for something else.

Then there's Hemingway's fourth wife Mary's decision, at the end of the 1950s—while she was once again thinking of leaving him—to speak about her lack of a sex life with Hemingway. Hemingway always insisted, in private and public, that his sex life with Mary—as with all women—was great. It became clear in an entry, inserted by Hemingway into a diary Mary was writing in East Africa in 1953, that Mary—like the fictional Catherine Barkley in *A Farewell to Arms*—had become a real part of his sexual obsession with androgyny, emotional merging, and sexual flipping.

We can go no further without entering into the radiance and pure beauty of his words—his only real way of trying to transcend his disabilities and his pain. Hemingway "sees" what he writes in a way that makes it visible to us in an uncanny way. He imagines everything so vividly and with such clarity that he seems to slip out of imagining into direct seeing. His writing feels totally immediate as if he has actually been there, seen that, felt and known that scene, that woman, that man. And we, the reader, are part of his experience, right there with him as we read. He writes gorgeously about landscape and trees, mountains, the sea and rivers, fishes, food, wine and beauty with a feminine eye for small, telling detail, and at times he has penetrating insights that take one's breath away. In the first part of his extraordinary novel, *The Garden of Eden,* he begins to describe the first days of a young married couple who will carry us into the darkest alleys of Hemingway's androgynous and gender-merging sexuality:

> They were living at le Grau du Roi then and the hotel was on a canal that ran from the walled city of Aigues Mortes straight down to the sea. They could see the towers of Aigues Mortes across the low plain of the Camargue and they rode there on their bicycles at some time of nearly every day along the white road that borders the canal. In the evenings and the mornings when there was a rising tide sea bass would come into it and they would see the mullet jumping wildly to escape from the bass and watch the swelling bulge of the water as the bass attacked.

He can bring France, Spain, and Italy up like a Monet or Cezanne and gives us the lovely detail of a face, a room, the precise rendering of daily life, a striped shirt, the aftermath of love and sex, the violence about to blow in passionate love affairs, the sorrow of parting. Hemingway's exuberance and appetite for life, his appreciation of food and drink makes one's mouth water; the descriptions of the gazpacho, spicy dark sausage, anchovies, steak and mashed potatoes makes one long to be there with him, to lift those beaded glasses of champagne and martinis, absinthe and cognac, to perhaps take the risk of telling him to quit being such a monster when he has been given the gift of creating such life out of mere words.

> On this morning there was brioche and red raspberry preserve and the eggs were boiled, and there was a pat of butter that melted as they stirred them and salted them lightly and ground pepper over them in the cups. They were big eggs and fresh and the girl's were not cooked quite as long as the young man's. He remembered that easily and he was happy with his, which he diced up with the spoon and ate with only the flow of the butter to moisten them and the fresh early morning texture and the bite of the coarsely ground pepper grains and the hot coffee and the chicory-fragrant bowl of café au lait.

They had made love when they were half awake with the light bright outside but the room still shadowed and then had lain together and been happy and tired and then made love again. Then they were so hungry that they did not think they would live until breakfast and now they were in the café eating and watching the sea and the sails and it was a new day again.

And then the darkness begins

"I'm the destructive type," she said. "And I'm going to destroy you . . . I'm going to wake up in the night and do something to you that you've never even heard of or imagined."

"She came quickly to the table and sat down and lifted her chin and looked at him with the laughing eyes and the golden face with the tiny freckles. Her hair was cropped as short as a boy's. It was cut with no compromises.

"You see," she said. "That's the surprise. I'm a girl. But now I'm a boy too and I can do anything and anything and anything."

And here Hemingway spells it out:

"Where I'm holding you you are a girl," he said. He held her tight around her breasts and he opened and closed his fingers feeling her and the hard erect freshness between his fingers." . . ."He had shut his eyes and he could feel the long light weight of her on him and her breast pressing against him and her lips on his. He lay there and felt something and then her hand holding him and searching lower and he helped with his hands and then lay back in the dark and didn't think at all and only felt the weight and the strangeness inside and she said, "Now you can't tell who is who can you? . . . You are changing," she said. "Oh you are. You are. Yes you are and you're my girl Catherine. Will you change and be my girl and let me take you?"

And this is how Hemingway writes about a fish:

He tried to hold it as lightly as he could and the long pole was bent to the breaking point of the line and trace by the fish which kept trying to go toward the open sea . . . The waiter had come from the café and was very excited. He was talking by the young man's side saying, "Hold him. Hold him. Hold him as softly as you can. He'll have to tire. Don't let him break. Soft with him. Softly. Softly." . . . Then he came up thrashing at the surface and then was down again and the young man found that although the fish felt as strong as ever the tragic violence was lessened and now he could be led around the end of the jetty and up the canal.

"How is he?" asked the waiter.

"He's fine but we've beaten him."

Then they all went out to see him laid out on the side of the road silver as a salmon and dark gunmetal shining on his back. He was a handsome beautifully built fish with great live eyes and he breathed slowly and brokenly.

Here is Hemingway with one of his perfect lines: "Remember everything is right until it's wrong. You'll know when it's wrong."

> And when he woke it was in the moonlight and she had made the dark magic of the change again and he did not say no when she spoke to him and asked the questions and he felt the change so that it hurt him all through and when it was finished after they were both exhausted she was shaking and she whispered to him, Now we have done it. Now we really have done it. Yes, he thought, now we have really done it. . . . But he was very worried now and he thought what will become of us if things have gone this wildly and this dangerously and this fast? What can there be that will not burn out in a fire that rages like that?

And now it's wrong:

> "Didn't you hear me say I did it? Didn't you watch me do it? Do you want me to wrench myself around and tear myself in two because you can't make up your mind? Because you won't stay with anything?"
>
> "Would you hold it down?"
>
> "Why should I hold it down? You want a girl don't you? Don't you want everything that goes with it? Scenes, hysteria, false accusations, temperament isn't that it? I'm holding it down. I won't make you uncomfortable in front of the waiter. I won't make the waiter uncomfortable. I'll read my damned mail."[17]

And then there's the bullfighting, which, perhaps of all his writing, most tellingly conveys Hemingway's identifications and splitting, his terror, his excitement, and, above all, his desire for death and oblivion. Hemingway watched the gore and horror, the monstrous male world of matadors, and the killing of large beautiful animals, with a particular dark mania and ecstasy. He makes us look, close up and unblinking, and often it's unbearable. Part of Hemingway's description of a bullfight in a feature article for the *Star Weekly* is as follows:

> He seemed like some great prehistoric animal, absolutely deadly and absolutely vicious. He charged silently and with a soft galloping rush. When he turned he turned on his four feet like a cat. . . . The bull came in on his rush, refused to be shaken off, and in full gallop crashed into the animal from the side, ignored the horse, drove one of his horns high into the thigh of the picador, and tore him, saddle and all, off the horse's back.[18]

Hemingway came to bullfights at a time when he was angry and depressed: His first two books were receiving reviews that infuriated him, he was unable to place his stories with a US publisher and had to resort to small literary magazines in Europe. It was a time when Hemingway's writing style was undergoing a striking transformation: Gertrude Stein had pretty much taught him how to write. Her influence helped Hemingway replace his early, wordy, wandering style with a new, detached, ambivalent way of writing. And what she taught was American literature, distinct from English literature. It was brand new, and he claimed it as his own.

Hemingway was now throwing out long, loping lines of simple, natural language, using colloquial dialogue and a taut, tense narrative style full of suspense and tension. He had deepened his understanding of character and was able to convey profound emotions and states of mind. The simplification and sparseness of his word-play gave his prose a powerful, distilled and original quality, very short on punctuation, very American, very edgy and harrowing, very beautiful, and far removed from the traditional English prose he had read as a child.

And so a very gloomy, depressed Hemingway, trying to get his foot in the door of the publishing houses and dejected by the rejection letters that kept coming, left Paris and traveled with Bob McAlmon, a publisher friend, to see their first bullfight. Hemingway, exhilarated and pumped now the despair had lifted, was about to meet his greatest passion and terror, the primitive and violent side of himself represented by a beast: "Heavily-muscled, amazingly fast on their feet and armed with dagger-sharp horns that they can wield with terrifying dexterity, they are truly awesome concentrations of male power."[19] Hemingway got caught up in the sexual imagery: the slim young matador with his elegant dance of enticement and the sweep of his scarlet cape, close and closer to the bull he comes, drawing the bull into a battle that will end with the beast's horns penetrating the man's frail body, tossing him into the air—impaled or gouged and trampled—or the matador able only to thrust his sword deep between the horns of the beast who will fall on his knees in surrender and death.

All this physicality reveals a merging not only with the bull's brutality and the matador's courage but also with their fate: death and glory. And part of the spectacle is the cruelty of the kill and the terrible risk the matador takes as he moves so intimately in and around the bull, risking the greatest male horror—that the sharp horns will rip off his penis or the soft, swinging cojones will be impaled or tossed into the air. Hemingway was hooked for life and wrote five extraordinary and wildly enthusiastic pieces about bullfighting before producing *The Undefeated,* a story that he, at that time, thought was his finest piece of fiction and that many reviewers thought overblown and sentimental. In retrospect, it would seem the book came from a literary flip arising out of mania.

In the late 1950s, Hemingway, now married to his fourth and last wife, Mary, had reached a time of fame and fortune. The critics loved *The Old Man and the Sea* and it sold over five million copies in two days; it was a best-seller, was awarded a Pulitzer Prize, and later was made into a movie. In the same year, he was awarded the Nobel Prize. He had all the acclaim a man could possibly want, but he knew his health was failing. He decided to return to Africa as the great white hunter one more time. And it was on this trip that he suffered two different plane crashes. The second was so serious that he was reported dead in all the world newspapers, giving Hemingway the extraordinary experience of being able to read his own obituaries. It shook him up, his fear and grandiosity escalated. He wanted to write and could not. He was forbidden to drink but could not stop, even though continuing would do even more damage to his failing kidneys and liver. His health was now in serious decline, but he was sick and tired of doctors and psychiatrists telling him what was wrong with him. He went back to a collection of documents and drafts from his Paris years, when his writing had been at its most sublime and his life was in full swing, and decided to tell his life and story in his own words. What he produced out of this time of terror, depression, and physical failure was *A Moveable Feast*. It was regarded as his single best piece of nonfiction work, but after writing it he was exhausted and emptied out, done for.

He was losing his hair. He was deteriorating mentally and physically. His body was giving up on him and his mind had cracked. He was told he had a form of diabetes that would leave him blind and impotent, and, whenever he was hospitalized, for depression or mania, he was given multiple treatments of ECT, which left him even more paranoid, delusional, and depressed than before. He was impotent, desperate, and tormented, his memory emptied out, unable to write. A few years earlier, a series of deaths had deeply depressed and disturbed him: his mother and his first grandchild, and, most agonizingly, Pauline, the mother of his two younger sons, had, after a brutal conversation with him, died on the operating table. Charles Scribner, his publisher and one of his closest and oldest friends died suddenly, leaving him lonely and bereft.

On a summer morning in the Boulder Mountains of Idaho, July 2, 1961, Ernest Hemingway woke before six, as was his custom, and left his bed. He was in terrible pain. His body was emaciated, he was gaunt and drained: he had hepatitis and hypertension and his mind was completely shot: he was hearing voices, his heart was broken—all passion spent, all illusions gone, face to face with his own death. He went first to the kitchen and then down into the basement. Mary had locked all the guns in the house in a storeroom in the basement, but—and how interesting—she had left the key in plain sight on the windowsill in the kitchen. Hemingway took it, unlocked the storeroom, selected his favorite twelve-gauge, double-barreled English shotgun made by Abercrombie & Fitch, pushed two shells into it, walked upstairs into the foyer where he knew Mary would find him, and shot himself in the head. The explosion blew away his entire cranial vault and Mary had to step over his head to reach what was left of him.

It is too hard to leave him like this. It is too sad to condemn him to the horrific violence of his self-murder. Norman Mailer tries to reconcile Hemingway's life with his death:

> It may even be that the final judgement on his work may come to the notion that what he failed to do was tragic, but what he accomplished was heroic, for it is possible that he carried a weight of anxiety with him which would have suffocated any man smaller than himself.[20]

Notes

1. Marcelline Hemingway, *At the Hemingways: With Fifty Years of Correspondence between Ernest and Marcelline Hemingway* (Moscow: University of Idaho, 1999), 622.

2. Ernest Hemingway, *The Letters of Ernest Hemingway*, Vol. 2: 1923–1925 (Cambridge, UK: Cambridge University Press, 2013), 1923–1925.

3. Ernest Hemingway, *Selected Letters 1917–1961*, edited by Carlos Baker, "Ernest Hemingway to Francis Scott Fitzgerald, 1934" (New York: Scribner, 1981), 408.

4. Ernest Hemingway, *The Nick Adams Stories* (New York: Amereon House, 1955), 33.

5. Hemingway, *Nick Adams Stories*, 13–14.

6. Grace Hall Hemingway to Ernest Hemingway, February 9, 1920; Ernest Hemingway Collection, John F. Kennedy Library.

7. Grace Hall Hemingway Scrapbooks, Ernest Hemingway Collection, John F. Kennedy Library.

8. Ernest Hemingway, "Fathers and Sons," *The Short Stories of Ernest Hemingway* (New York: Scribner, 1966), 496.

9. Kenneth S. Lynn, *Hemingway* (Cambridge, MA: Harvard University Press, 1987), 53.

10. Hemingway, "The Last Good Country," *Nick Adams Stories*, 121–122.

11. Hemingway, "Ernest to Arthur Mizener, 1950," *Selected Letters, 1917–1961*, 697.

12. Kenneth S. Lynn, *Hemingway* (Cambridge, MA: Harvard University Press 1995), 527.

13. Jeffrey A. Kottler, *Divine Madness* (San Francisco: Jossey-Bass, 2006), 89.

14. Archibald MacLeish, *The Letters of Archibald MacLeish, 1907–1982* (Boston: Houghton Mifflin, 1983), 261.

15. F. Scott Fitzgerald, *The Correspondence of F. Scott Fitzgerald*, edited by Matthew J. Bruccoli et al. (New York: Random House, 1980), 241.

16. Ernest Hemingway, *A Moveable Feast* (New York: Simon & Schuster, 2010), 125.

17. Ernest Hemingway, *The Garden of Eden* (New York: Scribner, 1986), 1, 4, 5, 8–9, 14–15, 17, 20–21, 65, 70.

18. Ernest Hemingway, *By-Line: Ernest Hemingway: Selected Articles and Dispatches of Four Decades*, edited by William White (New York: Scribner, 1998), 94.

19. Lynn, *Hemingway*, 212.

20. Norman Mailer, "Punching Papa." *New York Review of Books* 1 (August 1963), 13.

CONTRIBUTOR BIOGRAPHIES

Daniela S. Barberis is an assistant professor of history of science and social science at Shimer College in Chicago. Among her research projects is a study of the development of French epistemology in the late nineteenth and early twentieth centuries.

Robert Bogdan is a distinguished professor emeritus of social science and disability studies at Syracuse University. He is the author of *Freak Show: Presenting Human Oddities for Amusement and Profit* (1988, with Arnold Arluke), *Beauty and the Beast: Human-Animal Relations as Revealed in Real Photo Postcards, 1905–1935* (2010), and, with Martin Elks and James L. Knoll, *Picturing Disability: Beggar, Freak, Citizen, and Other Photographic Rhetoric* (2011).

Kathleen M. Brian is a lecturer in the Liberal Studies Department at Western Washington University. Her articles have appeared in the *History of Psychiatry, Journal of Literary and Cultural Disability Studies*, and the *Bulletin of the History of Medicine*.

Anna Creadick is an associate professor of English at Hobart and William Smith Colleges. She is the author of *Perfectly Average: The Pursuit of Normality in Postwar America* (2010).

Rebecca Ellis completed her PhD degree at the University of New Mexico in 2016. She is a postdoctoral teaching fellow with the Roots of Contemporary Issues program at Washington State University in Pullman, Washington.

Ivy George is a professor of sociology at Gordon College. Her writings include *Child Labour and Child Work* (1990) and, with Margaret Masson, *An Uncommon Correspondence* (1998).

Meghan Henning is an assistant professor of Christian origins in the Department of Religious Studies at the University of Dayton. Her writings have appeared in the *Journal of Early Christian Studies* and the *Journal of Late Antiquity*.

Lawrence E. Holcomb was an associate professor of sociology at Gordon College.

John M. Kinder is an associate professor of history at Oklahoma State University. He is the author of *Paying with Their Bodies: American War and the Problem of the Disabled Veteran* (2015).

Whitney E. Laemmli completed her PhD degree in the history and sociology of science at the University of Pennsylvania in 2015 and is currently a postdoctoral fellow at the Society of Fellows at Columbia University.

Beth Linker is an associate professor in the Department of the History and Sociology of Science at the University of Pennsylvania. She is the co-editor (with Nancy Hirschmann) of *Civil Disabilities: Citizenship, Theory, and the Body* (2015) and the author of *War's Waste: Rehabilitation in World War I America* (2011).

Jessica Meyer is a University Academic Fellow in Legacies of War at the University of Leeds. She is the author of *Men of War: Masculinity and the First World War in Britain* (2009).

Susan Schweik is a professor of English and associate dean of arts and humanities at the University of California, Berkeley. Her writings include *A Gulf So Deeply Cut: American Women Poets and the Second World War* (1991) and *The Ugly Laws: Disability in Public* (2009).

David Serlin is an associate professor of communication and science studies at the University of California, San Diego. His writings include *Replaceable You: Engineering the Body in Postwar America* (2004), and he has edited *Artificial Parts, Practical Lives: Modern Histories of Prosthetics* (with Katherine Ott and Stephen Mihm, 2002), *Imagining Illness: Public Health and Visual Culture.* (2010), and *Keywords for Disability Studies* (with Rachel Adams and Benjamin Reiss, 2015).

Murray K. Simpson is a reader and program director at the School of Education, Social Work, and Community Education at the University of Dundee. He is the author of *Modernity and the Appearance of Idiocy: Intellectual Disability as a Regime of Truth* (2014).

Carolyn Slaughter is a novelist and psychotherapist in Princeton, New Jersey. Her writings include *Before the Knife: Memories of an African Childhood* (2002), *A Black Englishman* (2004), and *Dresden, Tennessee* (2007).

James W. Trent Jr. is the editor (with Steven Noll) of *Mental Retardation in America: An Historical Reader* (2004) and the author of *The Manliest Man: Samuel G. Howe and the Contours of Nineteenth-Century American Reform* (2012) and *Inventing the Feeble Mind: A History of Intellectual Disability in the United States* (1994, 2016). He is a visiting scholar at the Heller School at Brandeis University.

Mary S. Trent completed her PhD degree in visual studies at the University of California, Irvine. She is an adjunct professor in art history and an advisement counselor at the College of Charleston. Her work has appeared in *American Art*.

INDEX

Note: Page references followed by an *f* indicate figure.